Computational Models of Learning in Simple Neural Systems

Computational Models of Learning in Simple Neural Systems

Edited by **Robert D. Hawkins** and **Gordon H. Bower**

Center for Neurobiology and Behavior
College of Physicians and Surgeons
Columbia University and
New York State Psychiatric Institute
New York, New York

Department of Psychology
Stanford University
Stanford, California

THE PSYCHOLOGY OF
LEARNING AND MOTIVATION, VOLUME 23
Advances in Research and Theory

ACADEMIC PRESS, INC.
Harcourt Brace Jovanovich, Publishers

San Diego   New York   Berkeley   Boston
London   Sydney   Tokyo   Toronto

ACADEMIC PRESS, INC.
San Diego, California 92101

United Kingdom Edition published by
ACADEMIC PRESS LIMITED
24-28 Oval Road, London NW1 7DX

LIBRARY OF CONGRESS CATALOG CARD NUMBER: 66-30104

ISBN   0-12-543323-9   (alk. paper)(hardcover)
ISBN   0-12-531958-4   (alk. paper)(paperback)

PRINTED IN THE UNITED STATES OF AMERICA
89   90   91   92   9   8   7   6   5   4   3   2   1

CONTENTS

QUANTITATIVE MODELING OF SYNAPTIC PLASTICITY
David C. Tam and Donald H. Perkel

COMPUTATIONAL CAPABILITIES OF SINGLE NEURONS: RELATIONSHIP TO SIMPLE FORMS OF ASSOCIATIVE AND NONASSOCIATIVE LEARNING IN *APLYSIA*
John H. Byrne, Kevin J. Gingrich, and Douglas A. Baxter

v

A BIOLOGICALLY BASED COMPUTATIONAL MODEL FOR SEVERAL SIMPLE FORMS OF LEARNING

Robert D. Hawkins

INTEGRATING BEHAVIORAL AND BIOLOGICAL MODELS OF CLASSICAL CONDITIONING

Nelson H. Donegan, Mark A. Gluck, and Richard F. Thompson

SOME RELATIONSHIPS BETWEEN A COMPUTATIONAL MODEL (SOP) AND A NEURAL CIRCUIT FOR PAVLOVIAN (RABBIT EYEBLINK) CONDITIONING

Allan R. Wagner and Nelson H. Donegan

SIMULATION AND ANALYSIS OF A SIMPLE CORTICAL NETWORK

Gary Lynch and Richard Granger

A COMPUTATIONAL APPROACH TO HIPPOCAMPAL FUNCTION

William B Levy

CONTRIBUTORS

Numbers in parentheses indicate the pages on which the authors' contributions begin.

Douglas A. Baxter, Department of Neurobiology and Anatomy, The University of Texas Medical School, Houston, Texas 77225 (31)

John H. Byrne, Department of Neurobiology and Anatomy, The University of Texas Medical School, Houston, Texas 77225 (31)

Nelson H. Donegan, Department of Psychology, Yale University, New Haven, Connecticut 06520 (109, 157)

Kevin J. Gingrich, Department of Anesthesiology, National Naval Medical Center, Bethesda, Maryland 20814 (31)

Mark A. Gluck, Department of Psychology, Stanford University, Stanford, California 94305 (109)

Richard Granger, Center for the Neurobiology of Learning and Memory, and Department of Information and Computer Science, University of California, Irvine, California 92717 (205)

Robert D. Hawkins, Center for Neurobiology and Behavior, College of Physicians and Surgeons, Columbia University, and New York State Psychiatric Institute, New York, New York 10032 (65)

William B Levy, Department of Neurological Surgery, Health Sciences Center, University of Virginia, Charlottesville, Virginia 22908 (243)

Gary Lynch, Center for the Neurobiology of Learning and Memory, University of California, Irvine, California 92717 (205)

Donald H. Perkel,[1] Department of Physiology and Biophysics, and Department of Psychobiology, University of California, Irvine, California 92717 (1)

[1]Deceased.

David C. Tam,[2] Department of Physiology and Biophysics, and Department of Psychobiology, University of California, Irvine, California 92717 (1)

Richard F. Thompson, Department of Psychology, University of Southern California, Los Angeles, California 90007 (109)

Allan R. Wagner, Department of Psychology, Yale University, New Haven, Connecticut 06520 (157)

[2]Present address: Laboratory for Cellular and Molecular Neurobiology, National Institute of Neurological Disorders and Stroke, National Institutes of Health, Bethesda, Maryland 20892.

FOREWORD

This volume of *The Psychology of Learning and Motivation* represents a slight departure from the traditional composition of such volumes. The objective of the series remains as before, namely, to provide a forum in which experimental psychologists and neuroscientists can write about significant bodies of research in which they are involved. The operating procedure has been to invite contributions from interesting, active investigators, and then allow them essentially free rein and the space they need to present their research and theoretical ideas as they see fit. The result of such invitations over the past two decades has been collections of papers which have been remarkable for the nature of their integrative summation, since the usual response to this challenge has been the presentation of a series of experimental results integrated around some particular problem and theory.

From the perspective of the editor, the process of obtaining contributions runs smoothly: A number of active scientists are selected and invited to contribute a chapter; it is then left to them to determine exactly which of their several topics they will write about and when they will send in their chapter. The process of issuing groups of invitations and allowing those who accept to choose a topic and date has resulted in volumes that include a diverse range of topics. Recent standard volumes, for instance, have had chapters ranging from a physiological analysis of the fear-potentiated startle reflex in rats to a computer simulation model of language understanding, from experiments on foraging behavior in mammals to studies of social scientists solving problems of governmental economic policy. Although the range of topics in each volume properly reflects the diversity and vitality of the field, there are fewer chapters per volume that are of direct concern to special interest groups.

Therefore, in order to attend to some special-interest concerns and to balance the diversity of the standard volumes of *The Psychology of Learning and Motivation*, the publishers and editor have decided to begin a new policy.

We have agreed to publish occasional "focus" volumes that include selected contributors who write their papers around a single topic, problem, or theme. These focus volumes will be assembled from contributors selected by the editor and a special co-editor, the latter selected for his or her expertise in the topic of the focus volume. The topics of the focus volumes will vary according to the issues and areas that are active and current on the research agenda of the field. A few of them may be reports prepared by participants in a topical conference. We hope that in this manner we will have responded to the concerns voiced by some special-interest groups of readers.

All such focus volumes will be titled by their special topic, and subtitled as a volume in *The Psychology of Learning and Motivation* series. The focus volumes are expected to be "occasional" and to be in addition to the regular, topically diverse volumes of this series which have appeared every winter since 1967.

Gordon H. Bower

PREFACE

Computational neuroscience is an exciting new field that has emerged from the convergence of progress in three separate disciplines: artificial intelligence, experimental psychology, and neurobiology. In artificial intelligence, there has been a renewal of interest in networks of neuronlike elements, which have recently been shown to be capable of learning rather sophisticated cognitive tasks such as speech generation and recognition. In experimental psychology, research over the past two decades has shown that simple learning paradigms such as classical conditioning have a cognitive flavor (in the sense that the animal is thought to construct an internal representation of the world), and psychologists have proposed detailed theories to account for the behavioral regularities in these paradigms. And in neurobiology, there has been considerable progress in elucidating the neural circuits and physiological mechanisms which actually underlie learning in several relatively simple systems.

The contributions selected for this volume all represent efforts to combine these three disciplines by constructing computational models of learning in simple neural systems. Each of the chapters reviews research by the authors on the cellular substrates of learning in a real nervous system, and each describes a computational model based on that research. In the first two chapters, Tam and Perkel and Byrne *et al.* present detailed models of plasticity in single neurons, and Byrne *et al.* relate that plasticity to nonassociative and associative learning in *Aplysia*. In the next three chapters, Hawkins, Donegan *et al.*, and Wagner and Donegan present simple network models for higher-order features of classical conditioning and discuss ways in which psychological models which account for these features correspond to the neuronal models. Hawkins and Donegan *et al.* describe models based on the neural circuitry and physiology underlying classical conditioning of *Aplysia* gill- and siphon-withdrawal, and Donegan *et al.* and Wagner and Donegan describe models based on the neural circuitry underlying conditioning of the rabbit nictitating membrane response. In the final two chapters, Lynch and Granger and Levy present models of areas of mammalian cortex (piriform cortex and hippocampus) where long-term potentiation (LTP) is thought to be involved in more complex types of learning. In both chapters the models are used to try to understand the functions of the cortical regions.

Unlike artificial neural network models, the models described in this volume are all based on data from real neurons and circuits which are thought to be substrates of learning. The modeling therefore has two goals. First, to improve our understanding of the biological systems, by seeing what aspects of their behavior can and cannot be generated from current knowledge of the neurons and connections. Computational modeling is often the only way to make such predictions, given the complexity of even these relatively simple systems. Modeling is therefore an important tool for approaching the more long-term goal of understanding how real neurons and circuits account for complex mental phenomena. The second goal is to generate intelligent learning models for their own sake. This biologically realistic approach to generating learning models has practical disadvantages compared to a pure artificial intelligence approach, but it also has some advantages. Furthermore, nervous systems are still the best computers we have for many tasks, and we probably can learn much more from them. Artificial neural network models have been successful in achieving practical goals by copying biology to the extent of using parallel, distributed processing. They might profit further by copying biological neurons, learning rules, and network architecture. Although nervous systems have constraints which appear to be (and may actually be) restrictive, using biology as a guide in this manner may nevertheless turn out to be the best way to create computer models with some of the capabilities of real nervous systems. The models described in this volume represent a new interdisciplinary field's first steps toward these goals.

Robert D. Hawkins

QUANTITATIVE MODELING OF SYNAPTIC PLASTICITY

David C. Tam
*Donald H. Perkel**

I. Introduction

Learning of any sort involves a relatively long-lasting change in the behavior of an organism and, perforce, in the functioning of parts of its nervous system. To model learning in neural systems, therefore, requires two steps: (1) quantitative modeling of the involved neuron or circuit before the learning is induced, and (2) incorporation of the neuronal modifications that underlie learning—anatomical, electrical, or chemical—into the first model. Ideally, the modifications assumed as the substrate of learning should be fully consistent with the structures and mechanisms of the model of the neuronal system of the naive animal, rather than imposed in an ad hoc fashion; it must be emphasized, however, that the choice and description of the mechanisms for neuronal modification are questions of neurobiology rather than of modeling as such.

Recent renewed studies of artificial neural networks exhibiting "learning" phenomena (e.g., Ackley, Hinton, & Sejnowski, 1985; Anderson, Silverstein, Ritz, & Jones, 1977; Hopfield, 1982; Grossberg, 1975; McClelland & Rumelhart, 1986a,b; Rumelhart, Hinton, & Williams, 1986), based on the conceptual framework developed in the 1940s (Hebb,

*Deceased

1

1949; McCulloch & Pitts, 1943), suggest that learning may require changes in synaptic (or connection) weights. A correlation of learning with changes in synaptic efficacy has also been demonstrated experimentally in biological systems (e.g., Alkon, 1984, 1987; Castellucci & Kandel, 1976). This suggests that a comprehensive, biological, computational model using known physiological, physical, and chemical principles and assumptions may be necessary in order to understand fully the dynamics and interactions of the subsystems.

In this article we first describe the quantitative approach to neuronal modeling through a compartmental description of synapses, nerve cells, and small circuits of neuronal networks. We then go on to illustrate specific examples of different mechanisms underlying synaptic plasticity in different systems. We conclude with a discussion of some general strategies for quantitative modeling. The model described in this chapter is implemented in a family of programs collectively termed MANUEL. These programs were written in FORTRAN and have been developed over the last two decades.

II.   Functional Reconstruction through Compartmental Models

Modeling of neurons and neuronal circuits can be undertaken at a variety of levels of simplification, ranging from the structureless logical switching element of McCulloch and Pitts (1943) to the most elaborate and detailed description involving voltage-dependent ion channels and a three-dimensional model of Ca^{2+} diffusion in the cytoplasm (Zucker, 1985). By *functional reconstruction* we refer to that level of realism and detail of modeling that attempts to include the functionally important features of neuronal morphology, transmembrane ionic currents, and associated chemical kinetics. A functional reconstruction is thus a working model of the neuron or circuit, intended to furnish reliable, quantitative predictions of the behavior of the system based on a distillation of its neurobiological characteristics.

One highly useful and versatile form of functional reconstruction uses a compartmental description of the neuron's structure. In this approach, the membrane of the neuron is divided into a finite number of regions (patches), each of which is judged to be small enough so that the transmembrane electrical potential at the center of the region is representative of the potential throughout the region. This use of equipotential regions of membrane for neuronal modeling was introduced by Rall (1964); it is a particular instance of a well-known approximation to continuous physical systems by discretizing a continuous structure, thereby converting a partial differential equation into a system of coupled ordinary differential equations.

Each region is treated in accordance with its equivalent electrical circuit, in which the membrane capacitance is in parallel with a number of transmembrane ionic current pathways, typically nonlinear. The cytoplasmic current pathways to adjoining regions are described by ohmic conductances.

To describe realistically the mechanisms of synaptic and dendritic information processing, a model must include the known physical principles governing the electrical and chemical events occurring at the membrane level. These include (1) voltage- and time-dependent conductances for various ion channels; (2) secondary events such as calcium-activated conductance changes and calcium ion dynamics, including competitive mechanisms for calcium removal; (3) processes for synthesis and release of presynaptic neurotransmitter, using either deterministic or stochastic dynamics for release; (4) receptor and neurotransmitter kinetics producing time-dependent synaptic conductances; and (5) conduction delay of action potentials by axons.

We first present the fundamental differential equation for a region of neuronal membrane and then show the modifications and additions required to represent dendritic structures, voltage-dependent ion channels, calcium ion dynamics, transmitter release and receptor dynamics, and the generation and actions of second messengers.

A. Equivalent Circuit and Fundamental Equation

The equivalent electrical circuit for an isopotential (or space-clamped) patch (or region) of neuronal membrane is shown in Fig. 1. The membrane potential E is measured from a point in the cytoplasm (inside the cell) to a ground in the extracellular fluid, that is, inside with respect to the outside of the cell. The circuit components shown extend across the membrane. The membrane capacitance C_{mem}, arising from the dielectric properties of the lipid bilayer, lies in parallel with a number of ionic conductances g. The instantaneous capacitive current I_{cap} measured across the capacitance is given by elementary circuit theory as

$$I_{cap} = C_{mem} \, dE/dt \qquad (1)$$

assuming that the capacitance is constant.

Each of the six current pathways, represented by a resistance in series with an electromotive force (emf), corresponds to a particular class of transmembrane ionic current carried by its corresponding population of

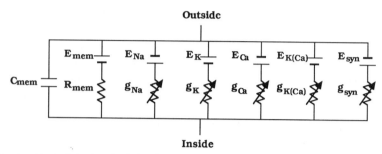

Fig. 1. Equivalent electrical circuit for an isolated isopotential region of neuronal membrane. Circuit elements include membrane capacitance (C_{mem}), membrane "leakage" resistance (R_{mem}) and its associated electromotive force (emf) (E_{mem}), plus four voltage-dependent conductances for sodium (Na), potassium (K), calcium (Ca), and calcium-activated potassium [K(Ca)], synaptic conductance (g_{syn}), and their associated emfs.

ion channels. The first current pathway is indicated by a fixed membrane resistance R_{mem} and an emf E_{mem}. This corresponds to the leakage current

$$I_{mem} = (E - E_{mem})/R_{mem} \qquad (2)$$

which is derived by taking the circuit diagram literally and applying Ohm's law. Note that a net outward current from the cytoplasm has a positive sign.

The resistances in the remaining current pathways are indicated as variable. This corresponds to the voltage dependence of the permeabilities or conductances of the Na^+, K^+, and Ca^{2+} channels, as well as to the dependence of the resistance (or conductance) of the calcium-activated K^+ channel on the cytoplasmic Ca^{2+} concentration, as discussed below. (Conductance is defined as the reciprocal of resistance.) Each conductance is in series with its equilibrium potential E_j, where the subscript j is used to represent the corresponding ion channel. Assuming the validity of an extended version of Ohm's law (for which the Ca^{2+} current is the chief exception; see Section II,B,2), we may write each of the transmembrane currents in the following generic form:

$$I_j = g_j(E, t)(E - E_j) \qquad (3)$$

where, following the usual convention, we use the conductance g_j rather than its reciprocal, the resistance R_j. The arguments for g_j reflect the reality that most ion channel permeabilities are dependent on membrane potential and its time course and often on concentrations of both intracellular and extracellular compounds, including neurotransmitters in the case of postsynaptic ion channels. That is, in the most general case, each conductance is a function of both membrane potential and time. Synaptic conductances are a special kind of ionic conductance in which activation is modulated by the presence of neurotransmitter.

At this point we apply Kirchhoff's current law (an expression of the conservation of charge) which states that the algebraic sum of all currents entering or leaving a point in a circuit—here the representative location lies in the cytoplasm—is zero. In generic terms, the resulting fundamental equation for a single, isolated region of membrane is given by the following differential equation:

$$C \, dE/dt + \sum_j I_j = 0 \qquad (4)$$

where C is the membrane capacitance, E is the membrane potential (voltage difference between the cytoplasm and the extracellular fluid), and each I_j represents a current flowing across the membrane. Substituting Eq. (3) into Eq. (4) we get

$$C \, dE/dt + \sum_j g_j(E, t)(E - E_j) = 0 \qquad (5)$$

Extended structures for which different portions do not have the same potential must be broken up into multiple regions, each of which is isopotential. The equivalent circuits of adjacent regions are connected through the cytoplasm; electrically, these intracellular pathways may be treated as a resistance. This additional source of current must then be included in the fundamental equation for each region. For region i, each of the regions k connected to it have resistive paths with resistance r_{ik}. The potential difference across that resistance is the difference between the membrane potentials in the two regions, $E_i - E_k$. Adding the cytoplasmic term to the fundamental equation, we have

$$C_i \, dE_i/dt + \sum_j g_{ij}(E_i, t)(E_i - E_{ij}) + \sum_k (E_i - E_k)/r_{ik} + I_{\mathrm{inj}} = 0 \qquad (6)$$

The first term represents the capacitive current. The second term sums over all ionic currents, including synaptic currents; the third term sums over all directly adjoining regions of membrane. We have also added a fourth term, which refers to current injected by the experimenter, as through the use of a current clamp or voltage clamp circuit. The sign convention for membrane potential implies that depolarizing or inward currents are negative, and hyperpolarizing or outward current are positive. Thus, each isopotential region i of the neuron or neurons represented in the model circuit can be described by a fundamental equation like that of Eq. (6). In addition, supplementary differential equations are required for the membrane conductances $g_{ij}(E_i, t)$ and for the dynamics of calcium ion, neurotransmitter effects, and second messenger action, as outlined in subsequent sections.

In our implementation of a general purpose compartmental model, we distinguish four kinds of currents in the summation of Eq. (6). The first is that associated with voltage-dependent ion channels in the membrane, such as the Hodgkin–Huxley Na^+ and K^+ channels. Constant conductance channels, such as leakage, are special cases of this type. The second type of current is a synaptic current, in which the conductance follows a time course determined by the kinetics of the binding interaction between the receptor and the corresponding neurotransmitter; a voltage dependence may be superimposed on the conductance as an option. A third type of current is the ohmic cytoplasmic current to or from the immediately adjacent regions. Finally, experimentally imposed currents, in pulses, ramps or sinusoidal patterns, may also be included using either current clamp or voltage clamp regimes.

1. Dendritic Structures and Spines

Dendritic branching structures in compartmental models may be conveniently represented by cylindrical segments or, when necessary, by related shapes such as tapered cylinders, truncated spheres, or truncated ellipsoids of revolution. Our implementation of the geometric shape of the various regions includes the following shapes: cylinder, tapered cylinder (truncated cone), truncated sphere, and truncated ellipsoid. Based on these elementary geometric membrane patches nearly any dendritic or axonal structure can be constructed by linking these components together with appropriately dimensioned elements of these pieces. A dendritic or axonal branching structure may be readily constructed by branching and coalescing regions together.

The membrane potential of a compartment is taken to be that of the center of the membrane patch it represents. The effective electric center of a region is defined by the plane perpendicular to the axis of the region that bisects the lateral surface area (i.e., the cell membrane area); this provides a better approximation of membrane current interrelationships than using simply the midpoint of the axis. From this point, essential parameters for modeling include the membrane surface area, the cross-sectional area at each end, and the electrical resistance from the center section to each of the end surfaces. For most shapes, closed form solutions can be used to find this position; the truncated ellipsoid, however, requires an iterative technique.

For an unbranched portion of a dendrite, the coupling resistance r_{ik} between any two adjoining regions is simply the sum of the cytoplasmic resistances from the center sections of each region to the conjoined ends (see Fig. 2). For a bifurcation point, where a dendrite forks distally into two branches, there are three cytoplasmic current pathways linking the three pairs of regions. For higher-order branch points in which N regions join, there are $N(N - 1)/2$ pairs of adjoining regions; each pathway is associated with the corresponding cytoplasmic resistance R_{ik}.

For a dendritic spine, the spine is represented by a single region of membrane, but the narrow stem generally need not be represented by separate regions of membrane. Rather it can be adequately modeled as a cytoplasmic resistance (Perkel, 1982–1983; Miller, Rall, & Rinzel, 1985; Perkel & Perkel, 1985). For most purposes, several spines originating within a given region of dendritic shaft can be represented as being coupled through their respective stem resistances to the electrical centerpoint of the dendritic shaft region.

2. Cytoplasmic Currents

A final contribution to the overall current flow into a region is the total flow through cytoplasmic pathways from different regions. The cytoplasmic current is calculated according to Ohm's law from the resistance and the voltage difference between the two regions. The cytoplasm is assumed to be an ohmic conductor, with specific resistivity ρ. The coupling resistance connecting each region i with adjoining region k is given by

$$R_{ik} = \rho \int_u^v dx/a(x) \qquad (7)$$

where x is the axial position through a region and $a(x)$ is the cross-sectional area as a function of axial position. The limits of integration are the

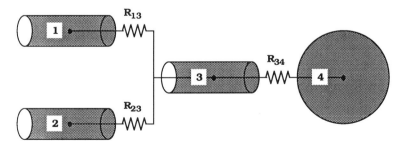

Fig. 2.   Schematic diagram showing the connections among membrane regions. The regions are connected by cytoplasmic resistances connecting between the midpoints of adjoining regions. The diagram also illustrates how a compartmental model can be constructed to model the dendritic tree structure of a neuron.

effective midpoints of the two regions. Electrical connections such as gap junctions may be formed between regions of different cells by specifying a cytoplasmic resistance between those regions.

B. DYNAMICS OF VOLTAGE-DEPENDENT ION CHANNELS

1. Voltage- and Time-Dependent Ion Channels

The classical approach to represent voltage- and time- dependent transmembrane ion channels is the gate model of Hodgkin and Huxley (1952). A generalized Hodgkin and Huxley approach considers each channel as having a number of on-off gates in series. Each gate is either open or closed; the channel as a whole is open (permeable or conducting) when all gates are in the open configuration. Each gate is assumed to operate independently of the others. Suppose there are two kinds of gates, and that each channel has p identical gates of a first kind and q gates of a second kind. Then if the (instantaneous) probability that a gate of the first kind is open is designated by m, and of the second kind by h, the probability that the channel is conducting is given by $m^p h^q$. For a population of independent channels, assuming that each gate behaves independently, this probability is equivalent to the fraction of channels in the conducting state. These gate variables (m and h) represent the probability or proportion that the gate is open, and the average conductance is proportional to the product of these probabilities. Therefore, if the conductance of the population of channels when fully open is designated g_{max}, then the effective conductance $g(E, t)$ is given by

$$g(E, t) = g_{max} m^p h^q \qquad (8)$$

for ion channels having two types of gates. Similarly, if there is only one type of gate for a particular ion channel, then the effective conductance is given by

$$g(E, t) = g_{max} n^r \qquad (9)$$

where the gate variable n is the probability of the gate being open and r is the number of identical gates in the channel. Finally, if the membrane has no voltage- or time-dependent conductance change, the effective conductance is simply given by

$$g(E, t) = g_{max} \qquad (10)$$

In the Hodgkin–Huxley (1952) model of the membrane of the squid giant axon, the Na^+ conductance is of the form of Eq. (8), where the first gate m is referred to as the *activation* gate because it is typically defined as opening (increasing) with depolarization; the second gate h is an *inactivation* gate because it closes or decreases with depolarization. In order for the voltage and time dependence of the predicted currents to match those measured in the squid axon, the Hodgkin–Huxley model assigned values of 3 and 1 to p and q, respectively. K^+ conductance was found to be satisfactorily fit to the form of Eq. (9), with the exponent $r = 4$, assuming only an activating gate, and the leakage conductance was of the form of Eq. (10).

The maximum or limiting conductance g_{max} is proportional to the area of membrane A_{mem} in the region:

$$g_{max} = G_{max}A_{mem} \qquad (11)$$

where G_{max} is the corresponding specific conductivity per unit area.

In the Hodgkin–Huxley model, gate transitions between the open and closed forms follow reactions of the following type:

$$m_{closed} \underset{\beta}{\overset{\alpha}{\rightleftharpoons}} m_{open} \qquad (12)$$

Because the gate variables are interpreted as probabilities, it follows that $m_{open} = m$ and $m_{closed} = 1 - m$. In this formulation, the gates obey first-order chemical kinetics with voltage-dependent reaction rates, giving rise to the differential equation of the form

$$dm/dt = \alpha - (\alpha + \beta)m \qquad (13)$$

The rate coefficients α and β are instantaneous functions of membrane potential E (in the region in which the channel lies). Alternatively, the first-order linear differential equation may be rewritten as

$$dm/dt = \alpha(1 - m) - \beta m \qquad (14)$$

It states that the rate of change of the probability that a gate is open is dependent on both the probability of the gate being in the open state m and the closed state $(1 - m)$. For the Hodgkin–Huxley and most other channels, the voltage dependence of α or β may be represented by the five-parameter generic formula

$$\alpha(E) = (a + bE)/\{c + \exp[(d + E)/f]\} \tag{15}$$

with the constraint that if $c = -1$, the numerator and denominator must vanish simultaneously when $E = -d$.

Smith (1978) and Thompson (1976) use an alternative form to Eqs. (14) and (15), in which the time constants and steady states of the gates are expressed in parametric expressions somewhat like those of Eq. (15), rather than the rate constants themselves. Their formulation expresses the voltage dependence of the steady-state gate opening m_s and the time constant τ_m rather than of rate constants. Specifically, their equations may be written in the form:

$$m_s = \{1 + \exp[(E + b)/c]\}^{-\phi} \tag{16}$$

$$\tau_m = a/\{1 + \exp[(E + b')/c']\} + d \tag{17}$$

and, alternatively, Eq. (13) can be expressed in the form:

$$dm/dt = (m_s - m)/\tau_m \tag{18}$$

where the steady-state gate opening m_s is given by

$$m_s = \alpha/(\alpha + \beta) \tag{19}$$

and the gate time constant τ_m is given by

$$\tau_m = 1/(\alpha + \beta) \tag{20}$$

The opening and closing rate constants can be recovered from the quantities given in Eqs. (16) and (17) by solving Eqs. (19) and (20) to obtain

$$\alpha = m_s/\tau_m \tag{21}$$

and

$$\beta = 1/\tau_m - \alpha \tag{22}$$

For many currents or channels, it is more straightforward to fit experimentally determined kinetic parameters by the Smith–Thompson formulation than to convert to rate constants before fitting, as is required with the Hodgkin–Huxley formulation. Our implementation allows either formulation for a given membrane type.

In our program, it is possible to circumvent the time dependence of specified gates while preserving their voltage dependence. An instantaneous gate can be used to set the gate openings to their steady-state values as determined by the present membrane potential. This simplification may result in considerable savings of execution time during simulation if the slow time course of other processes in the membrane are sufficiently rate-limiting to justify the approximation.

Finally, a generalized Ohm's law is used, in which the voltage drop across the equivalent conductor (the driving force) is the difference between the membrane potential and the Nernst potential for the ion to which the channel is permeable. Nernst potential is the equilibrium potential at which the electrical potential is balanced by the chemical potential between the membrane as a result of a difference in concentration of the ion permeable to that membrane. The Nernst potential E_Q for the ion Q is given by

$$E_Q = (RT/zF) \log_e([Q]_o/[Q]_i) \qquad (23)$$

where R is the gas constant, T is the absolute temperature, z is the ionic charge, and F is the Faraday constant; [Q] is the concentration of the permeant ion Q outside and inside the cell, as indicated by the subscripts o and i, respectively.

For conductances that are not perfectly selective to one ion, the user can simply provide the equilibrium (or reversal) potential measured for a particular current. The current passing through the population of ion channels of a particular type j is given by

$$I_j = g_{max}m^ph^q(E - E_Q) \qquad (24)$$

where E_Q is the equilibrium potential for the permeant ion(s).

2. Calcium Ion Currents

For calcium ion currents, two modifications may be necessary. Calcium is treated differently from other ionic species that contribute to the net membrane current for two reasons. First, its internal concentration may vary significantly during action potentials, changing the driving force on the ions. Second, it participates in other chemical and electrical processes, notably release of neurotransmitter and activation of other ionic conductances. Following the procedure used by Smith (1978) and Thompson (1976) for the *Tritonia* burster neuron, our model keeps track of the calcium ion concentration in a thin user-specified (usually 1–3 nm) shell of cytoplasm immediately subjacent to the membrane. That concentration is used, for example, to calculate the reversal level for calcium current according to the Nernst equation:

$$E_{Ca} = (RT/zF) \log_e \frac{[Ca^{2+}]_o}{[Ca^{2+}]_i} \tag{25}$$

where $z = 2$ for the divalent calcium ion. The reversal potential is continually updated during the numerical integration. Influx of calcium ion to this shell is directly proportional to calcium current:

$$J_{Ca} = -I_{Ca}/(zFA_{mem}) \tag{26}$$

where J_{Ca} is the calcium flux per unit area, A_{mem} is membrane area, and the minus sign and other parameters convert a negative (inward) current to a positive source term. Our implementation does not incorporate the detailed diffusion equations of Smith and Thompson, nor does it explicitly follow the multiple buffering reactions for calcium ion within the neuron. Instead, it makes use of the following approximation (suggested by P. A. Getting, personal communication): Entering calcium ion is divided proportionally into pools, each having its own decay properties. Specifically, the total calcium ion concentration in the shell is the sum of a basal level plus three labile pools:

$$[Ca^{2+}]_i = C_r + C_1 + C_2 + C_3 \tag{27}$$

Each of the labile pools decays exponentially according to its own time constant, τ_j. Inflowing calcium ion is divided among the three pools according to partition coefficients d_j (which sum to unity). Thus, each labile pool obeys the differential equation

$$dC_j/dt = -C_j/\tau_j + d_j J_{Ca}/w \tag{28}$$

where w is the shell thickness. Although this formulation may appear to be overly simplified, in practice it has reproduced the repeated burst pattern of *Tritonia* neurons (Thompson, 1976; Smith, 1987). In addition, experimental evidence (Barish, 1980) indicates that, in *Tritonia* neuron somata, the time course of calcium ion concentration is independent of the initial level of calcium ion, to the first approximation; a finding that justifies the simplifications used. An alternative more realistic treatment of the fate of entering calcium involves specifying an arbitrary number of calcium binding substrates. Each substrate is characterized by three time constants: Two of these describe the process of association and dissociation of calcium. The third process allows removal from the cell, for example, pumping or diffusion from the thin shell into the interior of the cell.

Any of the ionic currents may be designated by the user as flowing through a calcium channel. If a channel carries two ions (e.g., Na^+ as well as Ca^{2+}) it must be described as two separated channels with an appropriate partitioning of G_{max}. The calcium current I_{Ca} is simply the sum of the ionic currents designated as bearing calcium ions. Each such current is the product of the voltage-dependent conductance and the driving force, like any other ionic membrane current; our implementation does not incorporate the constant field expression of calcium current. The only difference between the dynamics of calcium currents and those of other ions lies in the continuous updating of the equilibrium potential, as described above. A discussion of the difficulties and uncertainties in describing calcium currents quantitatively is given by Hagiwara and Byerly (1981).

If the generalized Ohm's law expression of Eq. (24) is used, the Nernst potential may need to be continually updated as simulation proceeds since $[Ca^{2+}]_i$ varies with time due to accumulation of calcium ions, which may trigger a chain of secondary events. Alternatively, Eq. (24) may be replaced by the Goldman equation for calcium ion:

$$I_{Ca} = P_{Ca}(zFc)E\{[Ca^{2+}]_o - k[Ca^{2+}]_i\}/(k - 1) \qquad (29)$$

where $c = zF/RT$, $k = \exp(cE)$, and P_{Ca} is the permeability of calcium ion.

3. Calcium Ion Dynamics

Calcium ion regulation and removal follow first-order kinetics. Internal calcium ion concentration in any region can be considered as enveloped in a thin shell of cytoplasm adjacent to the membrane. Calcium ion enters (or leaves) via the calcium current in the appropriate ion channels in the membrane; it is also bound reversibly by each of a specified number of substrates S_i:

$$Ca^{2+} + S_i \rightleftharpoons CaS_i \rightarrow X \qquad (30)$$

The forward and backward rate constants for the reversible reaction and the rate constant for the irreversible removal term may be determined experimentally. The steady-state calcium concentrations for initial conditions may be determined by the amount of each substrate in each calcium-containing region. This description provides more than sufficient flexibility to fit experimental data or to test hypotheses such as the role of calcium accumulation in synaptic facilitation or to provide realistic Ca^{2+} dynamics for calcium-modulated K^+ or other currents.

C. SYNAPTIC MECHANISMS

For electrical synapses, the electrical coupling may be considered exactly as a cytoplasmic coupling (see Section II,A,2) between regions of membrane lying in different cells. For chemical synapses, the current flows through channels in the postsynaptic membrane mediated by the presence of neurotransmitters bound to the receptors. We describe the assumptions for synaptic currents in the context of the entire sequence of mechanisms underlying chemical synapses.

1. Neurotransmitter Release

The nerve terminal can be modeled as a single region of presynaptic membrane. The presynaptic membrane contains at least one ion channel that is permeable to calcium ion. In addition, other parameters must be specified, including those for calcium ion dynamics (see Section II,B,3) and neurotransmitter dynamics.

We assume that release takes place at some number of neurotransmitter release sites, S_o, each of which binds one vesicle of transmitter and a specific number of calcium ions. When the site is fully occupied, the contents of the vesicle are released into the synaptic cleft. The total number of vesicles of neurotransmitter in the presynaptic region is X_o, the sum of the number of free vesicles X and the number bound to release sites, X^*. The corresponding concentrations are defined as vesicles (or quanta) per release site, and are dimensionless quantities:

$$x_o = X_o/S_o$$
$$x = X/S_o \quad (31)$$
$$x^* = X^*/S_o$$

The total concentration is then the sum of the free and bound fractions:

$$x_o = x + x^* \quad (32)$$

Similarly, the total number of release sites is the sum of those unbound and those bound to vesicles:

$$S_o = S + S^* \tag{33}$$

The concentration of unbound vesicles is assumed to follow first-order kinetics, so that if no neurotransmitter were being released, the free vesicle concentration would approach its steady-state value x_∞ with a time constant τ_x for replenishment, according to the differential equation

$$
\begin{aligned}
dx/dt &= -(x - x_\infty)/\tau_x \\
&= -(x_o - x^* - x_\infty)/\tau_x
\end{aligned}
\tag{34}
$$

That is, the population of neurotransmitter available for binding to release sites, in units of vesicles (or quanta) is the solution of the above differential equation. This model can produce a form of synaptic depression through depletion of neurotransmitter.

Each release site (or active zone) in the membrane of the nerve terminal region has a binding site for a vesicle of transmitter and a specified number n (commonly assigned a value of 4) of calcium ion binding sites. Binding of vesicles and of calcium ions to the release sites is assumed to be fast and hence specified by the dissociation constants K_x and K_s. The fraction of calcium binding sites occupied by Ca^{2+} is then given by the rectangular hyperbolic expression $[Ca^{2+}]/(K_c + [Ca^{2+}])$; the fraction of release sites in which all n calcium-binding sites are occupied is the nth power of this expression. If we designate S as the population of unbound release sites, S^* the release sites fully bound by calcium, and X the population of available vesicles containing neurotransmitters, then the release kinetics are summarized as follows:

$$
nCa^{2+} + X + S \underset{K_x}{\overset{K_s}{\rightleftharpoons}} S^* \rightarrow Q \rightarrow T + S
\tag{35}
$$

The release site that binds a vesicle and n calcium ions irreversibly enters a "sequestered" state Q, which then irreversibly releases transmitter T into the cleft. The two irreversible reactions have their own rate constants. Our current model assumes no additional delay for the conversion of the release site after exocytosis into a site available for binding additional calcium and transmitter. This reaction is assumed to be fast, so the fraction of release sites bound to vesicles is given by

$$x^* = S^*/S_o$$
$$= x/(x + K_s) \tag{36}$$

By substituting Eq. (32) into Eq. (36) we arrive at the quadratic equation

$$x^{*2} - x^* (1 + x_o + K_s) + x_o = 0 \tag{37}$$

The appropriate root of this equation is calculated by the formula

$$x^* = 2x_o/\{1 + x_o + K_s + [(1 + x_o + K_s)^2 - 4x_o]^{1/2}\} \tag{38}$$

which has been arranged to minimize truncation error.

The binding of calcium ion to release sites is also assumed to be rapid and reversible. Each release site is assumed to have n calcium binding subsites; n is usually thought to be 4, but in our implementation the value is specified by the user. Letting B_o represent the total number of calcium binding sites, we have

$$B_o = nS_o$$
$$= B + B^* \tag{39}$$

with the same notation conventions for free and bound fractions as used above. At each subsite, the reaction

$$Ca^{2+} + B \underset{}{\overset{K_c}{\rightleftharpoons}} B^* \tag{40}$$

at equilibrium gives the fraction of subsites bound by calcium ion as

$$f_c = B^*/B_o$$
$$= [Ca^{2+}]_i/([Ca^{2+}]_i + K_c) \tag{41}$$

where the subscript i denotes (as above) the calcium ion concentration within the shell subjacent to the membrane.

Assuming independence among the calcium and vesicle binding sites, the fraction of release sites bound by the full complement n of calcium ions and by a vesicle of neurotransmitter is given by

$$f_x = x^* S_o f_c^n \tag{42}$$

If we then assume that such a fully bound release site goes through an irreversible reaction resulting in exocytosis of the quantum of neurotransmitter, with a rate constant $1/\tau_s$, then the differential equation for total vesicle concentration, including both the free-vesicle dynamics and the (continuous and deterministic) release into the synaptic cleft, is given by

$$dx_o/dt = -(x_o - x^* - x_\infty)/\tau_x - x^* f_c{}^n/\tau_s \qquad (43)$$

Note that our definition of vesicle concentration in terms of number of binding sites removes the quantity S_o from the last term of Eq. (43).

In our implementation of these mechanisms, we treat the free and bound moieties of neurotransmitter as a single state variable for numerical integration. In order to determine the partition between free and bound populations, the program must solve a quadratic equation. The general principle is that whenever an instantaneous equilibrium appears in a reaction scheme such as that of Eq. (35), the two species in the equilibrium are lumped as a single variable. If more than two species are linked through equilibria, the degree of the polynomial equation goes up correspondingly. The equations are solved through special means. For a linear or cyclic reaction sequence, an iterative technique is most efficient; for a general scheme of first-order reactions, a matrix technique is effective. Recourse to such special techniques is essential to avoid "stiffness" in the set of differential equations. Stiffness arises when there is a large disparity among effective time constants in the system, and it causes severe slowing down of any numerical integration algorithm that varies step size so as to confine truncation error within prescribed bounds (Gear, 1971). Combining components of a moving equilibrium is the best method for avoiding stiffness.

Ordinarily, sequestering of the vesicle within the membrane and subsequent exocytosis are treated as continuous processes; that is, in this case, the fractions of vesicles that can be released. However, it is also possible to treat them more realistically as stochastic processes. The probability of release in a time step is the product of the rate constant for sequestering or release and the duration of the time step. This probability and the number of eligible release sites determine the binomial distribution parameters, and the actual number of vesicles sequestered or released is drawn from the corresponding binomial distribution. The duration of the time step is kept small enough so that release events are nearly all isolated in time. Although stochastic release of neurotransmitter in a nerve terminal can be modeled, alternatively, as an approximation, the release of neurotransmitter can be modeled as a continual release of small amounts of transmitter even in the absence of an action potential. When an action potential invades the terminal, the depolarization-induced influx of Ca^{2+}

vastly increases the fraction f_c'', thereby resulting in a significant rate of release of transmitter into the synaptic cleft.

2. Transmitter–Receptor Dynamics

The fate of neurotransmitter after release from the nerve terminal is summarized by the following reaction scheme:

$$f_c''x^* \xrightarrow{1/\tau_s} X_c + R \underset{K_r}{\overset{1/\tau_g}{\rightleftharpoons}} C \rightarrow H \tag{44}$$

Bound transmitter is released into the cleft at a rate $x^*S_o f_c''/\tau_s$ (quanta per millisecond). Transmitter in the cleft is removed by diffusion and/or enzymatic degradation to the state X_x, represented by a single time constant τ_d. Binding of transmitter in the cleft with vacant receptor sites R is assumed to be rapid, and to have a dissociation constant K_r. The transmitter–receptor complex C is assumed to give rise to a conducting channel H through an irreversible reaction having rate constant $1/\tau_g$. The conducting form H then reverts to the nonconducting, unbound form R through a single irreversible reaction whose rate constant is $1/\tau_h$. During the process of opening and closing of the conducting channels, the bound neurotransmitter may, as specified by the user, be removed intracellularly, or reintroduced into the cleft. In this and some other details, our model differs from that proposed by Magleby and Stevens (1972).

Qualitatively, when neurotransmitter is released rapidly and briefly into the cleft, much of it binds rapidly to the receptors, after which the synaptic conductance, proportional to the conducting-channel population H, rises to a maximum and then, more slowly, decreases to a very low value; that value is not zero because of the small but persistent basal rate of transmitter release from the terminal.

In quantitative terms, we first define the total receptor population to be the sum of the populations in the three states (unbound, bound–nonconducting, and conducting):

$$R_o = R + C + H \tag{45}$$

Then we normalize the three populations to represent fractions, as in the presynaptic terminal, so that

$$r = R/R_o$$
$$c = C/R_o$$

$$h = H/R_o$$

$$r + c + h = 1 \qquad (46)$$

We also define $Z = X_c + C$, the total amount of transmitter, including that in the cleft and bound to the postsynaptic receptors. We normalize the transmitter to the receptor population, so that

$$t = X_c/R_o$$

$$z = Z/R_o \qquad (47)$$

$$z = t + c$$

Then the equilibrium between free and bound transmitter yields the fraction of transmitter bound to receptors as

$$
\begin{aligned}
\phi &= C/Z \\
&= c/z \\
&= tR/ZK_r \\
&= tr/zK_r \\
&= (1 - c/z)r/K_r \\
&= r/(r + K_r)
\end{aligned}
\qquad (48)
$$

Note that K_r is dimensionless; a small value (e.g., 0.0001) means that virtually all the transmitter released is bound to postsynaptic receptors.

The fraction of receptors in the bound but nonconducting state, designated by c, is found by substituting the last expression of Eq. (46) into Eq. (48) to yield

$$
\begin{aligned}
\phi &= c/z \\
&= (1 - c - h)/(1 - c - h + K_r)
\end{aligned}
\qquad (49)
$$

The appropriate solution to the quadratic equation in c is then

$$c = [2z(1 - h)]/\{W + [W^2 - 4z(1-h)]^{1/2}\} \qquad (50)$$

where

$$W = 1 - h + z + K_r \qquad (51)$$

By use of these equations, which derive from the equilibrium between transmitter in the cleft and the postsynaptic receptors, our implementation uses only the two state variables z and h for numerical integration. The corresponding differential equations are

$$dz/dt = (x^* f_c^{\,n}/\tau_s)(S_o/R_o) - (z - c)/\tau_d - c/\tau_g \qquad (52)$$

and

$$dh/dt = c/\tau_g - h/\tau_h \qquad (53)$$

in which c is given algebraically in terms of z, h, and the fixed parameters by Eqs. (50) and (51).

Finally, the synaptic conductance is then proportional to the fraction of conducting gates h:

$$g_{syn} = G_{syn} R_o\, h \qquad (54)$$

where G_{syn} is the conductance that would result if the channels bound by one quantum of transmitter were open. Note that h, and therefore g_{syn}, are functions of time but not of membrane potential. The corresponding synaptic current is given, as usual, by

$$I_{syn} = g_{syn}\, (E - E_{syn}) \qquad (55)$$

3. Second Messenger Effects

Modulation of channels and their currents by calcium ion or other second messengers is accomplished in a physiologically simplified manner. For Ca^{2+} activation of channels, as described above, the participation of calcium ion lies in the gate-opening reaction; this preserves the voltage and time dependence of calcium-activated channels. In effect, the forward rate constant α is replaced by the product $\alpha[Ca^{2+}]_i$ in Eq. (12); the physical units and numerical value of α must be adjusted appropriately.

In addition to the role Ca^{2+} plays as a second messenger, activated postsynaptic receptors can produce other second messengers that can act on conductances in the membrane. We have implemented this type of process using the same formalism as for receptors that conduct current with the exception that the receptor in state H instead modulates a voltage-dependent channel. Customarily this has taken the form of a fractional blockade, but activation of currents is possible as well. In the case in which a second messenger is reducing a conductance, the fraction of the channels blocked is given as a rectangular hyperbolic function of the second messenger concentration; the single parameter required is the concentration of second messenger that blocks half the channels of the specified type.

III.   Application to Synaptic Plasticity

Since, as described above, a large number of processes contribute to synaptic transmission, there are many ways in which changes can take place. For example, loci of modification could lie in presynaptic depolarization, calcium entry, vesicle production, release mechanisms, cleft dynamics, postsynaptic receptors, conductances, second messenger systems, or dendritic spine morphology. In order to illustrate how one may apply the techniques of functional reconstruction to problems of synaptic plasticity, we have chosen three sample phenomena involving a range of different mechanisms.

A.   FACILITATION THROUGH CALCIUM ACCUMULATION

It has been known for many years that in a number of experimental preparations (Katz & Miledi, 1967a, 1967b) when two impulses arrive at a nerve terminal at an interval in the range of tens of msec, the second one provokes a larger postsynaptic response than the first (Zucker, 1989). This phenomenon, known as paired-pulse facilitation, results from the accumulation of Ca^{2+} in the presynaptic terminal. After the first action potential and its associated calcium influx, the calcium concentration is elevated over a period of approximately 100 msec. During this time a subsequent action potential can cause a further increase in the calcium concentration to a level greater than that attained following the preceding impulse.

Although the phenomenon can be accounted for qualitatively using simply the above explanation, full understanding at the quantitative level requires a predictive model. We illustrate here an example in which a presynaptic terminal containing Hodgkin–Huxley squid axon membrane supplemented with voltage-dependent calcium channels and mechanisms for transmitter release forms a synapse onto a single patch of postsynaptic membrane. A brief depolarization caused a first action potential in the presynaptic element (Fig. 3A), resulting in an increase in the calcium concentration (Fig. 3B) and an excitatory postsynaptic potential (EPSP) (Fig. 3C). After a delay of 15 msec, another action potential was elicited. The residual calcium at the time of the second impulse resulted in a large peak level of calcium, which, due to the fourth-order dependence of release assumed here, caused a larger (facilitated) EPSP. In cases in which calcium had returned to basal levels before stimulation of the second action potential, no facilitation was exhibited. Three calcium removal processes

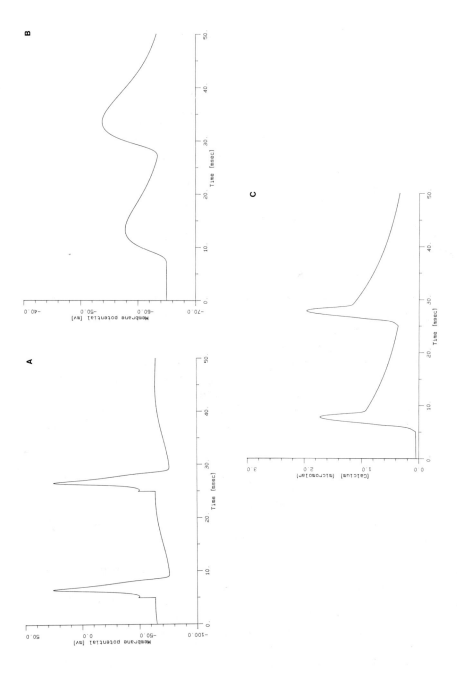

were used in this example with a range of capacities, affinities for calcium, and capabilities for removing calcium from the cytoplasm.

It is clear that paired-pulse facilitation can be explained by calcium accumulation and that this phenomenon that can be observed under a wide
range of different physiological conditions. Perhaps the relative ease with
which parameters can be found that produce paired-pulse facilitation is
related to the fact that almost every synapse exhibits this form of short-
term plasticity.

B. PRESYNAPTIC FACILITATION OF THE SENSORY NEURON–MOTOR NEURON SYNAPSE IN THE ABDOMINAL GANGLION OF *Aplysia*

One example of a system in which synaptic plasticity and behavioral
modification have been linked strongly is the gill-withdrawal reflex of
Aplysia (Castellucci & Kandel, 1976). In that monosynaptic reflex arc,
synaptic transmission between the sensory and motor neuron is enhanced
by tail shock or application of certain neurotransmitters and second messengers. It has been shown that the stimuli producing the enhancement
also broaden the action potential recorded in the soma of the sensory
neuron by reducing a potassium conductance.

We have sought to reproduce this finding in a reduced system. Two
regions of membrane, one presynaptic and the other postsynaptic, were
modeled. The presynaptic terminal region contained Hodgkin–Huxley
squid axon membrane, as well as calcium channels and release mechanisms. A single impulse was given in the terminal, and the membrane
potentials of the two regions were recorded. In addition, we monitored
the presynaptic calcium concentration. The manipulation was repeated
after reducing the maximum conductance (g_{max}) for the Hodgkin–Huxley
potassium current by 40%. As illustrated in Fig. 4A, this resulted in a
considerable broadening of the action potential, and increased EPSP size
(Fig. 4B) due to the larger calcium concentration in the terminal (Fig. 4C).
Further refinement of this model using assumptions closer to the observed physiology would provide for more realistic simulations. Nonetheless, the model serves to generate specific demands for measurements
of parameters and to identify the parameter ranges in which particular
phenomena are observed.

Fig. 3.   Paired-pulse facilitation through accumulation of calcium. A, Membrane potential in the presynaptic region of a two-region structure. Action potentials were elicited at
an interval of 15 msec. B, Membrane potential in the postsynaptic region. The excitatory
postsynaptic potential is larger following the second impulse. C, Presynaptic calcium concentration does not decay back to resting level before arrival of the second impulse. The
calcium level thus rises higher as a result of the second action potential.

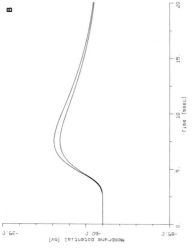

A

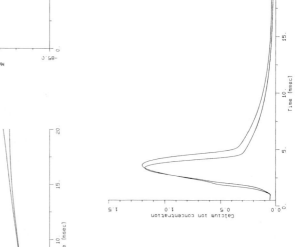

B

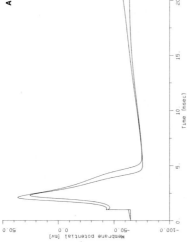

C

C.   Long-Term Potentiation and N-Methyl-d-Aspartate Receptors in the Hippocampus

In cases of synaptic plasticity in which it is not possible to record both pre- and postsynaptic elements directly, the role of quantitative predictions may be considerably enhanced. An example may be found in the case of long-term potentiation (LTP) of synaptic transmission in the hippocampus. This phenomenon is an enhancement of synaptic transmission lasting days or weeks following a brief, high-frequency train of stimulation to a bundle of afferent fibers (Bliss & Lomo, 1973). LTP has attracted considerable attention as a cellular change that might be related to mammalian learning and memory because of its properties of specificity, associativity, and long duration (for review see Bliss & Lynch, 1987; Nicoll, Kauer, & Malenka, 1988).

However, despite the success that has been achieved in observing the phenomenon over a period of hours in reduced preparations such as the hippocampal slice, mechanistic analysis has proven remarkably difficult. Indirect evidence has been presented arguing in favor of a presynaptic or a postsynaptic locus of modification. Specifically, measurements of long-lasting increases in glutamate levels in the hippocampus *in vivo* following tetanus of afferent pathways would suggest increased presynaptic transmitter release (Dolphin, Errington, & Bliss, 1982). On the postsynaptic side, an increase in the number of glutamate receptors has been proposed as the mechanism (Lynch & Baudry, 1984).

It is intuitively clear that either of these proposed specific mechanisms could account for the observed enhanced synaptic transmission. However, it is not obvious whether changes in the EPSP waveform are to be expected from either mechanism. It is in this type of situation, in which intuition becomes somewhat less reliable than would be expected, that quantitative modeling can provide predictions that are valuable in distinguishing among competing alternative possibilities. In this vein, we have applied functional reconstruction techniques to the problem of LTP by simulating the response of a pyramidal cell soma and dendrite to activation of an excitatory synapse on a remote dendritic spine. The input resistance measured at the soma was 50 MΩ.

Fig. 4.   Model of presynaptic facilitation in *Aplysia*. A, After a 40% reduction in potassium conductance in the presynaptic terminal, the action potential is broadened to the point that it rises sooner and falls later than the control trace. B, The presynaptic spike broadening causes an enhanced EPSP in the postsynaptic membrane. C, The calcium concentration in the terminal reaches a higher peak concentration but also remains elevated longer with reduced potassium conductance.

The membrane of the spine head contained glutamate receptors of the
N-methyl-D-aspartate (NMDA) type and the non-NMDA type, as well as
the same leakage channels as the rest of the purely passive structure. The
voltage dependence of the NMDA receptors was calibrated based on the
current–voltage measurements of NMDA responses in cultured mouse
CNS neurons (Mayer & Westbrook, 1984). Non-NMDA receptors had
linear current–voltage relations. If the ratio of non-NMDA to NMDA
conductances in the membrane are varied systematically, it has been
found that a ratio of approximately 10 : 1 gives a relation of peak synaptic
current to voltage that approximates the relation reported (Mayer &
Westbrook, 1984; Forsythe & Westbrook, 1988; Cotman & Stevens,
1988).

Using this synaptic structure, we have performed simulations of EPSPs
measured in the soma for various amounts of transmitter release and for
various ratios of non-NMDA to NMDA conductances. Figures 5 illus-

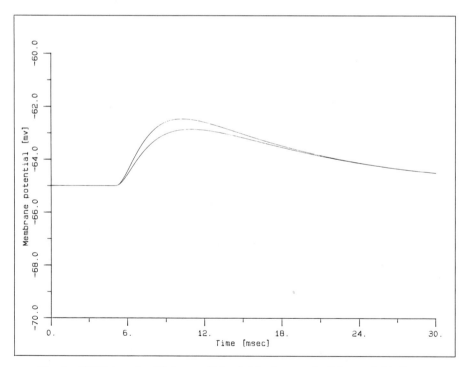

Fig. 5.   EPSPs in a simplified pyramidal cell. Membrane potential recorded in the soma.
A remote synapse located on a dendritic spine activated non-NMDA- and NMDA-type glutamate receptors in different ratios. Above, ratio of 5:1. Below, ratio of 1:2. The change in
ratio caused a change in the waveform of the EPSP.

trates our findings for two ratios of non-NMDA to NMDA receptor populations in the postsynaptic membrane. Because of the shorter channel lifetime for the non-NMDA receptor, the EPSP has a larger early component for the case with the larger ratio of non-NMDA to NMDA conductance. This EPSP shape difference is observed in the spine as well as in the soma, although the attenuation factor is approximately 2.5.

When parameters are lacking and techniques are unavailable for making particular types of measurements, this quantitative approach is useful for setting boundaries on parameter values and determining which phenomena are robust and which depend on relatively precise combinations of parameter values.

IV. Strategies for Quantitative Modeling: Numerical Implementation

Beside the specific implementation considerations discussed and developed in the earlier sections, there are some general numerical algorithms crucial to the computational accuracy of the simulation that cannot be overlooked. The choice of the numerical integration method and the random number generator employed in the simulation program may produce different simulation results if the accuracy of these algorithms is insufficient.

The numerical integration scheme used in our implementation is a slightly modified version of the Merson fifth-order variant of the Runge–Kutta algorithm (Gear, 1971). The extra derivative evaluation step provides an error estimate for automatic step size modification at each time step. Thus the error criteria may be modified depending on the particular simulation accuracy.

Most pseudo-random number generators supplied by the computer operating system libraries have the side effect of serial correlation and short period of recursion. An algorithm for producing a uniform random number sequence with immeasurably long period and no detectable serial correlation is described by Press, Flannery, Teukolsky, and Vetterling (1986), and is used in our implementation.

V. Conclusion

The process of detailed physiological neural modeling is not necessarily an end to itself. Rather it is a tool to help test, verify, and confirm the findings and hypotheses based on experimental results collected in the studies of biological nervous systems. The results produced by the quantitative modeling of the synaptic events illustrate vividly the underlying principles that may result in synaptic plasticity. Furthermore, the quantitative approach in simulation of biological nervous systems may guide experimentalists in designing new sets of experimental protocols when biological experimentation is time-consuming and is constrained by technical limitations. For a theoretician, such detailed biological models may provide insights to develop theories underlying learning and synaptic interactions given the simulation results. Since the model described in this article is a compartmental model from which one could construct a rather complicated neuronal structure or network, complex interactions among neurons may be studied with known connections and physiological parameters. Such detailed anatomical and physiological knowledge of the neural net is often unavailable to an experimentalist trying to make firm inferences about the underlying interactions of the system under study. The availability of such detailed biological models will augment the understanding of the nervous system, neuronal interactions, and synaptic plasticity both theoretically and experimentally.

ACKNOWLEDGMENTS

We are greatly indebted to David J. Perkel for valuable suggestions and technical assistance in the preparation of this manuscript. We also thank Wm. Seth Tucker for his assistance in performing simulation runs. The research and development of the MANUEL programs is supported by System Development Foundation Grant G283 and NIH Grant NS25210.

REFERENCES

Ackley, D. H., Hinton, G. E., & Sejnowski, T. J. (1985). A learning algorithm for Boltzmann machines. *Cognitive Science, 9,* 147–169.

Alkon, D. L. (1984). Calcium-mediated reduction of ionic currents: a biophysical memory trace. *Science,* **226,** 1037–1045.

Alkon, D. L. (1987). *Memory traces in the brain.* New York: Cambridge University Press.

Anderson, J. A., Silverstein, J. W., Ritz, S. A., & Jones, R. S. (1977). Distinctive features, categorical perception, and probability learning: Some applications of a neural model. *Psychological Review,* **84,** 413–451.

Barish, M. E. (1980). *Calcium regulation in the extreme peripheral cytoplasm of Molluscan neuron somata.* Unpublished doctoral dissertation, Stanford University, Stanford, CA.

Bliss, T. V. P. and Lomo, T. (1973). Long-lasting potentiation of synaptic transmission in the dentate area of the anaesthetized rabbit following stimulating the perforant path. *Journal of Physiology (London)* 232: 331–356.

Bliss, T. V. P. and Lynch, M. A. (1987). Long-term potentiation of synaptic transmission in the hippocampus: Properties and mechanisms. In P. W. Landfield and S. A. Deadwyler

(Eds.), *Long-term potentiation: From biophysics to behavior* (pp. 3–72). New York: Alan R. Liss.

Castellucci, V. F., & Kandel, E. R. (1976). Presynaptic facilitation as a mechanism for behavioral sensitization in *Aplysia*. *Science*, **194**, 1176–1178.

Cotman, C. W., & Stevens, D. R. (1988). Excitatory amino-acid receptors: Anatomical organization and functional implications. In E. A. Cavalheiro, J. Lehman and L. Turski (Eds.), *Frontier in excitatory amino acid research* (pp. 117–123). New York: Alan R. Liss.

Dolphin, A. C., Errington, M. L., & Bliss, T. V. P. (1982). Long-term potentiation of the perforant path in vivo is associated with increased glutamate release. *Nature (London)* **297**, 496–498.

Forsythe, I. D., & Westbrook, G. L. (1988). Slow excitatory postsynaptic currents mediated by *N*-methyl-D-aspartate receptors on cultured mouse central neurones. *Journal of Physiology (London)*, **396**, 515–533.

Gear, C. W. (1971). *Numerical initial value problems in ordinary differential equations.* Englewood Cliffs, NJ: Prentice-Hall.

Grossberg, S. (1975). A neural model of attention, reinforcement, and discrimination learning. *International Review of Neurobiology*, **18**, 263–327.

Hagiwara, S., & Byerly, L. (1981). Calcium channel. *Annual Review of Neuroscience*, **4**, 69–125.

Hebb, D. O. (1949). *The organization of behavior.* New York: Wiley.

Hodgkin, A. L., & Huxley, A. F. (1952). A quantitative description of membrane current and its application to conduction and excitation in nerve. *Journal of Physiology (London)*, **117**, 500–544.

Hopfield, J. J. (1982). Neural networks and physical systems with emergent collective computational abilities. *Proceedings of the National Academy of Sciences U.S.A.*, **79**, 2554–2558.

Katz, B., & Miledi, R. (1967a). The study of synaptic transmission in the absence of nerve impulses. *Journal of Physiology (London)*, **192**, 407–436.

Katz, B., & Miledi, R. (1967b). The timing of calcium action during neuromuscular transmission. *Journal of Physiology (London)*, **189**, 535–544.

Lynch, G., & Baudry, M. (1984). The biochemistry of memory: A new and specific hypothesis. *Science*, **224**, 1057–1063.

Magleby, K. L., & Stevens, C. F. (1972). A quantitative description of end-plate currents. *Journal of Physiology (London)*, **223**, 173–197.

Mayer, M. L., & Westbrook, G. L. (1984). Mixed-agonist action for excitatory amino acids on mouse spinal cord neurones under voltage clamp. *Journal of Physiology (London)*, **354**, 29–53.

McClelland, J. L. and Rumelhart, D. E. (1986a). *Parallel distributed processing. Vol. 1: Foundations.* Cambridge, MA: MIT Press.

McClelland, J. L. and Rumelhart, D. E. (1986b). *Parallel distributed processing. Vol. 2: Psychological and Biological Models.* Cambridge, MA: MIT Press.

McCulloch, W. S., & Pitts, W. H. (1943). A logical calculus of the ideas immanent in nervous activity. *Bulletin of Mathematical Biophysics*, **5**, 115–133.

Miller, J. P., Rall, W., & Rinzel, J. (1985). Synaptic amplification by active membrane in dendritic spines. *Brain Research*, **325**, 325–330.

Nicoll, R. A., Kauer, J. K., & Malenka, R. C. (1988). The current excitement in long-term potentiation. *Neuron*, **1**, 97–103.

Perkel, D. H. (1982–1983). Functional role of dendritic spines. *Journal de Physiologie (Paris)*, **78**, 695–699.

Perkel, D. H., & Perkel, D. J. (1985). Dendritic spines: role of active membrane in modulating synaptic efficacy. *Brain Research,* **325,** 331–335.

Press, W. H., Flannery, B. P., Teukolsky, S. A., & Vetterling, W. T. (1986). *Numerical recipes: The art of scientific computing.* New York: Cambridge University Press.

Rall, W. (1964). Theoretical significance of dendritic trees for neuronal input–output relations. In R. F. Reiss (Ed.), *Neural theory and modeling* (pp. 73–97). Stanford, CA: Stanford University Press.

Rumelhart, D. E., Hinton, G. E., & Williams, R. J. (1986). Learning representations by back-propagating errors. *Nature (London),* **323,** 533–536.

Smith, S. J. (1978). *The mechanism of bursting pacemaker activity in neurons of the mollusc Tritonia diomedia.* Unpublished doctoral dissertation, University of Washington, Seattle.

Thompson, S. H. (1976). *Membrane currents underlying bursting in molluscan pacemaker neurons.* Unpublished doctoral dissertation, University of Washington, Seattle.

Zucker, R. S. (1985). Calcium diffusion models and transmitter release in neurons. *Federation Proceedings,* **44,** 2950–2952.

Zucker, R. S. (1989). Short-term synaptic plasticity. *Annual Review of Neuroscience,* **12,** 13–31.

COMPUTATIONAL CAPABILITIES OF SINGLE NEURONS: RELATIONSHIP TO SIMPLE FORMS OF ASSOCIATIVE AND NONASSOCIATIVE LEARNING IN *APLYSIA*

John H. Byrne
Kevin J. Gingrich
Douglas A. Baxter

I. Introduction

From analyses of simple forms of learning performed in a variety of vertebrate and invertebrate model systems, it is becoming increasingly clear that learning involves changes in existing synaptic connections (see numerous chapters in this volume and Byrne, 1987, for review). Synaptic transmission, however, is by no means a simple process, and changes in the efficacy of synaptic transmission (synaptic plasticity) can be due to a number of factors acting either independently or in concert. Transmitter release can be considered the product of two variables. One is the number of vesicles of transmitter available for release (N), and the second is the probability of release (P) (Katz, 1966). Factors affecting the number of vesicles include synthesis of transmitter, reuptake of released transmitter, and mobilization of vesicles from storage or reserve pools to release sites in the presynaptic terminal. The probability of release can be affected by any factor that regulates Ca^{2+} influx into the terminal [such as the ability of the presynaptic action potential (spike) to invade the terminal or changes in spike height or width], the regulation of levels of intracellular Ca^{2+}, or any other step in the excitation–secretion process. Synaptic plasticity can have a postsynaptic locus as well. For example, the

31

effectiveness of a fixed amount of transmitter released by a presynaptic cell could be enhanced in several ways: by increasing the number of postsynaptic receptors for the transmitter, by increasing the affinity of the receptor for the transmitter, by increasing the input resistance of the postsynaptic cell so that a fixed synaptic current produces a greater change in membrane potential, or by a change in dendritic morphology such that the postsynaptic potential is propagated more effectively to some integrative area of the cell. Changes in morphology of the pre- and/or postsynaptic regions could also result in alterations of the synaptic cleft so that the released transmitter more effectively reaches receptor sites on the postsynaptic cell (see Tam & Perkel, this volume). Changes in synaptic transmission need not be limited to strictly a pre- or a postsynaptic locus—they could occur at both loci.

Given this diversity of possible loci for synaptic plasticity, a fundamental question is, Can a proposed mechanism account quantitatively for a given example of plasticity (and ultimately a particular behavior)? One way of addressing this issue is to formulate mathematical descriptions of the proposed mechanisms and examine whether a simulation of the resultant model can account for features of the plasticity and the behavior. Modeling and simulation studies have additional benefits as well. First, they provide a concise formulation of current hypotheses regarding complex interactions between multiple subcellular systems and processes, thus facilitating an understanding of the consequences of those interactions. Second, models make predictions that can be tested subsequently at the cellular and behavioral level, which helps to identify critical parameters that warrant experimental examination in greater detail. Third, models of simple forms of synaptic plasticity and learning at the cellular level can be used as building blocks for incorporation into neural networks. This synthetic and more theoretical approach provides the opportunity to examine the ability of such networks to exhibit complex features of learning and computational capabilities. In this article, we review some attempts to model mathematically the cellular and molecular bases of synaptic plasticity that contribute to nonassociative and associative learning in the marine mollusk *Aplysia*. The article by Hawkins (this volume) describes some of the consequences of incorporating single-cell models into a network consisting of multiple plastic cells.

Before describing the details of the mechanisms for synaptic plasticity contributing to several simple forms of learning in *Aplysia*, we first briefly review some of the basic conditioning procedures. This is done both for completeness and to provide some background for subsequent chapters in this volume.

A. PROCEDURES FOR MODIFYING BEHAVIOR

Many investigators interested in a cellular analysis of learning have employed both nonassociative and associative learning paradigms. Associative learning involves a wide range of behavioral modifications, but one that has been extensively studied is classical conditioning. In classical conditioning, two events are temporally paired. In contrast, nonassociative learning is not dependent on pairing. Examples of nonassociative learning are habituation, dishabituation, and sensitization. The importance of nonassociative learning should not be overlooked, because in at least one case the cellular mechanisms underlying associative learning seem to be an elaboration of mechanisms involved in nonassociative learning (see below).

1. Habituation

Habituation, perhaps the simplest form of nonassociative learning, is a decrement of responsiveness due to repetition of a stimulus. It is generally distinguished from simple fatigue since responsiveness can be rapidly restored (dishabituated) by the presentation of a novel stimulus to the animal. The parametric features of habituation have been described by Thompson and Spencer (1966).

2. Sensitization and Dishabituation

Sensitization is also a form of nonassociative learning and is generally defined as the enhancement of a nondecremented behavioral response as a result of applying a novel stimulus to the animal. The stimulus may be of the same modality and applied at the same site as a test stimulus used to elicit the response, or it may be of a different modality, applied to a different locus. *Dishabituation* is the restoration of a previously habituated response and, like sensitization, is produced by applying a novel stimulus to the animal. Previously, it was believed that sensitization and dishabituation involved a common mechanism (Carew, Castellucci, & Kandel, 1971). It has, however, become clear that multiple processes and mechanisms are involved (Hochner, Klein, Schacher, & Kandel, 1986b; Marcus, Nolen, Rankin, & Carew, 1988; Rankin & Carew, 1988; see also below).

3. Classical Conditioning

Classical conditioning is an example of associative learning in which presentation of a reinforcing (unconditioned) stimulus is made contingent on that of a preceding (conditioned) stimulus. The change in behavior produced by repeated pairing of the two stimuli can be measured in a number of ways. An example of classical conditioning involves the training procedure originally described by Pavlov (1927) to condition salivation in dogs. Before training, meat powder, referred to as the unconditioned stimulus (US), reliably elicited salivation, referred to as the unconditioned response (UR). The signal for the presentation of the US is called the conditioned stimulus (CS), and in the original experiments of Pavlov the CS was a metronome. Traditionally, the CS does not evoke a response similar to the UR and is typically referred to as a neutral stimulus. During training, the US was made contingent on the CS by repeatedly pairing the presentations of CS and US. After training, the response to the CS alone had changed such that the sound elicited salivation (the conditioned response, CR). The persistence of a conditioned response after training is called *retention*. When the contingency between CS and US was eliminated by repeatedly presenting the metronome in the absence of the meat powder (US), the ability of the CS to elicit the CR (salivation) gradually diminished. This process is called *extinction*.

In Pavlovian conditioning, contingency is generally established by the close temporal pairing (contiguity) of CS and US. (For a more detailed discussion, see Mackintosh, 1974, 1983; Rescorla, 1967.) Delivering the CS prior to the US is known as forward conditioning (as described above), whereas delivery of the CS after the US is known as backward conditioning. In some examples of classical conditioning, the temporal relationship between the presentation of the CS and US is graded such that there is an optimum time interval for conditioning. Shorter or longer intervals between the two stimuli, thus, result in less effective conditioning. The interval between CS onset and US onset is called the CS–US interval or the interstimulus interval (ISI). Most conditioning procedures involved repeated pairings of the CS and US. The interval between these pairings is called the intertrial interval (ITI).

Specificity of behavioral change as a consequence of pairing can be shown most clearly by using a differential conditioning procedure. In this procedure, two different conditioned stimuli are used in the same animal; one is specifically paired with the US and is therefore called the CS[+], whereas the other, the CS[-], is specifically unpaired. Learned changes in behavior can be assessed by comparing the response to the CS[+] with that to the CS[-].

In Pavlov's experiments the metronome (the CS), when initially presented alone, did not produce salivation. In some examples of conditioning procedures, the CS initially produces a small response similar to that evoked by the US. After pairing, the response to the CS is enhanced.

This type of conditioning is known as α-conditioning, a form of classical conditioning. Both are similar in that they require a close temporal relationship between the CS and the US. In classical conditioning, however, the neutral CS initially does not produce a response similar to the UR, whereas in α-conditioning the CS produces a weak response that is subsequently enhanced. Some have argued that the distinction between α-conditioning and classical conditioning is somewhat arbitrary, and in principle the two could be mediated by identical cellular mechanisms (Kandel, 1976; Patterson, Cegavske, & Thompson, 1973).

α-Conditioning and sensitization also resemble one another. Both involve a modification of a previously existing response to a stimulus. They differ, however, in their temporal requirements. α-Conditioning requires a close temporal association between the CS and US. Sensitization does not.

B.   NEURAL MECHANISMS OF HABITUATION, DISHABITUATION, AND SENSITIZATION IN *Aplysia*

Invertebrates such as the marine mollusk *Aplysia* are particularly useful for analyzing the neural and molecular events that give rise to changes in neural function underlying learning. The nervous systems of many invertebrates contain only several thousand cells (compared with the billions of cells in the vertebrate nervous system). Cellular properties of invertebrate neurons are similar to those of vertebrates. Despite the small number of cells, an invertebrate ganglion can mediate a variety of different behaviors. A given behavior may therefore be mediated by 100 neurons or less, allowing one potentially to determine the entire neural circuit generating the behavior. Many neurons are large and can be repeatedly identified as unique individuals, permitting one to examine the functional properties of an individual cell and to relate these properties to a specific behavior mediated by the cell. Changes in cellular properties that occur when a behavior is modified by learning can then be related to specific changes in behavior. Molecular and biophysical events underlying the changes in cellular properties can then be determined.

The neuronal mechanisms contributing to nonassociative and associative learning have been analyzed extensively in two defensive behaviors of the marine mollusk *Aplysia:* the siphon withdrawal and the tail withdrawal reflexes (for reviews see Byrne, 1985, 1987; Carew, 1987; Hawkins, Clark, & Kandel, 1986; Kandel & Schwartz, 1982). Of the various sites in the neural circuits for these behaviors, the sensory neurons that mediate these reflexes appear particularly susceptible to modulation through a variety of cellular mechanisms. Habituation of the reflex is paralleled by depression of neurotransmitter release from the presynaptic terminals of the sensory neurons. The depression leads to progressively less activation of the motor neurons, which in turn leads to a decreased behavioral response (Byrne, 1982; Byrne, Castellucci, & Kandel, 1978; Castellucci & Kandel, 1974; Castellucci, Pinsker, Kupfermann, & Kandel, 1970; Kupfermann, Castellucci, Pinsker, & Kandel, 1970). Synaptic depression is correlated with cumulative inactivation of the sensory neuron Ca^{2+} current (Klein, Shapiro, & Kandel, 1980) and depletion of neurotransmitter (Bailey & Chen, 1988; Gingrich & Byrne, 1984, 1985, 1987). The sensory neurons are also a cellular locus for dishabituation and sensitization. Dishabituation and sensitization have been associated with increased transmitter release from the presynaptic terminals of the sensory neurons *(presynaptic facilitation)* (Carew *et al.,* 1971; Castellucci & Kandel, 1976; Castellucci *et al.,* 1970). Presynaptic facilitation is correlated with an enhanced Ca^{2+} influx produced indirectly by a cAMP-dependent reduction in a membrane K^+ conductance (Klein & Kandel, 1978, 1980; Klein *et al.,* 1980). Mobilization of transmitter also appears to play a role in presynaptic facilitation (Gingrich & Byrne, 1984, 1985, 1987; Hochner, Schacher, Klein, & Kandel, 1985; Hochner, Klein, Schacher, & Kandel, 1986a; Hochner *et al.,* 1986b). Presynaptic facilitation leads to enhanced activation of motor neurons and an enhanced behavioral response.

II.   Mathematical Model of Subcellular Processes Contributing to Dishabituation and Sensitization in *Aplysia*

A.   COMPONENTS OF THE NONASSOCIATIVE MODEL

The current understanding of the various biochemical and biophysical mechanisms that contribute to plasticity within the sensory neurons has allowed us to develop formal descriptions of these processes. The approach was to transform the processes into mathematical formalisms, assign values to the parameters which agree with published data, and fit the components together to create a model of transmitter release.

The general features of the model are illustrated in Fig. 1. In Fig. 1A, the presynaptic terminal is shown as a varicosity of a sensory neuron (Bailey, Thompson, Castellucci, & Kandel, 1979). The active zone is represented by a grid of Ca^{2+} channels and release sites in the presynaptic membrane. Figure 1B shows a portion of the active zone and the underlying cytosol, which we refer to as a slab. The presynaptic membrane is present on the front face of the slab and illustrates the arrangement of the Ca^{2+} channels and the release sites. We assume that the channels and

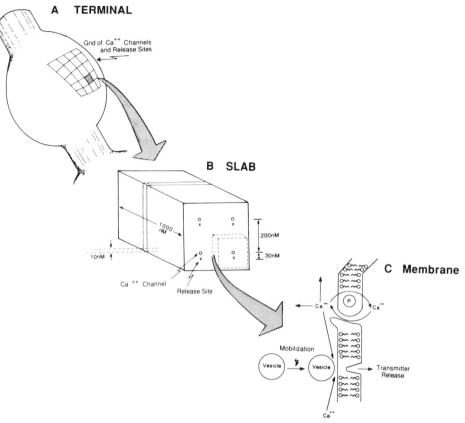

Fig. 1.   Schematic representation of the major features of the nonassociative model. A, Active zones in the presynaptic varicosities of sensory neurons are thought to represent regions of the terminal where transmitter is preferentially released. Active zones are characterized, in part, by focal regions of intramembranous specializations that are believed to be Ca^{2+} channels and sites for exocytosis, and by accumulations of synaptic vesicles immediately adjacent to the membrane (Bailey, Thompson, Castellucci, & Kandel, 1979). B, Within the active zone, Ca^{2+} channels (○), and release sites (X) are assumed to be dispersed uniformly. The dimensions indicated on the enlargement of a portion of the active zone (slab) were used in the solution of the diffusion equation. C, The simulations were based upon a single subsection of a slab that contained all of the basic elements of the model: a release site, Ca^{2+} channel, Ca^{2+} pump, and a pool of releasable vesicles that undergoes depletion and mobilization. The physiological properties of the basic elements in the subsection were considered to be uniform throughout both this terminal and other terminals of the sensory neuron. Therefore, a simulation of a single subsection is assumed to reflect the responses of all terminals. Note that the diagrams are not drawn to scale. Reprinted with permission from Gingrich, Baxter, & Byrne (1988).

release sites are arranged in a regular fashion and therefore base our calculations on a subsection of the slab which contains a single Ca^{2+} channel
and release site. An orthogonal view through the cell membrane from
such a subsection is shown in Fig. 1C. The cut is through a release site,
a Ca^{2+} channel, and a Ca^{2+} pump. During an action potential in the presynaptic terminal or a depolarizing pulse, Ca^{2+} enters through discrete
voltage-gated channels in the membrane. Once Ca^{2+} has entered the cell,
it diffuses in three dimensions. Ca^{2+} is removed from the cell by a membrane pump or buffered by the cytosol. The Ca^{2+} that reaches the release
sites triggers release of transmitter-containing vesicles that are in close
proximity to the inner surface of the membrane. Release occurs by exocytosis. The vesicles in close proximity to the membrane are called the
releasable pool. A flux of vesicles, which is referred to as *mobilization*,
moves transmitter from a storage pool into the releasable pool.

1.   Transmitter Storage and Release

The release of transmitter is modeled as a normalized flux of vesicles
(T_R) into the synaptic cleft that is determined by the number of vesicles
(N_R) within a releasable pool (P_R) and the concentration of Ca^{2+} at the
release site raised to the third power.

$$T_R = N_R \times [K_R \times Ca]^3 \tag{1}$$

The parameter K_R is simply a scaling multiplier. The power relationship
between the concentration of Ca^{2+} in the submembrane compartment at
the release site and release is consistent with data from the squid giant
synapse (Augustine & Charlton, 1986; Augustine, Charlton, & Smith,
1985). During various simulations, the initial value of N_R prior to any
stimulus-evoked release is adjusted such that depletion reduces the value
of N_R, while mobilization increases the value of N_R. Thus, the model does
not include explicit descriptions of processes regulating mobilization.
Such processes, however, are included in the model for associative conditioning (see below). In the absence of depletion or mobilization (i.e., a
normal synapse), the value of N_R was normalized to 100.

The change in the size of the releasable pool of transmitter during a
presynaptic depolarizing pulse (simulated action potential) was determined by solving the first-order differential equation

$$\frac{dN_R}{dt} = -T_R \tag{2}$$

2. Calcium Influx

The general description for the average influx of Ca^{2+} (I_{Ca}) through a single channel is

$$I_{Ca} = G_{Ca}(V,t) \times (V_m - E_{Ca}) \qquad (3)$$

where G_{Ca} is the average voltage- and time-dependent conductance of a Ca^{2+} channel, V_m is the membrane voltage, and E_{Ca} is the Nernst equilibrium potential for Ca^{2+}. It is assumed that the Ca^{2+} channel does not exhibit inactivation. Presynaptic action potentials are simulated by depolarizing pulses that shift V_m from a resting level of -50 mV to $+12$ mV. The durations of the presynaptic depolarizations were varied in order to simulate the spike broadening that is induced by procedures analogous to dishabituation and sensitization (Baxter & Byrne, 1987; Hochner et al., 1986b; Klein & Kandel, 1980; Pollock, Bernier, & Camardo, 1985; Walters, Byrne, Carew, & Kandel, 1983).

a. Calcium Channel Activation. The average kinetics of the Ca^{2+} channel are described in a form similar to that used by Hodgkin and Huxley (1952) to describe the kinetics of voltage-gated channels. In gastropods, activation of G_{Ca} can be approximated by a second-order process (Byerly, Chase, & Stimers, 1984; Byerly & Hagiwara, 1982; Chad, Eckert, & Ewald, 1984; Eckert & Ewald, 1983; Kostyuk, Krishtal, & Pidoplichko, 1981; Kostyuk, Krishtal, & Shakhovalov, 1977). Therefore the activation of G_{Ca} during a depolarizing pulse to some voltage (V_D) is given by

$$G_{Ca}(V_D,t) = G_{max} \times (1 - \exp(-t/T_m))^2 \qquad (4)$$

where G_{max} is the maximum average conductance of a Ca^{2+} channel at V_D, t is time during the depolarizing pulse, and T_m is a voltage-dependent time constant for activation. Substitution of Eq. (4) into Eq. (3) describes the influx of Ca^{2+} during the depolarization.

b. Calcium Channel Deactivation. The Ca^{2+} channels activated by the membrane depolarization exhibit time-dependent deactivation in response to repolarization. The deactivation of Ca^{2+} channels can be approximated by the sum of two decaying exponentials (Byerly et al., 1984; Eckert & Ewald, 1983). Therefore, the deactivation of G_{Ca} following repolarization to the resting potential (V_R) is given by

$$G_{Ca}(V_R,t) = G_{Ca}(V_D,t_p) \times [K_F \times \exp(-t/T_F) + K_S \times \exp(-t/T_S)] \quad (5)$$

where $G_{Ca}(V_D, t_p)$ is the magnitude of the conductance achieved at the end of the depolarizing pulse [see Eq. (4)], K_F and K_S are the individual contributions to deactivation by the fast and slow components respectively, and t is the time after the end of the pulse. Substitution of Eq. (5) into Eq. (3) describes the decay of the influx of Ca^{2+} following repolarization. This formulation ignores any steady-state current after deactivation, but this is small relative to that during depolarization (Eckert & Ewald, 1983).

3. Calcium Diffusion

To trigger the release of transmitter, Ca^{2+} must diffuse through the cytoplasm from an open Ca^{2+} channel to a release site at which exocytosis occurs. We developed a three-dimensional model of Ca^{2+} diffusion based on previously published models for diffusion in cytoplasm (e.g., Berg, 1983; Chad & Eckert, 1984; Crank, 1975; Fogelson & Zucker, 1985; Moore, Ramon, & Joyner, 1975; Simon & Llinas, 1985; Zucker & Fogelson, 1986; Zucker & Stockbridge, 1983). In this model, Ca^{2+} diffuses in three dimensions away from discrete channels to a release site that is 30 nm from the mouth of the Ca^{2+} channel (see Fig. 1B). Other factors that influence the concentration of Ca^{2+} include extrusion by membrane pumps and cytoplasmic buffering. We employed an explicit, backward difference numerical approximation to evaluate the partial differential equation that describes diffusion in Cartesian coordinates (for details see Gingrich, Baxter, & Byrne, 1988).

4. Postsynaptic Potential

The postsynaptic potential (V_{PSP}) that is produced by the release of transmitter was approximated as a resistance–capacitance (RC) network with a time constant (T_M) of 30 msec;

$$\frac{dV_{PSP}}{dt} = \frac{(K_V \times T_R) - V_{PSP}}{T_M} \tag{6}$$

where K_V is a constant that relates the release of transmitter to a change in the postsynaptic potential.

B. RESPONSE OF THE NONASSOCIATIVE MODEL TO A SIMULATED ACTION POTENTIAL IN THE SENSORY NEURON

The responses of some of the variables of the model during a 2-msec depolarization are shown in Fig. 2. During the depolarizing pulse that simulates an action potential in the presynaptic terminal, activation of the

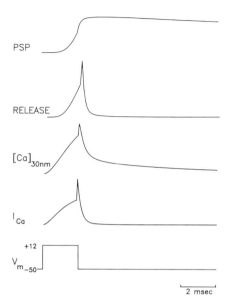

Fig. 2. Simulation of synaptic transmission at a sensory synapse. Displayed are the presynaptic membrane voltage (V_m), Ca^{2+} current (I_{Ca}), concentration of Ca^{2+} at the release site ([Ca]$_{30nm}$), the release of transmitter [T_R in Eq. (1)], and the simulated postsynaptic potential (PSP). Reprinted with permission from Gingrich, Baxter, & Byrne (1988).

Ca^{2+} channel results in an influx of Ca^{2+} (I_{Ca}). At the end of the pulse, there is a sharp increase in I_{Ca} due to the rise in the driving force while the channel remains open during its deactivation. The dynamics of deactivation then return the Ca^{2+} channel to its resting state and Ca^{2+} influx is terminated as the channel closes. The concentration of Ca^{2+} at the release site, [Ca$_{30nm}$], rises with activation of the Ca^{2+} channel during the pulse. The sharp increase in the concentration of Ca^{2+} at the end of the pulse is due to the corresponding increase in I_{Ca}. The rapid rise, exaggerated peak, and rapid decay of the release of transmitter reflect the fact that release is related to the cube of the concentration of Ca^{2+} [see Eq. (1)]. Finally, transmitter release (T_R) drives the RC network approximation of the postsynaptic membrane to generate the postsynaptic potential (PSP).

C. CONTRIBUTION OF SPIKE BROADENING AND MOBILIZATION TO DISHABITUATION AND SENSITIZATION

1. Input–Output Relationships

Presynaptic facilitation contributing to dishabituation and sensitization appears to be due to both spike broadening and mobilization. In order to separate the relative contributions of the two processes, it is necessary to hold one of the processes constant while the other is manipulated. This can be done experimentally by voltage clamping the presynaptic neuron. In this way, it is possible to alter the duration of the presynaptic potential systematically and therefore simulate spike broadening that is normally produced by a sensitizing or dishabituating stimulus. A plot of the magnitude of the postsynaptic potential (PSP) versus the duration of the presynaptic depolarization is known as the input–output (I–O) relationship. Similarly, by holding the duration of the presynaptic pulse constant during the modulatory effects of a sensitizing or dishabituating stimulus, the separate effects of mobilization can be determined. Obviously, the same manipulations can be done readily with a simulation of the mathematical model.

The relationship between the duration of presynaptic depolarizations and the amplitude of the PSP for empirical data (Hochner *et al.*, 1986b) and simulated results are plotted in Fig. 3. Responses for a normal synapse (neither depressed nor facilitated) are given in Fig. 3A. Both the stimulated and empirical data display a steep relationship between the

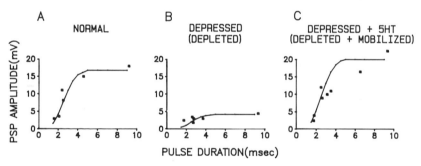

Fig. 3. Empirical and simulated input–output relationships. The equations and their respective parameters lead to a fit of empirical data. The model simulates changes in PSP amplitude produced by broadening of the presynaptic pulse. In all panels, the solid squares are the empirical data collected by Hochner, Klein, Schacher, and Kandel (1986b) from sensory neurons and follower neurons in dissociated cell culture, and the solid lines are the responses of the model. The empirical data was collected by delivering voltage clamp pulses from −50 mV to +12 mV at a series of different duration. The model parameters chosen to simulate these different release conditions are discussed in the text. A, Broadening the pulse duration without modulating the releasable pool enhances release in normal synapses. B, In depressed synapses increasing pulse duration alone does little to enhance the PSP. C, Application of 5-HT to the depressed synapse causes facilitation that is independent of pulse duration. Thus, presynaptic facilitation induced by 5-HT under these circumstances must involve some other process, which we refer to as mobilization. We could simulate this action by increasing the initial value of N_R. Once this second process increases the size of the releasable pool of transmitter, the steep relationship between pulse duration and PSP is restored. Reprinted with permission from Gingrich, Baxter, & Byrne (1988).

amplitude of the PSP and pulse durations between 2 and 4 msec. However, as pulse durations exceed 5 msec, further broadening produces little additional enhancement. Depletion of the pool of releasable transmitter during the pulse underlies this effect in the model. Figure 3B shows empirical and simulated results for a depressed or habituated synapse. Since our model accounts for synaptic depression by depletion of releasable transmitter (Gingrich & Byrne, 1985), such a simulation is referred to as *depleted*. Reducing the initial value of N_R by 75% reflects this depletion and yields an accurate simulation of the empirical data. In both simulated and empirical responses, increasing the duration of the pulse is ineffective in increasing release from a depressed synapse. Figure 3C shows the empirical responses of the depressed synapse after exposure to serotonin (5-HT). In our model, 5-HT triggers mobilization by producing an increase in the value of N_R (Gingrich & Byrne, 1987). Consequently, such a simulation is termed *depleted plus mobilized,* and the initial value of N_R is increased to 120% of normal. In both empirical and simulated responses, the steep relationship between pulse duration and the amplitude of the PSP is restored. Indeed, the magnitude of the PSPs is greater than that of the normal synapse (e.g., Fig. 3A).

The model provides an accurate description of the input–output relationship for normal, depressed, and facilitated synapses. Two key results are evident from the results illustrated in Fig. 3. First, the enhancement of PSPs at nondepressed synapses (analogous to sensitization) can be accounted for by increases in the duration of presynaptic action potentials, which are observed experimentally. Second, increases in the duration of presynaptic action potentials fail to enhance PSPs at depressed synapses. For enhancement of depressed synapses (analogous to dishabituation) there must be mobilization. Thus, these results indicate that broadening of the action potential can contribute significantly to sensitization but that mobilization of transmitter is necessary for dishabituation.

2. Changes in the Shape of PSPs during Presynaptic Facilitation

By independently manipulating the initial value of N_R and the duration of the presynaptic pulse in the model, it is possible to compare the relative contributions of the two processes underlying presynaptic facilitation to the shape of the PSP. The effect of changes in the value of N_R on the shape of the PSP is illustrated in Fig. 4. In Fig. 4A, the lowest trace shows a 2-msec depolarizing pulse that is used to generate the family of PSPs shown directly above. The only difference in the calculation of each PSP is an increase in the value of N_R by a fixed amount, which increases as one moves from the smallest to the largest PSP. Note that the time to peak of the PSP is unchanged but the rate of rise becomes greater as N_R

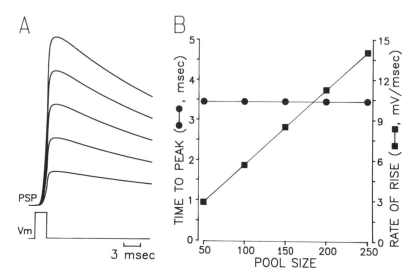

Fig. 4.   Effect of varying the initial size of the pool of releasable transmitter on the shape of simulated PSPs. A, The effect of mobilization on the shape of the PSP was evaluated by generating a family of PSPs using a constant duration presynaptic depolarizing pulse (2 msec) but with increases in the initial size of the releasable pool [N_R in Eq. (1)]. B, It is clear that increasing the pool size increases the rate of rise of the PSP and does not alter the time to peak of the PSP. These results are consistent with empirical data in which an increase in the rate of rise of PSPs during facilitation of depressed synapses is observed (Hochner, Klein, Schacher, & Kandel, 1986b). Reprinted with permission from Gingrich, Baxter, & Byrne (1988).

is increased. Figure 4B is a plot of these results. Changes in the value of N_R have no effect on the time to peak, but increases in the value of N_R produce a linear increase in the rate of rise of the PSP. This is so because release is proportional to N_R [Eq. (1)] and the concentration of Ca^{2+} at the release site is raised to the third power. Since only the value of N_R is changing and not the dynamics of Ca^{2+} influx, then only the magnitude of the PSP will change and not its time to peak.

The effect of varying pulse duration on the shape of the PSP is illustrated in Fig. 5. In Fig. 5A, the PSPs were generated by increasing the duration of the depolarizing pulses from 2 msec to 6 msec (in all cases the initial value of N_R was 100). As the pulse duration increases, there is both an increase in the amplitude of the PSP and its time to peak. The rate of rise, however, changes little for the PSPs shown. Figure 5B is a plot of the effect of pulse duration on time to peak and rate of rise. Time to peak varies nearly linearly with pulse durations of up to 7 msec. Beyond 7 msec there is no further increase because of complete depletion of the releasable pool during the pulse [see Eq. (2)]. There is only a small

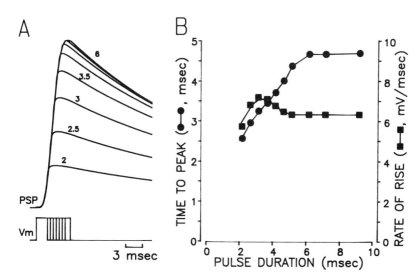

Fig. 5. Effect of varying the duration of the presynaptic pulse on the shape of the simulated PSP. A, The effect of spike broadening on the shape of the PSP was evaluated by
generating a family of PSPs using a constant initial value for N_R (N_R = 100) but with increasing durations for the presynaptic depolarizing pulse. B, Pulse broadening alone is associated
primarily with enhanced PSPs with an increased time to peak. Empirically, prolonging voltage clamp depolarizing pulses progressively increases the time-to-peak of PSPs with little
change in the rate-of-rise (Klein & Kandel, 1980; Hochner, Klein, Schacher, & Kandel,
1986a). Reprinted with permission from Gingrich, Baxter, & Byrne (1988).

change in the rate of rise as pulse durations increase. Initially, there is a
slight rise, followed by a decline and plateau. This is explained by the
interaction between increasing influx of Ca^{2+} and waning releasable
stores and their combined effect on release. Overall, the effect of pulse
duration on time to peak is by far the more prominent.

Finally, we examined the response of the model during both increases
in spike width and mobilization. This condition simulates the response of
the neuron to reinforcing stimuli that activate both processes. Figure 6
illustrates how these two mechanisms can interact to enhance the amplitude of the PSP to a magnitude greater than that produced in normal conditions (e.g., Fig. 3C). Initially, the effects of pulse widening and increasing N_R were evaluated independently. A control response (PSPa) is
generated using a pulse duration of 3.5 msec and an initial pool size (N_R)
of 100. Broadening the pulse to 5 msec while keeping the initial pool size
constant produces little additional enhancement (PSPb). As explained
above (Figs. 3A and 5A), the release of transmitter is limited by the initial
value of N_R at pulse durations greater than about 4 msec. Increasing N_R

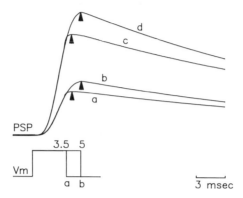

Fig. 6. Combined effects of increasing both pulse duration and pool size. The effect of pulse broadening and mobilization were evaluated independently and together. The duration of the presynaptic pulses are shown in the lower panel and simulated PSPs are shown in the upper panel. The arrowheads indicate the peaks of the PSPs. The enhancement of the PSPs induced by increasing the pulse duration from 3.5 msec (PSPa) to 5 msec (PSPb) is associated with a change in the time to peak of the corresponding PSPs. The enhancement of the PSPs induced by increasing the initial value of N_R (i.e., mobilization) for the 3.5-msec duration pulse is associated with a change in the rate of rise (PSPc). Combining the two processes of spike broadening and mobilization results in presynaptic facilitation that is associated with increases in both the time to peak and rate of rise (PSPd). Reprinted with permission from Gingrich, Baxter, & Byrne (1988).

by 200% while holding the duration fixed at 3.5 msec greatly increases the amplitude of the response (PSPc). Combining both pulse widening and mobilization produces a facilitated response (PSPd) that is enhanced beyond a simple summation of responses b and c. The resulting PSP showed an increase in the time to peak related to the greater pulse duration. The rate of rise is increased primarily by the larger releasable pool. These results are consistent with previous experimental data (see Fig. 3 in Hochner *et al.*, 1986b).

In summary, the nonassociative model can predict how the processes of mobilization and spike broadening affect the shape of the PSP. Mobilization of transmitter alone is associated with enhanced PSPs that have a constant time to peak and an increased rate of rise. Increasing the duration of the presynaptic pulses alone is associated with enhanced PSPs that have an increased time to peak and little change in rate of rise. Thus, the model indicates that the shape of the PSP can be used to gain insight into the relative contribution of spike broadening and mobilization to presynaptic facilitation, which contributes to dishabituation and sensitization.

Several lines of recent experimental evidence support the basic assumptions and conclusions of our model. First, a developmental analysis of learning in *Aplysia* revealed that dishabituation and sensitization can be distinguished ontogenetically (Rankin & Carew, 1988; see also Marcus *et al.*, 1988). The developmental separation of dishabituation and sensitization suggests that presynaptic facilitation, which contributes to both forms of plasticity, must be accomplished by multiple, developmentally distinct mechanisms. Second, Hochner *et al.* (1986b) compared the ability of spike broadening to mediate presynaptic facilitation in both normal and depressed synapses (e.g., Fig. 3). They found that prolonging the duration of the action potential could account for much of the presynaptic facilitation only in normal synapses (analogous to sensitization) but inferred that a second process was necessary to mediate presynaptic facilitation in depressed synapses (analogous to dishabituation). Moreover, they showed that prolonged durations of the action potential are associated with an increase in the time to peak of the PSP, whereas increasing transmitter release without changing spike duration affected only the rate of rise of the PSP (Hochner *et al.*, 1986a, 1986b; Klein *et al.*, 1980).

III. Mathematical Model of Subcellular Processes Contributing to Associative Learning in *Aplysia*

A. NEURAL MECHANISMS FOR ASSOCIATIVE CONDITIONING IN *Aplysia*

Studies on *Aplysia* indicate that a cellular mechanism called *activity-dependent neuromodulation* (Hawkins, Abrams, Carew, & Kandel, 1983; Walters & Byrne, 1983a) may contribute to classical conditioning observed on a behavioral level (Carew, Hawkins, & Kandel, 1983; Hawkins, Carew, & Kandel, 1986). A proposed general cellular scheme of activity-dependent neuromodulation is illustrated in Fig. 7A. Two sensory neurons (1 and 2), which constitute the pathways for the conditioned stimulus (CS), make weak subthreshold connections to a response system (e.g., a motor neuron). Delivering a reinforcing or unconditioned stimulus (US) alone has two effects. First, the US activates the response system and produces the unconditioned response (UR). Second, the US activates a diffuse modulatory system that nonspecifically enhances transmitter release from all the sensory neurons. This nonspecific enhancement contributes to sensitization (see above). Temporal specificity, characteristic of associative learning, occurs when there is pairing of the CS and thus spike activity in one of the sensory neurons (sensory neuron 1) with the US, causing a selective amplification of the modulatory effects in that specific sensory neuron (Hawkins *et al.*, 1983; Walters & Byrne, 1983a). Unpaired activity does not amplify the effects of the US in sensory neuron 2. The amplification of the modulatory effects in the paired sensory neu-

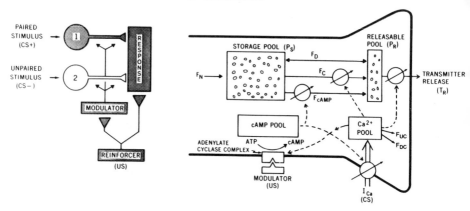

Fig. 7.   Cellular models for associative learning: A, Network model. Two sensory neurons (1 and 2) make subthreshold connections to a response system. Reinforcing stimuli
(US) cause direct activation of the response system and also activate a diffuse modulatory
system. Pairing of CS and US (indicated by stippling) enhances the modulatory effects over
that of unpaired stimulation. B, Single-cell model. The CS (spike activity) increases the level
of intracellular Ca^{2+}, which triggers transmitter release (T_R), mobilization of transmitter (F_C)
from a storage pool (P_S) to a releasable pool (P_R) and primes the adenylate cyclase complex.
Ca^{2+} is removed from the Ca^{2+} pool by F_{UC}, active uptake, and by F_{DC}, passive diffusion. F_D
represents diffusion of vesicles between the storage and releasable pools. The US activates
adenylate cyclase to increase cAMP levels that enhance mobilization of transmitter (F_{cAMP})
and increase Ca^{2+} influx (I_{Ca}). Increased Ca^{2+} influx is achieved indirectly through changes
in duration of the action potential. Association of CS with the US occurs when Ca^{2+} levels
are high at the time of the US. Paired application of the CS and US results in increased
levels of cAMP due to Ca^{2+} priming of the adenylate cyclase complex. The elevated cAMP
triggers increased mobilization of transmitter and subsequent enhanced Ca^{2+} influx and
transmitter release with the next test stimulus. F_N represents the delivery of vesicles to the
storage pool from unmodeled sources and results from transport from other storage pools
or synthesis triggered by depletion of the storage pool. F_N replenishes the storage pool
slowly because it is small relative to the volume of the pool. Its magnitude is proportional
to the difference between the initial and instantaneous concentration of vesicles in the storage pool. The circles with arrows through their center represent elements of the model
which are modulated positively by other variables. Modified from Gingrich & Byrne (1987).

ron leads to an enhancement of the ability of sensory neuron 1 to activate
the response system and produce the conditioned response (CR).

As indicated above, experimental analyses of sensitization of defensive
reflexes in *Aplysia* have shown that the neuromodulator released by the
reinforcing stimulus acts, at least in part, by reduction potassium currents
in the sensory neurons. Consequently, action potentials elicited after the
reinforcing stimulus are broader (due to less repolarizing K^+ current)
causing an enhanced influx of Ca^{2+}. Enhanced influx of Ca^{2+} triggers

greater release of transmitter from the sensory neurons, which causes increased activation of motor neurons and, thus, sensitization of the reflex. The effects of the natural modulatory transmitter released by sensitizing stimuli (Bernier, Castellucci, Kandel, & Schwartz, 1982; Ocorr, Tabata, & Byrne, 1986) can be mimicked by application of serotonin (5-HT) (Bernier *et al.*, 1982; Brunelli, Castellucci, & Kandel, 1976). This agent exerts its effects on action potential duration and transmitter release through changes in the level of the intracellular second messenger cAMP (Bernier *et al.*, 1982; Ocorr & Byrne, 1985). In addition to enhancing influx of Ca^{2+}, the neuromodulator released by the reinforcing stimulus leads to mobilization of transmitter in the sensory neurons (see above). The pairing specificity in the associative conditioning is due, at least in part, to an enhancement of cAMP levels beyond that produced by the modulator alone (Abrams, Bernier, Hawkins, & Kandel, 1984; Ocorr, Walters, & Byrne, 1983, 1985). Furthermore, it appears that influx of Ca^{2+} associated with the CS (spike activity) amplifies the US-mediated modulatory effect (Abrams, Carew, Hawkins, & Kandel, 1983) by interacting with a Ca^{2+}-sensitive component of the adenylate cyclase (Abrams, Eliot, Dudai, & Kandel, 1985). Evidence supporting the interaction of Ca^{2+} with adenylate cyclase is provided by studies of vertebrate neural tissue where a Ca^{2+}/calmodulin-dependent activation of neurotransmitter-stimulated adenylate cyclase has been demonstrated (Brostom, Brostom, Breckenridge, & Wolff, 1978; Gnegy, Muirhead, Robert-Lewis, & Treisman, 1984; Gnegy & Treisman, 1981; Malnoe, Stein, & Cox, 1983). Recent evidence indicates the presence of a Ca^{2+}-sensitive cyclase in *Aplysia* as well (Abrams *et al.*, 1985; Schwartz *et al.*, 1983; Weiss & Drummond, 1985). A critical role for Ca^{2+}-stimulated cyclase is also provided by studies of *Drosophila* in which it has been shown that the particulate adenylate cyclase of a mutant deficient in associative learning exhibits a loss of Ca^{2+}/calmodulin sensitivity (Aceves-Pina *et al.*, 1983; Dudai, 1985; Livingstone, 1985).

In order to model and account for many of the associative features of synaptic plasticity exhibited by the sensory neurons, it was necessary to construct a more complex model than that for dishabituation and sensitization. This extended model includes descriptions of additional subcellular processes. At the same time, some simplifications were introduced to limit the computation time in running the simulations. Details of the model are described in Gingrich and Byrne (1985, 1987). A general overview is presented below.

Figure 7B illustrates some of the major components of the associative model and their interactions. The model contains equations describing two pools of transmitter, a readily releasable pool (P_R) (as described previously) and a storage pool (P_S). Vesicles move from one pool to the other via three fluxes, one driven by diffusion (F_D), another driven by Ca^{2+} (F_C), and the third driven by levels of cAMP (F_{cAMP}). There are also equations describing the regulation of the levels of cAMP and Ca^{2+}. Action potentials lead to influx of Ca^{2+} (I_{Ca}), release of transmitter (T_R), and accumulation of Ca^{2+}. Application of the US leads to increased synthesis of cAMP, which leads to mobilization of transmitter (F_{cAMP}) and modulation of the spike parameters such that subsequent action potentials are broader, thus allowing for greater influx of Ca^{2+} and enhanced release of transmitter. When the CS (a burst of spikes) precedes the US, the elevated levels of Ca^{2+} regulate the adenylate cyclase complex such that when a subsequent US is delivered, there is greater synthesis of cAMP.

B. Ca^{2+} CHANNEL AND REGULATION OF THE LEVELS OF Ca^{2+}

To avoid the complexities of solving the three-dimensional diffusion equations described earlier and used for the nonassociative model, Ca^{2+} is assumed to be contained in discrete compartments (Fig. 7B). The pool of Ca^{2+} in Fig. 7B is actually contained in two volumes called the submembrane and interior compartments. The submembrane compartment represents the fraction of the cytosol lining the membrane; it has a thickness of a few vesicle diameters. The interior compartment represents the larger fraction of the cytosol interior to the submembrane compartment, which contains cellular organelles and systems that affect intracellular Ca^{2+}. During an action potential, Ca^{2+} (I_{Ca}) enters the submembrane compartment through voltage-dependent Ca^{2+} channels and rapidly diffuses into the larger interior compartment. Here the processes responsible for Ca^{2+} uptake and buffering exert their effect. These processes are represented as fluxes that remove Ca^{2+} from the interior compartment in accordance with two equations. One equation represents a flux (F_{UC}) that removes Ca^{2+} from the interior compartment by active processes in organelles such as the endoplasmic reticulum. A second equation represents removal of Ca^{2+} from the interior compartment due to diffusion (F_{DC}).

The concentration of Ca^{2+} (C_{Ca}) is determined by solving the differential equation:

$$\frac{dC_{Ca}}{dt} = (I_{Ca} - F_{UC} - F_{DC}) \times 1/V_C \qquad (7)$$

where I_{Ca} is the membrane Ca^{2+} current, F_{UC} the Ca^{2+} removed by active processes, F_{DC} the Ca^{2+} removed by diffusion, and V_C the volume of the interior compartment.

In the associative model, the duration of the action potential is modulated as a function of cAMP levels. While the details of this relationship are not fully understood, we assume, as a first approximation, that spike duration (given in seconds) is a linear function of the concentration of cAMP, where

$$\text{spike duration} = 0.003 + K_{DC} \times C_{cAMP} \tag{8}$$

K_{DC} is a constant, and C_{cAMP} is the concentration of cAMP. The unmodified (normal) spike duration is set at 3 msec.

C. REGULATION OF cAMP

The associative model also includes equations describing the concentration of cAMP and its effects on the release of transmitter from the sensory neuron. The cAMP cascade is a sequence of multiple events which includes the binding of a modulatory transmitter such as 5-HT to receptors, activation and decay of the activity of adenylate cyclase, synthesis and hydrolysis of cAMP, and protein phosphorylation and dephosphorylation. While many steps are involved, some evidence indicates that the rate-limiting step is the decay of adenylate cyclase activity (Castellucci, Nairn, Greengard, Schwartz, & Kandel, 1982; Schwartz et al., 1983). As a first approximation, we therefore assumed that the concentration of cAMP (C_{cAMP}) is described by a single lumped-parameter dynamic equation. We simulated the effects of the CS (a burst of spikes) on the level of cAMP by making the concentration of cAMP dependent on the intracellular concentration of calcium (C_{Ca}). In the presence of the US

$$\frac{dC_{cAMP}}{dt} = (-C_{cAMP}/T_{cAMP}) + K_{SC} + (K_{EC} \times C_{Ca}) \tag{9}$$

T_{cAMP} is the overall time constant for the regulation of cAMP levels (primarily decay of the activity of adenylate cyclase). K_{SC} is a constant that describes the degree of activation of the cAMP cascade in the presence of resting levels of intracellular Ca^{2+} during application of the US. K_{EC} is a constant that describes the additional activation of the cAMP cascade in the presence of intracellular Ca^{2+} (C_{Ca}) beyond resting level. C_{Ca} represents the Ca^{2+} concentration of the interior compartment [see Eq. (7)]. The first term in Eq. (9) describes the decay of cAMP levels, while the remaining terms describe the activation of adenylate cyclase during application of the US. In the absence of the US

$$\frac{dC_{cAMP}}{dt} = (-C_{cAMP}/T_{cAMP}) \tag{10}$$

If intracellular Ca^{2+} does not by itself lead to significant stimulation of adenylate cyclase (Ocorr *et al.*, 1985), then Eq. (10) applies even when the level of intracellular Ca^{2+} is altered as a result of test stimuli or CS presentations in the absence of the US.

D. RELEASE, STORAGE, AND MOBILIZATION OF TRANSMITTER

Perhaps the most significant conclusion to be drawn from the nonassociative models (Gingrich & Byrne, 1985; Gingrich *et al.*, 1988) is that processes regulating the availability of transmitter (i.e., depletion and mobilization) contribute significantly to synaptic plasticity in sensory neurons. During simulations of single action potentials, as described above, we simply reduced the number of vesicles (N_R) in the releasable pool (P_R) to model depletion and increased N_R to model mobilization. However, more explicit descriptions for these two processes are required in order to model the interactions between multiple stimuli and associative plasticity in sensory neurons.

1. Transmitter Release, Depletion, and Determination of Excitatory Postsynaptic Potentials

The releasable pool (P_R) contains vesicles that are in close proximity to release sites where the influx of Ca^{2+} (I_{Ca}) during an action potential causes the release of transmitter (T_R). The number of vesicles (N_R) within the releasable pool (P_R) is the product of the concentration of vesicles (C_R) in P_R and the volume (V_R) of P_R. As a consequence of release, this pool is depleted. An equation that reflects these principles is

$$T_R = (C_R \times V_R) \times (I_{Ca} \times K_R) \tag{11}$$

The product of I_{Ca} and K_R is proportional to the Ca^{2+} concentration in the submembrane compartment [see Eq. (7)]. A simpifying assumption used here is that the kinetics of I_{Ca} are equivalent to those of the concentration of Ca^{2+} at the release sites (see Fig. 2).

In the associative model, we also simplify the calculation of the PSP and assume that it is proportional to the total amount of transmitter that is released during an action potential in the sensory neuron. The differential equation describing this relationship is

$$\frac{dPSP}{dt} = T_R \tag{12}$$

where T_R is determined from Eq. (11).

2. Mobilization of Transmitter

In order to offset depletion, transmitter is delivered (mobilization) to the releasable pool. Mobilization may occur by the synthesis or translocation of transmitter. It seems likely that these diverse processes may have different kinetics and be regulated by multiple biochemical mechanisms. Given that mobilization occurs, it is reasonable to assume that a storage pool (P_S) acts as a reservoir from which vesicles can be removed to replenish the releasable pool. In the model, the storage pool also undergoes depletion, which is replenished slowly by synthesis of new vesicles or transport from other storage pools (Flux F_N in Fig. 7B).

Mobilization of transmitter from the storage pool to the releasable pool occurs via three fluxes. F_D is a flux of vesicles due to a difference in the concentration of vesicles in the storage pool and releasable pool. The magnitude of this current is a linear function of the concentration difference. F_C is a Ca^{2+}-mediated mobilization of vesicles from the storage to the releasable pool. F_C actually represents two Ca^{2+}-dependent fluxes, one that is fast in its response to changes in intracellular Ca^{2+} concentration and a second that is slower (see Gingrich & Bryne, 1985, for details). Finally, F_{cAMP} is a flux of transmitter which is regulated by the levels of cAMP.

In the model, US-stimulated increases in the level of cAMP modulate transmitter release in two ways. First, cAMP closes resting K^+ channels (Klein, Camardo, & Kandel, 1982; Shuster, Camardo, Siegelbaum, & Kandel, 1985; Siegelbaum, Camardo, & Kandel, 1982), which results in spike broadening and prolonged influx of Ca^{2+} with subsequent action potentials [see above and Eq. (8)]. Second, cAMP enhances mobilization of vesicles (F_{cAMP}) from the storage pool to the releasable pool (Gingrich & Bryne, 1984, 1985, 1987; see also Hochner et al., 1986b). This can be described as

$$F_{cAMP} = K_{FC} \times C_S \times C_{cAMP} \qquad (13)$$

where K_{FC} is a constant, C_S represents the concentration of vesicles in the storage pool, and C_{cAMP} is the concentration of cAMP. A role for mobilization of transmitter during synaptic facilitation is suggested by recent experimental work (see Section II,C).

With the individual fluxes specified, it is possible to write differential equations describing the concentration of vesicles in both pools: for the storage pool (P_S)

$$\frac{dC_S}{dt} = (F_N - F_C - F_{cAMP} - F_D) \times (1/V_S) \qquad (14)$$

where C_S is the concentration of vesicles in P_S and V_S is the volume of P_S, and for the releasable pool (P_R)

$$\frac{dC_R}{dt} = (F_{cAMP} + F_C + F_D - T_R) \times (1/V_R) \qquad (15)$$

where C_R is the concentration of vesicles in P_R and V_R is the volume of P_R.

The parameters in the various equations were adjusted by a combination of nonlinear parameter estimation and by trial and error to obtain an optimal fit to some of the available experimental data.

E. SIMULATION AND PREDICTIONS OF THE ASSOCIATIVE MODEL

Figure 8 illustrates the ability of the model to simulate the empirical data on associative neuronal plasticity. Figure 8A shows the results of a previous experimental analysis (Walters & Byrne, 1983a), and Fig. 8B

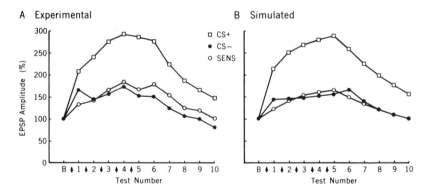

Fig. 8. Associative modifications of transmitter release: A, experimental data. Three phase test–train–test procedure for paired (CS⁺, CS precedes US by 600 msec), explicitly unpaired training (CS⁻, CS follows US by 2 min) and US alone (SENS) training. Point B on the abscissa is the normalized baseline EPSP evoked in a motor neuron in response to a test stimulus (single action potential in a sensory neuron). Training trials occur between test numbers B and 5 at the arrows. EPSPs produced by the training trials are not shown. Test numbers 5–10 represent posttraining period. Paired training (CS⁺) results in significant enhancement of the test EPSP compared to unpaired (CS⁻) and US alone (SENS) training. B, simulation of experimental data. Simulation captures salient qualities of empirical data of part A. From Gingrich & Byrne (1987).

shows the results of the computer simulation of the model. As in the experimental analysis, the simulation study had a three-phase test–train–test procedure. The first test phase consisted of simulating single action potentials in the model sensory neuron at 5-min intervals and establishing the baseline EPSP (labeled B in Fig. 8A,B). Three training conditions were simulated: paired CS and US with the CS occurring 600 msec before the US (CS$^+$), explicitly unpaired CS and US with the CS occurring 2 min after the US (CS$^-$), and presentation of the US alone (SENS). The CS was simulated with a 400-msec train (25 Hz) of spikes in the model sensory neuron and the US (simulated as activation of the cyclase) was applied for 200 msec. The training phase was repeated five times at 5-min intervals (arrows on Fig. 8). During the training phase the single test stimuli were still delivered, but 4 min after the US. After the training phase, the delivery of single test action potentials was continued to monitor the effectiveness of conditioning. Each of the conditioning procedures (CS$^+$, CS$^-$, SENS) produced enhancement of transmitter release. The CS$^+$ group, however, was enhanced beyond that of the CS$^-$ and SENS groups while there was little difference between the CS$^-$ and SENS groups (Fig. 8).

Changes in some of the variables of the model in response to paired and explicitly unpaired presentations of the CS and US for the first training trial are illustrated in Fig. 9. Two test pulses, one prior to pairing (at 1440 sec) and one after pairing (at 1740 sec), are also illustrated. Thus, Fig. 9 is a representation in continuous time of the first two values of the abscissa (test numbers B and 1) in Fig. 8. Paired presentations of the CS and US (Fig. 9A) lead to greater levels of cAMP than unpaired presentations (Fig. 9B) because the influx of Ca^{2+} preceding the US has amplified the synthesis of cAMP. Increased levels of cAMP cause greater spike broadening and mobilization of transmitter than that produced by unpaired presentations and thus greater facilitation of transmitter release [compare the transmitter release (T_R) at 1740 sec in Fig. 9C].

As illustrated in Fig. 8, a characteristic of the acquisition phase of the learning is that the amplitude of the EPSPs for the paired group increases as a function of trials and approaches an asymptote at approximately 300% of control. The results of the simulation suggest that the rising phase of the acquisition process is due to increasing levels of cAMP while the asymptote is a result of the establishment of a steady-state level of cAMP.

A characteristic feature of associative learning is the requirement for a close temporal association between the CS and US for effective conditioning. For conditioning of many simple reflex responses, the optimal ISI is generally about 400 msec. Longer ISIs are less effective and backward

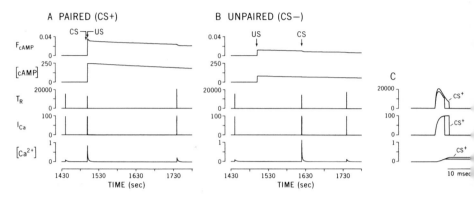

Fig. 9.   Model variables during paired and unpaired stimulation. F_{cAMP} is cAMP-mediated mobilization of transmitter [cAMP] is the concentration of cAMP, T_R is the transmitter release, I_{Ca} is the influx of Ca^{2+} and $[Ca^{2+}]$ is the concentration of Ca^{2+}. A, simulation of paired stimulation. Prior to pairing simulated spike activity with the US (activation of cyclase), five test stimuli (single 3-msec spikes) at 5-min intervals were generated in order to obtain stable responses. The response at 1440 sec was the fifth baseline response. Sixty sec after the fifth control response the CS (a train of simulated action potentials) was applied (first arrow). This was followed 600 msec later by application of the US (second arrow). The resultant elevation of Ca^{2+} levels by the CS at the time of the US caused increased synthesis of cAMP, which resulted in increased mobilization (F_{cAMP}) and spike widening. B, simulation of unpaired stimulation. The CS was delivered 120 sec after the US. cAMP levels are not enhanced by Ca^{2+} and they are smaller than the levels achieved with the paired stimulation shown in A. Consequently, the enhancement of transmitter release (T_R) (at 1740 sec) is less than that resulting from paired presentations of the CS and US. Note that for both A and B the peak of T_R is less during the CS than for the preceding test stimuli at 1440 sec, which results from depletion of transmitter by the test stimulus at the time of the CS. For the case of the CS⁻, there is greater Ca^{2+} influx and rise of $[Ca^{2+}]$ with the first CS because of cAMP-mediated broadening of spikes, which was induced by the preceding US. C, superimposed responses from parts A and B to test stimuli at 1740 sec are displayed on an expanded time base. Transmitter release is greater (top trace; increased magnitude and duration of T_R) for paired training due to enhanced mobilization and spike broadening. Modified from Gingrich & Byrne (1987).

conditioning is generally ineffective. We were therefore interested in determining whether the model could demonstrate a dependence on ISI similar to that observed in conditioning studies in *Aplysia* and other animals (Clark, 1984; Hawkins *et al.*, 1986a; Hull, 1943, 1952; Smith, Coleman, & Gormezano, 1969). Figure 10 illustrates the results. An ISI of 170 msec is optimal while longer or shorter ISIs are less effective. The optimal ISI is affected by both changes in spike frequency and duration of the CS and the duration of the US. Backward conditioning is ineffective. The ISI function in the model is a direct consequence of the kinetics of the buffering of intracellular Ca^{2+}. When the ISI is short, high levels of Ca^{2+} are

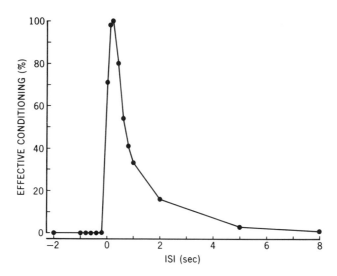

Fig. 10.   Interstimulus interval (ISI) function for model. The effective conditioning is the normalized difference between responses to the second test pulse after training in paired (CS$^+$) and explicitly unpaired (CS$^-$) simulations as a function of the time period between paired CS and US applications (ISI). In this simulation 10 training trials were presented so that the changes in transmitter release reached asymptotic levels. The relationship between the effectiveness of conditioning and the CS–US interval is due to the time course of the accumulation and buffering of Ca^{2+} in the cytoplasm. From Gingrich & Byrne (1987).

present at the time of the US and therefore the CS-mediated amplification of the effects of the US are greatest. As the interval between the CS and US increases, Ca^{2+} levels are buffered; consequently, with longer ISIs there is less amplification of the effects of the US. Thus, the elevation of intracellular Ca^{2+} levels produced by the CS serves as a trace that becomes associated with a closely paired US.

F.   FEATURES AND LIMITATIONS OF THE ASSOCIATIVE MODEL

We have used formalisms to describe complex processes such as the regulation of cAMP levels, spike broadening, and mobilization of transmitter that are necessarily simplifications of the actual processes. While the descriptions of these subcellular processes are rather coarse, we believe that these descriptions provide for a more substantial biological underpinning for models of learning than has heretofore been feasible.

The model demonstrates that associative learning at the single-cell level can be produced by a simple elaboration of mechanisms that contribute to nonassociative learning. The fact that this particular mathematical formulation leads to a fit of empirical data it was designed to fit does not validate the model. However, the utility of the model is demonstrated by its predictive value and its ability to account for empirical data not addressed during its construction. Additional studies will be necessary to determine the extent to which the proposed processes play a physiological role in synaptic plasticity of the sensory neuron and to obtain independent measurements of the parameters. One critical component of the model is the Ca^{2+}-triggered amplification of US-mediated synthesis of cAMP. If this feature is deleted from the model, the associative effect is abolished. A major unresolved issue that must be examined, however, is whether the proposed interaction of Ca^{2+}/calmodulin with the adenylate cyclase complex has intrinsic temporal specificity such that increases in levels of Ca^{2+} after modulation by the US (backward conditioning) do not amplify cAMP production. Temporal specificity, if not intrinsic to the cyclase, could be achieved by a second messenger-mediated down-regulation of Ca^{2+}/calmodulin effects. Alternatively, interneurons in the circuit which inhibit the sensory neurons may help endow the system with temporal specificity (Cleary & Byrne, 1986; Hawkins, Castellucci, & Kandel, 1981; Walters & Byrne, 1983b).

While our mathematical model is capable of predicting some features of associative learning, it cannot predict aspects of associative learning that depend on an interplay of multiple stimuli at different sites or upon more than one stimulus modality. This limitation, however, is due to the fact that the model is based only on a single neuron. By incorporating the present single-cell model into a circuit that includes multiple sensory neurons as well as modulatory or faciltatory interneurons, it will be possible to test its ability to predict more complex features of associative learning (see Hawkins, this volume; Donegan *et al.,* this volume; Gluck & Thompson, 1987; Hawkins & Kandel, 1984; Sutton & Barto, 1981). Indeed, much theoretical work by others has shown that artificial neural networks based on relatively simple learning rules have rather interesting computational properties. An intriguing question that we hope to pursue is what new properties might emerge as both the learning rules and the circuitry are made more physiological.

Acknowledgments

We thank Dr. L. Cleary for his comments on an earlier draft of this chapter. This research was sponsored by the Air Force Office of Scientific Research, Air Force Systems Command, USAF, under Grant Numbers AFOSR 84-0213 and 87-NL-0274 and National Institute of Mental Health Award K02 MH00649.

REFERENCES

Abrams, T. W., Bernier, L., Hawkins, R. D., & Kandel, E. R. (1984). Possible roles of Ca^{++} and cAMP in activity-dependent facilitation, a mechanism for associative learning in *Aplysia*. *Society for Neuroscience Abstracts,* **10,** 269.

Abrams, T. W., Carew, T. J., Hawkins, R. D., & Kandel, E. R. (1983). Aspects of the cellular mechanism of temporal specificity in conditioning in *Aplysia:* Preliminary evidence for Ca^{2+} influx as a signal of activity. *Society for Neuroscience Abstracts,* **9,** 168.

Abrams, T. W., Eliot, L., Dudai, Y., & Kandel, E. R. (1985). Activation of adenylate cyclase in *Aplysia* neural tissue by Ca^{2+}/calmodulin, a candidate for an associative mechanism during conditioning. *Society Neuroscience Abstracts,* **11,** 797.

Aceves-Pina, E. O., Booker, R., Duerr, J. S., Livingston, M. S., Quinn, W. G., Smith, R. F., Sziber, P. P., Tempel, B. L., & Tully, T. P. (1983). Learning and memory in *Drosophila*, studied with mutants. *Cold Spring Harbor Symposia of Quantitative Biology,* **48,** 831–840.

Augustine, G. J., & Charlton, M. P. (1986). Calcium dependence of presynaptic calcium current and post-synaptic response at the squid giant synapse. *Journal of Physiology (London),* **381,** 619–640.

Augustine, G. J., Charlton, M. P., & Smith, S. J. (1985). Calcium entry and transmitter release at voltage-clamped nerve terminals of squid. *Journal of Physiology (London),* **367,** 163–181.

Bailey, C. H., & Chen, M. (1988). Morphological basis of short-term habituation in *Aplysia*. *Journal of Neuroscience,* **8,** 2452–2457.

Bailey, C. H., Thompson, E. B., Castellucci, V. F., & Kandel, E. R. (1979). Ultrastructure of the synapses of sensory neurons that mediate the gill-withdrawal reflex in *Aplysia*. *Journal of Neurocytology,* **8,** 415–444.

Baxter, D. A., & Byrne, J. H. (1987). Modulation of membrane currents and excitability by serotonin and cAMP in pleural sensory neurons of *Aplysia*. *Society for Neuroscience Abstracts,* **13,** 1440.

Berg, H. C. (1983). *Random walks in biology*. Princeton, NJ: Princeton University Press.

Bernier, L., Castellucci, V. F., Kandel, E. R., & Schwartz, J. H. (1982). Facilitatory transmitter causes a selective and prolonged increase in adenosine 3′ : 5′-monophosphate in sensory neurons mediating the gill and siphon withdrawal reflex in *Aplysia*. *Journal of Neuroscience,* **2,** 1682–1691.

Brostrom, M. A., Brostrom, C. O., Breckenridge, B. M., & Wolff, D. J. (1978). Calcium-dependent regulation of brain adenylate cyclase. *Advances in Cyclic Nucleotide Research,* **9,** 85–99.

Brunelli, M., Castellucci, V., & Kandel, E. R. (1976). Synaptic facilitation and behavioral sensitization in *Aplysia:* Possible role of serotonin and cyclic AMP. *Science,* **194,** 1178–1181.

Byerly, L., Chase, P. B., & Stimers, J. R. (1984). Calcium current activation kinetics in neurones of the snail *Lymnea stagnalis*. *Journal of Physiology (London),* **348,** 187–207.

Byerly, L., & Hagiwara, S. (1982). Calcium currents in internally perfused nerve cell bodies of *Limnea stagnalis*. *Journal of Physiology (London),* **322,** 503–528.

Byrne, J. H. (1982). Analysis of the synaptic depression contributing to habituation of gill-withdrawal reflex in *Aplysia californica*. *Journal of Neurophysiology,* **48,** 431–438.

Byrne, J. H. (1985). Neural and molecular mechanisms underlying information storage in *Aplysia:* Implications for learning and memory. *Trends in Neuroscience,* **8,** 478–482.

Byrne, J. H. (1987). Cellular analysis of associative learning. *Physiological Review,* **67,** 329–439.

Byrne, J. H., Castellucci, V. F., & Kandel, E. R. (1978). Contribution of individual mechanoreceptor sensory neurons to defensive gill-withdrawal reflex in *Aplysia. Journal of Neurophysiology,* **41,** 418–431.

Carew, T. J. (1987). In J.-P. Changeux & M. Konishi (Eds.), *The neural and molecular cellular bases of learning: Dahlem konferenzen.* Chichester, Eng: Wiley.

Carew, T. J., Castellucci, V. F., & Kandel, E. R. (1971). An analysis of dishabituation and sensitization of the gill-withdrawal reflex in *Aplysia. International Journal of Neuroscience,* **2,** 79–98.

Carew, T. J., Hawkins, R. D., & Kandel, E. R. (1983). Differential classical conditioning of a defensive withdrawal reflex in *Aplysia californica. Science,* **219,** 397–400.

Castellucci, V. F., & Kandel, E. R. (1974). A quantal analysis of the synaptic depression underlying habituation of the gill-withdrawal reflex in *Aplysia. Proceedings of the National Academy of Sciences U.S.A.,* **71,** 5004–5008.

Castellucci, V. F., & Kandel, E. R. (1976). Presynaptic facilitation as a mechanism for behavioral sensitization in *Aplysia. Science,* **194,** 1176–1178.

Castellucci, V. F., Nairn, A., Greengard, P., Schwartz, J. H., & Kandel, E. R. (1982). Inhibitor of adenosine 3' : 5'-monophosphate-dependent protein kinase blocks presynaptic facilitation in *Aplysia. Journal of Neuroscience,* **2,** 1673–1681.

Castellucci, V. F., Pinsker, H., Kupfermann, I., & Kandel, E. R. (1970). Neuronal mechanisms of habituation and dishabituation of the gill-withdrawal reflex in *Aplysia. Science,* **167,** 1745–1748.

Chad, J. E., & Eckert, R. (1984). Calcium domains associated with individual channels can account for anomalous voltage relations of Ca-dependent responses. *Biophysical Journal,* **45,** 993–999.

Chad, J. E., Eckert, R., & Ewald, D. (1984). Kinetics of calcium-dependent inactivation of calcium current in voltage-clamped neurones of *Aplysia californica. Journal of Physiology (London),* **347,** 279–300.

Clark, G. A. (1984). A cellular mechanism for the temporal specificity of classical conditioning of the siphon-withdrawal response in *Aplysia. Society for Neuroscience Abstracts,* **10,** 268.

Cleary, L. J., & Byrne, J. H. (1986). Associative learning of the gill and siphon withdrawal reflex in *Aplysia:* Interneurons mediating the unconditioned response. *Society Neuroscience Abstracts,* **12,** 397.

Crank, J. (1975). *The mathematics of diffusion.* London: Oxford University Press (Clarendon).

Dudai, Y. (1985). Genes, enzymes and learning in *Drosophila. Trends in Neuroscience,* **8,** 18–21.

Eckert, R., & Ewald, D. (1983). Calcium tail currents in voltage-clamped intact nerve cell bodies of *Aplysia californica. Journal of Physiology (London),* **345,** 533–548.

Fogelson, A. L., & Zucker, R. S. (1985). Presynaptic calcium diffusion from various arrays of single channels: Implications for transmitter release and synaptic facilitation. *Biophysical Journal,* **48,** 1003–1017.

Gingrich, K. J., Baxter, D. A., & Byrne, J. H. (1988). Mathematical model of cellular mechanisms contributing to presynaptic facilitation. *Brain Research Bulletin,* **21,** 513–520.

Gingrich, K. J., & Byrne, J. H. (1984). Simulation of nonassociative and associative neuronal modifications in *Aplysia. Society for Neuroscience Abstracts,* **10,** 270.

Gingrich, K. J., & Byrne, J. H. (1985). Simulation of synaptic depression, posttetanic potentiation and presynaptic facilitation of synaptic potentials from sensory neurons mediating gill-withdrawal reflex in *Aplysia. Journal of Neurophysiology,* **53,** 652–669.

Gingrich, K. J., & Byrne, J. H. (1987). Single-cell neuronal model for associative learning. *Journal of Neurophysiology*, **57**, 1705–1715.

Gluck, M. A., & Thompson, R. F. (1987). Modeling the neural substrates of associative learning and memory: A computational approach. *Psychological Review*, **94**, 176–191.

Gnegy, M. E., Muirhead, N., Roberts-Lewis, J. M., & Treisman, G. (1984). Calmodulin stimulates adenylate cyclase activity and increases dopamine activation in bovine retina. *Journal of Neuroscience*, **4**, 2712–2717.

Gnegy, M., & Treisman, G. (1981). Effect of calmodulin on dopamine-sensitive adenylate cyclase activity in rat striatal membranes. *Molecular Pharmacology*, **19**, 256–263.

Hawkins, R. D., Abrams, T. W., Carew, T. J., & Kandel, E. R. (1983). A cellular mechanism of classical conditioning in *Aplysia:* Activity-dependent amplification of presynaptic facilitation. *Science*, **219**, 400–405.

Hawkins, R. D., Carew, T. J., & Kandel, E. R. (1986). Effects of interstimulus interval and contingency on classical conditioning of the *Aplysia* siphon withdrawal reflex. *Journal of Neuroscience*, **6**, 1695–1701.

Hawkins, R. D., Castellucci, V. F., & Kandel, E. R. (1981). Interneurons involved in mediation and modulation of gill-withdrawal reflex in *Aplysia*. I. Identification and characterization. *Journal of Neurophysiology*, **45**, 304–314.

Hawkins, R. D., Clark, G. A., & Kandel, E. R. (1986). In F. Plum (Ed.), *Handbook of physiology, Section I. The Nervous System. Vol. 6. Higher functions of the nervous system*. Bethesda, MD: American Physiological Society.

Hawkins, R. D., & Kandel, E. R. (1984). Is there a cell-biological alphabet for simple forms of learning? *Psychological Review*, **91**, 375–391.

Hochner, B., Klein, M., Schacher, S., & Kandel, E. R. (1986a). Action-potential duration and the modulation of transmitter release from the sensory neurons of *Aplysia* in presynaptic facilitation and behavioral sensitization. *Proceedings of the National Academy of Sciences U.S.A.*, **83**, 8410–8414.

Hochner, B., Klein, M., Schacher, S., & Kandel, E. R. (1986b). Additional component in the cellular mechanisms of presynaptic facilitation contributing to behavioral dishabituation in *Aplysia*. *Proceedings of the National Academy of Sciences U.S.A.*, **83**, 8794–8798.

Hochner, B., Schacher, S., Klein, M., & Kandel, E. R. (1985). Presynaptic facilitation in *Aplysia* sensory neurons. A process independent of K$^+$ current modulation becomes important when transmitter release is depressed. *Society for Neuroscience Abstracts*, **11**, 29.

Hodgkin, A. L., & Huxley, A. F. (1952). A quantitative description of membrane current and its application to conduction and excitation in nerve. *Journal of Physiology (London)*, **117**, 500–544.

Hull, C. L. (1943). *Principles of behavior*. New York: Appleton-/Century-Crofts.

Hull, C. L. (1952). *A behavior system*. New Haven, CT: Yale University Press.

Kandel, E. R. (1976). *Cellular basis of behavior*. San Francisco: Freeman.

Kandel, E. R., & Schwartz, J. H. (1982). Molecular biology of learning: Modulation of transmitter release. *Science*, **218**, 433–443.

Katz, B. (1966). *Nerve, muscle and synapse*. New York: McGraw-Hill.

Klein, M., Camardo, J., & Kandel, E. R. (1982). Serotonin modulates a specific potassium current in the sensory neurons that show presynaptic facilitation in *Aplysia*. *Proceedings of the National Academy of Sciences U.S.A.*, **79**, 5713–5717.

Klein, M., & Kandel, E. R. (1978). Presynaptic modulation of voltage-dependent Ca^{2+} current: Mechanism for behavioral sensitization in *Aplysia californica*. *Proceedings of the National Academy of Sciences U.S.A.*, **75**, 3512–3516.

Klein, M., & Kandel, E. R. (1980). Mechanism of calcium current modulation underlying presynaptic facilitation and behavioral sensitization in *Aplysia. Proceedings of the National Academy of Sciences U.S.A.,* 77, 6912–6916.

Klein, M., Shapiro, E., & Kandel, E. R. (1980). Synaptic plasticity and the modulation of the Ca^{2+} current. *Journal of Experimental Biology,* 89, 117–157.

Kostyuk, P. G., Krishtal, O. A., & Pidoplichko, V. I. (1981). Calcium inward current and related charge movements in the membrane of snail neurones. *Journal of Physiology (London),* 310, 403–421.

Kostyuk, P. G., Krishtal, O. A., & Shakhovalov, Y. A. (1977). Separation of sodium and calcium currents in the somatic membrane of mollusc neurones. *Journal of Physiology (London),* 270, 545–568.

Kupfermann, I., Castellucci, V., Pinsker, H., & Kandel, E. R. (1970). Neuronal correlates of habituation and dishabituation of the gill-withdrawal reflex in *Aplysia. Science,* 167, 1743–1745.

Livingstone, M. S. (1985). Genetic dissection of *Drosophila* adenylate cyclase. *Proceedings of the National Academy of Sciences U.S.A.,* 82, 5992–5996.

Mackintosh, N. J. (1974). *Conditioning and associative learning.* London: Oxford University Press (Clarendon).

Mackintosh, N. J. (1983). *The psychology of animal learning.* New York: Academic Press.

Malnoe, A., Stein, E. A., & Cox, J. A. (1983). Synergistic activation of bovine cerebellum adenylate cyclase by calmodulin and β-adrenergic agonists. *Neurochemistry International,* 5, 65–72.

Marcus, E. A., Nolen, T. G., Rankin, C. H., & Carew, T. J. (1988). Behavioral dissociation of dishabituation, sensitization and inhibition in *Aplysia:* Evidence for a multi-process view of non-associative learning. *Science,* 241, 210–213.

Moore, J. W., Ramon, F., & Joyner, R. W. (1975). Axon voltage-clamp simulations. I. Methods and test. *Biophysical Journal,* 15, 11–24.

Ocorr, K. A., & Byrne, J. H. (1985). Membrane responses and changes in cAMP levels in *Aplysia* sensory neurons produced by serotonin, tryptamine, FMRFamide and small cardioactive peptide B (SCP_B). *Neuroscience Letters,* 55, 113–118.

Ocorr, K. A., Tabata, M., & Byrne, J. H. (1986). Stimuli that produce sensitization lead to elevation of cyclic AMP levels in tail sensory neurons of *Aplysia. Brain Research,* 371, 190–192.

Ocorr, K. A., Walters, E. T., & Byrne, J. H. (1983). Associative conditioning analog in *Aplysia* tail sensory neurons selectively increases cAMP content. *Society for Neuroscience Abstracts,* 9, 169.

Ocorr, K. A., Walters, E. T., & Byrne, J. H. (1985). Associative conditioning analog selectively increases cAMP levels of tail sensory neurons in *Aplysia. Proceedings of the National Academy of Sciences U.S.A.,* 82, 2548–2552.

Patterson, M. M., Cegavske, C. F., & Thompson, R. F. (1973). Effects of a classical conditioning paradigm on hind-limb flexor nerve response in immobilized spinal cats. *Journal of Comparative and Physiological Psychology,* 84, 88–97.

Pavlov, I. P. (1927). *Conditioned reflexes: An investigation of the physiological activity of the cerebral cortex.* London: Oxford University Press.

Pollock, J. P., Bernier, L., & Camardo, J. S. (1985). Serotonin and cyclic adenosine 3' : 5'-monophosphate modulate the potassium current in tail sensory neurons in the pleural ganglion of *Aplysia. Journal of Neuroscience,* 5, 1862–1871.

Rankin, C. H., & Carew, T. J. (1988). Dishabituation and sensitization emerge as separate processes during development in *Aplysia. Journal of Neuroscience,* 8, 197–211.

Rescorla, R. A. (1967). Pavlovian conditioning and its proper control procedures. *Psychological Review,* 74, 71–80.

Schwartz, J. H., Bernier, L., Castellucci, V. F., Polazzola, M., Saitoh, T., Stapleton, A., & Kandel, E. R. (1983). What molecular steps determine the time course of the memory for short-term sensitization in *Aplysia? Cold Spring Harbor Symposia of Quantitative Biology*, **48**, 811–819.

Shuster, M. J., Camardo, J. S., Siegelbaum, S. A., & Kandel, E. R. (1985). Cyclic AMP-dependent protein kinase close serotonin-sensitive K$^+$ channels of *Aplysia* sensory neurons in cell-free membrane patches. *Nature (London)*, **313**, 392–395.

Siegelbaum, S. A., Camardo, J. S., & Kandel, E. R. (1982). Serotonin and cyclic AMP close single K$^+$ channels in *Aplysia* sensory neurons. *Nature (London)*, **299**, 413–417.

Simon, S. M., & Llinas, R. R. (1985). Compartmentalization of the submembrane calcium activity during calcium influx and its significance in transmitter release. *Biophysical Journal*, **48**, 485–498.

Smith, M. C., Coleman, S. R., & Gormezano, I. (1969). Classical conditioning of the rabbit's nictitating membrane response at backward, simultaneous, and forward CS–US intervals. *Journal of Comparative and Physiological Psychology*, **69**, 226–231.

Sutton, R. S., & Barto, A. G. (1981). Toward a modern theory of adaptive networks: Expectation and prediction. *Psychological Review*, **88**, 135–170.

Thompson, R. F., & Spencer, W. A. (1966). Habituation: A model phenomenon for the study of neuronal substrates of behavior. *Psychological Review*, **73**, 16–43.

Walters, E. T., & Byrne, J. H. (1983a). Associative conditioning of single sensory neurons suggests a cellular mechanism for learning. *Science*, **219**, 405–408.

Walters, E. T., & Byrne, J. H. (1983b). Slow depolarization produced by associative conditioning of *Aplysia* sensory neurons may enhance Ca^{2+} entry. *Brain Research*, **280**, 165–168.

Walters, E. T. Byrne, J. H., Carew, T. J., & Kandel, E. R. (1983). Mechanoafferent neurons innervating the tail of *Aplysia*. II. Modulation by sensitizing stimulation. *Journal of Neurophysiology*, **50**, 1543–1559.

Weiss, S., & Drummond, G. I. (1985). Biochemical properties of adenylate cyclase in the gill of *Aplysia californica. Comparative Biochemistry and Physiology*, **80B**, 251–255.

Zucker, R. S., & Fogelson, A. L. (1986). Relationship between transmitter release and presynaptic calcium influx when calcium enters through discrete channels. *Proceedings of the National Academy of Sciences U.S.A.*, **83**, 3032–3036.

Zucker, R. S., & Stockbridge, N. (1983). Presynaptic calcium diffusion and the time courses of transmitter release and synaptic facilitation at the squid giant synapse. *Journal of Neurosciences*, **3**, 1263–1269.

A BIOLOGICALLY BASED COMPUTATIONAL MODEL
FOR SEVERAL SIMPLE FORMS OF LEARNING

Robert D. Hawkins

I. Introduction

Since the publication of *Origin of Species* in 1859, scholars have debated whether the mental abilities of animals and men could be explained by the theory of evolution. Darwin recognized that this was a critical issue for his theory and argued that the instinctual behavior of animals was consistent with it:

> To my imagination it is far more satisfactory to look at such instincts as the cuckoo ejecting its foster-brothers, ants making slaves, the larvae of ichneumonidae feeding within the live bodies of caterpillars, not as specially endowed or created instincts, but small consequences of one general law leading to the advancement of all organic beings—namely, multiply, vary, let the strongest live and the weakest die. (p. 234)

Darwin also realized that the evolution of instinctual behavior must be due to a corresponding evolution of the brain:

> Indeed, I suppose that it will hardly be doubted, when an instinctive action is transmitted by inheritance in some slightly modified form, that this must be caused by some slight change in the organization of the brain. (cited in Romanes, 1884, p. 264)

In a later publication, Darwin suggested that these arguments could logically be extended to include man's mental powers, language, moral faculties, and religion: That is, that every aspect of the mental life of animals and men has evolutionary origins (Darwin, 1871). This implication

THE PSYCHOLOGY OF LEARNING
AND MOTIVATION, VOL. 23

65

Copyright © 1989 by Academic Press, Inc.
All rights of reproduction in any form reserved.

of the theory of evolution has provoked strong opposition. For example, in an unsigned review of *Origin of Species* published in 1860, Bishop Samuel Wilberforce went through a series of scientific arguments against evolution, but for the final, most telling argument, he wrote:

> Man's derived supremacy over the earth; man's power of articulate speech; man's gift of reason; man's free-will and responsibility; man's fall and man's redemption; the incarnation of the Eternal Son; the indwelling of the Eternal Spirit—all are equally and utterly irreconcilable with the degrading notion of the brute origin of him who was created in the image of God, and redeemed by the Eternal Son.

These arguments are echoed today in debates over the continuity of mental abilities across species, over the use of language by animals, over the ideas of sociobiology, and over the teaching of evolution in public schools.

One difficulty for Darwin's position was the paucity of evidence about intermediate stages between animal instinct and man's reason. This gap in the evidence motivated the first systematic studies of intelligent animal behavior. For example, in the preface to one of the first texts on comparative psychology, Romanes wrote in 1882:

> It will thus be apparent that the present volume, while complete in itself as a statement of the facts of Comparative Psychology, has for its more ultimate purpose the laying of a firm foundation for my future treatise on Mental Evolution. (p. vii)

More than 100 years of the scientific study of animal behavior has produced a taxonomy of different types of learning in which the major categories are associative learning, which includes classical and operant conditioning, and nonassociative learning, which includes habituation and sensitization. However, there is still little agreement on how these different forms of learning relate to one another, and therefore correspondingly little understanding of how they might have evolved.

In this article, I hope to make a contribution to the ongoing debate over the evolution of mind by considering a relatively new source of evidence, information about the cellular mechanisms of several simple forms of learning. During the past two decades there has been substantial progress in identifying cellular mechanisms for habituation, sensitization, and conditioning in simple vertebrate systems and in more complex invertebrates such as *Aplysia, Drosophila, Hermissenda,* locusts, and crayfish (for reviews see Carew & Sahley, 1986; Byrne, 1987; Hawkins, Clark, & Kandel, 1987). Results from both *Aplysia* and *Drosophila* studies indicate that a cellular mechanism of classical conditioning, an associative form of learning, is an elaboration of a mechanism of sensitization, a nonassociative form of learning, and therefore might plausibly have evolved from it (Duerr & Quinn, 1982; Hawkins, Abrams, Carew, & Kandel, 1983). I review results from *Aplysia* studies in Section II.

The finding that sensitization and classical conditioning appear to be mechanistically related suggested the hypothesis that yet more complex forms of learning might in turn be generated from combinations of an alphabet of the mechanisms of these elementary forms of learning (Hawkins & Kandel, 1984). The higher-order features of classical conditioning provide an attractive area in which to investigate this hypothesis for two reasons. First, these features of conditioning have a cognitive flavor (in the sense that the animal's behavior is thought to depend on a comparison of current sensory input with an internal representation of the world) and they may therefore provide a bridge between basic conditioning and more advanced forms of learning (Kamin, 1969; Rescorla, 1978; Wagner, 1978; Mackintosh, 1983; Dickinson, 1980). Second, some of these features of conditioning have been demonstrated in invertebrates, in which a cellular analysis of their mechanisms may be feasible (Sahley, Rudy, & Gelperin, 1981; Colwill, 1985; Hawkins, Carew, & Kandel, 1986; Farley, 1987).

In a theoretical paper, Eric Kandel and I suggested how several of the higher-order features of conditioning could be accounted for by combinations of the mechanisms of habituation, sensitization, and classical conditioning in the basic neural circuit for the *Aplysia* gill-withdrawal reflex (Hawkins & Kandel, 1984). Since the arguments in that paper were entirely qualitative, however, quantitative modeling seemed desirable. In Sections III–VI of this chapter, I describe a computer model incorporating basic features of the cellular mechanisms and neural circuitry known to underlie learning in *Aplysia* and show that the model can simulate a broad range of behavioral properties of habituation, sensitization, basic classical conditioning, and higher-order features of conditioning. The results suggest that these different forms of learning may all be mechanistically related and therefore might represent the first few steps in an evolutionary sequence. While these proposals are clearly highly speculative and may be wrong in many respects, I hope that they suggest a useful framework for further investigations into the relationship between different forms of learning.

II. Behavioral and Cellular Studies of Learning in *Aplysia*

Studies of learning in *Aplysia* have focused on the defensive withdrawal reflexes of the external organs of the mantle cavity. In *Aplysia* and in other mollusks, the mantle cavity, a respiratory chamber housing the gill, is covered by a protective sheet, the mantle shelf, which terminates in a fleshy spout, the siphon. When the siphon or mantle shelf is stimulated by touch, the siphon, mantle shelf, and gill all contract vigorously and withdraw into the mantle cavity. This reflex is analogous to vertebrate defensive escape and withdrawal responses, which can be modified by experience. Unlike vertebrate withdrawal reflexes, however, the *Aplysia* withdrawal reflex is partly monosynaptic: Siphon sensory neurons synapse directly on gill and siphon motor neurons (Fig. 1). Nonetheless, this simple reflex can be modified by two forms of nonassociative learning, habituation and sensitization, as well as two forms of associative learning, classical and operant conditioning. The neural mechanisms of habituation, sensitization, and classical conditioning have been partially analyzed at the cellular and molecular levels.

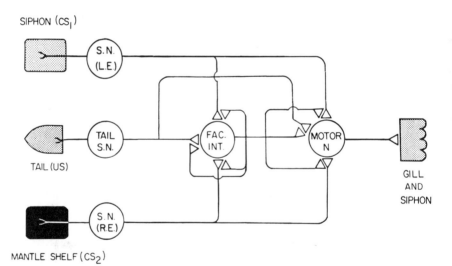

Fig. 1.   Partial neuronal circuit for the *Aplysia* gill- and siphon-withdrawal reflex and its modification by tail stimulation. Mechanosensory neurons (S.N.) from the siphon (LE cluster), mantle (RE cluster), and tail excite gill and siphon motor neurons. The sensory neurons also excite facilitator interneurons which produce presynaptic facilitation at all of the terminals of the sensory neurons. Approximately 25 siphon sensory neurons, 25 gill and siphon motor neurons, and 5 facilitator neurons have been identified (Byrne, Castellucci, & Kandel, 1974; Kupfermann, Carew, & Kandel, 1974; Perlman, 1979; Frost, Clark & Kandel, 1985; Hawkins, Castellucci, & Kandel, 1981; Mackey, Kandel, & Hawkins, 1989). Several other interneurons which are not included in this figure have also been described (Hawkins, Castellucci, & Kandel, 1981; Byrne, 1981; Mackey *et al.*, 1987).

A. HABITUATION

In habituation, perhaps the simplest form of learning, an animal learns to ignore a weak stimulus that is repeatedly presented when the consequences of the stimulus are neither noxious nor rewarding. Thus, an *Aplysia* will initially respond to a tactile stimulus to the siphon by briskly withdrawing its gill and siphon. With repeated exposure to the stimulus, however, the animal will exhibit reflex responses that are reduced to a fraction of their initial value. Habituation can last from minutes to weeks, depending on the number and pattern of stimulations (Carew, Pinsker, & Kandel, 1972; Pinsker, Kupfermann, Castellucci, & Kandel, 1970).

At the cellular level, the short-term (minutes to hours) form of habituation involves a depression of transmitter release at the synapses that the siphon sensory neurons make on gill and siphon motor neurons and interneurons (Castellucci & Kandel, 1974; Castellucci, Pinsker, Kupfermann, & Kandel, 1970). This depression is thought to involve a decrease in the amount of Ca^{2+} that flows into the terminals of the sensory neurons with each action potential (Klein, Shapiro, & Kandel, 1980). Since Ca^{2+} influx determines how much transmitter is released, a decrease in Ca^{2+} influx would result in decreased release (Fig. 2A). Recent evidence suggests that habituation may also involve depletion of releasable transmitter pools (Bailey & Chen, 1988; Gingrich & Byrne, 1985).

B. SENSITIZATION

Sensitization is a somewhat more complex form of nonassociative learning in which an animal learns to strengthen its defensive reflexes and to respond vigorously to a variety of previously weak or neutral stimuli after it has been exposed to a potentially threatening or noxious stimulus. Thus, if a noxious sensitizing stimulus is delivered to the neck or tail, the siphon and gill withdrawal reflexes will be enhanced, as will inking, walking, and other defensive behaviors (Pinsker *et al.*, 1970; Walters, Carew, & Kandel, 1981). This enhancement persists from minutes to weeks depending on the number and intensity of the sensitizing stimuli (Pinsker, Hening, Carew, & Kandel, 1973; Frost, Castellucci, Hawkins, & Kandel, 1985).

The short-term (minutes to hours) form of sensitization involves the same cellular locus as habituation, the synapses that the sensory neurons make on their central target cells, and again the learning process involves an alteration in transmitter release: in this case an enhancement in the amount released (Castellucci & Kandel, 1976; Castellucci *et al.*, 1970).

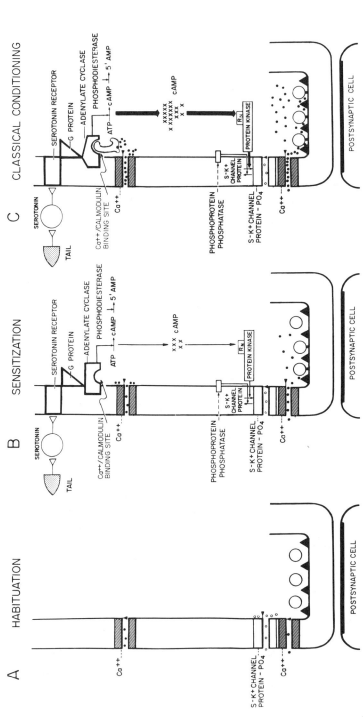

Fig. 2. Cellular mechanisms contributing to habituation, sensitization, and classical conditioning of the *Aplysia* gill- and siphon-withdrawal reflex. A. Habituation: Repeated stimulation of a siphon sensory neuron, the presynaptic cell in the figure, produces prolonged inactivation of Ca²⁺ channels in that neuron (represented by the closed gates), leading to a decrease in Ca²⁺ influx during each action potential and decreased transmitter release. B. Sensitization: Stimulation of the tail produces prolonged inactivation of K⁺ channels in the siphon sensory neuron through a sequence of steps involving cAMP and protein phosphorylation. Closing these K⁺ channels produces broadening of subsequent action potentials, which in turn produces an increase in Ca²⁺ influx and increased transmitter release. C. Classical conditioning: Tail stimulation produces amplified facilitation of transmitter release from the siphon sensory neuron if the tail stimulation is preceded by action potentials in the sensory neuron. This effect may be due to priming of the adenyl cyclase by Ca²⁺ that enters the sensory neuron during the action potentials, so that the cyclase produces more cAMP when it is activated by the tail stimulation.

Sensitization, however, uses more complex molecular machinery. This machinery has at least five steps (Figs. 1 and 2B):

1. Stimulating the tail activates a group of facilitator neurons which synapse on or near the terminals of the sensory neurons and act there to enhance transmitter release. This process is called *presynaptic facilitation*.

2. The transmitters released by the facilitator neurons, which include serotonin, a small peptide (SCP), and an unknown transmitter, activate an adenylate cyclase which increases the level of free cyclic AMP in the terminals of the sensory neurons.

3. Elevation of free cyclic AMP, in turn, activates a second enzyme, a cAMP-dependent protein kinase.

4. The kinase acts by means of protein phosphorylation to close a particular type of K^+ channel and thereby decreases the total number of K^+ channels that are open during the action potential.

5. A decrease in K^+ current leads to broadening of subsequent action potentials, which allows a greater amount of Ca^{2+} to flow into the terminal and thus enhances transmitter release (Kandel & Schwartz, 1982; Klein & Kandel, 1980; Siegelbaum, Camardo, & Kandel, 1982; Castellucci, Nairn, Greengard, Schwartz, & Kandel, 1982; Bernier, Castellucci, Kandel, & Schwartz, 1982; Hawkins, Castellucci, & Kandel, 1981; Kistler *et al.*, 1985; Abrams, Castellucci, Camardo, Kandel, & Lloyd, 1984; Glanzman, Mackey, Hawkins, Dyke, Lloyd, & Kandel, 1989; Mackey, Kandel, & Hawkins, 1989).

Recent evidence suggests that sensitization may also involve mobilization of transmitter to release sites, perhaps through Ca^{2+}–calmodulin- or Ca^{2+}–phospholipid-dependent protein phosphorylation (Gingrich & Byrne, 1985; Hochner, Braha, Klein, & Kandel, 1986; Hochner, Klein, Schacher, & Kandel, 1986; Boyle, Klein, Smith, & Kandel, 1984; Sacktor, O'Brian, Weinstein, & Schwartz, 1986). The neural circuit for the gill- and siphon-withdrawal reflex also includes other sites of plasticity that could contribute to sensitization (Jacklet & Rine, 1977; Kanz, Eberly, Cobbs, & Pinsker, 1979; Hawkins *et al.*, 1981; Frost, Clark, & Kandel, 1988). Finally, in addition to producing sensitization, noxious stimuli can also produce transient *inhibition* of the gill- and siphon-withdrawal reflex (Mackey *et al.*, 1987; Marcus, Nolen, Rankin, & Carew, 1988; Krontiris-Litowitz, Erickson, & Walters, 1987). This effect appears to be due in part to activation of Phe-Met-Arg-Phe-NH$_2$ (FMRFamide) neurons which produce presynaptic inhibition of the siphon sensory cells by acting through a different second messenger system, the metabolites of arachidonic acid (Piomelli *et al.*, 1987; Mackey *et al.*, 1987).

C. CLASSICAL CONDITIONING

Classical conditioning resembles sensitization in that the response to a stimulus in one pathway is enhanced by activity in another. In classical conditioning an initially weak or ineffective conditioned stimulus (CS) becomes highly effective in producing a behavioral response after it has been paired temporally with a strong unconditioned stimulus (US). Often a reflex can be modified by both sensitization and classical conditioning. In such cases, the response enhancement produced by classical conditioning (paired presentation of the CS and US) is greater and/or lasts longer than the enhancement produced by sensitization (presentation of the US alone). Moreover, whereas the consequences of sensitization are broad and affect defensive responses to a range of stimuli, the effects of classical conditioning are specific and enhance only responses to stimuli that are paired with the US.

In conditioning of the *Aplysia* withdrawal response, the unconditioned stimulus is a strong shock to the tail that produces a powerful set of defensive responses; the conditioned stimulus is a weak stimulus to the siphon that produces a feeble response. After repeated pairing of the CS and US, the CS becomes more effective and elicits a strong gill and siphon withdrawal reflex. Enhancement of this reflex is acquired in less than 15 trials, is retained for days, extinguishes with repeated presentation of the CS alone, and recovers with rest (Carew, Walters, & Kandel, 1981). The siphon withdrawal reflex can also be differentially conditioned using stimuli to the siphon and mantle shelf as the discriminative stimuli. Using this procedure, we have found that a single training trial is sufficient to produce significant learning and that the learning becomes progressively more robust with more training trials (Carew, Hawkins, & Kandel, 1983). We also found significant conditioning when the onset of the CS preceded the onset of the US by 0.5 sec and marginally significant conditioning when the interval between the CS and the US was extended to 1.0 sec. In contrast, no significant learning occurred when the CS preceded the US by 2 or more sec, when the two stimuli were simultaneous, or, in backward conditioning, when the US onset preceded the CS by 0.5 or more sec (Hawkins *et al.*, 1986). Thus, conditioning in *Aplysia* resembles conditioning in vertebrates in having a steep interstimulus interval (ISI) function, with optimal learning when the CS precedes the US by approximately 0.5 sec (e.g., Gormezano, 1972).

What cellular processes give classical conditioning this characteristic stimulus and temporal specificity? Evidence obtained over the past several years indicates that classical conditioning of the withdrawal reflex involves a pairing-specific enhancement of presynaptic facilitation. In classical conditioning the sensory neurons of the CS pathway fire action potentials just before the facilitator neurons of the US pathway become active. Using a reduced preparation we have found that if action potentials are generated in a sensory neuron just before the US is delivered, the US produces substantially more facilitation of the synaptic potential from the sensory neuron to a motor neuron than if the US is not paired with activity in the sensory neuron or if the order of the two stimuli is reversed (Hawkins *et al.*, 1983; Clark, 1984). Pairing spike activity in a sensory neuron with the US also produces greater broadening of the action potential and greater reduction of the outward current in the sensory neuron than unpaired stimulation, indicating that the enhancement of facilitation occurs presynaptically (Hawkins *et al.*, 1983; Hawkins & Abrams, 1984). Thus, at least some aspects of the mechanism for classical conditioning occur within the sensory neuron itself. We have called this type of enhancement *activity-dependent amplification of presynaptic facilitation*. Similar cellular results have been obtained independently by Walters and Byrne (1983), who have found activity-dependent synaptic facilitation in identified sensory neurons that innervate the tail of *Aplysia*. By contrast, Carew, Hawkins, Abrams, and Kandel (1984) have found that a different type of synaptic plasticity, first postulated by Hebb (1949) and often thought to underlie learning, does *not* occur at the sensory neuron–motor neuron synapses in the siphon withdrawal circuit. Plasticity at other sites in the reflex circuit may, however, also contribute to conditioning (Lukowiak, 1986; Colebrook & Lukowiak, 1988).

These experiments indicate that a mechanism of classical conditioning of the withdrawal reflex is an elaboration of the mechanism of sensitization of the reflex: presynaptic facilitation caused by an increase in action potential duration and Ca^{2+} influx in the sensory neurons. The pairing specificity characteristic of classical conditioning results because the presynaptic facilitation is augmented or amplified by temporally paired spike activity in the sensory neurons. We do not yet know which aspect of the action potential in a sensory neuron interacts with the process of presynaptic facilitation to amplify it, nor which step in the biochemical cascade leading to presynaptic facilitation is sensitive to the action potential. Preliminary results suggest that the influx of Ca^{2+} with each action potential provides the signal for activity and that it interacts with the cAMP cascade so that serotonin produces more cAMP (Fig. 2C). Thus, brief application of serotonin to the sensory cells can substitute for tail shock as the US in the cellular experiments, and Ca^{2+} must be present in the external medium for paired spike activity to enhance the effect of the serotonin (Abrams, 1985; Abrams, Carew, Hawkins, & Kandel, 1983). Furthermore, serotonin produces a greater increase in cAMP levels in siphon sensory cells if it is preceded by spike activity in the sensory cells than if it is not (Kandel et al., 1983; see also Occor, Walters, & Byrne, 1985, for a similar result in Aplysia tail sensory neurons). Finally, experiments on a cell-free membrane homogenate preparation have shown that the adenyl cyclase is stimulated by both Ca^{2+} and serotonin, consistent with the idea that the cyclase is a point of convergence of the CS and US inputs (Abrams, Eliot, Dudai, & Kandel, 1985).

III.   A Computational Model for Several Simple Forms of Learning

The quantitative model I have developed to simulate various aspects of learning incorporates the neural circuit shown in Fig. 1 and the basic cellular processes diagrammed in Fig. 2. On the cellular level, my model is very similar to the single-cell model for conditioning of Gingrich and Byrne (1987; see also Byrne et al., this volume). Basically, I have attempted to plug a simplified version of Gingrich and Byrne's single-cell model into a small neural circuit to see whether the resulting circuit properties could account for a variety of features of learning. Unlike Gingrich and Byrne, I have not tried to fit a particular set of empirical data, since some of the features of learning addressed have not yet been tested in Aplysia. Rather, my goal is to show that a variety of features of habituation, sensitization, and classical conditioning could in principle be generated in the manner I suggest.

The cellular processes in my model were made as simple as possible to reduce both free parameters and computation time and are therefore only approximations of reality. Thus, most of the cellular processes are assumed to be linear, which is probably not accurate. Also, in the version described in this paper, habituation is assumed to be due solely to Ca^{2+} channel inactivation and sensitization to spike broadening, although experimental evidence suggests that transmitter depletion and mobilization are also involved. This choice was not critical, however, since an alternate version based solely on transmitter handling produced similar results for most of the features of learning discussed. Free parameters in the model were adjusted by trial and error so that one set of parameters would produce strong conditioning with as many higher-order features as possible. None of the parameter values appeared to be critical within a factor of two, although this point was not investigated systematically.

Time is modeled as a series of discrete units, which are conceived of as being the same length as the stimulus durations. No attempt has been made to model events (such as the interstimulus interval function) with a greater time resolution. In each time unit CS1, CS2, the US, or any combination of these stimuli can occur. A stimulus produces one or more action potentials in the corresponding sensory neuron. Stimulus strength is coded by the number of action potentials produced: In most of the simulations shown, CS1 and CS2 each have strengths of one arbitrary unit and produce one action potential, and the US has a strength of six arbitrary units and produces six action potentials. Synaptic depression is assumed to be independent of the number of action potentials produced. [This is approximately true since the depression is partially offset by a homosynaptic facilitatory process not modeled here (see Gingrich & Byrne, 1985).] Thus, if a sensory neuron is activated, the number (N) of available calcium channels in that neuron decreases by a fixed percentage

$$\Delta N = -C_1 \times N \qquad (1)$$

where C_1 is a constant, and this number recovers by another fixed percentage during each time unit:

$$N(t + 1) = N(t) + C_2 \times [N_{max} - N(t)] \qquad (2)$$

The duration (D) of each action potential in a sensory neuron is assumed to be proportional to the cAMP level in that neuron plus one:

$$D = 1 + C_3 \times C_{cAMP} \qquad (3)$$

and calcium influx per action potential is proportional to the action potential duration times the number of available calcium channels:

$$I_{Ca} = D \times N/N_{max} \qquad (4)$$

To keep the equations as simple as possible, transmitter release from each sensory neuron is assumed to be linear with calcium influx, and the resultant postsynaptic potential (PSP) in both the motor neuron and the facilitator neuron is linear with the total transmitter released by all of the sensory neurons:

$$PSP = C_4 \times \Sigma I_{Ca} \qquad (5)$$

The facilitator neuron fires a number of action potentials (S) equal to the difference between the PSP and a threshold T:

$$S = PSP - T \text{ if } PSP > T, 0 \text{ otherwise} \qquad (6)$$

The facilitator neuron threshold is variable and is set equal to a fraction of the PSP level during the *previous* time unit:

$$T(t) = C_5 \times PSP (t - 1) \tag{7}$$

This has the effect of causing accommodation of facilitator neuron firing during a prolonged input. Spikes in the facilitator release transmitter, which causes an increase in cAMP levels in the sensory neurons according to the following equation:

$$\Delta C_{cAMP} = C_6 \times S \times \{1 + [C_7 \times I_{Ca} (t - 1)]\} \tag{8}$$

where $\{1 + [C_7 \times I_{Ca} (t - 1)]\}$ represents "priming" of the adenyl cyclase by calcium influx in the sensory neuron during the *previous* time unit. cAMP levels then decay by a fixed percentage during each time unit:

$$C_{cAMP} (t + 1) = C_8 \times C_{cAMP} (t) \tag{9}$$

In the simulations shown in this paper, the initial values are as follows: $N = N_{max}$, $C_{cAMP} = 0$, $T = 0$, $I_{Ca} = 0$; and the parameter values are as follows: $C_1 = .15$, $C_2 = .005$, $C_3 = 1$, $C_4 = 7.5$, $C_5 = 0.9$, $C_6 = .002$, $C_7 = 15$, $C_8 = .9975$. To minimize computation time, the time unit is 10 sec (very similar results were obtained in Fig. 6 with a 1-sec unit, which is more realistic). With these parameters, the time constant for decay of cAMP levels is approximately 1 hour, and the time constant for recovery from calcium channel inactivation is approximately 30 min. The output of the model is the amplitude of the PSP in the motor neuron. I have not specified the function which relates PSP amplitude to behavior (gill and siphon contraction), but for most purposes this is assumed to be linear.

IV.   Simulations of Habituation and Sensitization

In an influential paper published in 1966, Thompson and Spencer described nine parametric features of habituation which are widely observed in the animal kingdom: (1) a decrease in responding with repeated stimulation, (2) recovery with rest, (3) more rapid rehabituation, (4) faster habituation with weaker stimuli, (5) faster habituation with shorter interstimulus intervals, (6) subzero habituation, (7) generalization of habituation, (8) dishabituation by presentation of a strong stimulus to another site, and (9) habituation of dishabituation. The model described in the preceding section successfully simulates seven of these nine features of habituation (Table I).

A. HABITUATION, RECOVERY, AND REHABITUATION

Figure 3 shows a simulation of habituation of responding to a stimulus presented repeatedly at 1-min intervals, recovery following a 60-min rest, and rehabituation. In this simulation, habituation is due to prolonged inactivation of Ca^{2+} channels in the sensory neurons [Eq. (1)], and recovery is due to recovery from that inactivation [Eq. (2)]. Both the habituation and recovery approximate those seen in real *Aplysia* (Pinsker *et al.*, 1970). However, the model fails to show another feature of real habituation, which is that rehabituation is typically more rapid than the original habituation (Carew *et al.*, 1972).

TABLE I

PARAMETRIC FEATURES OF HABITUATION AND SENSITIZATION
OBSERVED IN THE LITERATURE

Feature	Simulation by model?[a]	*Aplysia* reference[b]
1. Repeated stimulation → habituation	Yes	1
2. Recovery with rest	Yes	1
3. Faster rehabituation	No	2
4. Stronger stimulation		
→ Less habituation	Yes	1
→ Possible facilitation or biphasic	Yes	
→ More habituation with constant test stimulation	No	
5. Longer ITI		
→ Less habituation	Yes	1
→ More habituation with constant test interval	(Yes)	
6. Subzero habituation	Yes	
7. Generalization of habituation	Yes	
8. Second stimulus → dishabituation	Yes	1
Stronger stimulus → greater dishabituation	Yes	
Can go above baseline	Yes	3
Prehabituation not necessary ("sensitization")	Yes	3
Dishabituation > sensitization	(Yes)	3
9. Habituation of dishabituation	(Yes)	1

[a] Parentheses indicate that the feature can be simulated with modifications to the model.
[b] Key: 1, Pinsker, Kupfermann, Castellucci, & Kandel (1970); 2, Carew, Pinsker, & Kandel (1972); 3, Carew, Castellucci, & Kandel (1971).

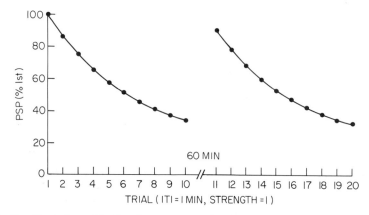

Fig. 3. Simulations of habituation, recovery with rest, and rehabituation. The ordinate shows the amplitude of the PSP produced in the motor neuron each time a stimulus occurs, expressed as a percentage of the response to the stimulus on the first trial. Stimulus strength, 1 arbitrary unit; ITI, 1 min.

B. EFFECT OF STIMULUS STRENGTH

Figure 4A shows a simulation of habituation of responding to stimuli of three different strengths (1, 12, and 20 arbitrary units). In the simulation, as in real *Aplysia,* stronger stimuli produce less habituation than weaker ones (Pinsker *et al.,* 1970) and very strong stimuli may produce either a progressive increase in responding or an initial increase followed by habituation. [This effect is seen in long-term sensitized *Aplysia,* which react to the stimulus as if it is very strong (Pinsker *et al.,* 1973).] Spencer, Thompson, and Nielson (1966a, 1966b) and Groves and Thompson (1970) observed these effects of stimulus strength in habituation of the cat hind-limb flexion reflex and suggested that they might be explained if the stimulus excites two opposing cellular processes: homosynaptic depression, leading to habituation, and an unspecified facilitatory process, leading to an increase in responding. Hawkins *et al.* (1981) proposed a variation on this idea based on the known circuitry of the *Aplysia* gill- and siphon-withdrawal reflex (see Fig. 1). Stimulation of sensory neurons produces both homosynaptic depression, leading to habituation, and excitation of facilitatory interneurons, leading to presynaptic facilitation of the sensory neurons and an increase in responding. The net outcome depends on the balance of these two opposing cellular processes. Increasing stimulus strength increases excitation of the facilitatory interneurons, tipping the balance towards facilitation. As illustrated in Fig. 4A, a computer model incorporating these ideas successfully simulates these effects of stimulus

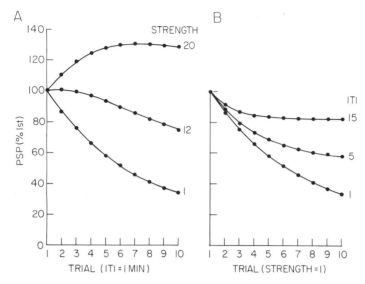

Fig. 4. Simulations of the effects on habituation of stimulus strength and intertrial interval. A, Habituation with three different stimulus strengths (1, 12, and 20 arbitrary units). ITI, 1 min. B, Habituation with three different intertrial intervals (1, 5, and 15 min). Stimulus strength, 1.

strength. However, the model fails to simulate another reported effect of stimulus strength, which is that whereas stronger stimuli produce less habituation when training and testing are performed with the same stimuli, they may produce more habituation when testing is performed with a constant stimulus (Davis & Wagner, 1968).

C. Effect of Intertrial Interval

There is typically less habituation the longer the intertrial interval (ITI) (Pinsker et al., 1970). In the simulation shown in Fig. 4B, this is simply because the Ca^{2+} channel inactivation on each trial is constant [Eq. (1)], and a longer interval allows more recovery from inactivation before the next trial [Eq. (2)]. Like the effect of stimulus strength, the effect of intertrial interval depends on how it is tested. Whereas longer intervals produce less habituation during training, they may produce more habituation when tested a constant time after training (Davis, 1979). The model described here does not successfully simulate that result. However, a similar model described by Gingrich and Byrne (1985) is able to simulate the dual effect of intertrial interval by including an additional cellular process, posttetanic potentiation (PTP), in the sensory neurons.

D.   SUBZERO HABITUATION AND GENERALIZATION

Subzero habituation refers to the fact that even if the response to a stimulus has habituated to zero, continued presentation of that stimulus can continue to produce additional habituation as measured in a retention test following a recovery period. This effect can be simulated with the additional assumption that there is a discrete threshold in the function relating motor neuron excitatory postsynaptic potential (EPSP) amplitude to behavioral output such that depression of the sensory neuron–motor neuron EPSP continues after the behavioral response has reached zero.

Generalization of habituation refers to the fact that repeated presenta- tion of one stimulus can produce a decrease in responding to a second, similar stimulus. This effect can be simulated by supposing that the two stimuli excite overlapping sets of sensory neurons. This idea will be de- veloped more fully in the context of generalization of conditioning.

E.   DISHABITUATION AND SENSITIZATION

The response to an habituated stimulus can be increased following pre- sentation of a second strong or noxious stimulus (Pinsker et al., 1970). This effect, called dishabituation, was originally thought to be due to the removal of habituation (Pavlov, 1927). However, Spencer et al. (1966a), working on the cat hindlimb flexion reflex, and Carew, Castellucci, and Kandel (1971), working on the Aplysia gill- and siphon-withdrawal reflex, showed that (1) the dishabituated response could be larger than the origi- nal, rested response, and (2) the same second stimulus that produced dis- habituation could also produce an increase in responding to a nonhabitu- ated stimulus, or sensitization. They therefore argued that dishabituation is a special case of sensitization and is due to the activation of an indepen- dent facilitatory process, rather than the removal of habituation.

Figure 5 shows simulations of dishabituation and sensitization using the quantitative model described above. In these simulations, both dishabitu- ation and sensitization are accounted for by activation of facilitatory in- terneurons which produce presynaptic facilitation of the sensory neurons (Fig. 1). In agreement with the results of Spencer et al. (1966a) and Carew et al. (1971), a moderate stimulus (50 arbitrary units) produces some dis- habituation and a stronger stimulus (100 units) produces greater dishabit- uation which goes above the level of the original, rested response (Fig. 5A). Moreover, either stimulus can produce sensitization of a nonhabitu- ated response (Fig. 5B). The model fails to simulate another result re- ported by Carew et al. (1971) and by Marcus et al. (1988), which is that dishabituation tends to be larger and more reliable than sensitization. This result can be simulated by either (1) making the function relating motor

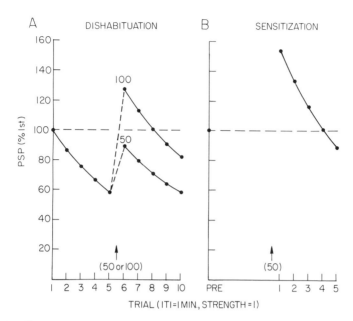

Fig. 5.   Simulations of dishabituation and sensitization. A, Dishabituation by a strong second stimulus (either 50 or 100 arbitrary units) which occurs between trials 5 and 6 (arrow). B, Sensitization by a strong stimulus (50 arbitrary units) which occurs before trial 1 (arrow).

neuron firing to behavior decelerating, so that dishabituation and sensitization approach a common ceiling; (2) adding processes representing vesicle depletion and mobilization, so that dishabituation involves two processes (spike broadening and mobilization) whereas sensitization involves only one (spike broadening) (see Gingrich & Byrne, 1985); or (3) adding a presynaptic inhibitory process which decreases in strength during habituation, so that sensitization is offset by inhibition whereas dishabituation is not (see Mackey et al., 1987).

Finally, the model also fails to simulate another common feature of habituation, which is that a dishabituating stimulus tends to become less effective with repeated use (Pinsker et al., 1970). In the simulations, a stimulus which is strong enough to produce significant dishabituation also sensitizes itself, preventing it from habituating (see Fig. 4A). It should be possible to simulate habituation of dishabituation if the model were changed to make dishabituation more powerful than sensitization by one of the methods mentioned above. In that case, a stimulus which was just strong enough to produce dishabituation would not be strong enough to sensitize itself, allowing it to habituate.

V. Simulations of Parametric Features of Conditioning

As reviewed in Section II, cellular evidence from *Aplysia* suggests that
a mechanism of classical conditioning, an associative form of learning, is
an elaboration of a mechanism of sensitization, a nonassociative form of
learning. One of the major goals of the modeling described in this chapter
is to explore this idea by seeing to what extent a single model based on
the *Aplysia* data could explain features of both nonassociative and associative learning. Like habituation and sensitization, classical conditioning
has a number of parametric features which are commonly observed
throughout the animal kingdom (see Kimble, 1961; Mackintosh, 1974, for
reviews). In this section I show that the model I have described can account at least qualitatively for most of these features of conditioning (Table II).

TABLE II

PARAMETRIC FEATURES OF CONDITIONING OBSERVED IN THE
LITERATURE

Feature	Simulation by model?[a]	*Aplysia* reference[b]
1. Acquisition	Yes	4
α vs. β	Yes	
Sigmoidal	Yes	4
2. Extinction	Yes	4
3. Spontaneous recovery	Yes	4
4. "Disinhibition"	Yes	
5. Forgetting	Yes	
6. Paired > US alone > unpaired > CS alone	Yes	4
7. Differential	Yes	5
Response to CS⁻ biphasic	Yes	
8. Generalization	Yes	
9. Effect of CS strength	Yes	
10. Effect of US strength	Yes	
11. Effect of ITI	Yes	
12. Effect of ISI	Yes	6
13. Delay > trace	Yes	
14. Shift in timing CR	(Yes)	
15. CR resembles UR	No	

[a]Parentheses indicate that the feature can be simulated with modifications to the model.
[b]Key: 4, Carew, Walters, & Kandel (1981); 5, Carew, Hawkins, & Kandel (1983); 6,
Hawkins, Carew, & Kandel (1986).

A. ACQUISITION AND EXTINCTION

Figure 6 shows a simulation of acquisition and extinction of a conditioned response by the model described in Section III. The results of the simulation are qualitatively similar to results obtained with *Aplysia* (Carew *et al.*, 1981), but they have been made quantitatively more dramatic for illustrative purposes. In the hypothetical experiment shown in Fig. 6, there is a pretest, five paired trials with the CS preceding the US by one time unit, five extinction trials, and a posttest. The intertrial interval is 5 min. The ordinate shows the amplitude of the PSP produced in the motor neuron each time a stimulus (CS or US) occurs. Conditioning in this simulation is due to activity-dependent amplification of presynaptic facilitation of the PSP from the CS sensory neuron to the motor neuron [Eqs. (3, 4, 5, 6, and 8).]

Psychologists sometimes distinguish between increasing the amplitude of a preexisting response to the CS (α-conditioning) and learning a new response (β-conditioning). In the simulation, conditioning produces an enhancement of a preexisting PSP in the motor neuron (α-conditioning).

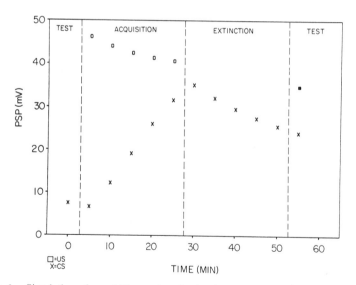

Fig. 6.   Simulation of acquisition and extinction in classical conditioning. The ordinate shows the amplitude of the PSP produced in the motor neuron each time a stimulus (CS or US) occurs in a hypothetical conditioning experiment with five training trials and five extinction trials. □, US; X, CS, ■, response to the CS at that time if the five extinction trials are omitted; CS strength, 1 arbitrary unit; US strength, 6; ITI, 5 min.

However, if there were a threshold PSP amplitude for producing a behavioral response (of, for example, 15 mV), conditioning would lead to the development of a new response to the CS at the behavioral level ("β-conditioning"). These results suggest that there is no fundamental difference between α and β-conditioning, but rather the apparent difference between the two may depend on how the response is measured.

As in many instances of real conditioning (e.g., Carew et al., 1981), the acquisition function illustrated in Fig. 6 is slightly S-shaped. The initial acceleration (which is more evident with weaker CSs) (see Fig. 18) is due to positive feedback in the calcium priming process: The first conditioning trial produces broadening of the action potential in the sensory neuron and hence an increase in calcium priming of the cAMP cascade on the second conditioning trial [Eqs. (3, 4, and 8)]. This produces greater broadening of the action potential and greater calcium priming on the third and subsequent trials. The deceleration in acquisition occurs as the response evoked by the CS approaches that evoked by the US. This leads to decreased effectiveness of the US due to accommodation in the facilitator neuron (see the discussion of blocking, below), such that the response to the CS reaches an asymptote at approximately the level of the response to the US.

Extinction in this model is assumed to have the same cellular mechanism as habituation: synaptic depression due to inactivation of Ca^{2+} channels [Eq. (1)]. Extinction has a number of features in common with habituation which are thus readily simulated by the model. For example, if the CS is not presented for some time following extinction, the animal's response to the CS recovers, indicating that the animal remembers the original training (Carew et al., 1981). This effect, which is called *spontaneous recovery*, can be accounted for by recovery from Ca^{2+} channel inactivation [Eq. (2)]. The response to the CS can also be restored by presentation of a strong extraneous stimulus. Pavlov (1927) referred to this phenomenon as disinhibition, because he thought that extinction was due to inhibition which the extraneous stimulus removed. In the model described here, however, disinhibition is accounted for by the same cellular process as dishabituation: presynaptic facilitation of the sensory neuron.

A conditioned response may lose its strength not only through extinction, but also through the simple passage of time or forgetting. The filled square in Fig. 6 shows the small amount of forgetting that would have occurred in this simulation if the five extinction trials had been omitted. Forgetting in the simulation is due to the gradual decline in cAMP levels in the sensory neuron following training [Eq. (9)].

B. CONTROL PROCEDURES

The simulation shown in Fig. 6 illustrates the effect of paired training on the response to the CS. However, control procedures are necessary to demonstrate that an increase in responding to the CS is associative in nature. The model successfully simulates a number of control procedures that have been used in *Aplysia* (Carew *et al.*, 1981, 1983; Hawkins *et al.*, 1986). For example, simulations with the CS and US occurring either by themselves or explicitly unpaired produce little or no increase in responding to the CS (posttest = 62, 126, and 84% of pretest, respectively). Moreover, the rank order of effectiveness of various training procedures (Paired > US alone > No Training ≈ Unpaired > CS alone) is the same in the simulations as in real experiments (Carew *et al.*, 1981). In the simulations this is because CS-alone training produces habitation, US-alone training produces sensitization, unpaired training produces a combination of the two, and paired training produces an amplification of sensitization.

Figure 7 shows a simulation of another type of control procedure, differential conditioning. In this experiment, two CSs which activate different sensory neurons are used (see Fig. 1). During training, one CS is paired with the US and the other CS is given unpaired with the US. The

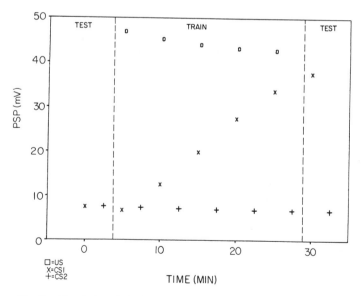

Fig. 7. Simulation of differential conditioning. □, US; X, CS$_1$; +, CS$_2$.

response to the paired CS shows a large increase whereas the response to the unpaired CS shows none, demonstrating the associative nature of the learning. In differential conditioning in *Aplysia*, there is frequently also some increase in responding to the unpaired CS, which can be attributed to the nonassociative process of sensitization (e.g., Carew *et al.*, 1983). An interesting result of the model is that the relative amounts of conditioning and sensitization depend entirely on the priming factor, C_7. Thus, differences in the magnitude of that factor could explain why conditioning produces different amounts of sensitization in different animals or different experiments. Another result which is frequently observed in differential conditioning experiments is an initial increase in responding to the unpaired CS, followed by a decrease. This effect is not observed in the simulation shown in Fig. 7, in which each CS excites one sensory neuron. However, it can be simulated if the two CSs are assumed to excite overlapping sets of sensory neurons ($CS_1 = SN_1$, SN_2 and $CS_2 = SN_2$, SN_3) (see Fig. 8). As previously suggested by Rescorla and Wagner (1972), the shared sensory neuron may be thought of as responding to the stimuli that are always present in the experimental situation (the background stimuli).

C. STIMULUS SPECIFICITY AND GENERALIZATION

As demonstrated by differential conditioning, animals learn to respond to the conditioned stimulus and not to other irrelevant stimuli. Activity-dependent enhancement of presynaptic facilitation readily confers this stimulus specificity: Only those sensory neurons that are active preceding the US undergo the amplified form of presynaptic facilitation, and thus only the response to the paired conditioned stimulus is selectively enhanced (Fig. 7).

Stimulus specificity is not generally complete, however. After conditioning, animals will respond to stimuli other than the conditioned stimulus, and the strength of the response will depend on the degree of similarity between the test stimulus and the conditioned stimulus. The model includes two cellular explanations for stimulus generalization. The first is sensitization: An aversive unconditioned stimulus will produce some enhancement of defensive responses to *all* stimuli, whether they are paired with it or not. This enhancement will simply be greater for the paired stimuli. The second explanation [which is basically similar to those proposed by Bush and Mosteller (1951) and Atkinson and Estes (1963)] is that there will be some overlap in the sensory neurons and interneurons excited by different stimuli (Fig. 8). Thus, conditioning of one stimulus will produce amplified presynaptic facilitation of some (but not all) of the neurons that are excited by a second stimulus and will therefore produce

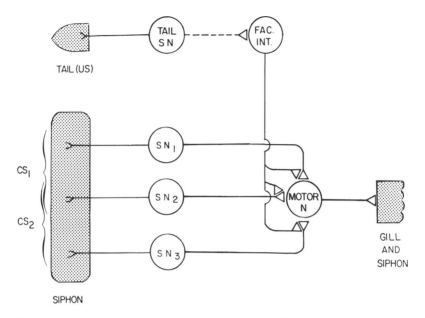

Fig. 8. Proposed cellular mechanisms of stimulus specificity and generalization. CS_1 excites sensory neurons 1 and 2, and CS_2 excites neurons 2 and 3. Only those sensory neurons that are active preceding the US undergo the amplified form of presynaptic facilitation. Thus, conditioning of CS_1 produces partial, but not complete, generalization to CS_2. Some of the synaptic connections shown in Fig. 1 have been omitted to simplify the wiring diagram.

partial enhancement of the response to the second stimulus. The greater the similarity between the stimuli, the more overlap there will be in the neurons they excite, and consequently the more generalization.

A simulation of generalization based on these ideas is shown in Fig. 9. In this simulation, CS_1 excites sensory neurons 1 and 2 and CS_2 excites sensory neurons 2 and 3. Conditioning CS_1 leads to an increase in responding to CS_2 in part because of sensitization caused by presentation of the US during training and in part because the two stimuli excite a common sensory neuron that undergoes activity-dependent enhancement of presynaptic facilitation during conditioning (see Fig. 8). Clearly, this mechanism could account for a wider range of generalization if it occurred at sensory interneurons as well as primary sensory neurons.

D.   EFFECTS OF CS STRENGTH, US STRENGTH, AND ITI

The rate of acquisition of a conditioned response is typically an increasing function of CS strength, US strength, and intertrial interval (ITI). As

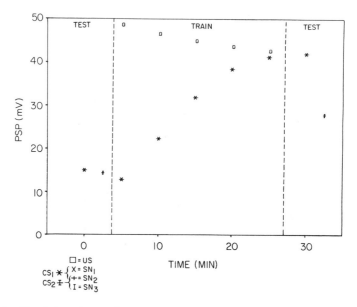

Fig. 9. Simulation of generalization. □, US; X, SN₁ (sensory neuron 1); +, SN₂; I, SN₃. CS₁ excites SN₁ and SN₂, and CS₂ excites SN₂ and SN₃.

shown in Fig. 10, the model successfully simulates each of these effects. In these simulations, a stronger CS produces more spikes in the CS sensory neuron and thus greater Ca^{2+} influx and greater priming of the adenyl cyclase [Eq. (8)]. A stronger US produces more spikes in the facilitatory interneuron and thus greater activation of the adenyl cyclase in the sensory neuron [Eq. (8)]. In either case the result is greater synthesis of cAMP, greater spike broadening [Eq. (3)], and greater facilitation of transmitter release from the CS sensory neuron [Eq. (4 and 5)]. Since each trial produces some habituation of the effectiveness of both the CS and the US due to inactivation of Ca^{2+} channels in the sensory neurons [Eq. (1)], a longer intertrial interval permits greater recovery from this habituation [Eq. (2)], and thus more effective training on the next trial and more rapid acquisition.

E. CS–US TIMING

Conditioning is also often critically dependent on the exact timing of the CS and US during training. For example, in many preparations conditioning is optimal when the CS onset precedes the US onset by approximately 0.5 sec, and there is little or no conditioning if the interstimulus interval is longer or if the order of the two stimuli is reversed (Hawkins

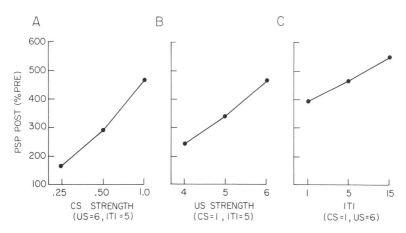

Fig. 10. Simulation of the effects on acquisition of CS strength, US strength, and intertrial interval. A, Graph of the amplitude of the PSP in the motor neuron on the first posttest, expressed as a percent of its value on the pretest, following five training trials with a CS strength of either 0.25, 0.50, or 1.0 arbitrary units. US strength, 6; ITI, 5 min. B, Similar graph of learning as a function of US strength (4, 5, or 6 arbitrary units). CS strength, 1; ITI, 5 minutes. C, Learning as a function of intertrial interval (1, 5, or 15 min). CS strength, 1; US strength, 6.

et al., 1986). The model described in Section III was not designed to handle events with this time resolution, but it does qualitatively simulate these effects: Conditioning occurs if the CS precedes the US by one time unit, but not if the interval is longer or if the order of the stimuli is reversed. In this model these effects are assumptions, but in the similar but more detailed model of Gingrich and Byrne (1987), they are derived from more basic assumptions about Ca^{2+} handling and priming of the cyclase.

Conditioning often depends not only on the timing of the stimulus onsets, but also on the timing of their offsets. For example, delay conditioning, in which the CS and US overlap during training, is generally more effective than trace conditioning, in which the CS terminates before the US starts. The model qualitatively simulates this effect because in delay conditioning the late part of the CS sums with the US in the facilitator neuron. Thus, in delay conditioning the effective US gets stronger as the response to the CS gets stronger, whereas in trace conditioning this does not happen.

F. THE CONDITIONED RESPONSE

The model can account for both the stimulus and temporal specificity of classical conditioning, but it has little to say about the conditioned response. For example, the timing of the conditioned response frequently shifts during training such that the response occurs shortly before the expected onset of the US. The model does not provide an explanation for this effect, although it could account for a decrease in response latency with increased CS strength if it included more biophysical detail. It also fails to explain why the conditioned response frequently resembles the unconditioned response (for example, salivation with food as the US or withdrawal with shock as the US). Behavioral and cellular experiments on *Aplysia* are currently addressing this question (Frost *et al.,* 1988; Erickson & Walters, 1986; Hawkins, Lalevic, Clark, & Kandel, 1989).

VI. Simulations of Higher-Order Features of Conditioning

In addition to the parametric features described above, classical conditioning has several higher-order features which are thought to have a cognitive flavor. Some of these were first described by Pavlov and the early students of associative learning; others have more recently been described by Kamin, Rescorla, Wagner, and others who have been interested in the cognitive or information-processing aspects of learning. According to this view, in a classical conditioning experiment the animal builds an internal representation of the external world, compares this representation with reality (with the view of the world as validated by current sensory information) and then modifies its behavior accordingly (Dickinson, 1980; Kamin, 1969; Mackintosh, 1983; Rescorla, 1978; Wagner, 1978).

In light of the evidence for a cellular relationship between habituation, sensitization, and classical conditioning, it is interesting to examine the possibility that combinations of the elementary mechanisms used in these simple forms of learning can account for additional higher-order aspects of associative learning, without requiring additional cellular mechanisms. Here I shall consider five higher-order features: (1) second-order conditioning, (2) blocking, (3) overshadowing, (4) contingency effects, and (5) pre- and postexposure effects (Table III). The explanations proposed for these phenomena are not meant to be exclusive. Rather, I wish only to indicate how simple cellular processes such as synaptic depression and facilitation could be used in different combinatorial ways to contribute to these higher-order features of behavior.

A. SECOND-ORDER CONDITIONING

A second-order conditioning experiment has two stages: In stage I CS_1 is paired with the US, and then in stage II a second CS (CS_2) is paired

TABLE III

HIGHER-ORDER FEATURES OF CONDITIONING OBSERVED IN THE
LITERATURE

Feature	Simulation by model?[a]	*Aplysia* reference[b]
1. Second-order	Yes	
2. Blocking	Yes	7
3. Overshadowing		
Different strengths	Yes	
Different probabilities of reinforcement	Yes	
4. Contingency		
Extra USs	Yes	8
Extra CSs (partial reinforcement)	Yes	
Both	Yes	
5. Preexposure		
CS (latent inhibition)	Yes	
US	Yes	
Both	Yes	9
6. US postexposure	(Yes)	
7. Sensory preconditioning	No	
8. Conditioned inhibition	No	

[a]Parentheses indicate that the feature can be simulated with modifications to the model.
[b]Key: 7, Colwill (1985); 8, Hawkins, Carew, & Kandel (1986); 9, Lukowiak (1986).

with CS_1. As Pavlov (1927) noted, this procedure can lead to an associative increase in responding to CS_2. Thus, in effect, as a result of the conditioning in stage I, CS_1 acquires the ability to act as a US in stage II. Second-order conditioning is thought to be ubiquitous in everyday life and to bridge the gap between laboratory experiments and complex natural behavior, which often does not have obvious reinforcers. Second-order conditioning also illustrates the interchangeability of the CS and US, since the same stimulus can serve as either a CS or a US in a conditioning experiment.

Second-order conditioning might be explained by two features of the neural circuit shown in Fig. 1. First, in addition to being excited by the US, the facilitator neuron is also excited by the CS sensory neurons. Second, the facilitator neuron produces facilitation not only at the synapses from the sensory neurons to the motor neurons but also at the synapses from the sensory neurons to the facilitator neuron itself. This fact has the interesting consequence that the sensory–facilitator synapses (unlike the sensory–motor synapses) should act like Hebb synapses. According to this idea, firing a sensory neuron just before firing the facilitator produces selective strengthening of the synapse from that sensory neuron to the facilitator. As a result, during stage I conditioning, CS_1 acquires a greater ability to excite the facilitator, allowing it to act as a US in stage II.

Figure 11 shows a simulation of second-order conditioning based on this mechanism. During stage II, the response to CS_2 increases while CS_1 undergoes extinction. As controls, CS_2 does not condition in stage II if CS_1 is presented unpaired with the US in stage I, of if CS_2 is presented unpaired with CS_1 in stage II.

Rescorla and his colleagues have found that habituating the US following second-order conditioning decreases the response to CS_1, but habituating either the US or CS_1 does not decrease the response to CS_2 (Rescorla, 1973). Rescorla has interpreted these results as showing that first-order conditioning is predominantly S–S (that is, CS_1 is associated with the US, which in turn is associated with the response), while second-order conditioning is predominately S–R (that is, CS_2 is associated directly with the response). The model described in Section III fails to simulate Rescorla's results (see also the discussion of postexposure, below). Hawkins and Kandel (1984) have suggested how it might be modified to do so, based on ideas similar to Rescorla's, but these ideas have not been incorporated in the present model.

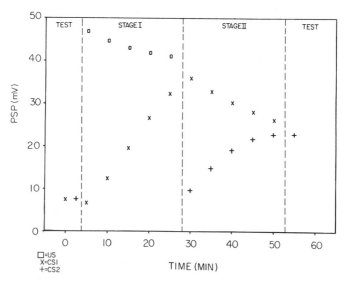

Fig. 11.   Simulation of second-order conditioning. $\square$, US; X, CS_1; +, CS_2.

B. BLOCKING AND OVERSHADOWING

Like a second-order conditioning experiment, a blocking experiment has two stages. In stage I, CS_1 is paired with the US as usual. In stage II, CS_2 is added to CS_1 and the compound stimulus CS_1CS_2 is paired with the US. As Kamin (1969) noted, this procedure generally produces little conditioning of CS_2, even though good conditioning of CS_2 occurs if CS_1 is omitted in stage II or if CS_1 was not previously conditioned in stage I. Thus, simultaneous presentation with a previously conditioned stimulus (CS_1) blocks conditioning of a naive stimulus (CS_2).

The discovery of blocking was very influential in the history of thinking about conditioning, because blocking demonstrates that animals may not acquire a conditioned response despite many pairings of the CS and US. This result suggests that conditioning is not simply an automatic outcome of stimulus pairing but may instead involve cognitive processes. For example, Kamin (1969) proposed that an animal forms expectations about the world, compares current input with those expectations, and learns only when something unpredicted occurs. Because CS_1 comes to predict the US in the first stage of training, in the second stage the compound CS_1CS_2 is not followed by anything unexpected and, therefore, little conditioning occurs.

Rescorla and Wagner (1972) have formalized this explanation by suggesting that the associative strength of a CS in effect subtracts from the strength of a US with which it is paired. In the neural model, this substraction function is accomplished by accommodation of firing in the facilitator neuron (Fig. 12). Thus, as the synapses from CS1 to the facilitator become strengthened during stage I training the facilitator fires progressively more during CS1 and less during the US, due to accommodation caused by CS1 [Eq. (6 and 7)]. This process reaches an asymptote when there is just enough firing left during the US to counteract CS1 habituation. When training with the compound stimulus CS_1CS_2 starts in the second stage of training, CS_2 is followed by very little firing in the facilitator neuron and therefore does not become conditioned. Firing of the facilitator neuron at the onset of CS_2 does not produce activity-dependent facilitation, because that process requires a delay between CS onset and the onset of facilitation [Equation (8)].

This example illustrates how the model incorporates in very rudimentary forms the notions of predictability and internal representation. The predicted effect of CS_1 is represented internally as the strength of the synapse from CS1 to the facilitator neuron. The actual consequences of CS_1 are compared to this prediction through the process of accommodation, which in effect subtracts the associative strength of CS_1 from the

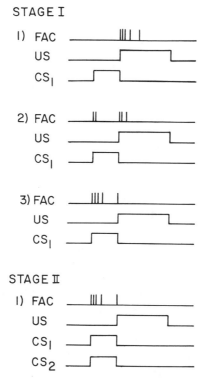

Fig. 12. Proposed cellular mechanism of blocking. As conditioning of CS_1 proceeds (stage I, trials 1, 2, and 3) the facilitator neuron fires more during the conditioned stimulus (CS) period. This firing produces accommodation which reduces firing during the US period. When compound conditioning starts (stage II), CS_2 is followed by little firing of the facilitator neuron and therefore does not become conditioned.

strength of the US that follows it. As these two strengths become equal, CS_1 can be said to predict the US, which thus loses its reinforcing power, and no further learning occurs. This subtraction process also explains why the response to the CS reaches an asymptote at approximately the response to the US during normal acquisition (see Fig. 6).

Figure 13 shows a simulation of blocking. Following stage II training there is very little conditioning of CS_2, while CS_1 retains the associative strength it acquired in stage I. As controls, CS_2 undergoes substantially more conditioning during stage II if CS_1 occurs unpaired with the US in stage I, or if CS_1 occurs separately from CS_2 and the US during the stage II.

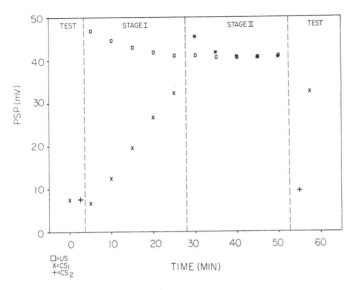

Fig. 13. Simulation of blocking. *, Simultaneous occurrence of CS_1 and CS_2.

Gluck and Thompson (1987) have reported some difficulty in simulating blocking with a quantitative model based on the ideas suggested by Hawkins and Kandel (1984). Although the Gluck and Thompson model is basically similar to the one described here, it differs in many details. In particular, it is formulated at the level of algebraic synaptic learning rules rather than molecular processes. Gluck and Thompson (1987) note that blocking is much more successful in their model if they assume an S-shaped acquisition function, rather than a decelerating acquisition function (which was their initial assumption). This observation may help explain why the model described here simulates blocking with little difficulty. An S-shaped acquisition function is a natural consequence of the molecular processes (in particular, calcium priming of the cAMP cascade) upon which this model is based. However, the model described here still produces some blocking if the acquisition function is artificially changed to a decelerating one (by holding priming constant), although in that case blocking is less complete.

Overshadowing is similar to blocking but involves training with CSs which differ in salience or probability of reinforcement rather than previous association with the US. As Pavlov (1927) noted, if CS_1 is more salient (stronger) than CS_2 and the compound stimulus CS_1CS_2 is paired with the US, there will tend to be little conditioning of CS_2, even though good conditioning of CS_2 occurs if it is paired with the US by itself. Thus, a strong CS overshadows a weaker CS when they are presented simultaneously, preventing conditioning of the weak CS. Overshadowing of CS_2 when it is part of the compound stimulus CS_1CS_2 also occurs if the two CSs have the same salience but CS_1 has a higher probability of reinforcement (i.e., is a better predictor of the US) than CS_2.

The model described here simulates both types of overshadowing. Figure 14 shows a simulation of overshadowing with two different CS strengths (CS_1, 1.75 and CS_2, 1.00). The explanation of this effect is similar to the explanation proposed for blocking: CS_1 conditions more rapidly than CS_2 initially (since it has more action potentials and hence greater calcium priming of the cAMP cascade) and conditioning of both CSs decelerates as their combined associative strengths approach the US strength. In the simulation this occurs by the second paired trial, before there has been much conditioning of CS_2. As training continues, the CS strengths actually habituate slightly, with the response to CS_1 remaining near asymptote and the response to CS_2 remaining at a low level.

Figure 15 shows a simulation of overshadowing with two different probabilities of reinforcement. During training, trials on which the compound CS_1CS_2 is paired with the US alternate with trials on which CS_2 is

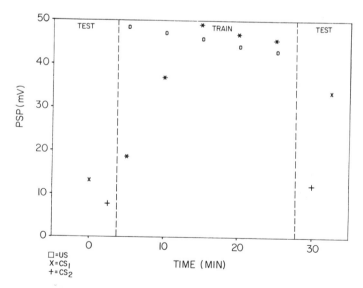

Fig. 14.   Simulation of overshadowing by a CS with greater salience. CS_1 strength, 1.75; CS_2 strength, 1.00; *, simultaneous occurrence of CS_1 and CS_2.

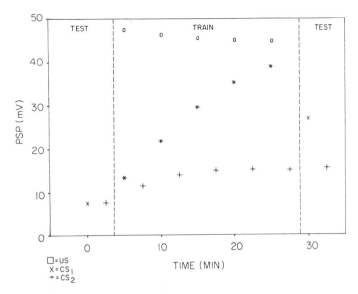

Fig. 15. Simulation of overshadowing by a CS with a higher probability of reinforcement. *, Simultaneous occurrence of CS_1 and CS_2.

presented alone. Thus CS_1 is always followed by the US, whereas CS_2 is followed by the US only half of the time. As a result, CS_1 conditions more rapidly than CS_2 (see the discussion of partial reinforcement below). Conditioning of both CSs decelerates as the associative strength of the compound CS_1CS_2 approaches the US strength. As in the previous example, this asymptote occurs before there has been much conditioning of CS_2, which is thus overshadowed by the more rapidly conditioning CS_1.

C.   THE EFFECT OF CONTINGENCY

Like blocking, the effect of contingency illustrates that animals do not simply learn about the pairing of events, but also learn about their correlation or contingency, that is, how well one event predicts another. Rescorla (1968) demonstrated this effect by showing that adding additional, unpaired CSs or USs to a conditioning procedure decreases learning, although the animals receive the same number of pairings of the CS and US. A similar effect of extra USs has been demonstrated for conditioning of gill and siphon withdrawal in *Aplysia* (Hawkins *et al.*, 1986). Hawkins and Kandel (1984) suggested that habituation of US effectiveness might contribute to the effect of extra USs. Thus, just as CS effectiveness habituates with repeated presentations of the CS, so might US effectiveness habituate with repeated presentations of the US. Adding additional, un-paired USs would therefore cause greater habituation of the US, leading to decreased US effectiveness on the paired trials and decreased learning.

The neuronal model includes US habituation, since the US pathway is not treated any differently than the CS pathways. Figure 16 shows a simulation in which additional, unpaired USs are presented during train-ing. This procedure causes extra US habituation and decreased condition-ing of the CS.

Rescorla and Wagner (1972) proposed a different explanation for the effect of extra USs, which is that it could be explained by an extension of the argument they advanced for blocking and overshadowing by in-cluding in the analysis the stimuli that are always present in the experi-mental situation (the background stimuli). Thus an experiment with extra USs (alternating trials of CS_1–US and US alone) can be thought of as an experiment with alternating trials of CS_1CS_2–US and CS_2–US, where CS_2 represents the background stimuli. In this case CS_2 conditions more rapidly than CS_1 (since it receives twice as many paired trials) and there-fore tends to overshadow conditioning of CS_1. This explanation of the effect of extra USs and the explanation based on US habituation (Fig. 16) are not mutually exclusive, and both may contribute. Thus, if a "back-ground" stimulus (CS_2 in the argument above) is added to the simulation

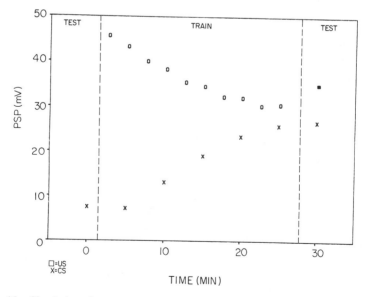

Fig. 16. Simulation of extra USs (partial warning). ■, Response to the CS at that time if the five extra USs are omitted.

shown in Fig. 16, degradation of conditioning of the extra USs is more profound.

Presenting additional, unpaired CSs during training (partial reinforcement) also decreases conditioning, as illustrated in the simulation shown in Fig. 17. This effect has two explanations: extinction (CS habituation) caused by the unpaired CSs, and a consequent decrease in calcium priming of the cAMP cascade on the paired trials. As might be expected, presenting both additional, unpaired USs and CSs causes an even greater decrease in conditioning than either procedure by itself.

D. PRE- AND POSTEXPOSURE EFFECTS

Learning can be disrupted by presenting extra, unpaired stimuli before paired training, as well as during it. For example, presentation of unpaired CSs in stage I of an experiment causes a retardation of conditioning during paired training in stage II. This effect, which is referred to as latent inhibition, has a formal similarity to the effect of partial reinforcement described above, and it may have a similar neural explanation. Figure 18 shows a simulation of latent inhibition in which inactivation of Ca^{2+} current during stage I leads to a decrease in Ca^{2+} priming of the cAMP cascade and hence retardation of conditioning in stage II. This

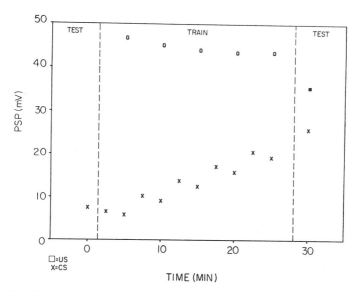

Fig. 17.   Simulation of extra CSs (partial reinforcement). ■, Response to the CS at that time if the five extra CSs are omitted.

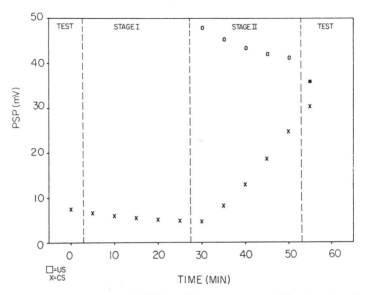

Fig. 18. Simulation of latent inhibition. ■, Response to the CS at that time if stage I training is omitted.

effect is most evident during the early part of stage II (compare with Fig. 6). With continued training, conditioning eventually reaches the same asymptote as it would have without stage I training.

For reasons similar to those described above for the effect of extra USs, presentation of unpaired USs in stage I (US preexposure) also decreases conditioning during paired training in stage II. Furthermore, unpaired presentation of both CSs and USs in stage I produces an even greater decrease in conditioning than presentation of either stimulus by itself.

In addition to these preexposure effects, posttraining exposure to the experimental stimuli can also reduce or degrade learning. Degradation of conditioning by posttraining exposure to the CS (extinction) was discussed in Section V. Conditioning can also be reduced by repeated presentation (habituation) of the US following training (Rescorla, 1973). Rescorla (1978) has suggested that this procedure weakens the animal's internal representation of the US, which in turn weakens its response to a CS associated with that US. The model described in Section III does not simulate this posttraining US exposure effect with simple stimuli. However, the model can simulate this effect if the CS is thought of as a compound stimulus, one component of which represents the stimuli that are always present in the experimental situation (the background stimuli), and special assumptions are made about habituation of those stimuli.

E. Sensory Preconditioning and Conditioned Inhibition

Although the model I have described can qualitatively simulate many of the higher-order features of conditioning, there are a few other features which it does not explain. One of these is sensory preconditioning. A sensory preconditioning experiment has two stages: In stage I, the compound stimulus CS_1CS_2 is repeatedly presented, and in stage II one of the stimuli (CS_1) is paired with the US. A frequent result of stage II training is an increase in responding to both CS_1 and CS_2, suggesting that the stage I training resulted in the formation of an association between the two CSs. The model I have described does not include any mechanism for such stimulus association.

Another higher-order feature of conditioning which the model does not explain is conditioned inhibition. One way to demonstrate conditioned inhibition is to intermingle trials on which CS_1 is paired with the US and trials on which the compound stimulus CS_1CS_2 is presented without the US. In this situation CS_2 signals that the US will *not* occur. Following such training, animals frequently learn to respond to CS_1 but not to the compound stimulus CS_1CS_2, suggesting that CS_2 has acquired negative strength. The model I have described cannot account for conditioned inhibition because it does not include any mechanism that can give a CS negative strength. Unlike many psychological models in which positive and negative learning are treated symmetrically (e.g., Rescorla & Wagner, 1972), this model utilizes a separate mechanism, synaptic depression, for all negative learning. The relative success of the model demonstrates that this mechanism may contribute to a wider range of learning phenomena than has generally been appreciated. However, depression cannot account for conditioned inhibition and related learning phenomena, since the lowest it can go is zero. To explain those phenomena, it will presumably be necessary to add inhibitory interneurons to the neuronal circuit shown in Fig. 1. Neurons which produce inhibition in this circuit have been identified, and their properties are currently being investigated (Hawkins *et al.*, 1981; Mackey *et al.*, 1987; Small, Kandel, & Hawkins, 1989).

VII. Discussion

The finding that a molecular mechanism of conditioning of the *Aplysia* withdrawal reflex appears to be an extension of a mechanism of sensitization suggests two hypotheses: First, that higher forms of learning may utilize the mechanisms of lower forms of learning as a general rule, and second, that this may occur because the mechanisms of higher forms of learning have evolved from those of lower forms of learning. The alternative possibility is that fundamentally new types of learning mechanisms have appeared during evolution. It is easy to imagine how the cellular mechanism of conditioning in *Aplysia* might have evolved from the mechanism of sensitization. For example, a small change in the adenyl cyclase molecule might have made it sensitive to Ca^{2+} that enters the cell during an action potential, thus giving rise to the activity dependence of facilitation. This example suggests that the mechanisms of yet higher forms of learning may similarly have evolved from the mechanism of conditioning. Higher forms of learning may also utilize the mechanisms of lower forms of learning within an individual animal. Thus, whereas single neurons may possess only a few fundamental types of plasticity which are used in all forms of learning, combining the neurons in large numbers with specific synaptic connections (as occurs, for example, in mammalian cortex) may produce the much more subtle and varied processes required for more advanced types of learning.

In this article I have attempted to illustrate these ideas by showing how several higher-order features of classical conditioning might be generated from combinations of the cellular mechanisms used in simpler forms of learning. The model I have presented is similar in many respects to (and was guided by) mathematical models proposed by modern behaviorists to account for the same phenomena. In particular, it provides a neuronal version of a concept central to many of those models, which is that learning depends on the degree to which the US is surprising or unpredicted (e.g., Rescorla & Wagner, 1972; Wagner, 1978, 1981; Mackintosh, 1975). The model differs from most mathematical models, however, in that it is based on known physiology and neural circuitry. As a consequence, it utilizes separate mechanisms (facilitation and depression) for positive and negative learning.

Although the model I have described successfully simulates a wide range of phenomena in habituation, sensitization, basic classical conditioning, and higher-order features of conditioning, it fails to explain several other important learning phenomena, including sensory preconditioning, conditioned inhibition, and the nature of the conditioned response. An optimist might look at these results and say that the model must be close to the truth and simply needs improvement, whereas a pessimist might say that if a model fails to simulate a single important phenomenon it must be fundamentally wrong. Since no model will ever simulate all behavioral phenomena, one's position will ultimately depend on how sympathetic one is to the philosophy of the model. In any case, the failures of a model are often as instructive as its successes, since they identify the areas in which either additional or different ideas are necessary.

In addition to these failures to simulate a number of behavioral phenomena, the model has several other limitations. First, some of the behavioral phenomena which it can explain have not yet been tested in *Aplysia*, so the relevance of *Aplysia* physiology and circuitry to those phenomena is not demonstrated. Second, although the simulations demonstrate the sufficiency of the model to explain several features of learning, they do not demonstrate its necessity, that is, they do not show that those features of learning *are* generated in the manner suggested. Third, even if the model is correct, it does not demonstrate either that the relation between these different forms of learning results from evolution or that this process can be extended to yet more complex forms of learning.

A virtue of the model I have presented is that it should be testable by recording from the relevant neurons during learning in *Aplysia* (for preliminary results consistent with the model, see Hawkins & Schacher, 1989). Those tests cannot shed any direct light on the role of evolution, but they should provide additional insights into the ways in which several simple forms of learning (habituation, sensitization, classical conditioning, and higher-order features of conditioning) are related on the level of their basic cellular mechanisms. Whatever the outcome of those tests, the simulations described in this chapter support the more general hypothesis that relatively advanced types of learning may result from combinations of the mechanisms of more basic forms of learning in simple neural circuits.

ACKNOWLEDGMENTS

I am grateful to Greg Clark, Lise Eliot, and Irving Kupfermann for their comments and criticisms, to Kathrin Hilten and Louise Katz for preparing the figures, and to Harriet Ayers and Andy Krawetz for typing the manuscript. Preparation of this article was supported by a grant from the National Institute of Mental Health (MH-26212).

REFERENCES

Abrams, T. W. (1985). Activity-dependent presynaptic facilitation: An associative mechanism in *Aplysia*. *Cell and Molecular Neurobiology*, **5**, 123–145.

Abrams, T. W., Carew, T. J., Hawkins, R. D., & Kandel, E. R. (1983). Aspects of the cellular mechanism of temporal specificity in conditioning in *Aplysia*: Preliminary evidence for Ca^{2+} influx as a signal of activity. *Society for Neuroscience Abstracts*, **9**, 168.

Abrams, T. W., Castellucci, V. F., Camardo, J. S., Kandel, E. R., & Lloyd, P. E. (1984). Two endogenous neuropeptides modulate the gill and siphon withdrawal reflex in *Aplysia* by presynaptic facilitation involving cAMP-dependent closure of a serotonin-sensitive potassium channel. *Proceedings of the National Academy of Sciences U.S.A.*, **81**, 7956–7960.

Abrams, T. W., Eliot, L., Dudai, Y., & Kandel, E. R. (1985). Activation of adenylate cyclase in *Aplysia* neural tissue by Ca^{2+}/calmodulin, a candidate for an associative mechanism during conditioning. *Society for Neuroscience Abstracts*, **11**, 797.

Atkinson, R. C., & Estes, W. K. (1963). Stimulus sampling theory. In R. D. Luce, R. R. Bush, & E. Galanter (Eds.), *Handbook of mathematical psychology* (vol. 2, pp. 121–268). New York: Wiley.

Bailey, C. H., & Chen, M. (1988). Morphological basis of short-term habituation in *Aplysia*. *Journal Neuroscience*, **8**, 2452–2459.

Bernier, L., Castellucci, V. F., Kandel, E. R., & Schwartz, J. H. (1982). Facilitatory transmitter causes a selective and prolonged increase in adenosine 3′ : 5′-monosphosphate in sensory neurons mediating the gill and siphon withdrawal reflex in *Aplysia*. *Journal of Neuroscience*, **2**, 1682–1691.

Boyle, M. B., Klein, M., Smith, S. J., & Kandel, E. R. (1984). Serotonin increases intracellular Ca^{2+} transients in voltage-clamped sensory neurons of *Aplysia californica*. *Proceedings of the National Academy of Sciences U.S.A.*, **81**, 7642–7646.

Bush, R. R., & Mosteller, F. (1951). A model for stimulus generalization and discrimination. *Psychological Review*, **58**, 413–423.

Byrne, J. (1981). Comparative aspects of neural circuits for inking behavior and gill withdrawal in *Aplysia californica*. *Journal of Neurophysiology*, **45**, 98–106.

Byrne, J. (1987). Cellular analysis of associative learning. *Physiological Review*, **67**, 329–439.

Byrne, J., Castellucci, V., & Kandel, E. R. (1974). Receptive fields and response properties of mechanoreceptor neurons innervating siphon skin and mantle shelf in *Aplysia*. *Journal of Neurophysiology*, **37**, 1041–1064.

Carew, T. J., Castellucci, V. F., & Kandel, E. R. (1971). An analysis of dishabituation and sensitization of the gill-withdrawal reflex in *Aplysia*. *International Journal of Neuroscience*, **2**, 79–98.

Carew, T. J., Hawkins, R. D., Abrams, T. W., & Kandel, E. R. (1984). A test of Hebb's postulate at identified synapses which mediate classical conditioning in *Aplysia*. *Journal of Neuroscience*, **4**, 1217–1224.

Carew, T. J., Hawkins, R. D., & Kandel, E. R. (1983). Differential classical conditioning of a defensive withdrawal reflex in *Aplysia californica*. *Science*, **219**, 397–400.

Carew, T. J., Pinsker, H. M., & Kandel, E. R. (1972). Long-term habituation of a defensive withdrawal reflex in *Aplysia*. *Science*, **175**, 451–454.

Carew, T. J., & Sahley, C. L. (1986). Invertebrate learning and memory: From behavior to molecules. *Annual Review of Neuroscience*, **9**, 435–487.

Carew, T. J., Walters, E. T., & Kandel, E. R. (1981). Classical conditioning in a simple withdrawal reflex in *Aplysia californica*. *Journal of Neuroscience*, **1**, 1426–1437.

Castellucci, V. F., & Kandel, E. R. (1974). A quantal analysis of the synaptic depression underlying habituation of the gill-withdrawal reflex in *Aplysia*. *Proceedings of the National Academy of Sciences U.S.A.*, **71**, 5004–5008.

Castellucci, V., & Kandel, E. R. (1976). Presynaptic facilitation as a mechanism for behavioral sensitization in *Aplysia*. *Science*, **194**, 1176–1178.

Castellucci, V. F., Nairn, A., Greengard, P., Schwartz, J. H., & Kandel, E. R. (1982). Inhibitor of adenosine 3′ : 5′-monophosphate-dependent protein kinase blocks presynaptic facilitation in *Aplysia*. *Journal of Neuroscience*, **2**, 1673–1681.

Castellucci, V., Pinsker, H., Kupfermann, I., & Kandel, E. R. (1970). Neuronal mechanisms of habituation and dishabituation of the gill-withdrawal reflex in *Aplysia. Science,* **167,** 1745–1748.

Clark, G. A. (1984). A cellular mechanism for the temporal specificity of classical conditioning of the siphon-withdrawal response in *Aplysia. Society for Neuroscience Abstracts,* **10,** 268.

Colebrook, E., & Lukowiak, K. (1988). Learning by the *Aplysia* model system: Lack of correlation between gill and gill motor neurone responses. *Journal of Experimental Biology,* **135,** 411–429.

Colwill, R. M. (1985). Context conditioning in *Aplysia californica. Society for Neuroscience Abstracts,* **11,** 796.

Darwin, C. (1859). *On the origin of species by means of natural selection.* New York: Appleton.

Darwin, C. (1871). *The descent of man and selection in relation to sex.* New York: Appleton.

Davis, M. (1979). Effects of interstimulus interval length and variability on startle response habituation. *Journal of Comparative and Physiological Psychology,* **72,** 177–192.

Davis, M., & Wagner, A. R. (1968). Startle responsiveness after habituation to different intensities of tone. *Psychonomic Science,* **12,** 337–338.

Dickinson, A. (1980). *Contemporary animal learning theory.* London: Cambridge University Press.

Duerr, J. S., & Quinn, W. G. (1982). Three *Drosophila* mutants that block associative learning also affect habituation and sensitization. *Proceedings of the National Academy of Sciences U.S.A.,* **79,** 3646–3650.

Erickson, M. T., & Walters, E. T. (1986). Pseudoconditioning, alpha conditioning, and stimulus–response learning in *Aplysia. Society for Neuroscience Abstracts,* **12,** 398.

Farley, J. (1987). Contingency learning and causal detection in *Hermissenda:* I. Behavior. *Behavioral Neuroscience,* **101,** 13–27.

Frost, W. N., Castellucci, V. F., Hawkins, R. D., & Kandel, E. R. (1985). Monosynaptic connections made by the sensory neurons of the gill- and siphon-withdrawal reflex in *Aplysia* participate in the storage of long-term memory for sensitization. *Proceedings of the National Academy of Sciences U.S.A.,* **82,** 8266–8269.

Frost, W. N., Clark, G. A., & Kandel, E. R., (1985). Changes in cellular excitability in a new class of siphon motor neurons during sensitization in *Aplysia. Society for Neuroscience Abstracts,* **11,** 643.

Frost, W. N., Clark, G. A., & Kandel, E. R. (1988). Parallel processing of short-term memory for sensitization in *Aplysia. Journal of Neurobiology,* **19,** 297–334.

Gingrich, K. J., & Byrne, J. H. (1985). Simulation of synaptic depression, posttetanic potentiation, and presynaptic facilitation of synaptic potentials from sensory neurons mediating gill-withdrawal reflex in *Aplysia. Journal of Neurophysiology,* **53,** 652–669.

Gingrich, K. J., & Byrne, J. H. (1987). Single-cell neuronal model for associative learning. *Journal of Neurophysiology,* **57,** 1705–1715.

Glanzman, D. L., Mackey, S., Hawkins, R. D., Dyke, A., Lloyd, P. E., & Kandel, E. R. (1989). Depletion of serotonin in the nervous system of *Aplysia* reduces behavioral enhancement of gill- and siphon-withdrawal as well as the heterosynaptic facilitation produced by tail shock. *Journal of Neuroscience,* in press.

Gluck, M. A., & Thompson, R. F. (1987). Modeling the neural substrates of associative learning and memory: A computational approach. *Psychological Reviews,* **94,** 176–191.

Gormezano, I. (1972). Investigations of defense and reward conditioning in the rabbit. In A. H. Black & W. F. Prokasy (Eds.), *Classical conditioning II: Current research and theory* (pp. 151–181). New York: Appleton-Century-Crofts.

Groves, P. M., & Thompson, R. F. (1970). Habituation: A dual-process theory. *Psychological Review*, **77**, 419–450.

Hawkins, R. D., & Abrams, T. W. (1984). Evidence that activity-dependent facilitation underlying classical conditioning in *Aplysia* involves modulation of the same ionic current as normal presynaptic facilitation. *Society for Neuroscience Abstracts*, **10**, 268.

Hawkins, R. D., Abrams, T. W., Carew, T. J., & Kandel, E. R. (1983). A cellular mechanism of classical conditioning in *Aplysia:* Activity-dependent amplification of presynaptic facilitation. *Science, 219*, 400–405.

Hawkins, R. D., Carew, T. J., & Kandel, E. R. (1986). Effects of interstimulus interval and contingency on classical conditioning of the *Aplysia* siphon withdrawal reflex. *Journal of Neuroscience, 6*, 1695–1701.

Hawkins, R. D., Castellucci, V. F., & Kandel, E. R. (1981). Interneurons involved in mediation and modulation of gill-withdrawal reflex in *Aplysia*. II. Identified neurons produce heterosynaptic facilitation contributing to behavioral sensitization. *Journal of Neurophysiology, 45*, 315–326.

Hawkins, R. D., Clark, G. A., & Kandel, E. R. (1987). Cell biological studies of learning in simple vertebrate and invertebrate systems. In F. Plum (Ed.), *Handbook of physiology. Sect. 1. The nervous system. Vol. V: Higher functions of the brain.* (pp. 25–83). Bethesda, MD: American Physiological Society.

Hawkins, R. D., & Kandel, E. R. (1984). Is there a cell biological alphabet for simple forms of learning? *Psychological Review*, **91**, 375–391.

Hawkins, R. D., Lalevic, N., Clark, G. A., & Kandel, E. R. (1989). Classical conditioning of *Aplysia* siphon withdrawal involves the development of a new response to the CS. *Society for Neuroscience Abstracts*, **15**, in press.

Hawkins, R. D., & Schacher, S. (1989). Identical facilitator neurons L29 and L28 are excited by cutaneous stimuli used in dishabituation, sensitization, and classical conditioning of *Aplysia*. *Journal of Neuroscience,* in press.

Hebb, D. O. (1949). *The organization of behavior.* New York: Wiley.

Hochner, B., Braha, O., Klein, M., & Kandel, E. R. (1986). Distinct processes in presynaptic facilitation contribute to sensitization and dishabituation in *Aplysia:* Possible involvement of C kinase in dishabituation. *Society for Neuroscience Abstracts, 12*, 1340.

Hochner, B., Klein, M., Schacher, S., & Kandel, E. R. (1986). Additional component in the cellular mechanism of presynaptic facilitation contributes to behavioral dishabituation in *Aplysia*. *Proceedings of the National Academy of Sciences U.S.A., 83*, 8794–8798.

Jacklet, J., & Rine, J. (1977). Facilitation at neuromuscular junctions: Contribution to habituation and dishabituation of the *Aplysia* gill withdrawal reflex. *Proceedings of the National Academy of Sciences U.S.A., 74*, 1267–1271.

Kamin, L. J. (1969). Predictability, surprise, attention and conditioning. In B. A. Campbell & R. M. Church (Eds.), *Punishment and aversive behavior* (pp. 279–296). New York: Appleton-Century-Crofts.

Kandel, E. R., Abrams, T., Bernier, L., Carew, T. J., Hawkins, R. D., & Schwartz, J. H. (1983). Classical conditioning and sensitization share aspects of the same molecular cascade in *Aplysia*. *Cold Spring Harbor Symposia on Quantitative Biology, 48*, 821–830.

Kandel, E. R., & Schwartz, J. H. (1982). Molecular biology of learning: Modulation of transmitter release. *Science, 218*, 433–443.

Kanz, J. E., Eberly, L. B., Cobbs, J. S., & Pinsker, H. M. (1979). Neuronal correlates of siphon withdrawal in freely behaving *Aplysia*. *Journal of Neurophysiology, 42*, 1538–1556.

Kimble, G. A. (1961). *Hilgard and Marquis' conditioning and learning.* New York: Apple-ton-Century-Crofts.

Kistler, H. B., Jr., Hawkins, R. D., Koester, J., Steinbusch, H. W. M., Kandel, E. R., & Schwartz, J. H. (1985). Distribution of serotonin-immunoreactive cell bodies and processes in the abdominal ganglion of mature *Aplysia. Journal of Neuroscience,* **5,** 72–80.

Klein, M., & Kandel, E. R. (1980). Mechanism of calcium current modulation underlying presynaptic facilitation and behavioral sensitization in *Aplysia. Proceedings of the National Academy of Sciences U.S.A.,* **77,** 6912–6916.

Klein, M., Shapiro, E., & Kandel, E. R. (1980). Synaptic plasticity and the modulation of the Ca^{++} current. *Jouranl of Experimental Biology,* **89,** 117–157.

Krontiris-Litowitz, J. K., Erickson, M. T., & Walters, E. T. (1987). Central suppression of defensive reflexes in *Aplysia* by noxious stimulation and by factors released from body wall. *Society for Neuroscience Abstracts,* **13,** 815.

Kupfermann, I., Carew, T. J., & Kandel, E. R. (1974). Local, reflex, and central commands controlling gill and siphon movements in *Aplysia. Journal of Neurophysiology,* **37,** 996–1019.

Lukowiak, K. (1986). *In vitro* classical conditioning of a gill withdrawal reflex in *Aplysia:* neural correlates and possible neural mechanisms. *Journal of Neurobiology,* **17,** 83–101.

Mackey, S. L., Glanzman, D. L., Small, S. A., Dyke, A. M., Kandel, E. R., & Hawkins, R. D. (1987). Tail shock produces inhibition as well as sensitization of the siphon-withdrawal reflex of *Aplysia:* Possible behavioral role for presynaptic inhibition mediated by the peptide Phe-Met-Arg-Phe-NH_2. *Proceedings of the National Academy of Sciences U.S.A.,* **84,** 8730–8734.

Mackey, S. L., Kandel, E. R., & Hawkins, R. D. (1989). Identified serotonergic neurons in the cerebral ganglion of *Aplysia* produce presynaptic facilitation of siphon sensory neurons. *Journal of Neuroscience,* in press.

Mackintosh, N. J. (1974). *The psychology of animal learning.* London: Academic Press.

Mackintosh, N. J. (1975). A theory of attention: Variations in the associability of stimuli with reinforcement. *Psychological Reviews,* **82,** 276–298.

Mackintosh, N. J. (1983). *Conditioning and associative learning.* London: Oxford University Press.

Marcus, E. A., Nolen, T. G., Rankin, C. H., & Carew, T. J. (1988). Behavioral dissociation of dishabituation, sensitization, and inhibition in *Aplysia. Science,* **241,** 210–213.

Ocorr, K. A., Walters, E. T., & Byrne, J. H. (1985). Associative conditioning analog selectively increases cAMP levels of tail sensory neurons in *Aplysia. Proceedings of the National Academy of Sciences U.S.A.,* **82,** 2548–2552.

Pavlov, I. P. (1972). *Conditioned reflexes: An investigation of the physiological activity of the cerebral cortex* (G. V. Anrep, Trans.). London: Oxford University Press.

Perlman, A. J. (1979). Central and peripheral control of siphon withdrawal reflex in *Aplysia californica. Journal of Neurophysiology,* **42,** 510–529.

Pinsker, H. M., Hening, W. A., Carew, T. J., & Kandel, E. R. (1973). Long-term sensitization of a defensive withdrawal reflex in Aplysia. *Science,* **182,** 1039–1042.

Pinsker, H., Kupfermann, I., Castellucci, V., & Kandel, E. R. (1970). Habituation and dishabituation of the gill-withdrawal reflex in *Aplysia. Science,* **167,** 1740–1742.

Piomelli, D., Volterra, A., Dale, N., Siegelbaum, S. A., Kandel, E. R., Schwartz, J. H., & Belardetti, F. (1987). Lipoxygenase metabolites of arachidonic acid as second messengers for presynaptic inhibition of *Aplysia* sensory cells. *Nature (London),* **328,** 38–43.

Rescorla, R. A. (1968). Probability of shock in the presence and absence of CS in fear conditioning. *Journal of Comparative and Physiological Psychology,* **66,** 1–5.

108   **Robert D. Hawkins**

Rescorla, R. A. (1973). Second-order conditioning: Implications for theories of learning. In F. J. McGuigan & D. B. Hulse (Eds.), *Contemporary approaches to conditioning and learning* (pp. 127–150). Washington, DC: V. H. Winston.

Rescorla, R. A. (1978). Some implications of a cognitive perspective on Pavlovian conditioning. In S. H. Hulse, H. Fowler, & W. Honig (Eds.), *Cognitive processes in animal behavior* (pp. 15–50). Hillsdale, NJ: Erlbaum.

Rescorla, R. A., & Wagner, A. R. (1972). A theory of Pavlovian conditioning: Variations in the effectiveness of reinforcement and non-reinforcement. In A. H. Black & W. F. Prokasy (Eds.), *Classical conditioning II: Current research and theory.* (pp. 64–99). New York: Appleton-Century-Crofts.

Romanes, G. J. (1882). *Animal intelligence.* New York: Appleton.

Romanes, G. J. (1884). *Mental evolution in animals.* New York: Appleton.

Sacktor, T. C., O'Brian, C. A., Weinstein, J. B., & Schwartz, J. H. (1986). Translocation from cytosol to membrane of protein kinase C after stimulation of *Aplysia* neurons with serotonin. *Society for Neuroscience Abstracts,* **12,** 1340.

Sahley, C., Rudy, J. W., & Gelperin, A. (1981). An analysis of associative learning in a terrestrial mollusc. I. Higher-order conditioning, blocking, and a transient US pre-exposure effect. *Journal of Comparative Physiology,* **144,** 1–8.

Siegelbaum, S. A., Camardo, J. S., & Kandel, E. R. (1982). Serotonin and cyclic AMP close single K^+ channels in *Aplysia* sensory neurones. *Nature (London),* **299,** 413–417.

Small, S. A., Kandel, E. R., & Hawkins, R. D. (1989). Activity-dependent enhancement of presynaptic inhibition in *Aplysia* sensory neurons. *Science,* **243,** 1603–1609.

Spencer, W. A., Thompson, R. F., & Nielson, D. R., Jr. (1966a). Response decrement of the flexion reflex in the acute spinal cat and transient restoration by strong stimuli. *Journal of Neurophysiology,* **29,** 221–239.

Spencer, W. A., Thompson, R. F., & Nielson, D. R., Jr. (1966b). Decrement of ventral root electrotonus and intracellularly recorded PSPs produced by iterated cutaneous afferent volleys. *Journal of Neurophysiology,* **29,** 253–273.

Thompson, R. F., & Spencer, W. A. (1966). Habituation: A model phenomenon for the study of neuronal substrates of behavior. *Psychological Review,* **173,** 16–43.

Wagner, A. R. (1978). Expectancies and the priming of STM. In S. H. Hulse, H. Fowler, & W. Honig (Eds.), *Cognitive processes in animal behavior* (pp. 177–209). Hillsdale, NJ: Erlbaum.

Wagner, A. R. (1981). SOP: A model of automatic memory processing in animal behavior. In N. E. Spear & R. R. Miller (Eds.), *Information processing in animals: Memory mechanisms* (pp. 5–47). Hillsdale, NJ: Erlbaum.

Walters, E. T., & Byrne, J. H. (1983). Associative conditioning of single sensory neurons suggests a cellular mechanism for learning. *Science,* **219,** 405–408.

Walters, E. T., Carew, T. J., & Kandel, E. R. (1981). Associative learning in *Aplysia:* Evidence for conditioned fear in an invertebrate. *Science,* **211,** 504–506.

INTEGRATING BEHAVIORAL AND BIOLOGICAL MODELS OF CLASSICAL CONDITIONING

Nelson H. Donegan
Mark A. Gluck
Richard F. Thompson

I. Introduction

Considerable progress has been made in identifying the neural substrates of classical (Pavlovian) conditioning in both invertebrate preparations (e.g., Carew, Hawkins, & Kandel, 1983; Walters & Byrne, 1983; Alkon, 1984; Crow, 1985) and vertebrate preparations (e.g., Cohen, 1984; M. Davis, Hitchcock, & Rosen, 1987; Thompson, 1986). The primary focus of this work has been to identify the circuitry and, ultimately, the cellular mechanisms responsible for acquisition of learned behaviors. In addition to acquisition, however, a wide range of associative learning phenomena can be observed in classical conditioning, including blocking, overshadowing, extinction, conditioned inhibition, supernormal conditioning, and interstimulus interval effects. Thus, our successes in understanding acquisition bring us to a larger theoretical challenge: to develop neural models capable of deriving the full spectrum of behavioral phenomena observed in conditioning. One strategy for developing such models is to integrate neural models of acquisition with behavioral models capable of deriving classical conditioning phenomena. In this way, behavioral models can serve as concise embodiments of multiple constraints imposed by the behavioral phenomena on a biological model.

In spite of the successes of current behavioral models of conditioning,

109

there remain several problems in mapping these models onto identified neural circuits. First, there exists no single best model of conditioning; rather, one finds a variety of models, each cast of a different level of abstraction, accounting for different, but overlapping, sets of behavioral phenomena. Second, it is difficult to compare, contrast, or even integrate these models because each is expressed in a different formalism, generally that of the prevailing theoretical tradition in which it was first developed. Generating a common formalism, within which each of the major theoretical accounts of conditioning could be expressed, would seem a natural and helpful next step. Ideally, such a formalism would not only allow comparisons among the behavioral models, but also facilitate comparisons with the neural circuits presumed to implement these processing assumptions.

A. Overview

We have chosen to represent several classical conditioning models within a common formalism based on adaptive networks for associative learning. Similar connectionist network models are currently receiving intensive development in cognitive psychology and artificial intelligence (e.g., Gluck & Bower, 1988; Parker, 1986; Rumelhart & McClelland, 1986). In Section II, we reformulate the key ideas embodied by three influential models of classical conditioning within this adaptive network formalism: The first is the Rescorla–Wagner model (Rescorla & Wagner, 1972; Wagner & Rescorla, 1972), which can be taken as a version of the least mean- squares (LMS) algorithm of adaptive network theory (Widrow & Hoff, 1960) and has been shown to account successfully for a variety of phenomena of stimulus selection as well as conditioned inhibition in the Pavlovian conditioning literature. The basic premise of these error-correcting rules is that increments or decrements in the associative strength of a stimulus are determined by the discrepancy (error) between the outcome predicted by the collection of conditioned stimuli on a trial and the actual outcome of that trial (e.g., the presence of absence of the US). The second is the priming model developed by Wagner and colleagues (e.g., Wagner, 1976; 1978), which describes the ways in which US processing can be modulated by antecedent stimuli. The model addresses phenomena of stimulus selection as well as variation in the effectiveness of a stimulus in eliciting an unconditioned response (e.g. habituation). The third model is the SOP (sometimes opponent process) model (Donegan, 1980; Donegan & Wagner, 1987; Mazur & Wagner, 1982; Wagner, 1981), which is a quantitative, "real time," connectionist model that addresses a broad range of phenomena in the Pavlovian conditioning and habituation literatures.

We compare and contrast these models, identifying common and distinctive processing assumptions. We then show how the network representations inspired by these three models can all be viewed as having a common incremental learning rule but varying in the nature of their rules for decrementing associative strengths. This suggests that behavioral paradigms that clearly reflect decremental processes, such as extinction or conditioned inhibition, will be critical in distinguishing among models.

In Sections III and IV we focus on neural circuits in the *Aplysia* and mammalian cerebellum which have been identified as critical to the learning and expression of classically conditioned behaviors. We compare these neural circuits to the three adaptive network models and use our analyses of these models and their ability to generate various Pavlovian conditioning phenomena as a tool for evaluating the potential of the neural circuits for exhibiting the full range of conditioning phenomena addressed by the behavioral models.

To briefly summarize our conclusions: Our analyses of the known *Aplysia* circuitry in Section III suggest that the formal properties of this circuit have much in common with the assumptions of the priming model, rather than with the Rescorla–Wagner model as Hawkins and Kandel (1984) suggest. However, a network representation of the Rescorla–Wagner model, which does predict these phenomena, suggests possible extensions to the *Aplysia* circuitry which might generate a wider range of behavioral phenomena.

In Section IV we consider a mammalian system: the rabbit conditioned eyeblink preparation. We review the cerebellar–brain stem model of acquisition proposed by Thompson and colleagues and explore correspondences between features of the three network models and the known patterns of connectivity in these structures. These mappings suggest ways in which the neural circuitry for acquisition may be capable of generating a broader range of conditioning phenomena.

B. ADAPTIVE NETWORK MODELS OF CONDITIONING

In the last few years there has been an increased interest across the disciplines of cognitive psychology, computer science, and neurobiology in understanding the information processing capabilities of adaptive networks consisting of interconnected, neuronlike computing elements. These models are notable for their computational power and resemblance to psychological and neurobiological processes (e.g., Ackley, Hinton, & Sejnowski, 1985; Gluck & Bower, 1988; Hinton & Anderson, 1981; McClelland & Elman, 1986; Rosenberg & Sejnowski, 1986; Rumelhart & McClelland, 1986).

A typical adaptive network consists of processing units (nodes) connected by weighted unidirectional links. The state of each processing unit, at each moment in time, is described by its activation, which is determined by the sum of the weighted inputs to that unit from all its incoming connections. Presentation of a stimulus pattern to the system corresponds to activating a set of sensory units. These units pass their activation along their weighted connections either directly to the output units or to intermediate "hidden" units, which relay them to output units. The activation pattern over the layer of output units corresponds to some particular response of the system to that input. The weights in the network correspond to strengths of associations in classical learning theory, and the algorithm for changing the weights corresponds to learning rules in the theories.

We can formulate these ideas more precisely for a single adaptive element with n inputs. If the activity in input node i is a_i, then the output activity, g, is determined according to the following rule for the spread of activation:

$$g = f\left(\sum_{i=1}^{n} w_i a_i\right) \tag{1}$$

where the sum is over the n input nodes, and the w_is are real-valued numbers which represent the ability of activity in input node i to increase (or decrease) the activation of the adaptive element. The function f is a monotonic function which relates the weighted sum of the inputs to the output behavior of the adaptive element. We will consider two types of adaptive elements: linear elements, in which the output function is the identify map, $f(x) = x$, and nonlinear elements, in which the output function is constrained to be nonnegative according to

$$f(x) = \lfloor x \rfloor = \begin{cases} x & \text{if } x \geq 0 \\ 0 & \text{if } x < 0 \end{cases}$$

C. Classical Conditioning

We now consider how models of classical (Pavlovian) conditioning could be expressed within this formalism. In classical conditioning, a conditioned stimulus (CS), such as a tone, is paired with an unconditioned stimulus (US), such as food or an electric shock. Over the course of training, the CS develops the ability to elicit a conditioned response (CR) as a result of its association with the US. In addressing the facts of classical conditioning, we will be developing trial-level models; that is, models that describe the effects of a training trial—pairings of conditioned stimuli (CSs) with an unconditioned stimulus (US)—on the strengths of CS associations. These models can be viewed as rules that specify how the variables of CS and US intensity, and most importantly, the animal's expectancy for the US on a trial, combine to determine the changes in associative strengths produced by the trial.

By definition, trial-level models do not address many important real-time aspects of conditioning, such as the intratrial temporal relationship between the CS and the US and the temporal properties of response generation. As a heuristic for developing more general biological models of conditioning, we begin by exploring mappings of trial-level models onto neural circuits involved in acquisition. The simplicity, parsimony, and formal power of trial-level models motivate us to begin by attempting to map these models onto biological circuits before moving onto more complex real-time models.

Within our adaptive network formalism, we represent each potential CS_i by a unique sensory node. The activation of that node, a_i, is set to 0 if CS_i is not present on the trial and 1 if it is present. The US is represented by a special stimulus node whose activation is a function of US intensity and is denoted by a positive, continuous variable, λ. The associative strength of a CS is represented by its weight, w_i, which is a continuous variable that can take on positive, zero, or negative values. The output of an adaptive node, g, in response to a set of cues is presumed to be related to the CR by some monotonic transformation. Learning in these models is presumed to take place through modification of the CS weights. If w_i represents the association between CS_i and the adaptive node prior to a conditioning trial, then the change in association strengths produced by the trial can be represented as Δw_i.

The adaptive network models currently being studied by computer scientists and cognitive psychologists cover a wide range of assumptions regarding the sophistication of the individual processing elements (nodes). Many cognitive-level models presume that nodes are capable of computing complex functions for updating association weights according to various learning rules. In developing adaptive network representations of conditioning models, we have chosen to restrict the computational power of the individual units to simpler rules for incrementing and decrementing weights. The motivation behind this is to make the units more neuron like, wherein the behavioral properties of the system emerge through the connectivity and interaction of larger numbers of nodes. More specifically, we impose the constraint that associative changes be limited to conjunctive, or Hebbian, learning rules (Hebb, 1949). We then explore how the capacities of various behavioral models of conditioning could emerge from configurations of such elements. (For discussions of the neurobiological evidence for conjunctive or Hebb-like learning rules at the synaptic level, see Brown, Chapman, Kairias, & Keenan, 1988; Levy & Steward, 1979, 1983.) Within the adaptive network literature, the Hebbian rule is usually formulated as:

$$\Delta w_i = \beta a_i k \qquad (2)$$

where β is a positive valued learning rate parameter, a_i is as described above, and k, the reinforcing signal, can either be the output activity of the adaptive node or the activity of a special training signal. Note that the term "Hebbian" has been used in the literature in two distinct ways: first, as an algorithmic or behavioral rule for changing associative strengths and second, as a neurobiological term to denote a synapse at which strength changes are solely dependent on pre- and postsynaptic activity. Following adaptive network theorists, we use the term "Hebb rule" strictly in its algorithmic sense, to denote the learning rule in Eq. (2) which is sensitive only to the pairwise co-occurance of two events, similar to the earlier linear operator models of Hull (1943), Spence (1936), and Bush and Mosteller (1951). [We have chosen this more general form to allow a broader range of network implementations of this conjunctive rule, as in the case of pairing-specific presynaptic facilitation observed in *Aplysia* (e.g., Hawkins, Abrams, Carew, & Kandel, 1983).]

   This approach to developing elementary adaptive network models of conditioning can be contrasted with related work by Sutton and Barto (1981), who also proposed an adaptive network model of conditioning. In their model, individual elements (nodes) update associative weights according to a "temporally refined extension of the Rescorla–Wagner model" (Sutton & Barto, 1981, p. 135). This allowed their network model to address a wider range of phenomena than the Rescorla–Wagner model: that is, phenomena reflecting the effects of temporal variables on conditioning. Recent extensions or elaborations of this model were subsequently proposed by Sutton and Barto (1987), Klopf (1988), and Kehoe (1985). In contrast to our simplified trial-level networks, the approach in these models has been to propose learning capacities for individual nodes which *exceed* that of the Rescorla–Wager model, a trial-level conditioning model. Like the original formulations of the priming and SOP models, additional assumptions allow their models to capture a range of "real-time" conditioning phenomena.

II. Adaptive Network Representations of Behavioral Models

Contemporary theories of associative learning in animals have, to a large extent, been driven by several related issues: the problem of stimulus selection (see Rudy & Wagner, 1975) and the question of whether contiguous presentation of two stimuli is sufficient to promote associative learning (e.g., Rescorla, 1968). The problem of stimulus selection can be illustrated by the following question: If a significant event is proceeded by several stimuli, which stimuli will become strongly associated and which weakly associated with the target event? Earlier theories assumed that stimulus salience and number of pairings were the sole determiners of how much associative strength (control over behavior) a stimulus acquires. These assumptions were challenged by findings such as Kamin's blocking experiment (Kamin, 1969) and the work of Wagner (1969) and Rescorla (1968) on stimulus validity as a determinant of associative learning.

Early models designed to account for this body of findings appealed to variations in attentional processes controlling CS processing (e.g., Mackintosh, 1975) or were nonattentional and appealed to CS-produced variations in US processing (e.g., Rescorla & Wagner, 1972; Wagner & Rescorla, 1972). The scope of these models was limited to phenomena of stimulus selection and, in the case of the Rescorla–Wagner model, conditioned inhibition. Since then, models of conditioning have sought to address a broader range of learning phenomena. In addition to addressing the growing literature on stimulus selection and conditioned inhibition, these more recent models address associative phenomena such as interstimulus interval effects, latent inhibition, second-order conditioning, and nonassociative phenomena such as habituation. These models retain the character of the earlier models in being either attentional (e.g., Pearce & Hall, 1980) or nonattentional in nature (e.g., Donegan & Wagner, 1987; Mazur & Wagner, 1982; Sutton & Barto, 1981; Wagner, 1976, 1981).

In this paper, we will focus on three nonattentional models that share a common assumption that allows them to address a variety of phenomena of classical conditioning and habituation: Expected USs are less effective in promoting US processing necessary for conditioning and response generation than are unexpected USs. As noted previously, the models to be considered are the Rescorla–Wagner model (Rescorla & Wagner, 1972; Wagner & Rescorla, 1972), Wagner's priming model

(Wagner, 1976; 1978), and the SOP model (Donegan, 1980; Donegan & Wagner, 1987; Mazur & Wagner, 1982; Wagner, 1981).[1]In the remainder of this section we briefly characterize each of the models and show how their assumptions concerning US processing and associative learning can be represented by simple adaptive networks with precise rules for changes in associative weights.

A. RESCORLA–WAGNER MODEL

The Rescorla–Wagner model was designed to account for a variety of phenomena of associative learning observed in classical conditioning, especially phenomena of stimulus selection and conditioned inhibition. The model computes the effects of a training trial—pairings of conditioned stimuli (CSs) with an unconditioned stimulus (US)—on the strengths of CS associations. As we previously noted, the Rescorla–Wagner model can be viewed as a rule that specifies how the variables of CS and US intensity, and most importantly, the animal's expectancy for the US on a trial, combine to determine the changes in associative strengths produced by the trial. Of particular interest is its similarity to learning algorithms influential in adaptive network theories of cognition and artificial intelligence. We will first describe the Rescorla–Wagner model and show how it is formally equivalent to the least mean squares (LMS) algorithm of Widrow and Hoff (1960). We then show how the assumptions of the Rescorla–Wagner model can be represented within our adaptive network formalism using two instantiations of the Hebbian rule of Eq. (2).

The Rescorla–Wagner model proposes that phenomena of stimulus selection can be explained by assuming that the effectiveness of a US for producing associative learning depends on the relationship between the US and the expected outcome (Rescorla, 1968; Wagner, 1969; Kamin, 1969). In a critical experiment which well illustrates this principle, Kamin (1969) began by training animals with a light, the CS, which was paired with a shock US (see Table I).[2]In the second phase of training, a compound stimulus consisting of a light and a tone was paired with the shock. Surprisingly, subjects learned very little about the tone→shock relationship, compared to control subjects who had received identical numbers of tone + light→shock trials, but no pretraining to the light. Kamin de-

---

[1]The real-time models of Sutton and Barto (1981, 1987), Klopf (1988), and Kehoe (1985) may be considered, at the trial level, to be equivalent to the Rescorla–Wagner model and hence are not considered separately here.

[2]In the full experiment, the light and tone CSs were counterbalanced. In subsequent work, giving Group II element training with a third CS in order to control for the amount of US exposure prior to compound training has produced comparable results.

TABLE I

PARADIGM OF BLOCKING EXPERIMENTS[a]

Group	Phase		
	Element training	Compound training	Test
I	Light → US	Light + tone → US	Tone
II	—	Light + tone → US	Tone

[a] Adapted from Kamin (1969).

scribed this as a "blocking" effect because prior training of the light→ shock association blocked learning of the tone→shock association during the second stage of training.

To account for blocking and related phenomena, the Rescorla–Wagner model assumes that changes in the strength of an association between a particular CS and its outcome is proportional to the degree to which the outcome is unexpected (unpredicted) given all the stimulus elements present on that trial. To describe this assumption formally, Rescorla and Wagner used V_i to denote the strength of association between stimulus element CS_i and the US. If CS_i is followed by an unconditioned stimulus, then the change in association strength between CS_i and the US, ΔV_i, can be described by

$$\Delta V_i = \alpha_i \beta_1 (\lambda_1 - \sum_{s \in S} V_s),$$ (3)

where α_i is a learning rate parameter indexing the salience of CS_i, β_1 is a learning rate parameter that reflects the salience of the US, λ_1 is equated with the maximum possible level of association strength supported by the US intensity, and $\sum V_s$ is the sum of the associative strengths between all the stimulus elements present on that trial, including CS_i, and the US. If CS_i is presented and not reinforced, then the association between CS_i and the US decreases analogously by:

$$\Delta V_i = \alpha_i \beta_2 (\lambda_2 - \sum_{s \in S} V_s),$$ (4)

where λ_2 is generally taken to be 0, β_2 is a parameter which reflects the rate of learning on trials without US presentations, and the other parameters are as in Eq. (3).

The model accounts for the blocking effect as follows: In phase 1, CS_1

is paired with the US, and V_1 approaches the maximum associative value
(e.g., $\lambda_1 = 1$). In phase 2, CS_1 is presented in compound with a neutral
CS_2 (i.e., V_2 begins at zero), and the compound is followed by the US. In
a comparison group, CS_1 and CS_2 enter the compound phase with no prior
training (i.e., $V_1 = V_2 = 0$). By Eq. (3), increments in associative strength
accruing to the novel stimulus, CS_2, should be less in the blocking than
in the comparison condition. By a similar logic, the model also accounts
for such phenomena as contingency learning (Rescorla, 1968), multitrial
overshadowing (Wagner, 1969), and conditioned inhibition (Wagner &
Rescorla, 1972). Despite some limitations of the model in dealing with
phenomena such as latent inhibition and the extinction of conditioned inhibitors (see Zimmer-Hart & Rescorla, 1974), the Rescorla–Wagner
model continues to be an influential model of the associative changes occurring during classical conditioning.

In the following, we develop a network model capable of deriving the
range of conditioning phenomena addressed by the Rescorla–Wagner
model. One restriction that we impose on the network is that the changes
in weights be governed by the Hebbian learning rule of Eq. (2). The challenge is to develop network configurations such that the Rescorla–Wagner algorithm is, in a sense, embodied in the connectivity of the *network*.
We have found that reformulating the Rescorla–Wagner algorithm by algebraically rearranging the terms of Eqs. (3) and (4) provides insights into
how such a network can be developed.

Following Sutton and Barto (1981), we begin by noting that in Eqs. (3)
and (4) of the Rescorla–Wagner model, the summation is taken over only
those CSs which are present on a trial. With the introduction of a new
variable, a_i, which equals 1 if CS_i is present on a trial and 0 if CS_i is
absent, and assuming that $\beta = \beta_1 = \beta_2$, we can represent Eqs. (3) and
(4) as:

$$\Delta w_i = \beta a_i(\lambda - \Sigma w_j a_j), \qquad (5)$$

where the summation is now over all possible CSs; w_i, the weight from
CS-node i to the US, is equivalent to V_i in the Rescorla–Wagner formulation; and $\Sigma w_j a_j$ represents the summed strengths of all CSs present on
the trial, that is, it corresponds to $\Sigma_{s \in S} V_s$ of the Rescorla–Wagner model.[3]
(See Fig. 1 for a summary of all learning algorithms presented in this arti-

---

[3]For expository purposes, we have simplified the notation of the Rescorla–Wagner model
by equating β_1 and β_2 and not including α_i (we consider $\alpha_i = 1$ for all CS_i). The conditioning
phenomena that we address do not require differences in β values or α values. However, for
some phenomena, such as conditioning with partial reinforcement or pseudo-discrimination
training, it is necessary to assume that $\beta_1 > \beta_2$ (see, e.g., Wagner, Logan, Haberlandt, &

Model		Associative Changes	Equation
Rescorla–Wagner:	Reinforced	$\Delta V_i = \alpha_i \beta_1 (\lambda - \sum_{s \in S} V_s)$	(3)
	Nonreinforced	$\Delta V_i = \alpha_i \beta_2 (\lambda - \sum_{s \in S} V_s)$	(4)
LMS:		$\Delta w_i = \beta a_i (\lambda - \sum w_j a_j)$	(5)
LMS (reformulated)		$= \beta a_i \lambda - \beta a_i \sum w_j a_j$	(6)
Non-linear LMS		$\Delta w_i = \beta a_i \lambda - \beta a_i \lfloor \sum w_j a_j \rfloor$	(7)
Priming:	Reinforced	$\Delta w_i = \beta_1 a_i \lfloor (\lambda - \sum w_j a_j) \rfloor$	(8)
	Nonreinforced	$\Delta w_i = - \beta_2 w_i a_i$	(9)
Hawkins–Kandel:	Reinforced	$\Delta w_i = \beta_1 a_i \lfloor (\lambda - \sum w_j a_j) \rfloor - \beta_2 w_i a_i$	(11)
	Nonreinforced	$\Delta w_i = - \beta_2 w_i a_i$	(9)
SOP (reformulated)		$\Delta w_i = \beta_1 a_i \lfloor (\lambda - \sum w_j a_j) \rfloor - \beta_2 a_i \sum w_j a_j$	(10)
KEY:	$\Delta w_i, \Delta V_i$	Change in associative strength of CS_i	
	$\sum_{s \in S} V_s = \sum w_j a_j$	Summed strength for all CSs present.	
	λ	Variable which indicates presence or absence of US	
	a_i	Variable which indicates presence or absence of CS	
	β, β_1, β_2	Conditioning or learning rate parameters (US dependent)	
	α_i	Conditioning or learning rate parameter (CS dependent)	
	$\lfloor x \rfloor$	$\begin{cases} x & \text{if } x \geq 0 \\ 0 & \text{if } x < 0 \end{cases}$	

Fig. 1.   Learning algorithms for the Rescorla–Wagner, LMS, priming, Hawkins–Kandel, and SOP models.

Price, 1968). It should also be noted that α_i in Eqs. (3) and (4) of the Rescorla–Wagner model is not equivalent to a_i and a_j in Eq. (5) of the LMS rule. Both determine the rate of learning for a particular CS_i, but the a_j parameter in Eq. (5) also modulates the contribution of a presented cue CS_j to the expectation of the US, $\sum w_j a_j$. In contrast, α_i from the Rescorla–Wagner equations does not affect the contribution of CS_s to the expectation of a US, $\sum_{s \in S} V_s$.

cle.) The model now describes the associative changes prescribed for all CSs (present or absent). When the US is present $\lambda > 0$, otherwise $\lambda = 0$. Note that for CSs which are not present (i.e., when $a_i = 0$) no changes in associative strength are predicted.

As noted by Sutton and Barto (1981) this is the well-known least mean squares (LMS) algorithm of adaptive network theory (Widrow & Hoff, 1960), also sometimes referred to as the "delta rule" (Rumelhart, Hinton, & Williams, 1986). These rules are called error-correcting rules because associative changes are driven by a discrepancy (error) between what the system expects and what actually occurs. For a given task, these rules can be shown to find, asymptotically, the optimal set of association weights which minimize the magnitude of the expected (squared) error. Adaptive network models generally presume that individual elements or nodes in the network have the computational power of altering the association weights according to the LMS rule of Eq. (5). Within such a network, each adaptive element would have two types of inputs: multiple inputs corresponding to possible CSs and a single special "teaching" input corresponding to the US (see, e.g., Sutton & Barto, 1981). The weights associated with the different CSs would change over trials according to the LMS rule so that the weighted sum of the incoming activation from the CS inputs, $\Sigma w_j a_j$, will come to predict, as closely as possible, the US input, λ. Because we have restricted ourselves to networks that adapt according to Eq. (2) of the Hebbian rules, we now consider how such a network might have the emergent property of having its responses to *CS*s conform to the predictions of the Rescorla–Wagner/LMS rule. In such a network the node-to-node associations are altered according to the Hebbian rule of Eq. (2), but the input–output relations conform to the Rescorla–Wagner model.

B.   COMPARING THE RESCORLA–WAGNER/LMS AND HEBBIAN RULES

As noted earlier, there are at least two interpretations of the Hebbian rule of Eq. (2). One simply acknowledges that associative weights are incremented when one input signal co-occurs with another input signal. The other, more in the spirit of Hebb's original suggestion, proposes that associative (synaptic) weights are incremented when an input signal (presynaptic activity) is correlated with the output activity of the adaptive node (postsynaptic activity). For our purposes, we use the first, less restrictive, version. The most critical aspect of the rule is that associative changes are only influenced by the pairwise relationship between two signals: For example, weight changes are independent of the stimulus context in which these signals occur. In contrast, the Rescorla–Wagner model predicts that associations that develop between a cue (CS) and an outcome (US) depend on all the CSs that are present on the conditioning trial. As previously noted, this context sensitivity is a key aspect of the Rescorla–Wagner model, enabling it to account for a wide variety of stimulus selection phenomena (e.g., blocking) in which co-occuring cues compete with each other for associative strength.

Equation (5) of the Rescorla–Wagner/LMS rule (henceforth, R-W/LMS) has a number of well-known computational advantages as a learning rule over the simpler Eq. (2) of the Hebbian rule. When embedded within a network of associations, the R-W/LMS rule allows a system to learn complex discriminations which the Hebbian rule is unable to learn (for a more complete review of the differences between these algorithms, see Sutton & Barto, 1981). While the Hebbian rule has been used by adaptive network theorists to model associative memories (e.g., Amari, 1977; Anderson, Silverstein, Ritz, & Jones, 1977), most current connectionist models in cognitive psychology and artificial intelligence use the more powerful R-W/LMS rule for modeling associative changes. A further attraction of the R-W/LMS rule is that it has recently been generalized to train multilayer adaptive networks for solving complex learning tasks (LeCun, 1985; Parker, 1985, 1986; Rumelhart *et al.*, 1986). We turn now to seeing how the R-W/LMS rule might be realized within the adaptive network formalism, using Hebbian learning rules.

Turning back to Eq. (5) of the R-W/LMS rule, we note that it can be reexpressed as the sum of two, simpler, Hebbian rules. To illustrate, we begin by multiplying Eq. (5) through with β and a_i, to get:

$$\Delta w_i = \beta a_i \lambda - \beta a_i \Sigma w_j a_j \qquad (6)$$

We can consider the first term of Eq. (5) $\beta a_i \lambda$, to be a form of Hebbian learning in which the reinforcing activity, k in Eq. (2), is equated with the training signal, λ (which indicates the presence or absence of the US). Following a CS by a US allows for increments in associative strength proportional to λ. The second term indicates that presentation of CSs results in decrements in associative strength proportional to the summed associative strength of all the CSs presented, $\Sigma w_j a_j$. Note that this second, decremental, portion of Eq. (6), $- \beta a_i \Sigma w_j a_j$, can also be viewed as a form of Hebbian learning with the direction of learning reversed (i.e., with a negative β). In this "reverse-Hebbian" learning, the reinforcement signal, k, in Eq. (2) is equated with the expectation of the US generated by the CSs present on a particular trial, that is, $\Sigma w_j a_j$. Thus, on a reinforced trial, both incremental and decremental processes will interact to determine the net change in associative strength. This means that the more the US is expected, given all the CSs present on a trial, the less each CS's associative strength will increase on a paired trial, and the more it will decrease on a nonreinforced (ie., unpaired) CS-alone trial, where $\lambda = 0$.[4]

It should be noted that the rearrangement of terms in Eq. (6) suggests different assumptions about the stimulus-processing steps generated by a trial than does the formally equivalent, original version of the Rescorla–Wagner model in Eqs. (3) and (4). The formalism of the Rescorla–Wagner model was designed to capture a core assumption about US processing: that a US's ability to generate increments in associative strength can be modulated by CSs with which it has previously been paired. In the case of blocking, preceding a US by the pretrained CS blocks conditioning to the target CS by diminishing processing of the US on compound trials. This reduces the opportunity for the added target CS to gain associative strength. More generally, the Rescorla–Wagner model suggests that a conditioning trial produces one effect; an increment, decrement, or no change in a CS's associative strength. The effect is incremental when $V < \lambda$ and decremental when $V > \lambda$. In contrast, Eq. (6) has both incremental and decremental processes being generated on all reinforced conditioning trials. The incremental effects of US presentation are constant across trials ($\beta a_i \lambda$), but the decremental effects of signaling the US vary in proportion to the associative strengths of all CSs present on the trial (i.e., $-\beta a_i \Sigma w_j a_j$). Asymptotic levels of responding occur when the increment and decrement in associative strength produced by a trial are equal and thus cancel out. What is of particular interest to us is that Eq. (6) suggests how the behavioral predictions of the Rescorla–Wagner model can be formulated as a pair of opponent excitatory and inhibitory processes. This assumption, that the effect of a conditioning trial can be understood as a combination of opponent associative processes, is also a core feature of the SOP model (see, e.g., Mazur & Wagner, 1982).

The splitting of the R-W/LMS equation into the sum of two elementary components suggests a network representation that uses Hebbian rules to implement the R-W/LMS algorithm (see Figure 2A). In accordance with the terms of Eq. (6), US occurence, represented by λ, increments the associative strength of preceding CSs through presynaptic facilitation caused by coactivation of the CS pathway and the US projection onto the

---

[4]As noted by Andrew Barto (personal communication, July 1986), the effect of breaking the Rescorla–Wagner model into two opponent processes is similar to what happens in Hopfield networks (Hopfield, 1982) when the network is first trained with a Hebbian learning rule on the desired outputs and then is allowed to run freely with the learning rule reversed. A similar two-stage training procedure is also used in Boltzmann machines (Ackley, Hinton, & Sejnowski, 1985).

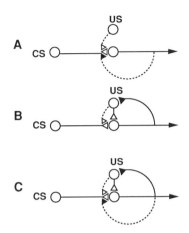

Fig. 2. Schematic of adaptive network representations of three behavioral models of conditioning: A, The Rescorla–Wagner Model: In accordance with the terms of Eq. (6), US occurence, represented by λ, increments the associative strength of preceding CSs through presynaptic facilitation caused by coactivation of the CS pathway and the US projection onto the CS pathway (dashed line, open triangle). The expectancy of the US generated by a CS, $\Sigma w_j a_j$, is coded by the output activation of the adaptive node. CS-evoked activity in the adaptive node causes a CR to be generated and the strength of the CS pathway to be decreased (dashed line, filled triangle). B, Priming: Conditioning of CS pathway occurs from concurrent activation of CS and US pathways, as in the reformulation of the Rescorla–Wagner model in A. Associatively produced decrements of US processing result from adaptive node activity which, through a negative feedback loop, inhibits activity in the US node. This network also includes a direct excitatory connection from the US to the adaptive node. C, SOP: This network combines the features and rules of the networks in A and B and represents basic assumptions of the SOP model, when characterized at the trial-level. Changes in a CS's associative strength are influenced by: (1) incremental processes as in A, (2) processes for decreasing the strength of CS associations through feedback from the adaptive node, and (3) attenuation in US processing, as in our network version of the priming model in B.

CS pathway. The subject's expectancy of the US generated by a CS, $\Sigma w_j a_j$, is coded by the output activation of the adaptive node. Activity in the adaptive node causes a CR to be generated and the strength of the CS pathway to be decreased. Activation of the feedback loop from the adaptive node decreases the strength of the CS association.[5] These decremen-

---

[5]In Fig. 2 we have chosen to illustrate convergence of the nodal inputs responsible for increasing and decreasing associative "synaptic" strengths in terms of presynaptic contacts (suggesting a mechanism of presynaptic facilitation) for ease of exposition only. The important point is that the synapse's strength can be increased by appropriately timed converging inputs from the CS node and the US node or decreased by input from the CS node and the recurrent feedback from the adaptive node. We assume that equivalent abstract network

tal effects generated by the CS are responsibile for extinction, conditioned inhibition, and blocking. In the previously mentioned example of blocking (see Table I), conditioning to the tone is blocked by the previously trained light CS because, in addition to the US's incrementing the associative strength of the tone (via $\beta a_i \lambda$), strong activation of the adaptive node by the light results in offsetting decrements in the tone's strength (via $- \beta a_i \Sigma w_j a_j$). That is, during compound training, the magnitude of the decremental process engaged on each compound trial ($- \beta a_i \Sigma w_j a_j$) will be larger for subjects pretrained on the light than for subjects for which the light is neutral at the outset of compound training.

As described above, this network model will possess the essential properties of the Rescorla–Wagner model, providing that the nodal activation values are allowed to exhibit both the positive and negative values [as in the corresponding parenthetical error term, $(\lambda - \Sigma w_j a_j)$, of Eq. (5) of the Rescorla–Wagner/LMS rule]. We now consider a slight modification of this network model in which the firing of the adaptive node is constrained to be nonnegative, as would be the case if the activation in the node were more closely equated with the firing behavior of a neuron. In this case the activation (output) of the adaptive node, g, would be a nonlinear function of the weighted sum of the inputs according to

$$g = \left\lfloor \sum w_j a_j \right\rfloor = \begin{cases} \sum w_j a_j & \text{if } \sum w_j a_j \geq 0 \\ 0 & \text{otherwise} \end{cases}$$

Learning in this nonlinear variation on the Rescorla–Wagner model would be described by

$$\Delta w_i = \beta a_i \lambda - \beta a_i \left\lfloor \sum w_j a_j \right\rfloor, \tag{7}$$

---

representations could be developed in which the increments in synaptic strength required activation of the pre- and postsynaptic elements within some window of time.

A second point is that the network representations presented in this paper focus on ways of developing representations that capture the essential character of the several learning algorithms we are considering. As a consequence, we have not made an effort to include all of the network properties necessary for response generation, in particular, the UR (e.g., Fig. 2A). One could represent the immediate UR generated by the US in terms of a second pathway exiting the US node and going to some output nodes responsible for response production. Since the Rescorla–Wagner model only specifies the effects of the US on associative weights, we have only represented the US's teaching input.

where the variables are as in Eq. (6). The input–output behavior of this nonlinear network will be equivalent to the Rescorla–Wagner model with one exception: In the Rescorla–Wagner model the net expectation can be negative if a cue which has previously been trained as a conditioned inhibitor is presented alone. In the Rescorla–Wagner model this results in the sum of the weights ($\Sigma w_j a_j$) being negative. However, in the nonlinear Rescorla–Wagner network model a conditioned inhibitor can offset the effects of a strong positive (excitatory) cue but cannot drive the adaptive node below the zero baseline if presented alone. This creates an interesting contrast between the original Rescorla–Wagner model and this network interpretation.

The Rescorla–Wagner model predicts that repeatedly presenting a conditioned inhibitor alone will result in a loss, or extinction, of its inhibitory properties. That is, just as a nonreinforced presentation of an excitatory CS results in a loss of its excitatory properties, there is a symmetrical loss of inhibition for conditioned inhibitors. According to Eq. (5)

$$\Delta w_i = \beta a_i (\lambda - \Sigma w_j a_j),$$

an inhibitory CS will become more neutral when presented alone because the change in strength, Δw_i, will be in the positive direction. That is, since w_i is negative, and $\lambda = 0$, the right side of Eq. (5) will have a positive value. In the nonlinear network model, however, conditioned inhibitors do not extinguish. Presentation of a conditioned inhibitor in the absence of US will not change the associative strength of that CS because there are neither US-mediated increments nor CS-evoked decrements (via the adaptive node). Thus, while this model was motivated by an attempt to develop an adaptive network capable of deriving the phenomena addressed by the Rescorla–Wagner model, the constraints of making adaptive networks more "neural-like" suggests a reformulation of the model which avoids a well-known flaw in the Rescorla–Wagner model's predictions.[6]

Another perspective on the relationship between the Rescorla–Wagner model, the Hebb rule, and alternative ways of developing networks whose behavior mimics that of the Rescorla–Wagner model can be seen by letting k, the error signal in Eq. (2) of the Hebb rule ($\Delta w_i = \beta a_i k$), be equated with the parenthetical error term ($\lambda - \Sigma w_j a_j$) from Eq. (5) of the R-W/LMS rule,

$$\Delta w_i = \beta a_i (\lambda - \Sigma w_j a_j)$$

[6]Sutton and Barto (1987) propose a similar modification to their real-time extension of the Rescorla–Wagner model.

Figure 3A shows an adaptive network representation of this idea. There are two inputs to the adaptive element, a CS input, which has an activation of a_i (1 or 0), and an error signal whose activity is $(\lambda - \Sigma w_j a_j)$, which can be either positive, negative, or zero. The error signal is shown making a "presynaptic" connection on the CS terminal to indicate that the CS activity is being correlated with the error signal and not with the activity in the adaptive node, which will equal $\Sigma w_j a_j$.

If the training input in Fig. 3A corresponds to the error term of the Rescorla–Wagner model, $(\lambda - \Sigma w_j a_j)$, then the changes in associative strength prescribed by the Rescorla–Wagner model could be accom-

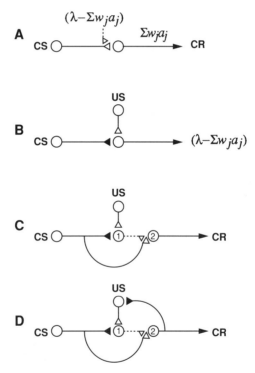

Fig. 3. A, An adaptive network with two inputs. B, A single Hebbian adaptive element for computing the LMS error signal. The changes in the CS association strength are proportional to the activity in the adaptive element. CS input is presumed to have an inhibitory impact on the element's activity. C, A model in which the output from network B serves as the error signal to network A. The input to this model is CS and US activity and the output (CR) is $\Sigma w_j a_j$ as predicted by Eq. (5) of the R-W/LMS rule. D, A combination of network C with the priming–negative feedback model from Fig. 2C.

plished using a single Hebbian rule in which the change in CS association, Δw_i, is proportional to the strength of the error signal. It should be remembered that the associative link between the CS and the adaptive node can take on a range of positive and negative values. The change in weighting will be positive when $(\lambda - \Sigma w_j a_j)$ is positive and negative when this parenthetical term is negative (as in extinction or conditioned inhibition training). The output of such a network would equal $\Sigma w_j a_j$, the predicted CR from the Rescorla–Wagner model.

The model in Fig. 3A begs the question of how the error signal $(\lambda - \Sigma w_j a_j)$ is computed or where it comes from. We will outline here one possible mechanism for computing this error signal, which also requires only a single Hebbian rule. Figure 3B shows a Hebbian adaptive element which is capable of computing the LMS error signal. In this network, changes in CS associative strengths are governed by activation of the CS node and the net activation of the adaptive node. The US node has a positive (excitatory) effect on the adaptive node when the US is presented $(\lambda > 0)$, but no effect in the absence of the US, that is, when $\lambda = 0$. Each CS input has a negative (i.e., inhibitory) impact on the adaptive node's activity proportional to its associative strength, w_i; that is, a strong CS→US association is represented as a strong inhibitory association. (Note that Fig. 3B shows the input from only one CS; it is presumed, however, that the adaptive node receives input from many similarly connected CSs.) The resulting activity (output) from the adaptive node in Fig. 3B will equal $(\lambda - \Sigma w_j a_j)$, the error signal in Eq. (5). To illustrate this, consider what happens over the course of repeated CS–US pairings. At the outset of training, the excitatory US input to the adaptive node is high (e.g., $\lambda = 1$) and the inhibitory CS input is small. Consequently, the net activity in the adaptive node will be high. This will cause a large increase in the inhibitory strength of the CS association. On succeeding trials the strength of CS_i will grow until $w_i \cong 1$, at which point the strong inhibitory input from CS_i will cancel out the excitatory input from the US node to the adaptive node (i.e., when $\Sigma w_j a_j \cong 1$), leaving the adaptive node with little or no net activation. As a result, increments in CS_i's associative strength will be small or zero. If a novel CS is then presented in compound with the previously trained CS and reinforced, as in the blocking paradigm, little conditioning will occur to the novel CS. Under these circumstances, activity in the adaptive element will be close to zero, making the teaching input onto the CS–CR pathway in Fig 3A close to zero.

Comparing the networks in Figs. 3A and 3B, we note that in both, changes in CS associations are governed by CS activity, a_i, being correlated with either a special error signal (Fig. 3A) or the activity (output) of the adaptive node (Fig. 3B), both of which can be described by $(\lambda -$

$\Sigma w_j a_j$). Hence, in both networks, the changes to the CS associations can be characterized by $\Delta w_i = \beta a_i(\lambda - \Sigma w_j a_j)$, the R-W/LMS rule.

Figure 3C shows a network representation of the R-W/LMS rule resulting from combining the network models in Figs. 3A and 3B. The output from network B serves as the error signal input to network A. The input to the network in Fig. 3C comes from CS and US nodal activation. The output comes from the adaptive node and is described by $\Sigma w_j a_j$, the predicted CR from the R-W/LMS rule. An interesting feature of this model is its redundancy; the associative strength of a single CS is represented in two places, with one being excitatory and the other inhibitory. One modulates US processing that is, it generates the appropriate error signal, while the other uses this error signal to modify weights in the CS–CR pathway and thus the expression of CRs. Thus, Fig. 3C represents another adaptive network model whereby the associative changes prescribed by the Rescorla–Wagner model can be computed using simple Hebbian learning rules.

From foregoing discussions of Figs. 3A and 3B, the model implies that Node 1 will show a large increase in activation to an unexpected US, i.e., when $\lambda >> (\Sigma w_j a_j = 0)$. Thus, on the first conditioning trial, the US will strongly activate node 1 (which is equivalent to the adaptive node in Fig. 3B). This will have two effects: First, the strength of the inhibitory CS pathway onto node 1 will be increased; second, the weight of the CS pathway onto the output (node 2), will show a positive increment due to the the reinforcing activity in node 1, which represents a positive error signal, that is, an unpredicted US. The activity in node 2, the output unit, will generate a CR proportional to the summated associative activation. A nonreinforced presentation of a previously trained CS will cause node 1 to have a negative net activation level since $(\lambda = 0) < \Sigma w_j a_j$. The convergence of activity in the CS→node 2 pathway with the negative output of node 1 will have a subtractive effect on the weighting of the CS→node 2 pathway. If the CS→node 2 pathway has a positive, excitatory weighting, it will become less positive, as in extinction training. If the pathway has a neutral (zero) weight, then it will take on a negative value and thus becomes inhibitory, that is, a neutral CS nonreinforced in compound with a CS previously paired with the US will become a conditioned inhibitor.

An important point of the preceding exercise is that learning algorithms expressed as formal equations can be equivalently represented by networks that have very different patterns of connectivity. In trying to understand how real neuronal circuits may accomplish particular computations, being familiar with the variety of ways that learning algorithms can be instantiated in abstract networks is likely to be helpful. This familiarity should make it easier for a neuroscientist to recognize the computational capacities of the variety of neuronal architectures that are being considered as candidate mechanisms of learning in particular preparations and species.

C. PRIMING MODEL

The development of the priming model by Wagner and colleagues (e.g., Pfautz & Wagner, 1976; Wagner, 1976, 1979) was motivated by two primary considerations. As previously noted, the Rescorla–Wagner model was developed expressedly to address phenomena of stimulus selection and conditioned inhibition. As a result, there are many conditioning phenomena that fall outside its scope, such as latent inhibition, second-order conditioning, interstimulus interval (ISI) effects, and conditioned diminution of the UR. Thus, one goal of the priming model was to make contact with these additional conditioning phenomena as well as phenomena of habituation. A second consideration was that the Rescorla–Wagner model explains conditioning phenomena at the level of individual conditioning trials. That is, it provides a rule that specifies the associative product of a trial but does not make assumptions about the processing of trial events: the CS and US. A second goal of the priming model was to specify rules of an information-processing system that would describe the ways in which the temporal dynamics of CS and US processing give rise to a variety of phenomena of excitatory conditioning and habituation attributed to temporal variables such as interstimulus interval (ISI).

In the priming model, the memory system is characterized as a set of representational nodes, which correspond to the possible CSs and USs, that are connected by associative linkages. The learning rules of the model consist of nonquantitative rules for nodal activation and the conditions necessary for incrementing and decrementing strengths of associative links. As stated by Wagner and Terry (1975):

> The net associative tendency accruing to a CS during any interval of time embracing a CS and UCS will depend upon the amount of joint CS and UCS rehearsal and the amount of CS alone rehearsal that is afforded: Joint rehearsal should increase the tendency for the CS to be acted toward as a signal for the UCS while CS-alone rehearsal should decrease this tendency. (p. 370).

The model, in its original formulation, distinguishes three states of activation: inactivity and two active states. When a node is inactive, presentation of the corresponding stimulus results in a special state of activation (rehearsal) that is particularly effective in generating a response inherent to that stimulus (e.g., a UR) and incrementing the strengths of associative links with other concurrently active nodes. If a node is inactive and an associated stimulus is presented, the node will enter some lower state of activation which has two important consequences: generation of a response (e.g., CR) and making the node refractory to full activation (rehearsal) by a presentation of the stimulus it represents. Thus, the priming model deduces a variety of conditioning phenomena in terms of variation in the effectiveness of a stimulus, e.g., a US, to promote activation of its corresponding representational node.

Figure 2B illustrates an adaptive network interpretation of Priming similar to that of Pfautz and Wagner (1976). The US pathway is shown making a "presynaptic" connection on the CS pathway to indicate that conditioning of the CS pathway occurs from concurrent activation of CS and US pathways, as in the reformulation of the Rescorla–Wagner model in Fig. 2A. Associatively produced decrements of US processing result from the CS activating the adaptive node which, through a negative feedback loop, inhibits activity in the US node.

Figure 2B also includes a direct excitatory connection from the US to the adaptive node. Thus, in contrast to the network representation of the Rescorla–Wagner model, the priming model makes predictions about the UR as well as the CR. For example, the priming model captures the fact that preceding a target US by a trained CS, or the same US, can diminish the UR to a subsequently presented US (Donegan, 1981; Pfautz, 1980). For this reason we have included this UR pathway in our network interpretation of the priming model. However, in developing an algorithmic interpretation of this network, we limit ourselves to describing the trial-level implications of the model for acquisition and CR generation. Thus, our formal characterization of the priming model does not address phenomena such as proactive effects of US presentations on conditioning (Terry, 1976).

Although the rules of the priming model for incrementing and decrementing associative strengths have never been formally stated, we can represent the principal assumptions in the formal notation of adaptive networks. As in Eq. (5) of the Rescorla–Wagner/LMS rule, we let w_i be the associative strength between CS_i and the US. On a trial in which CS_i occurs with the US, the change in w_i will be determined by

$$\Delta w_i = \beta_1 a_i \left\lfloor (\lambda - \Sigma w_j a_j) \right\rfloor, \tag{8}$$

where $\Sigma w_j a_j$ is the summed association strength for all CSs present, λ is the maximum level of conditioning supported by the US, β_1 is a learning rate parameter for reinforcement, and

$$\lfloor x \rfloor = \begin{cases} x & \text{if } x \geq 0 \\ 0 & \text{if } x < 0 \end{cases}$$

On nonreinforced CS presentations (i.e., when $\lambda = 0$), the associative strength of the CS will be decreased according to

$$\Delta w_i = -\beta_2 w_i a_i \qquad (9)$$

where β_2 is a learning rate parameter for nonreinforcement. It should be emphasized that these equations do not capture the full range of ideas expressed in the priming model, such as those regarding the temporal properties of CS and US activation, but they do allow us to capture, at the trial level, a subset of the model's predictions.

As in the original formulation of the Rescorla–Wagner model, the priming model derives phenomena such as blocking through an associative modulation of US processing. In the case of blocking (see Table I), prior training with the light (CS) causes the light to activate the adaptive node strongly on compound trials. This produces inhibition in the US node, making it more refractory to US activation and thus less effective in incrementing the associative strength of the added CS (not shown in Fig. 2B) during compound training. In terms of Eq. (8) of the priming model, this occurs as w_i approaches λ. As noted above, the priming model does not address phenomena of conditioned inhibition, which are captured by the Rescorla–Wagner model. If CS_A is paired with the US (so that $w_A > 0$) and subsequently nonreinforced in compound with a novel CS_x, CS_x will not become an inhibitor, although w_A will extinguish. That is, decrements in a CS's associative weight are not influenced by other CSs present on nonreinforced trials. The decrement in the weight of CS_i is proportional only to the value of w_i, which is bounded below by zero (see Fig. 1).

In comparing the network representations of our reformulations of the Rescorla–Wagner and priming models we note that both have a common component, a Hebbian incremental process which is sensitive only to the pairwise co-occurence of CSs and the US. Both models explain the blocking effect and related phenomena by having this incremental process offset by the system's expectation of the US. The models differ, however, in how this expectation offsets the incremental process. In our network reformulation of the Rescorla–Wagner model, the offset is conceived as an additional decremental process which operates directly on the associative strength of the CSs. In the priming model, however, expectation serves to attenuate the US's ability to promote an incremental associative change.

The models also differ regarding the decrement of associative weights on nonreinforced trials, that is, extinction trials. In the Rescorla–Wagner model, decrements associated with nonreinforcement are context-sensitive (i.e., influenced by the associative weights of co-occuring CSs), while in the priming model, decrements in extinction are not context-sensitive and depend only on the current associative strength of the CS.

D. SOMETIMES OPPONENT PROCESS MODEL

The sometimes opponent process (SOP) model (Donegan, 1980; Donegan & Wagner, 1987; Mazur & Wagner, 1982; Wagner, 1981) can be seen as an extension of the priming model in two ways. First, it provides a more formal distinction between states of nodal activation, which allows for the development of a quantitative, determinant model of classical conditioning and habituation. Second, it provides rules for decrementing associative strengths that allow the model to address phenonmena of conditioned inhibition.

As in the priming model, SOP treats memory as a set of representational nodes connected by associative links. For both CS and US nodes, SOP distinguishes among three states of nodal activation and specifies the ways in which overlapping patterns of activation in CS and US nodes act upon the strengths of the associative links. To characterize briefly the features of the SOP model relevant to the issues in this chapter, we first consider the consequences for nodal activation of presenting a single stimulus. We then consider the learning rules of the model by specifying the ways in which a CS–US pairing modifies associative strengths.

Presentation of a CS or US causes its corresponding nodal representation in memory to enter a primary state of activation (designated A1) from which it decays into a secondary state of activation (designated A2) before returning to a state of inactivity. On a CS–US trial, concurrent activation of the CS and US nodes to the A1 state causes their associative link to be strengthened proportional to the temporal overlap of A1 activation in the two nodes. As the CS gains associative strength, presenting the CS will cause the associated US node to enter into the A2 state of activation, with the level of activation being proportional to the strength of the CS–US association. Associative activation of the US node has three consequences. First, a CR characteristic of the late, A2, phase of US activation is generated to the CS (see Wagner & Brandon, in press). Second, the US node becomes more refractory to A1 activation by a subsequently presented US. Third, inhibitory associations are strengthened when A1 activation in the CS node overlaps with A2 activity in the US node. (For a more detailed description of SOP, see Wagner and Donegan, this volume.)

For purposes of the present discussion, the critical features of the SOP model are (1) an associatively produced diminution of US processing that diminishes the US's reinforcing and response-generating capabilities, and

(2) an associatively induced decrement in the excitatory strength of the CS–US associations due to the inhibition resulting from an overlapping of A1 activity in the CS node with A2 activity in the US node. In this way, SOP can be viewed as a composite of elements from our reformulation of the Rescorla–Wagner model and the Priming model. Figure 2C illustrates a network which combines the features and rules of the networks in Fig. 2A,B and represents the basic assumptions of the SOP model, when characterized at the trial level. Thus, in this simplified interpretation of SOP, changes in a CS's associative strength are influenced by (1) an associatively generated attenuation in US processing, as in our network version of the priming model in Fig. 2B and (2) an associative process for reducing the strength of CS associations as in our network version of the Rescorla–Wagner model in Fig. 2A. (In a similar fashion, Fig. 3D suggests how the network representation of the Rescorla–Wagner model in Fig. 3C might be combined with the network representation of the Priming model in Fig. 2B.)

By combining the abstract network representations inspired by the Rescorla–Wagner and priming models, the properties of SOP expressed in Fig. 2C that are important for conditioning can also be represented in the formal notation of adaptive networks as

$$\Delta w_i = \beta_1 a_i \left[(\lambda - \sum w_j a_j) \right] - \beta_2 a_i \sum w_j a_j \qquad (10)$$

It should be emphasized that SOP is a "real-time" model (Donegan & Wagner, 1987; Mazur & Wagner, 1982) and that the trial-level description in Eq. (10) does not represent all of the assumptions of the SOP model. Rather, it is meant to summarize features of the network in Fig. 2C.[7]

The purpose of this reformulation is to highlight the trial-level implica-

---

[7]As in the formalization of Fig. 2B by Eq. (8) of the Priming model, the formalization of Fig. 2C by Eq. (10) omits the influence of the direct US connection to the adaptive node illustrated in Fig. 2C. In the original formulation of SOP the presentation of a US on a paired trial produces both an early incremental process followed by a later decremental process caused by the early, A1, and late A2, states of activation, respectively. Differentiating these two effects is important, however, only if the temporal aspects of CS and US presentation are specified. For example, SOP correctly predicts that backward conditioning should in some circumstances produce excitatory conditioning, and in others inhibitory conditioning (Larew, 1986). With forward CS–US pairings at optimal ISIs, the effect of the later, decremental process is small relative to the incremental process. Thus, for describing the trial-level implications of SOP for CR generation, we can combine the incremental and decremental effects into one incremental process as suggested by the first term in Eq. (10).

tions of SOP suggested by our network representation so as to facilitate comparisons with the other models presented in this chapter. As in the priming model, increased expectation of the US (as represented by the output activation of the adaptive node, $\Sigma w_j a_j$) reduces the incremental (reinforcing) effect of US presentation according to $[(\lambda - \Sigma w_j a_j)]$. As in our network reformulation of the Rescorla–Wagner model, the expectation for the US decreases associative strengths according to $- \beta a_j \Sigma w_j a_j$.

From this combination of rules for increasing excitatory and inhibitory associations, we see that in SOP blocking is a multiply determined phenomenon. Prior training on the light results in the US node in Fig. 2C being inhibited by feedback from the adaptive node, which reduces the US's ability to promote excitatory associations with the CS. In addition, the firing of the adaptive node by the trained CS (i.e., the expectation of the US) reduces the associative strength between the CS and the US. Thus, the decreased opportunity for the *formation* of excitatory associations between the CS and the US, and the decreased associative strength between the CS and US generated by the pretrained CS, combine to produce a blocking effect.

E. SUMMARY

Having adopted a common adaptive network notation, we have reformulated, and in many places simplified, three influential models of classical conditioning. The simplification was necessary in order to focus on just those aspects of each model which are critical for describing behavior at the level of trial-by-trial changes in associative strengths. This exercise has highlighted several nonobvious similarities and differences among the models: First, each model can be conceived of as having a common Hebbian incremental process which is initiated by activity in the US pathway converging with activity in the CS pathway. Each of the three models also incorporates one or both of two possible decremental processes initiated by activity in the adaptive node. As noted earlier, our reformulation of the Rescorla–Wagner model presumes a decremental process that operates directly on the associative strength of the CS and is context-sensitive. That is, it is influenced by all CSs occuring on the trial. This is illustrated by the recurrent feedback loop from the adaptive node in Fig. 2A. In the priming model, one decremental process, which is context-sensitive, attenuates US processing and thereby retards conditioning (illustrated by the recurrent feedback loop from the adaptive node onto the US node in Fig. 2B). A second decremental process, which occurs only on trials in which the US is not present, underlies extinction and is not context-sensitive but rater context-free. Our trial-level adaptive network representation of the SOP model in Fig. 2C illustrates how the SOP model includes the common Hebbian incremental process in addition to both of the context-sensitive decremental processes from the other models: the *associative decrement* process from the Rescorla–Wagner model and the *increment attentuation* process from the priming model. In this way we can see how the central learning mechanism of SOP, when characterized at the level of a trial, can be viewed as a combination of the context-sensitive learning rules of the priming and Rescorla–Wagner models. As noted, the full representation of the SOP model, however, is able to address additional phenomena such as interstimulus interval effects, second-order conditioning, stimulus priming effects, and habituation, all of which are outside the scope of either the Rescorla–Wagner model or our simplified representation of the trial-level implications of SOP.

We turn now to two neural circuits which have been identified as critical to the learning and expression of classically conditioned behaviors. In the remaining sections, we compare these neural circuits to the three network models described above and use our analyses of these models and their ability to generate various conditioning phenomena as a tool for evaluating the potential of the neural circuits for exhibiting the the full range of Pavlovian phenomena addressed by the behavioral models.

III. Invertebrate Circuits: *Aplysia*

A. CLASSICAL CONDITIONING IN *Aplysia*

Hawkins and Kandel (1984) postulated the existence of a "cell-biological alphabet" for learning, in which the basic units may be combined to form progressively more complex learning processes. In particular, they hypothesized that several higher-order features of classical conditioning may be derivable from our understanding of the cellular mechanisms for associative learning in *Aplysia*. Gluck and Thompson (1987) developed a computational model of the *Aplysia* circuitry and used it to test Hawkins and Kandel's specific hypotheses regarding possible mechanisms for differential conditioning, second-order conditioning, blocking, and contingency learning.

The basic reflex studied in *Aplysia* is withdrawal of the siphon, mantle shelf, and gill to tactile stimulation of the siphon or mantle shelf. This withdrawal reflex is partly monosynaptic and can be obtained in a reduced preparation of the abdominal ganglion with sensory and motor neurons. Thus, siphon sensory neurons synapse directly on gill and siphon motor neurons and repeated activation of the sensory neurons results in habituation of the motor neuron response (Carew, Pinsker, & Kandel, 1972). If stimulation of sensory neurons (CS) is followed by strong shock to the tail (US), the synaptic potential of the motor neurons to the CS is facilitated (see Fig 4A). Further, the action potential in the sensory neurons is broadened, indicating a presynaptic effect, which has been termed a pairing-specific enhancement of presynaptic facilitation (Hawkins, Abrams, Carew, & Kandel, 1983). If repeated paired trials are given, this enhancement increases above the level produced by US sensitization alone, yielding a basic phenomenon of classical conditioning, an associatively induced increase in response of motor neurons to the CS. This conditioning depends critically on the time between presentation of the CS and the US.

Hawkins and Kandel propose that the phenomena of conditioning in *Aplysia* result from the interplay of habituation and sensitization [in much the same way as Groves and Thompson (1970) suggested that the two processes interact] together with a third process, namely pairing-specific enhancement of the excitability of the CS terminals. The mechanism is thought to be an enhancement of the sensitization process at the CS terminal, which is temporally dependent on the occurrence of an action potential in the CS terminal shortly before US presentation.

Gluck and Thompson's computational model of the *Aplysia* circuit confirmed that several of the higher-order features of classical conditioning do, as Hawkins and Kandel (1984) suggest, follow as natural elaborations of cellular mechanisms for associative and nonassociative learning. In particular they provided quantitative support for the Hawkins and Kandel models of acquisition, extinction, differential conditioning and second-order conditioning. In doing this, Gluck and Thompson found that they did not need to concern themselves with the biophysical properties of neurons (e.g., ionic membrane properties), fine-grained temporal properties and mechanisms of neurotransmitter release, or the kinetics of transmitter–receptor interactions. Rather, the models suggested by Hawkins and Kandel (1984) for differential and second-order conditioning appear to be robust at a cellular level of description comparable to the adaptive network models of conditioning presented here. Quantitative simulations of the Hawkins and Kandel models for blocking and contingency learning suggest, however, that these qualitative models are not sufficiently well detailed to predict robustly these higher-order features of classical conditioning.

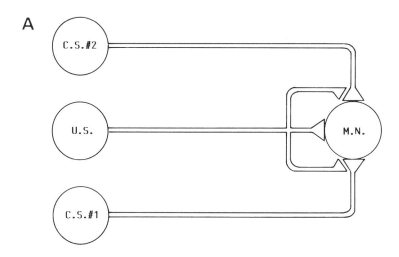

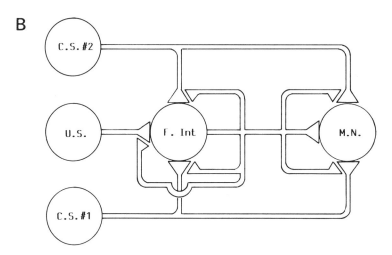

Fig. 4.   Schematic of the circuits proposed by Hawkins and Kandel to account for conditioning of the gill- and siphon-withdrawal responses in *Aplysia:* A, Basic circuit with sensory neurons and one motor neuron. B, Extended circuit model with putative interneuron between US sensory neuron and motor neuron.

B. The Hawkins and Kandel (1984) Model

Three basic mechanisms of plasticity interact in the Hawkins and Kandel (1984) model: *habituation,* which is presumed to occur at CS terminals whenever a CS is presented, *presynaptic facilitation,* which is caused by US presentation, and *pairing-specific enhancement* of presynaptic facilitation. Facilitation occurs for all CS terminals receiving input from facilitator interneurons activated by the US but is enhanced for terminals which have just previously been activated by CS presentation. Note that this associative increase in synaptic efficacy will be partially offset by the nonassociative habituation occuring during CS presentations. Hawkins and Kandel suggested that the asymptote of learning would occur when the increments and decrements just balance each other. While this basic model is sufficient to account for the most elementary learning phenomena of acquisition, retention, and extinction of learned responses, the Hawkins–Kandel *Aplysia* model, like the priming model, does not account for the full breadth of phenomena which motivated the Rescorla–Wagner model, such as, conditional inhibition.

Hawkins and Kandel (1984) also suggest an extended model of the *Aplysia* circuitry (see Fig. 4B) in which they postulated than an interneuron located between the US sensory neuron and the motorneuron might approximate the $(\lambda - \Sigma w_j a_j)$ component of Eq. (5) of the Rescorla–Wagner/LMS model as follows: Consider, again, the blocking paradigm in Table I in terms of Fig. 4B. The animal is first trained with $CS_1 \rightarrow US$ pairings. On the first presentation of a $CS_1 + CS_2$ compound trial, the CS_2 will have no effect but the CS_1 will activate the interneuron. This interneuron then becomes refractory to activation by the following US—caused perhaps by accomodation and/or recurrent inhibition. Hawkins and Kandel speculate that this could mediate the blocking effect if the firing of the interneuron by the CS_1, and its resulting inhibition, attenuated the increment in synaptic strength which accrues to the CS_2.

C. Gluck and Thompson's (1987) Computational Model

The Hawkins–Kandel neural model was inspired by an attempt to capture the salient features of the Rescorla–Wagner behavioral model (Hawkins & Kandel, 1984). We review here, however, some important differences between these two models, focusing primarily on their respective assumptions regarding the process for decrementing associative–synaptic weights.

As Hawkins and Kandel note (p. 386), their model's nonassociative decremental process for mediating extinction (i.e., habituation) is more closely in accord with the Groves–Thompson (1970) model of habituation than with the Rescorla–Wagner model. Adopting the formal assumptions of the Groves–Thompson behavioral model of habituation at the neuronal level, Gluck and Thompson (1987) modeled habituation in the Aplysia using the same context-free decremental process given by Eq. (9) of the priming model:

$$\Delta w_i = - \beta_2 w_i a_i$$

where the notation is as before.

Hawkins and Kandel, in contrast to the Rescorla–Wagner model, postulate a nonassociative mechanism for strength decrements which is *context-free;* it is unaffected by the context in which the CS occurs. Decrements in a CS's synaptic weight in the Hawkins–Kandel *Aplysia* model depend only on the current associative strength of a CS and whether or not it has been presented. Thus, the context-free decremental processes in the Hawkins–Kandel model and the priming model can both be characterized by Eq. (9) (see Wagner & Terry, 1975). In the priming model, however, this decremental process occurs only on nonreinforced trials, in contrast to Hawkins and Kandel's assumption that the process operates on both paired and extinction trials. Noting the functional similarity between Hawkins and Kandel's putative refractory interneuron and the negative feedback loop of the priming model, we can simplify the algorithms of Gluck and Thompson's (1987) computational interpretation of the Hawkins–Kandel model, recasting it at the trial level.[8] Combining the incremental process of the priming model from Eq. (8),

$$\Delta w_i = \beta_1 a_i \left[(\lambda - \sum w_j a_j) \right]$$

with the decremental habituation process characterized by Eq. (9),

$$\Delta w_i = - \beta_2 w_i a_i$$

we can model the effect of a trial in Hawkins and Kandel's extended *Aplysia* model (Fig. 4B) as

$$\Delta w_i = \beta_1 a_i \left[(\lambda - \sum w_j a_j) \right] - \beta_2 w_i a_i \tag{11}$$

[8] By having the CS activate, rather than inhibit, activity in the US pathway, the Hawkins and Kandel model is able to generate second-order conditioning whereas the network in Fig. 2A is not. In both cases, however, signaling the US (i.e., presentation of associated CSs) diminishes the ability of the US to promote increments in synaptic strengths.

where the variables are as before (see also Table I). Presentation of a CS alone (without reinforcement) will change the associative strength just according to Eq. (9) above. Thus, both the priming model and the Hawkins and Kandel model can be described using similar equations for decremental and incremental processing. The critical difference, however, is in when the decremental process in Eq. (9) occurs. It is important to emphasize that in Hawkins and Kandel's model decrements occur on both reinforced and nonreinforced trials, in contrast to the priming model, in which the decremental process occurs only on nonreinforced trials.

The Rescorla–Wagner model predicts that an asymptotic level of conditioning to a CS element will be reached when the sum of the CS elements equals the maximum level of conditioning supported by the US. As Hawkins and Kandel note (p. 386), their model differs in this regard in that the asymptotic level of conditioning is predicted to occur when there is an equilibrium between the associative process of pairing-specific enhancement of sensitization and the nonassociative process of habituation (Hawkins & Kandel, 1984, p. 386). While this is true for their simplified model (Fig. 4A), the ability of a conditioned CS element to prevent interneuron firing during US presentation in their second, extended, model (Fig. 4B) provides an additional source of modulation for the growth of CS synaptic strength. The asymptotic level of conditioning will occur when three interacting processes are in equilibrium: (1) habituation, (2) strengthening of the CS synapses via the facilitator interneuron (via sensitization and pairing specific enhancement), and (3) attenuation of facilitation of the CS synapses due to a reduction of facilitator interneuron activity by conditioning of the CS synapses.

What is the implication of this for the blocking paradigm? For blocking to occur, there must be an attenuation of conditioning to CS_2 due to prior training to CS_1. According to the Hawkins and Kandel hypothesis, this should occur because the presentation of the previously conditioned CS_1 stimulus will prevent, or reduce, firing of the facilitator interneuron during US presentation, eliminating the necessary source for pairing specific learning. As demonstrated by the simulations of Gluck and Thompson (1987), it is necessary that there be some activity in the facilitator interneuron to maintain an equilibrium between pairing-specific enhancement of sensitization (occuring during US presentations) and habituation (occuring during CS presentations). Gluck and Thompson showed that quantitative interpretations of the qualitative assumptions of the Hawkins–Kandel *Aplysia* model will not necessarily generate blocking when extended compound training is given (asymptotic blocking) because of a potential conflict between (1) the need to maintain interneuron firing during US presentation to maintain a learned association, and (2) the need to inhibit the interneuron from firing during the US presentation to resist the acquisition of a new association. Thus, the circuit-level assumptions of the Hawkins–Kandel model are not, by themselves, sufficient to predict blocking. Rather, additional biophysical details must also be specified (see, e.g., Hawkins, this volume). In comparing the Hawkins–Kandel model to the priming and Rescorla–Wagner models (both of which predict robust blocking effects), we see how assumptions about when and how decremental processes operate can have serious implications for differentiating models at both the behavioral and biological level. In particular, the rules for decreasing associative (synaptic) strength can strongly determine the magnitude and durability of blocking and conditioning.

D. *Aplysia* AND THE RESCORLA–WAGNER MODEL

An interesting comparison arises between the Hawkins–Kandel neural model and our adaptive network representations of the Rescorla–Wagner and priming models. As noted earlier, Eq. (11) of our trial-level interpretation of the Hawkins–Kandel model is derived from the priming model by combining the incremental process of Eq. (8) and the decremental process (Eq. 9) which operates—in the priming model—only on CS-alone trials. Structurally, however, it is evident that the connectivity of the basic Hawkins–Kandel model in Fig. 4A is similar to Fig. 2A of our network interpretation of the Rescorla–Wagner model for the generation of CRs. This suggests that the circuit connectivity of the basic *Aplysia* model (i.e., without the interneuron) in Fig. 4A might, with additional processing assumptions, be sufficient to implement the Rescorla–Wagner model and thereby generate a more complete range of conditioning phenomena.

Hawkins and Kandel suggest that the effect of a CS presentation is to cause a nonassociative context-free decrement of that CS strength on all trials. If instead, the decremental process was governed by the postsynaptic activity in the motorneuron (as in Fig. 2A of the Rescorla–Wagner network model), then the *Aplysia* circuitry would be sufficient to implement Eq. (7) of the modified version of the Rescorla–Wagner model.[9]

---

[9]Actually, for this circuit model to implement the Rescorla–Wagner model fully would require that the synapses be able to have both excitatory and inhibitory effects, a neurobiologically implausible idea. A more plausible interpretation of Fig. 2A is that each of the excitatory CS synapses is replaced by a pair of excitatory and inhibitory synapses. If each of the synapses in a pair begin with an equivalent strength, then the initial effect of novel CS activity will be to have no net effect on the postsynaptic neuron. Changes, both up or down, in just one of these synapses would allow the net effect of CS activity to range from inhibitory to excitatory, as in the Rescorla–Wagner model.

IV.   Vertebrate Circuits: Eyelid Conditioning in the Rabbit

A.   The Cerebellar and Brain Stem Circuit

Over the past several years, considerable progress has been made in identifying brain structures and pathways responsible for a well-studied form of conditioning in a vertebrate: the rabbit conditioned eyeblink response (Clark *et al.*, 1984; Marek, McMaster, Gormezano, & Harvey, 1984; Mauk, Steinmetz, & Thompson, 1986; McCormick, Clark, Lavond, & Thompson, 1982; McCormick *et al.*, 1981; Rosenfeld & Moore, 1983; Thompson, 1986). On the basis of these and related findings, Thompson and colleagues have proposed a cerebellar–brain stem model of acquisition which describes the critical brain structures in the CS–CR pathway, and the US pathways involved in UR generation and reinforcement (see Fig. 5). In this section, we explore ways in which this circuit-level model of acquisition can be expanded to address a broader range of associative learning phenomena. We first review the basic facts of eyelid conditioning and components of the cerebellar–brain stem circuit proposed by Thompson and colleagues. We then compare the network representations of the Rescorla–Wagner and Priming models with the cerebellar–brain stem model of simple acquisition. Correspondences between the behavioral and neural models can indicate ways in which the neural networks could, in principle, generate the broader range of associative learning phenomena addressed by the behavorial models.

In a typical conditioning session, rabbits receive pairings of an auditory CS with a corneal airpuff US. At the outset, the CS has no detectable effect on the eyelid or nictitating membrane (NM) response and the US produces a vigorous eyelid closure and NM extension. With repeated CS–US pairings, the tone comes to elicit an eyeblink CR that is well timed to occur just prior to US onset. Information about the tone is coded by the dorsal cochlear nucleus, which projects to pontine nuclei, which in turn project, via mossy fibers, to the cerebellar cortex and deep nuclei: This is termed the CS pathway (see Fig. 5). The cerebellum sends projections to the contralateral red nucleus, which sends projections back across the midline to the motor neurons in the accessory abducens and facial nuclei, which ultimately drive the measured responses: This is termed the CR pathway. Information about the corneal airpuff US is coded by activity in the trigeminal spinal nuclei. Projections from the spinal nuclei to the motor neurons in the accessory abducens and facial nuclei drive the immediate UR to the airpuff. The spinal nuclei also project to the dorsal accessory olive (DAO), which in turn projects, via climbing fibers, to the cerebellar cortex and deep nuclei. Mauk *et al.* (1986) have

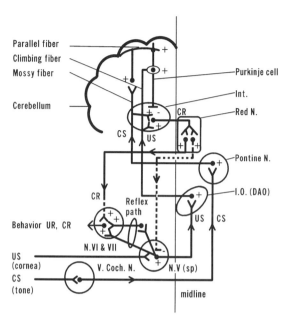

Fig. 5. Simplified schematic of hypothetical circuit for eyeblink conditioning in the rabbit. The US (corneal airpuff) pathway seems to consist of somatosensory projections to the dorsal accessory portion of the inferior olive (DAO) and its climbing fiber projections to the cerebellum. The tone CS pathway seems to consist of auditory projections to pontine nuclei (Pontine N.) and their mossy fiber projections to the cerebellum. The efferent (eyelid closure) CR pathway projects from the interpositus nucleus (Int.) of the cerebellum to the red nucleus (Red N.) and via the descending rubral pathway to act ultimately on motor neurons. The red nucleus may also exert inhibitory control over the transmission of somatosensory information about the US to the inferior olive (IO) such that when an eyeblink CR occurs, the red nucleus dampens US activation of climbing fibers. Pluses indicate excitatory and minuses inhibitory synaptic action. From Thompson, *Science* (1986). Copyright © 1986 by the AAS. Reprinted with permission.

described this as the reinforcement pathway. Pairing a CS with stimulation of the DAO can result in the development of discrete, striated muscle CRs (e.g., eyeblinks). In conventionally trained animals (tone → airpuff), small lesions in the DAO can be shown to have little immediate effect on CRs to the tone. However, with continued CS–US pairings, CRs to the tone decrease to pretaining levels. It appears that the tone extinguishes as a result of the reinforcing properties of the US having been abolished by the lesion. Steinmetz, Rosen, Chapman, and Thompson (1986) have also demonstrated that stimulation of lateral pontine nuclei (LPN) or the

middle cerebellar peduncle (i.e., sources of mossy fiber input to the cerebellum) can serve as an effective CS: When paired with corneal airpuff
or stimulation of the DAO, LPN stimulation comes to elicit normal eyeblink CRs. Training parameters known to be critical for conditioning with
tone–airpuff pairings, such as ISI, are similarly critical in the development of CRs when using LPN and DAO stimulation for the CS and the
US. From these and other observations, Thompson and colleagues have
proposed that the plasticity responsible for the development of conditioned striated muscle responses occurs in the interpositus nucleus and/
or in the overlying cortex. Activation of these cerebellar structures by
appropriately converging CS (mossy fiber) and US (climbing fiber) activity is assumed to induce plasticity in the cerebellar networks such that
the CS can eventually drive output neurons of the interpositus nucleus
and give rise to a behavioral CR.

Figure 6 depicts a more detailed view of a subset of the circuitry shown
in Fig. 5, including the afferents assumed to carry information about CS
and US occurrence, the connectivity of the cerebellar cortex and deep
nuclei, and the efferents from the cerebellum involved in the generation
of the eyeblink response. As we have previously noted, information about
CS occurrence comes from mossy fiber projections to the cerebellum via
the pontine nuclei (see discussion in Solomon, Lewis, LoTurco, Steinmetz, & Thompson, 1986; Steinmetz *et al.*, 1986). Mossy fibers project to
the cerebellar cortex and, we presume, the deep nuclei (Gerrits & Voogd,
1987). In the cortex, they excite granule cells, which in turn have dual
effects on the Purkinje cells. Granule cells have direct excitatory effects
on Purkinje cells through parallel fiber contacts and indirect inhibitory
effects through inhibitory interneurons (stellate cells). Thus, presentation
of a CS will generate excitatory and inhibitory input to Purkinje cells.
Altering the strength of one input could allow the net effect of a CS on
Purkinje cell activation to be excitatory (increase the rate of firing above
the baseline firing rate) or inhibitory (decrease the rate of firing below the
baseline firing rate.) Because the cerebellar cortex communicates with
the deep nuclei solely through the Purkinje cells (which exert an inhibitory influence on the deep nuclei), variation in CS-evoked activity in Purkinje cells could have important effects on learning and response
generation.

As previously noted, the reinforcement pathway, which carries information about the US, is taken to be the climbing fibers from the inferior
olive (Mauk *et al.*, 1986; McCormick *et al.*, 1982). Climbing fibers provide
strong synaptic input to Purkinje cells and also send collaterals to the
deep nuclei. As can be seen in Fig. 6, CS and US pathways converge in

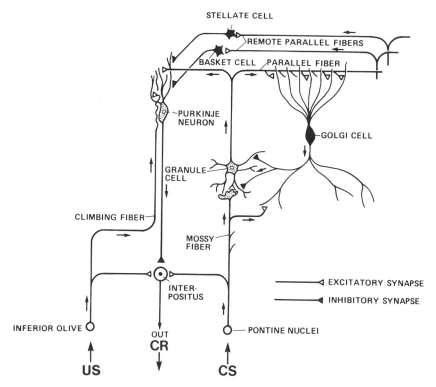

Fig. 6. Schematic of the cerebellar–brain stem circuit depicting the afferents assumed to carry information about CS and US occurrence, the connectivity of the cerebellar cortex and deep nuclei, and the efferents from the cerebellum involved in the generation of the conditioned eyeblink response (CR). Information about CS occurrence comes from mossy fiber projections to the cerebellum via the pontine nuclei. The reinforcement pathway, which carries information about the unconditioned stimulus (US), is taken to be the climbing fibers from the inferior olive. The efferent pathway for the conditioned response (CR) consists of projections from the interpositus nucleus which act ultimately upon motor neurons.

the cerebellar cortex and the deep nuclei. The efferent pathway for the conditioned response consists of projections from the interpositus nucleus which act ultimately upon motor neurons (Lavond, McCormick, Clark, Holmes, & Thompson, 1981).

In recordings from the cerebellar cortex in well-trained animals, one can find Purkinje cells that show a decrease in simple spike firing (simple spikes are evoked by parallel fiber activation) that precedes and models the conditioned eyeblink response (see Fig. 7see also Berthier & Moore,

PURKINJE CELL

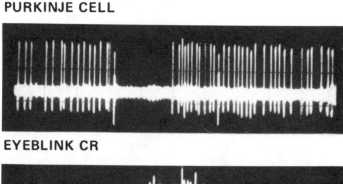

EYEBLINK CR

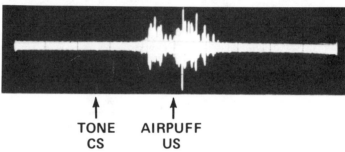

↑   ↑
TONE   AIRPUFF
CS   US

Fig. 7.   A Purkinje cell from a well-trained animal showing a decrease in simple spike firing that precedes and models the conditioned eyeblink response.

1986; Donegan, Foy, & Thompson, 1985; Foy & Thompson, 1986).[10] At the outset of training, tone CSs evoke increases or no change in Purkinje cell firing. However, with training, the tone-evoked decreases which model the conditioned response become much more prevalent. One possible model of cerebellar function in classical conditioning of striated muscle responses is that, over the course of learning, Purkinje cells that project to the region of the interpositus that control the appropriate behavioral response (e.g., eyeblink, leg flexion) develop a learning-induced decrement of simple spike firing in the CS period. The idea that, over the course of training, a CS starts by exciting Purkinje cells but ends by reducing Purkinje cell activity below baseline levels is in the spirit of proposals of Albus (1971) and Ito (1984) regarding the nature of learning-induced plasticity in the cerebellum. In this case, the CS generates excitatory input to a population of Purkinje cells through parallel fiber synapses and indirect inhibitory input through stellate cells. At the outset of

[10]Increases in Purkinje cell activity that precede and model the CR are also observed. In our speculations, we will focus on the conditioned decreases in Purkinje cell activity.

training, the net effect tends to be excitatory. With repeated CS–US pairings, it is proposed that the strength of the parallel fiber–Purkinje cell synapses decreases (Crepel & Krupa, 1988; Sakurai, 1987; Ito, 1984; Ekerot & Kano, 1985), resulting in the CS having a net inhibitory effect on Purkinje cell activity. This would result in the interpositus experiencing a momentary release from inhibition, which would allow the generation of a response to the CS.

As previously noted, we believe that the climbing fibers provide the teaching input to both the cortex and the deep nuclei. In the interpositus, the CS→CR pathway (mossy fiber collateral→output cell) would be strengthened by an appropriately timed convergence of CS-evoked activity in the mossy fiber collaterals with US-evoked activity in climbing fiber collaterals at the interpositus output cells (see Fig. 6). Thus, over the course of training, the CS will come to elicit a CR through the strengthened drive of mossy fiber collaterals onto the output cells in the interpositus and through a release of inhibition from the cortex produced by CS-generated decrements in Purkinje cell activity.

In considering correspondences between the abstract network representations suggested by the three learning models depicted in Fig. 2 and features of the cerebellar and brain stem circuit described above, what should be apparent is that one could generate mappings at several levels of analysis. On the one hand, regarding the convergence of information from the CS pathway and the US pathway responsible for excitatory conditioning, one could treat the US node as representing input from the dorsal accessory olive, the CS node as input from pontine nuclei, and the adaptive node as elements of the cerebellum. Appropriate convergence of activity in the CS and US pathways would increase the ability of the CS to drive the output neurons in the cerebellar deep nuclei. Such a scenario would emphasize the important structures, pathways, and sites of convergence but would be silent about the exact sites and cellular mechanisms of plasticity within the cerebellum. On the other hand, one could point to correspondences between the features of the abstract circuit and the cellular organization of the cerebellum as depicted in Fig. 6. The input from the US would be in the form of climbing fiber collaterals, input from the CS in the form of mossy fiber collaterals, and the adaptive node would correspond to the output neurons in the interpositus.[11] Strengthening of the mossy fiber and output cell synapse could be accomplished via a form

[11]One problem with such assumptions is that the connectivity within the interpositus nucleus of the afferents, excitatory and inhibitory interneurons (not shown), and output cells is not nearly as well understood as the organization of the cortex. Thus, the depiction of the interpositus circuitry in Fig. 6 is grossly simplified in comparison to the more accurate representation of the cortex.

of presynaptic facilitation (as suggested by the figure) or postsynaptic modifications (assuming that US input affected the adaptive node). In mapping the network onto the cerebellar cortex several obvious elaborations on the abstract network would be required: for example, reversing the sign of the plasticity rules and allowing converging activation of CS and US pathways to decrement synaptic strength, analogous to the synaptic depression observed at parallel fiber and Purkinje cell synapses described above. Obviously, additional elements would have to be added (interneurons equivalent to stellate cells) to allow the CS to momentarily release the deep nuclei from inhibition, for example, as described above. The utility of such mappings is that they can suggest how the neural system could, in principle, generate a variety of associative learning phenomena and the kinds of experiments that could evaluate the neural system's potential. The level at which the mapping is carried out would depend on the progress in characterizing the relevant neuronal circuitry and the physiological methods to be used.

The preceding mappings illustrate correspondences between features of the abstract networks and the cerebellar circuit that are responsible for some aspects of simple acquisition, that is, incrementing the associative strength of the CS. In considering decremental processes, the priming model (see Fig. 2B) proposes that on CS–US pairings, US processing is modulated by the CS as a function of its associative strength. That is, the ability of the US to generate a response and teaching input to relevant sites of plasticity will not be constant over training but will decrease as the associative strength of the CS increases. As we have noted, behavioral support comes from findings such as the conditioned diminution of the UR (e.g., Donegan 1981) and blocking (e.g., Kamin, 1969). Evidence for this proposal also can be found in the physiological literature in analyses of the ability of the US to activate portions of the US pathway over the course of training. For example, with repeated pairings of the CS and US, there is a marked decrease in US-evoked climbing fiber responses in the Purkinje cells (Foy & Thompson, 1986). In the following section we propose a mapping of the priming model onto the cerebellar and brain stem circuit. In particular, we consider how a significant associative modulation of a teaching input from the US pathways might result from recurrent inhibition provided by a feedback loop from the red nucleus to the trigeminal spinal nuclei (or from the interpositus to the DAO—not shown in Fig. 5).

B. THE RED NUCLEUS FEEDBACK LOOP AND PRIMING

Depicted in Fig. 5 is a projection from the red nucleus (part of the CR output pathway) to the spinal nuclei of the trigeminal nerve (part of the

US input pathway). Work with cats suggests that this projection can inhibit sensory evoked responses in the trigeminal spinal nuclei. Dostrovsky and colleagues have shown that stimulating the red nucleus inhibits activity in pars oralis and pars caudalis evoked by touching or pinching facial skin and by tooth pulp stimulation (K. D. Davis & Dostrovsky, 1986; Gray & Dostrovsky, 1971). Weiss (1986) has shown that red nucleus stimulation inhibits activity in the dorsal accessory olive evoked by tactile stimulation of forelimb regions, presumably through red nucleus projections to the dorsal column nuclei. The significance of the inhibitory loop from the red nucleus is that, in more abstract terms, it creates a network in which activation of the CS→CR pathway not only generates a CR, but also inhibits activity in structures coding the US. A second source of negative feedback onto the "reinforcement pathway" may be the projection from the interpositus to the DAO (not shown in Fig. 5), which is thought to be inhibitory (Andersson, Gorwicz, & Hesslow, 1987). If this is true for the rabbit, then this aspect of the cerebellar–brain stem network should function like the network representation of the priming model in Fig. 2B. That is, it should be capable of generating the variety of learning phenomena addressed by the priming model. In the case of blocking, a previously trained light CS would block conditioning to a contemporaneous tone CS as a result of the light activating the inhibitory feedback loop from the red nucleus. In such compound trials, US activation of the spinal nuclei would be diminished, thereby reducing the reinforcing potential of the US and consequently impairing conditioning to the tone. In more formal terms, associative activation in the CR pathway corresponds to the term $\Sigma w_j a_j$ in Eq. (8) and activity in the trigeminal nerve corresponds to the teaching input, λ. Given that the feedback loops from the red nucleus (and/or interpositus) are inhibitory, the relationship will be subtractive, $|\lambda - \Sigma w_j a_j|$, with the constraint that the activity in trigeminal nuclei–DAO, the teaching input, can not be driven below 0. As a result, the products of a conditioning trial will be described by Eq. (8) of the priming model, $\Delta w_i = \beta_1 a_i |\lambda - \Sigma w_j a_j|$ (see also Fig. 2B).

The foregoing exercise in mapping features of a hypothetical network onto the cerebellar–brain stem circuit represents an example of a larger set of possible mappings. The goal of such speculative exercises is to provide suggestions for how the brain structures responsible for acquisition of the conditioned eyeblink response could generate a broader range of associative learning phenomena. We again emphasize that the real utility of these speculations will be the empirical tests of the capacities of the cerebellar–brain stem circuit that they lead to (e.g., see Wagner & Donegan, this volume).

V. General Discussion

We have described an approach to the development of neural models of classical conditioning which integrates formalized learning rules derived from behavioral analyses with circuit-level descriptions of learning derived from physiological experiments. This is much in the spirit of Marr's framework for understanding complex information-processing systems, in which he distinguishes three distinct levels of explanation (Marr, 1982, pp. 19–29): the level of the *computation* performed, the level of the behavioral *algorithm* for this computation, and the level of the physical mechanisms which *implement* this algorithm. (For a more detailed discussion of Marr's ideas as applied to mappings between algorithmic and computational-level models of classical conditioning, see Granger & Schlimmer, 1986.) The approach we have developed is probably most applicable to model systems in which the behavioral properties of the learning processes have been characterized at a formal, algorithmic, level, but in which the neural circuitry (brain structures and connectivity) underlying this learning is only partially understood.

We have illustrated a strategy for mapping behavioral models of conditioning onto indentified neural circuits which might implement these algorithms. To do this, we have suggested a common formalism (abstract network representations) for representing, at the *trial level,* the core assumptions from a variety of distinct behavioral models which have been proposed for classical conditioning. Simple adaptive network models facilitate comparisons and contrasts among the models by restricting the networks to elementary associative processes for learning [i.e., the Hebb rule of Eq. (2)] and by having the behavioral properties of the algorithms expressed primarily through patterns of connectivity, which, in turn, suggest possible mappings onto neural circuits.

We have focused on three nonattentional models that share a common assumption that allows them to address a variety of phenomena of classical conditioning and habituation: the assumption that expected USs are less effective in promoting US processing necessary for conditioning than unexpected USs. The models we considered were the Rescorla–Wagner model, the priming model, and SOP. In comparing network representations inspired by these models, we have noted that all have a common component, a Hebbian or conjunctive incremental process. The models all explain the blocking effect and related phenomena by viewing this incremental process as being offset by the system's expectation of the US. The models differ, however, in how this expectation offsets the incremental process. In our adaptive network representation of the Rescorla–

Wagner model, the offset is conceived as an additional *decremental* process which operates directly on the associative strength of the CSs. In the priming model, however, expectation serves to *attenuate* the US's ability to promote an incremental associative change. The simplified network representation of the SOP model illustrates how SOP can be viewed as possessing the common incremental process in addition to associative decremental processes from both the Priming and Rescorla–Wagner models. At the level of behavioral analyses, the simple adaptive networks have illustrated the importance of decremental processes for distinguishing among the models.

In the second part of the chapter we focussed on two neural circuits which have been identified as critical to the learning and expression of classically conditioned behaviors. We compared these circuits to the three network models described above, and used our analyses of these models and their ability to generate various behaviors as a tool for evaluating the potential of the neural circuits for mediating a variety of conditioning phenomena that are central to contemporary models of associative learning in animals.

Hawkins and Kandel's (1984) model of conditioning in *Aplysia* can be viewed as an instantiation of the priming model in which the nonassociative decremental process (habituation) operates on every trial rather than on just nonreinforced trials. Gluck and Thompson's (1987) computational analyses of this model illustrated some of its potential advantages and limitations. Our (first) reexpression of the Rescorla–Wagner model as a sample adaptive network suggests how the basic circuit connectivity of the *Aplysia* circuit might more closely approximate the full power of the Rescorla–Wagner model if the decremental process were associative and context-sensitive, that is, influenced by the presence of other CSs.

We also illustrated how our network representation of the Rescorla–Wagner and Priming models might be mapped onto the identified circuits in the cerebellum and brain stem and how promising features of each might be combined. By identifying the red nucleus negative feedback loop with the priming model, we are also able to draw parallels with putative mechanisms in the *Aplysia* circuit. As in the priming model, the Hawkins–Kandel neural circuit model explains blocking by an attenuation of US processing by associated CSs.

In conclusion, we believe that formal behavioral models of conditioning, when expressed as adaptive networks, can provide an important theory-driven guide to identifying the neural substrates of conditioning. Our preliminary analyses have suggested the importance of assumptions about decremental processes, in both behavioral and biological models, for evaluating a model's ability to generate the full range of classical conditioning phenomena.

ACKNOWLEDGMENTS

For helpful suggestions on earlier drafts of this chapter, we are grateful to Andrew Barto, Tom Brown, Richard Granger, Misha Pavel, Gordon Shepherd, Richard Sutton, Allan Wagner, and Bill Whitlow. This research was supported by the Office of Naval Research (grant #N00014-83K-0238) and by a grant from the Sloan Foundation.

REFERENCES

Ackley, D. H., Hinton, G. E., & Sejnowski, T. J. (1985). A learning algorithm for Boltzmann machines. *Cognitive Science, 9,* 147–169.
Albus, J. S. (1971). A theory of cerebellar function. *Mathematical Biosciences, 10,* 25–61.
Alkon, D. L. (1984). Calcium-mediated reduction of ionic currents: A biophysical memory trace. *Science, 226,* 1037–1045.
Amari, S. (1977). Neural theory of association and concept formation. *Biological Cybernetics, 26,* 175–185.
Anderson, J. A., Silverstein, J. W., Ritz, S. A., & Jones, R. S. (1977). Distinctive features, categorical perception, and probability learning: Some applications of a neural model. *Psychological Review, 84,* 413–451.
Andersson, E., Gorwicz, M., & Hesslow, G. (1987). Inferior olive excitability after high frequency climbing fiber activation in the cat. *Experimental Brain Research, 67,* 523–532.
Berthier, N. E., & Moore, J. W. (1986). Cerebellar Purkinje cell activity related to the classically conditioned nictitating membrane response. *Experimental Brain Research, 63,* 341–350.
Brown, T. H., Chapman, P. F., Kairiss, E. W., & Keenan, C. L. (1988). Long-term synaptic potentiation. *Science, 242,* 724–728.
Bush, R., & Mosteller, F. (1951). A model for stimulus generalization and discrimination. *Psychological Review, 58,* 413–423.
Carew, T. J., Hawkins, R. D., & Kandel, E. R. (1983). Differential classical conditioning of a defensive withdrawal reflex in *Aplysia californica. Science, 219,* 397–400.
Carew, T. J., Pinsker, H. M., & Kandel, E. R. (1972). Longterm habituation of a defensive withdrawal reflex in *Aplysia. Science, 175,* 451–454.
Clark, G. A., McCormick, D. A., Lavond, D. G., Baxter, K., Gray, W. J., & Thompson, R. F. (1984). Effects of lesions of cerebellar nuclei on conditioned behavioral and hippocampal neuronal responses. *Brain Research, 291,* 125–136.
Cohen, D. H. (1984). Identification of vertebrate neurons modified during learning: Analysis of sensory pathways. In D. L. Alkon & J. Farley (Eds.), *Primary neural substrates of learning and behavioral change.* London: Cambridge University Press.
Crepel, F., & Krupa, M. (1988) Activation of protein kinase C induces a long-term depression of glutamate sensitivity of cerebellar Purkinje cells. An in vitro study. *Brain Research, 458,* 397–401.

Crow, T. (1985). Conditioned modification of phototatic behavior in *Hermissenda:* Differential light adaptation of B-photoreceptors. *Journal of Neuroscience,* **5,** 215–223.

Davis, K. D., & Dostrovsky, J. O. (1986). Modulatory influences of red nucleus stimulation on the somatosensory responses of cat trigeminal subnucleus oralis neurons. *Experimental Neurology,* **91,** 80–101.

Davis, M., Hitchcock, J. M., & Rosen, J. B. (1987). Anxiety and the amygdala: Pharmacological and anatomical analysis of the fear-potentiated startle paradigm. In G. H. Bower (Ed.), *The psychology of learning and motivation.* (Vol. 21). New York: Academic Press.

Desmond, J. E., & Moore, J. W. (1986). Dorsolateral pontine tegmentum and the classically conditioned nictitating membrane response: Analysis of CR-related single-unit activity. *Experimental Brain Research,* **65,** 59–74.

Donegan, N. H. (1980). *Priming produced facilitation or diminution of responding to a Pavlovian Unconditioned Stimulus.* Unpublished doctoral dissertation, Yale University, New Haven, CT.

Donegan, N. H., Foy, M. R., & Thompson, R. F. (1985). Neuronal responses of the rabbit cerebellar cortex during performance of the classically conditioned eyelid response. *Society for Neuroscience Abstracts,* **11,** 245.8.

Donegan, N. H., & Wagner, A. R. (1987). Conditioned dimunition and facilitation of the UCR: A sometimes-opponent-process interpretation. In I. Gormezano, W. Prokasy, & R. Thompson (Eds.), *Classical conditioning II: Behavioral, neurophysiological, and neurochemical studies in the rabbit.* Hillsdale, NJ: Erlbaum.

Ekerot, C. F., & Kano, M. (1985). Long-term depression of parallel fiber synapses following stimulation of climbing fibers. *Brain Research,* **342,** 357–367.

Foy, M. R., & Thompson, R. F. (1986). Single unit analysis of Purkinje cell discharge in classically conditioned and untrained rabbits. *Society for Neuroscience Abstracts,* **12,** 518.

Gerrits, N. M., & Voogd, J. (1987). The projection of the nucleus reticularis tegmentis pontis and adjacent regions of the pontine nuclei to the central cerebellar nuclei in the cat. *Journal of Comparative Neurology,* **258,** 52–69.

Gluck, M. A., & Bower, G. H. (1988). Evaluating an adaptive network model of human learning. *Journal of Memory and Language,* **27,** 166–188.

Gluck, M. A. & Thompson, R. F. (1987). Modeling the neural substrates of associative learning and memory: A computational approach. *Psychological Review,* **94,** 176–191.

Granger, R. H., & Schlimmer, J. C. (1986). The computation of contingency in classical conditioning. In G. H. Bower (Ed.), *The psychology of learning and motivation* (Vol. 20). New York: Academic Press.

Gray, B. G., & Dostrovsky, J. O. (1971). Modulation of the sensory responses of cat trigeminal and cuneate neurons by electrical stimulation of the red nucleus. *Society for Neuroscience Abstracts,* **9,** 247.

Groves, P. M., & Thompson, R. F. (1970). Habituation: A dual-process theory. *Psychological Review,* **77,** 419–450.

Hawkins, R. D., Abrams, T. W., Carew, T. J., & Kandel, E. R. (1983). A cellular mechanism of classical conditioning in Aplysia: Activity-dependent amplification of presynaptic facilitation. *Science,* **219,** 400–404.

Hawkins, R. D., & Kandel, E. R. (1984). Is there a cell-biological alphabet for simple forms of learning? *Psychological Review,* **91,** 376–391.

Hebb, D. (1949). *Organization of behavior.* New York: Wiley.

Hinton, G. E., & Anderson, J. A. (1981). *Parallel models of associative memory.* Hillsdale, NJ: Erlbaum.

Hopfield, J. J. (1982). Neural networks and physical systems with emergent collective computational abilities. *Proceedings of the National Academy of Sciences U.S.A.*, 2554–2558.

Hull, C. L. (1943). *Principles of behavior.* New York: Appleton-Century-Crofts.

Ito, M. (1984). *The cerebellum and neural control.* New York: Raven Press.

Kamin, L. J. (1969). Predictability, surprise, attention and conditioning. In B. A. Campbell & R. M. Church (Eds.), *Punishment and aversive behavior* (pp. 279–296). New York: Appleton-Century-Crofts.

Kehoe, E. J. (1985). *A neural network model of classical conditioning.* Paper presented at the twenty-sixth annual meeting of the Psychomic Society, Boston, MA.

Klopf, A. H. (1987). A neuronal model of classical conditioning. *Psychobiology,* **16**, 85–125.

Larew, M. B. (1986). *Inhibitory learning in Pavlovian backward conditioning procedures involving a small number of US–CS trials.* Unpublished doctoral dissertation, Yale University, New Haven, CT.

Lavond, D. G., McCormick, D. A., Clark, G. A., Holmes, D. T., & Thompson, R. F. (1981). Effects of ipsilateral rostral pontine reticular lesions on retention of classically conditioned nictating membrane and eyelid responses. *Physiologial Psychology,* **94**, 335–339.

LeCun, Y. (1985). Une procedure dapprentissage pour reseau a seuil assymetrique. *Proceedings of Cognitiva 85, Paris,* pp. 599–604.

Levy, W. B., & Steward, O. (1979). Synapses as associative memory elements in the hippocampal formation. *Brain Research,* **175**, 233–245.

Levy, W. B., & Steward, O. (1983). Temporal contiguity for long-term associative potentiation/depression in the hippocampus. *Neuroscience,* **8**, 791–797.

Mackintosh, N. J. (1975). A theory of attention: Variations in the associability of stimuli with reinforcement. *Psychological Review,* **82**, 276–298.

Marek, G. J., McMaster, S. E., Gormezano, I., & Harvey, J. A. (1984). The role of the accessory abducens nucleus in the rabbit nictitating membrane response. *Brain Research,* **299**, 215–229.

Marr, D. (1982). *Vision: A computational investigation into the human representation and processing of visual information.* San Francisco: Freeman.

Mauk, M. D., Steinmetz, J. E., & Thompson, R. F. (1986). Classical conditioning using stimulation of the inferior olive as the unconditioned stimulus. *Proceedings of the National Academy of Sciences U.S.A.*, **83**, 5349–5353.

Mazur, J. E., & Wagner, A. R. (1982). An episodic model of associative learning. In M. L. Commons, R. J. Herrnstein, & A. R. Wagner (Eds.), *Quantitative analyses of behavior: Vol III. Acquisition.* Cambridge, MA: Ballinger.

McClelland, J. L., & Elman, J. L. (1986). Interactive processes in speech perception: The TRACE model. In J. L. McClelland & D. E. Rumelhart (Eds.), *Parallel distributed processing: Explorations in the microstructure of cognition: Vol. 2. Psychological and biological models.* Cambridge, MA: Bradford Books/MIT Press.

McCormick, D. A., Clark, G. A., Lavond, D. G., & Thompson, R. F. (1982). Initial localization of the memory trace for a basic form of learning. *Proceedings of the National Academy of Sciences U.S.A.*, **798**, 2731–2742.

McCormick, D. A., Lavond, D. G., Clark, G. A., Kettner, R. E., Rising, C. E., & Thompson, R. F. (1981). The engram found?: Role of the cerebellum in classical conditioning of nictitating membrane and eyelid responses. *Bulletin of the Psychonomic Society,* **183**, 103–105.

Parker, D. (1985). *Learning logic* (Report No. 47). Cambridge, MA: MIT, Center for Computational Research in Economics and Management Science.

Parker, D. (1986). A comparison of algorithms for neuron-like cells. In *Proceedings of the Neural Networks for Computing Conference.* Snowbird, UT.

Pearce, J. M., & Hall, G. (1980). A model for Pavlovian learning: Variations in the effectiveness of conditioned and unconditioned stimuli. *Psychological Review*, **87**, 532–552.

Pfautz, P. L. (1980). *Unconditioned facilitation and diminution of the unconditioned response*. Unpublished doctoral dissertation, Yale University, New Haven, CT.

Pfautz, P. L., & Wagner, A. R. (1976). Transient variations in responding to Pavlovian conditioned stimuli have implications for mechanisms of "priming." *Animal Learning and Behavior*, **4**, 107–112.

Rescorla, R. A. (1968). Probability of shock in the presence and absence of CS in fear conditioning. *Journal of Comparative and Physiological Psychology*, **66**, 1–5.

Rescorla, R. A., & Wagner, A. R. (1972). A theory of Pavlovian conditioning: Variations in the effectiveness of reinforcement and non-reinforcement. In A. H. Black & W. F. Prokasy (Eds.), *Classical conditioning II: Current research and theory*. New York: Appleton-Century-Crofts.

Rosenberg, C. R., & Sejnowski, T. J. (1986). The spacing effect on Nettalk, a massively-parallel network. In *Proceedings of the 8th Annual Conference of the Cognitive Science Society*. Amherst, MA.

Rosenfeld, M. E., & Moore, J. W. (1983). Red nucleus disrupt the classically conditioned nictitating membrane response in the rabbit. *Behavioral Brain Research*, **10**, 393–398.

Rudy, J. W., & Wagner, A. R. (1975). Stimulus selection in associative learning. In W. K. Estes (Ed.), *Handbook of learning and memory* (Vol. 2). Hillsdale, NJ: Erlbaum.

Rumelhart, D. E., Hinton, G. E., & Williams, R. J. (1986). Learning internal representations by error propagation. In D. E. Rumelhart & J. L. McClelland (Eds.), *Parallel distributed processing: Explorations in the microstructure of cognition: Vol. 1. Foundations*. Cambridge, MA: MIT Press.

Rumelhart, D. E., & McClelland, J. L. (Eds.). (1986). *Parallel distributed processing: Explorations in the microstructure of cognition. Vol. 1. Foundations* Cambridge, MA: MIT Press.

Sakurai, M. (1987). Synaptic modification of parallel fibre–Purkinje cell transmission in *in vitro* guinea-pig cerebellar slices. *Journal of Physiology (London)*, **394**, 463–480.

Sejnowski, T. J. (1976). On global properties of neuronal interaction. *Biological Cybernetics*, **22**, 85–95.

Solomon, P. R., Lewis, J. L., LoTurco, J., Steinmetz, J. E., & Thompson, R. F. (1986). The role of the middle cerebellar peduncle in acquisition and retention of the rabbit's classically conditioned nictitating membrane response. *Bulletin of the Psychonomic Society*, **241**, 75–78.

Spence, K. W. (1936). The nature of discrimination learning in animals. *Psychological Review*, **43**, 427–449.

Steinmetz, J. E., Rosen, D. J., Chapman, P. F., & Thompson, R. F. (1986). Classical conditioning of the rabbit eyelid response with a mossy fiber stimulation CS. I. Pontine nuclei and middle cerebellar peduncle stimulation. *Behavioral Neuroscience*, **100**, 871–880.

Sutton, R. S., & Barto, A. G. (1981). Toward a modern theory of adaptive networks: Expectation and prediction. *Psychological Review*, **88**, 135–170.

Sutton, R. S., & Barto, A. G. (1987). A temporal-difference model of classical conditioning. In *Proceedings of the 9th Annual Conference of the Cognitive Science Society*. Seattle, WA.

Terry, W. S. (1976). The effects of priming US representation in short-term memory on Pavlovian conditioning. *Journal Of Experimental Psychology: Animal Behavior Processes*, **2**, 354–370.

Thompson, R. F. (1986). The neurobiology of learning and memory. *Science*, **233**, 941–947.

Wagner, A. R. (1969). Stimulus selection and a modified continuity theory. In G. Bower & J. Spence (Eds.), *The psychology of learning and motivation* (Vol. 3). New York: Academic Press.

Wagner, A. R. (1976). Priming in STM: An information-processing mechanism for self-generated depression in performance. In T. J. Tighe & R. N. Leaton (Eds.), *Habituation: Perspectives from child development, animal behavior, and neurophysiology.* Hillsdale, NJ: Erlbaum.

Wagner, A. R. (1978). Expectancies and the priming of STM. In S. H. Hulse, H. Fowler, & W. K. Honig (Eds.), *Cognitive processes in animal behavior.* Hillsdale, NJ: Erlbaum.

Wagner, A. R. (1979). Habituation and memory. In A. Dickinson & R. A. Boakes (Eds.), *Mechanisms of learning and motivation.* Hillsdale, NJ: Erlbaum.

Wagner, A. R. (1981). SOP: A model of automatic memory processing in animal behavior. In N. Spear & G. Miller (Eds.), *Information processing in animals: Memory mechanisms.* Hillsdale, NJ: Erlbaum.

Wagner, A. R., & Brandon, S. (in press). Evolution of a structured connectionist model of Pavlovian conditioning (AESOP). In S. B. Klein & R. R. Mowrer (Eds.), *Contemporary learning theories.* Hillsdale, NJ: Erlbaum.

Wagner, A. R., Logan, F. A., Haberlandt, K., & Price, T. (1968). Stimulus selection in animal discrimination learning. *Journal of Experimental Psychology, 76,* 171–180.

Wagner, A. R. & Rescorla, R. A. (1972). Inhibition in Pavlovian conditioning: Applications of a theory. In R. A. Boakes & S. Halliday (Eds.), *Inhibition and learning* (pp. 301–336). New York: Academic Press.

Wagner, A. R. & Terry, W. S. (1975). Backward conditioning to a CS following an expected vs. a surprising UCS. *Animal Learning and Behavior, 3,* 370–374.

Walters, E. T., & Byrne, J. H. (1983). Associative conditioning of single sensory neurons suggests a cellular mechanism for learning. *Science, 219,* 404–407.

Weiss, C. (1986). *The dorsal accessory olive: Inhibitory gating by rubrospinal conditioning stimulation; and physiology of its afferent neurons.* Unpublished doctoral dissertation, Northwestern University, Chicago, IL.

Widrow, G., & Hoff, M. E. (1960). Adaptive switching circuits. *Institute of Radio Engineers, Western Electronic Show and Convention, Convention Record, 4,* 96–194.

Zimmer-Hart, C. L., & Rescorla, R. (1974). Extinction of Pavlovian conditioned inhibition. *Journal of Comparative and Physiological Psychology, 86,* 837–845.

SOME RELATIONSHIPS BETWEEN A COMPUTATIONAL MODEL (SOP) AND A NEURAL CIRCUIT FOR PAVLOVIAN (RABBIT EYEBLINK) CONDITIONING

Allan R. Wagner
Nelson H. Donegan

I. Introduction

SOP is an abstract model of animal learning and performance that was developed in an attempt to integrate conceptually the principal behavioral regularities of Pavlovian conditioning (see Wagner, 1981). It is a computational model, designed to deduce such quantitative relationships as those summarized by the Rescorla–Wagner (1972) learning rule (see Mazur & Wagner, 1982). It is a mechanistic theory, intended to rationalize such empirical relationships as the similarity that obtains between US priming effects (e.g., Terry, 1976) and the blocking phenomenon (Kamin, 1969), in terms of presumed theoretical equivalences (see Donegan & Wagner, 1987). It is also a real-time model, formulated to account for such intra-trial phenomena as the variation in momentary conditioned responding with variation in the CS duration, as well as more molar phenomena (see Wagner & Larew, 1985). The basis of the acronym is discussed in Section II.

An abstract theory such as SOP is not, in principle, partial to any particular neurobiological realization. However, the research of Richard Thompson and his colleagues (e.g., Mauk, Steinmetz, & Thompson, 1986; McCormick & Thompson, 1983; Thompson, 1986) on eyeblink conditioning in the rabbit has presented us with some major insights into the neural circuitry involved in the Pavlovian conditioning of a vertebrate preparation. And we are impressed, thus far, with how gracefully some of the abstract theoretical processes of SOP appear to map onto this functional circuitry. Describing the major correspondences and some of their implications is the primary goal of the present article.

In the sections that follow we first present an introductory-level description of SOP, emphasizing the essence of its propositions and some of the fundamental regularities that it addresses. Then we will present a basic sketch of current knowledge concerning the essential neural circuitry involved in eyeblink conditioning in the rabbit. This sets the stage for the central section, which attempts to show how the abstract theoretical processes of SOP have apparent corollaries in the functional circuitry that is involved in this instance of Pavlovian conditioning. If one takes the mapping seriously, one can be encouraged to draw implications concerning what next steps might be profitable in further neuronal investigation as well as in further theoretical development. In the concluding sections we point to some possible implications as well as take the occasion to speak to several general issues concerning the relationship between abstract computational theories such as SOP and the neurobiological substrates of learning.

II. SOP

In current parlance SOP would be described as a connectionist model (Feldman & Ballard, 1982). That is, the knowledge system is conceived as a set of nodes that take on activity states and are capable of influencing each other according to the excitatory and/or inhibitory connections that obtain among them. Performance is attributed to a presumed tendency of activity in certain nodes to drive overt behavior, and the acquisition of conditioned responding is interpreted in terms of a presumed change in how some nodes do this via alteration in the linkages that they have with other nodes. It is inviting to think of nodes as neuronlike (Feldman & Ballard, 1982), but the thrust of the present chapter would encourage one to think of the nodes of SOP and their properties as identifiable with systems of neurons. That, of course, gets ahead of the story.

The acronym SOP was suggested in part by an apparent relationship between the model and the opponent process theory of R. L. Solomon and Corbit (1974), especially as the latter has been construed by Schull (1979). Solomon and Corbit suggested that many phenomena involving hedonic stimuli could be understood by assuming that such stimuli produce not only a direct process (called α) in line with the prominent affective tone of the stimulus, but also a "slave" reaction to the α process (called β) that is in opposition to the α process. Thus, for example, because the β process is slower to recruit and to dissipate than the α process, one can appreciate that a "pleasant" event might be followed by an "unpleasant" afterexperience. Schull proposed that many facts of conditioning involving aversive or appetitive USs might be explained by assuming that one of the CRs that a CS may become capable of eliciting is the secondary, β, process initiated by a US, but not the α process. Our view was that it might be useful to expand upon these notions in two ways. That is, we supposed that (a) it might be useful to assume that stimuli generally produce a sequence of a primary and a secondary unconditioned process, that is, that this feature is not restricted to hedonic stimuli, and (b) that *all* conditioning effects (e.g., all conditioned response tendencies) are mediated by the "conditioning" of the secondary component in such a sequence produced by a US. What we suggested then, however, is that in such a treatment it could not be assumed that the initial and secondary components are uniformly in opposition, as they are assumed to be in the more narrowly construed opponent process theory. They might appear to be in some of their effects and not in others. SOP is a *sometimes opponent process* theory (Donegan & Wagner, 1987; Mazur & Wagner, 1982; Wagner, 1981).

SOP characterizes the representational activity that may be produced directly by a stimulus or indirectly via associative connections in terms of the state dynamics of stimulus nodes as depicted for a CS and for a US in Fig. 1. A node is not an elemental theoretical unit but a functional grouping, within which one can distinguish different patterns of activity as a result of different conditions of stimulation. That is, each node is conceived of as consisting of a large but finite set of elements that can be variously distributed among the three states of inactivity (I), primary activity (A1), and secondary activity (A2). It is assumed that when a node is acted upon by the stimulus it represents, some proportion (p_1) of the elements in the I state will be promoted in each moment of stimulation to the A1 state, from which they will subsequently decay, first to the A2 state, and then back to inactivity. In contrast, it is assumed that when a node is acted upon via excitation propagated over associative connection(s), some proportion (p_2) of the elements in the I state will be promoted in each moment to the A2 state, from which they will also decay back to inactivity. Figure 1 summarizes these assumptions by way of an appropriate state-transition diagram within each node. SOP assumes that p_1 increases with increasing stimulus intensity and that p_2 increases with

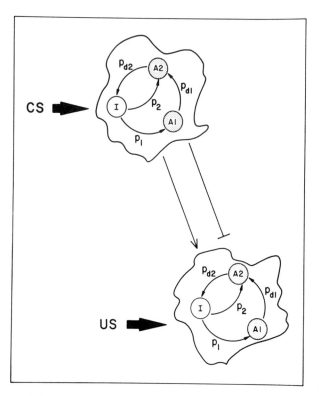

Fig. 1. A depiction of two nodes in the memory system of SOP, one presumed to be directly activated by a CS and the other by a US in a Pavlovian conditioning situation. The connected circles within each node represent the three activity states in which nodal elements may momentarily reside, and the connecting paths represent the allowable state transitions. The two nodes are joined to suggest the manner of directional excitatory (pointing arrow) and inhibitory (stopped line) linkages that are commonly assumed to be formed.

a measure of the summed products of the activity in connecting nodes, weighted by their relevant connection strengths, V_j. The momentary decay probabilities p_{d1} and p_{d2} are taken to increase with concurrent A1 and A2 activity in other nodes, according to general rules that make $p_{d1} > p_{d2}$. SOP adopts the stochastic assumptions that it does as deliberate simplifications that allow determinant quantitative specification. Given the initial activity values for a node such that $p_1 + p_{A1} + p_{A2} = 1.0$ and the parameters p_1, p_2, p_{d1} and p_{d2}, one can easily specify the variation in nodal activity occasioned by any episode of stimulation. To illustrate, Fig. 2 presents several simulations to which we will refer.

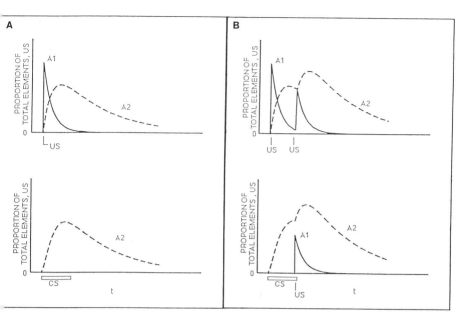

Fig. 2. A, Representative simulations describing the proportions of US nodal elements in the A1 and A2 states over successive amounts of time following a punctate US (top graph) or an extended excitatory CS (bottom graph). B, Simulation of the US nodal A1 and A2 states when a US presentation is preceded by the same US (top graph) or extended excitatory CS (bottom graph) occurring in the simulations in 2A.

A. UNCONDITIONED ACTIVITY DYNAMICS

The functions at the top of Fig. 2A depict the course of A1 and A2 nodal activity following a momentary presentation of a US to an inactive node. As can be seen, there is a period of predominately A1 activity followed by a period of predominately A2 activity before the node reverts to inactivity. If the US had been presented for more than a single moment, the functions would have been more complex but no less specifiable, sharing the sequential characteristics as shown.

There are three domains of data that have particularly encouraged this sequential-processes conceptualization. One domain concerns the character of responding observed in Pavlovian conditioning experiments. The second concerns certain refractory-like effects observed in studies of Pavlovian conditioning and habituation. The third concerns the training conditions that produce excitatory versus inhibitory conditioning. We will comment on each of these in turn in regard to the model's assertions concerning unconditioned activity dynamics before making analogous observations in regard to the model's assertions concerning conditioned activity dynamics.

1. *The Character of the Response*

SOP assumes that the A1 and A2 process each has its own behavioral consequences. In some instances this assumption is obviously invited by the nature of the unconditioned response to a stimulus, that is, when some US produces a clear sequence of first one behavior and then another. In other instances, the UR may not have salient descriptive discontinuities but may still be divisible into primary and secondary components on some functional basis.

A striking example of a UR in which the A1 and A2 processes appear to be associated with notably different behaviors is in the common laboratory case of a naive rat subjected to a brief footshock. The immediate response is agitated hyperactivity (e.g., Blanchard & Blanchard, 1969; Blanchard, Dielman, & Blanchard, 1968; Bolles & Riley, 1973) which then, characteristically, is followed by a secondary, longer-lasting hypoactivity or freezing response (Blanchard *et al.,* 1968; Blanchard & Blanchard, 1969; Bolles & Collier, 1976; Bolles & Riley, 1973). Similar examples can be found in the behavioral effects of certain drugs. For instance, the well-known prominent response to morphine injection is sedation. However, the initial sedation produced by morphine is also likely to be followed by a definite period of hyperactivity (Babbini & Davis, 1972; Fog, 1969).

The results of an experimental evaluation of the early and the late effects of morphine in the rat, reported by Paletta and Wagner (1986), are shown in the main body of Fig. 3. Mean activity counts in a stabilimeter device were taken in successive observation periods, from 30 min preinjection to 24 hours postinjection, in relation either to a morphine injection (5 mg/kg delivered sc) or a saline injection. As can be seen, there was little variation in the animals' activity on the different measurement occasions in the series associated with the saline injection. In contrast, the morphine injection produced not only an initial decrease in activity (observed in the first 5 min after injection and still prominent in the third postinjection measurement period beginning 60 min later), but also a subsequent period of marked hyperactivity (observed on the measure taken 4 hours after injection) before behavior returned to the saline baseline.

In contrast to these examples, some USs produce dissociable primary and secondary responses that are complimentary rather than antagonistic. Grau (1987) has suggested that this is exemplified in findings involving

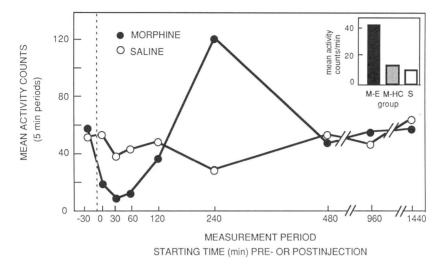

Fig. 3.   The line graph depicts activity changes produced by 5 mg/kg morphine injection in the rat, over a 24-hr postinjection period, compared to baseline activity following saline injection. The notable result is a biphasic UR with a period of sedation followed by a period of hyperactivity. Drawn from Paletta & Wagner (1986), Experiment 1. The bar graph insert shows the mean activity counts during a test session in the experimental environment, without morphine, for Group M-E, which previously had morphine injections paired with the experimental environment, Group M-HC, which experienced the same morphine but in the home cage, and Group S, which received only saline in training. Drawn from Paletta & Wagner (1986), Experiment 2.

the analgesic response exhibited by rats to intense stimulation. For a period of time following an episode of footshock the rat is less sensitive (hypoalgesic) to painful stimuli such as radiant heat applied to the tail (see, e.g., Chesher & Chan, 1977). Investigation of this unconditioned response has identified two components: an initial, short-duration hypoalgesia that is not modified by administration of the opiate antagonist naloxone, and a secondary, more persistent hypoalgesia that is removed or reduced by naloxone (Lewis, Cannon, & Liebeskind, 1980; Mayer & Watkins, 1981). The nonopioid component and the opioid component of the analgesic response consistently emerge sequentially (Drugan, Moye, & Maier, 1982; Grau, Hyson, Maier, Madden, & Barchas, 1981) in the manner of A1 and A2. On the basis of this and other observations, Grau (1987) has suggested that the initial, short-duration nonopioid form of postshock analgesia in the rat can be identified with the A1 process and the second, more persistent opioid form with the A2 process of SOP.

The unconditioned eyeblink response of the rabbit to a corneal air puff or paraorbital shock, which is of special interest here, appears, in gross measures such as lid displacement, to involve a single closure without discernable segments. However, the closure is the combined result of activity in several distinct neural pathways and involves several distinct muscular volleys (see, e.g., Harvey, Land, & McMaster, 1984; Holstege, Tan, van Ham, & Graveland, 1986; Sanes & Ison, 1979). EMG recordings from the orbicularis oculi muscles in the human reveal an early configuration of activity, designated R_1 and R_2, and a less regular, later component, designated, R_3 (Penders & Delwaide, 1973; Sanes & Ison, 1979). There is reason (see Section III) to think of these early and late components of the eyeblink UR as being associated with the A1 and A2 processes, respectively.

From analyses of the variety of URs that appear to have distinguishable initial (A1-generated) and secondary (A2-generated) components, one must conclude that the sequential behaviors are not uniformly in opposition. They are sometimes in opposition and sometimes complementary. SOP is silent on why this variability appears, but simply accepts the behavioral sequence as empirically exhibited.

2. Refractory-Like Effects

The stochastic assumptions of SOP concerning nodal dynamics do make the A1 and A2 processes consistent opponents in the following sense: To the degree that a node is in the A2 state, it is less accessible for activation to the A1 state by appropriate stimulation. Figures 2A and 2B illustrate the essential antagonism. The top graph of Fig. 2B presents a simulation identical to that in the top graph of Fig. 2A but now including a second US presentation during the later phase of processing initiated by the first US. As may be seen, when the US is presented during this phase it does not generate the same level of A1 activity that it otherwise would. The implication is that any behavioral consequence that is dependent upon A1 nodal activity initiated by a US should potentially witness the kind of refractory-like effect which is depicted in Fig. 2B.

Substantial evidence for such effects can be found in the literature on short-term habituation. For example, M. Davis (1970), studying the acoustic startle response in rats, found that the amplitude of rats' startle responses to the second of two punctate tones in a series was less than the response to the first, but the decrement became less apparent as the interval separating the stimuli was lengthened from 2 to 30 sec. Whitlow (1975) observed similar results in rabbits' vasomotor responses to sequential presentations of visual or auditory stimuli. In addition, he observed that the transient decremental effect was stimulus-specific. For example, shortly preceding a tone exposure by the same tone resulted in a reduced response to the second stimulus, whereas preceding a tone presentation by a light which evoked the same vasomotor response did not result in a reduced response to the tone. Related findings have been documented in other vertebrate preparations, such as leg flexion in spinal cats (Thompson & Spencer, 1966), and in invertebrate preparations, such as the defensive siphon and gill withdrawal response in *Aplysia* elicited by tactile stimulation of the skin (e.g., Castellucci & Kandel, 1976).

3. Excitatory versus Inhibitory Learning

SOP, like any learning model, must specify the conditions under which excitatory and inhibitory learning occur. The model assumes that both effects result from concurrent states of activation in the CS and US nodes. SOP assumes that an increment in the excitatory link from one node to another occurs only in moments in which both nodes have elements in the A1 state and that the size of the increment is proportional to a measure of the degree of joint A1 activity. Stated more specifically, for the linkage from a CS node to a US node, it is assumed that the increment in excitatory strength ($\Delta V^{+}_{\text{CS-US}}$) in any moment is the product of $p_{\text{A1,CS}}$, the proportion of CS elements in the A1 state, times $p_{\text{A1,US}}$, the proportion of US elements in the A1 state, multiplied by an excitatory learning rate parameter, L^{+}. It is correspondingly assumed that an increment in inhibitory linkage from one node to another occurs only in moments in which the former node has elements in the A1 state, while the latter node has elements in the A2 state. Stated specifically for the linkage from a CS node to a US node, it is assumed that the increment in inhibitory strength ($\Delta V^{-}_{\text{CS-US}}$) in any moment is the product of $p_{\text{A1,CS}}$, the proportion of CS elements in the A1 state, times $p_{\text{A2,US}}$, the proportion of US elements in the A2 state, multiplied by an inhibitory learning rate parameter, L^{-}. At any moment and over any episode of time both kinds of conjoint activity may occur so that the net change in associative will be

$$\Delta V_{\text{CS-US}} = (\Delta V^{+}_{\text{CS-US}}) - (\Delta V^{-}_{\text{CS-US}}).$$

To illustrate the mechanisms of SOP regarding the formation of excitatory and inhibitory associations, Mazur and Wagner (1982) reported a series of simulations of the model involving a variety of basic Pavlovian conditioning arrangements. One set of these is especially relevant to the present topic and is depicted in Fig. 4. The left column of graphs in Fig. 4A shows representative simulations of a forward, trace-conditioning trial, in which a momentary CS precedes by some interval a momentary

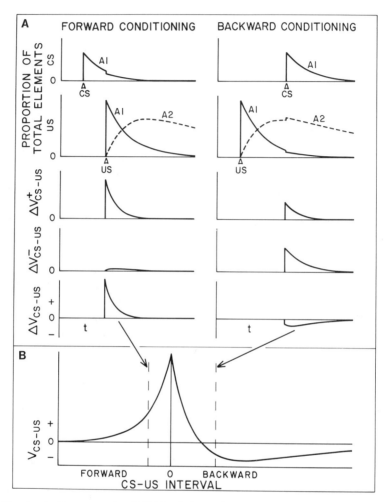

Fig. 4. A, Representative SOP simulations of single trials of forward and backward conditioning. Displayed are the simulated patterns of activity in CS and US nodes (top two graphs in each column) and the simulated changes in $V^+_{CS\text{-}US}$, $V^-_{CS\text{-}US}$, and net $V_{CS\text{-}US}$ (bottom three graphs in each column) over time. B, Predictions for the total $V_{CS\text{-}US}$ after a trial are shown for a range of forward and backward CS–US intervals. The broken vertical lines show where the two examples in panel A fall in relationship to the other intervals summarized. Reprinted from Mazur & Wagner (1982).

US. The right column of graphs in the same panel shows representative simulations of a similar backward conditioning trial in which the CS follows the US. The top two graphs in each case describe the relevant activity dynamics of the CS and US nodes over time. The three lower graphs in each column trace, in order, the momentary excitatory conditioning,

$\Delta V^+_{\text{CS-US}}$, the momentary inhibitory conditioning, $\Delta V^-_{\text{CS-US}}$, and the net momentary change in associative connection, $\Delta V_{\text{CS-US}}$, that result from the nodal activity in the two conditioning arrangements.

In the case of the forward conditioning example, the values of $\Delta V^+_{\text{CS-US}}$ are greater than those of $\Delta V^-_{\text{CS-US}}$, consistent with the preferential overlap that is afforded the A1 activity of the CS node with the initial A1 activity of the US node versus the later occurring A2 activity of that node. In comparison, in the backward conditioning case, where $p_{\text{A1,US}}$ has largely decayed but $p_{\text{A2,US}}$ is substantial at the time of application of the CS, the succeeding increments in excitatory association, $\Delta V^+_{\text{CS-US}}$, are consistently less than the corresponding increments in inhibitory association, $\Delta V^-_{\text{CS-US}}$. The result is that, whereas the algebraic consequence, $\Delta V_{\text{CS-US}}$, is uniformly positive in the forward conditioning example, it is uniformly negative in this backward conditioning example.

The overall associative outcomes of the two conditioning arrangements are obtained by summing the successive momentary values of $\Delta V_{\text{CS-US}}$ over the episodes depicted. Figure 4B summarizes the results of equivalent simulations with a range of CS–US relationships and indicates by broken vertical lines where the examples of Fig. 4A would fall in relationship to cases of greater or lesser asynchrony. As may be seen, all forward conditioning arrangements are expected to result in excitatory $V_{\text{CS-US}}$, with the magnitude of the excitatory learning decreasing exponentially as the CS–US interval increases. A somewhat unexpected prediction is that optimal conditioning occurs when the CS and US are presented simultaneously. In the case of backward conditioning, US–CS pairings can have either a net excitatory or inhibitory consequence, depending upon the US–CS interval.

Empirical support for these predictions comes from a variety of sources. For example, Kamin (1965) and Pavlov (1927) report that with a forward trace conditioning procedure, conditioning becomes less robust as the interstimulus interval (ISI) is lengthened. Although conventional evaluations of simultaneous conditioning have typically produced no evidence of excitatory conditioning (e.g., Schneiderman & Gormezano, 1964), such evaluations are problematic, in part because the opportunity for the US to interfere with CS processing is not equated across ISIs. When this confounding has been removed through special experimental arrangements (e.g., Rescorla, 1980a), SOP's prediction that simultaneous presentations of a CS and US should be more effective than forward presentations has received support. In a very clever experimental design, Rescorla (1980a) arranged for subjects (rats) to receive sequential presentations of two stimulus compounds, A and B followed by C and D where A, B, C, and D were distinctive flavors. He then evaluated whether stimulus A became more strongly associated with the simultaneously presented stimulus, B, or the subsequently presented stimulus, C or D. The evaluation was done via a sensory preconditioning design in which either B or D was paired with a toxin following the initial training. The finding of interest was that A appeared more aversive when B was paired with the toxin than when D was paired with the toxin. Following the logic of the sensory preconditioning design employed, the strength of the A–B association established by simultaneous pairing in the first phase was revealed to be stronger than the A–D association established by forward pairing. This important result deserves to be replicated in other conditioning preparations.

With regard to backward conditioning, until recently there has been considerable skepticism concerning the reality of any associative effects of backward, US–CS pairings per se (see, e.g., Mackintosh, 1974). However, it now seems clear that excitatory conditioning can result from sufficiently short intervals (e.g., Heath, 1976; Wagner & Terry, 1975), as SOP predicts. Inhibitory learning is also a genuine outcome (e.g., Mahoney & Ayres, 1976; Maier, Rapaport, & Wheatley, 1976). According to the simulation results in Fig. 4B, US–CS pairings should produce excitatory outcomes at short intervals, inhibition at intermediate intervals, and little or no conditioning at sufficiently long intervals. An investigation by Larew (1986) is especially instructive in that the experimenter asked, specifically, whether inhibitory backward conditioning occurs principally at intermediate US–CS intervals, as predicted by SOP in Fig. 4B. In a series of experiments, using a conditioned emotional response (CER) procedure with rats, Larew found that a CS acquired substantial inhibitory properties when it occurred at an intermediate US–CS interval (30 sec), but not when it occurred at a shorter or longer interval (1 or 600 sec, respectively).

B.   Conditioned Activity Dynamics

SOP makes the common assumption that a CS, as a result of Pavlovian conditioning, can become capable of influencing the activity in a node unconditionally representing another stimulus. But it also makes the strong assumption that a CS can thus only become capable of exciting (or inhibiting the excitement of) the A2 activity of such a US node. As previously noted, it is assumed that when a node is acted upon via excitation propagated over associative connection(s), some proportion (p_2) of the nodal elements in the I state will be promoted in each moment to the A2 state. And it is assumed that p_2 increases with a measure of net excitation (excitation minus inhibition) contributed by all CS nodes that are active (Mazur & Wagner, 1982).

The bottom diagram of Fig. 2A depicts the course of activity in a US node during and following the presentation of a protracted CS with which the US has acquired excitatory connections. The nodal activity shows a period of A2 recruitment, with the repeated moments of application of p_2, followed by a period of decay back to inactivity. The important principle emphasized by comparison of the two diagrams of Fig. 2A is that "conditioned" nodal activity (bottom diagram) includes only a secondary portion of the unconditioned nodal activity (top diagram). This principle has obvious implications for the conditioned response, the refractory-like effects, and the excitatory versus inhibitory learning that can come to be controlled by a Pavlovian CS.

1. The Character of the Response

From the preceding, it is expected that an excitatory CS will not produce the full A1 and A2 activity in a US node, but only the secondary, A2 activity. As a consequence, any CR that develops should not mimic the full UR but should mimic the secondary component of the UR. SOP thus calculates that if one looks beyond the relationship between the CR and the initial prominent component of the UR, CSs will have a quite varied, but lawful, behavior-producing relationship to potential USs.

Reference was previously made to the UR sequence observed in rats following an electric shock US, involving an initial period of agitated behavior followed by a longer period of freezing. What should the CR look like if a formerly neutral CS is paired with such a US? The notable fact is that the CR established to a CS paired with footshock consists of freezing, the secondary component of the UR, and not agitation, the primary component (Blanchard & Blanchard, 1969; Bolles & Collier, 1976; Fanselow, 1980; Fanselow & Baackes, 1982). The conditioned emotional response (CER) measure (Estes & Skinner, 1941) that has been so extensively used in investigation of Pavlovian conditioning presumably reflects such conditioned freezing.

Paletta and Wagner (1986) suggested that the relationship between CR and UR supposed by SOP is similarly exemplified in the case of conditioned activity changes produced with injection of morphine as the US. The well-known prominent response to morphine injection is sedation. One might thus be surprised by recent studies (e.g., Mucha, Volkovskis, & Kalant, 1981) in which morphine has been administered to rats in distinctive environments and it has been observed that the environmental cues (CS) come to produce an activity change (CR) that is just the opposite—hyperactivity. However, Paletta and Wagner (1986) pointed out that the initial sedation produced by morphine is followed by a period of hyperactivity (see Fig. 3). And, in comparison experiments they confirmed that the conditioned response based upon a morphine US mimicked the secondary response to morphine. Rats were given 10 daily injections of either morphine sulfate (5 mg/kg) in the experimental chamber (M-E), the same drug in the home cage (M-HC), or only saline (S) in both environments. All three groups were then tested for their levels of activity in the experimental chamber following a saline injection, that is, in the absence of morphine. The bar graph insert of Fig. 3 displays the essential findings: the activity level for Group M-E, in which the environment had been associated with morphine, was substantially higher than that for Group M-HC, which had equal drug exposure but not in the test context, or than that for Group S, which was drug-naive. Siegel (1979, 1981) has emphasized that the CR in studies like that of Paletta and Wagner, with pharmacological USs, will be "compensatory" to the prominent response to the US. This was certainly true in the Paletta and Wagner (1986) study. However, it is also true that the CR mimicked the secondary response to the drug, as anticipated by SOP. It remains to be seen whether the evidence for "conditioned compensatory responses" frequently observed with pharmacological USs will generally be found to be associated with biphasic URs with a secondary component antagonistic to the initial response.

When the primary and secondary components of the UR are similar to each other, the CR should likewise mimic the secondary component, although this relationship may be revealed only with more subtle observations than in cases involving antagonistic component URs. In a preceding example we noted that a nonopioid component and an opioid component of the analgesic response emerge sequentially following a noxious stimulus (Drugan et al., 1982; Grau et al., 1981) in the manner of A1 and A2. It is significant then that the analgesic response that can be conditioned to environmental cues appears to be prominently opioid in nature (i.e., to be blocked by naloxone) (Fanselow & Baackes, 1982; Fanselow & Bolles, 1979), just like the secondary UR component. This fact is central to Grau's (1987) suggestion that the initial, short-duration nonopioid form of postshock analgesia in the rat can be identified with the A1 process, and the second, more persistent (and conditionable) opioid form with the A2 process.

According to SOP, the conditioned response to the CS can be identified with a secondary response to the US, whether or not there is antagonism or other basis for distinguishing between the two presumed UR components. We have taken this on faith (Donegan & Wagner, 1987) to be the case in the rabbit eyeblink conditioned response. One of the points that we make in Section IV is that Thompson and colleagues (e.g., McCormick, Clark, Lavond, & Thompson, 1982) have supported our reasoning through observations that certain lesions abolish the eyeblink CR but do not affect the (immediate) UR.

2. Refractory-Like Effects

In the preceding section on unconditioned activity dynamics, we noted that to the degree that a US node is in the A2 state, it is less accessible for activation to the A1 state by the US. The top graphs in Fig. 2B versus 2A exemplified this theoretical corollary. The theory supposes that an excitatory CS, by similarly placing the US node in the A2 state, also has the ability to confer refractory-like effects on a subsequently presented US. This is illustrated in the lower graph of Fig. 2B. The simulation involves a presentation of the same US otherwise employed in Fig. 2 but now following the same CS employed in the companion lower graph of Fig. 2A. The obvious result is that the A1 activation of the US node is less than it would be in the absence of the CS, that is, is less than the activation generated by a US-alone presentation shown in the top graph of Fig. 2A. The supposition that an excitatory CS produces the same refractory-like effects as the US itself has been central to our theorizing for some time (Wagner, 1976, 1978) and is believed to be supported by a considerable amount of prior research in our laboratory and by others. Here we will mention but some of the more obvious research examples, concerned with the predictable variation in the UR to a US and with the equally predictable variation in the excitatory, associative learning occasioned by a US.

In a series of studies, Pfautz (1980) has shown how the amplitude of rabbit eyeblink URs to a paraorbital shock US can be modulated by a shortly preceding instance of the same US. In one experiment rabbits were run in a single session with pairs of USs irregularly presented and separated by either .5, 2, or 16 sec. Figure 5A summarizes one of the major findings by showing the mean amplitude eyelid closure to a 5-mA target US shock when that US was preceded by no shock (US) or by the same 5-mA shock 2-sec earlier (US–US). There was a clear decrement in responding to the target US when it was shortly preceded by the same US.

That a similar diminution of the UR can be produced by preceding the US by a CS[+] with which the US has been paired has been demonstrated by Donegan (1981). Rabbits were given training with auditory or visual CSs associated with US delivery (CS[+]). Following the development of conditioned responses, test trials were arranged in which the UR amplitude was measured. Figure 5B depicts the mean amplitude eyelid closure

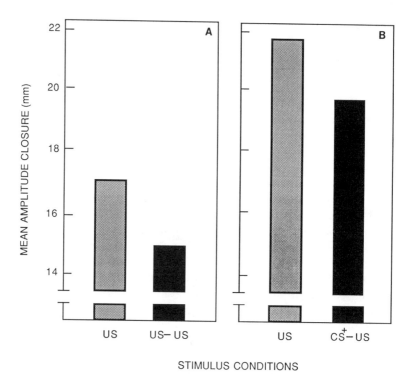

Fig. 5. A, Mean amplitude eyelid closure to a 5-mA shock US on trials when the designated target US was present in relative isolation (US) or was preceded by the same shock
(US–US). Drawn from Pfautz (1980). B, Mean amplitude eyelid closure to a 5-mA shock
US on trials when the designated target US was presented alone (US) or was preceded by
a CS⁺ (CS⁺–US). Drawn from Donegan (1981).

with a 5-mA US when that US was preceded by no CS (US) or the CS⁺
(CS⁺–US). As can been seen from this figure, diminution of the UR was
observed when the US was preceded by a CS⁺ relative to US-alone trials.
Other important comparisons were included in the Pfautz and the Donegan studies, for example, demonstrations that the same diminution was
not produced by a similar CS⁻ that was consistently nonreinforced (Donegan, 1981). But Fig. 5 makes the theoretical point that a CS⁺ produces
the same refractory-like effect on unconditioned responding as does the
US itself.

The A1 process of the US is presumed to be responsible for the excit-
atory associative learning as well as the initial UR produced by a US.
Such learning can be reduced by a preceding US (Terry, 1976) or CS⁺
(Savaadra; reported in Wagner, 1969b). A set of studies conducted by

Terry (1976) demonstrated that the acquisition of a conditioned eyeblink response reinforced by a paraorbital shock US is diminished if each CS–US pairing is shortly preceded by an application of the same US. Terry (1976) trained rabbits in one of his experiments with two CSs, one which was simply consistently reinforced by the presentation of a US, and a second which was similarly reinforced by a US but was also preceded 4 sec earlier by another, "priming" US. Figure 6A depicts the outcome of equivalent CS-alone test trials following the training described. As is suggested by this figure, the percentage of CRs was reliably less to that CS which was preceded by a US during (US, CS–US) than to that which was not (CS–US). Terry further supported the interpretation that the priming decrement was due to the initial US producing a refractory-like effect specific to the US involved by showing that the decrement did not occur if the priming and conditioning USs were not the same, that is, were directed to different eyes rather than the same eye.

A conceptually similar study was conducted by Savaadra (reported in Wagner, 1976), who demonstrated that acquisition of a conditioned eyeblink response reinforced by a paraorbital shock US is diminished by preceding the US with a CS^+ with which the US has previously been paired.

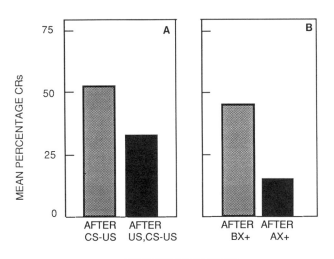

TRAINING CONDITIONS

Fig. 6.   A, Mean percentage conditioned responses to two CSs in a test session, following CS–US pairings that were preceded by a presentation of the same US (US,CS–US) or not (CS–US). Drawn from Terry (1976). B, Mean percentage conditioned responses to a cue X in a test session, following training in which X was compounded with a highly excitatory stimulus (AX +) or a less excitatory stimulus (BX +). Drawn from Wagner (1976).

Using an experimental design which produces an effect we now refer to as "blocking" (Kamin, 1968), Savaadra arranged for a novel CS (X) to be followed by a US when the X cue was in compound with (and, thus, the US was preceded by) either a stimulus that was highly trained as an excitatory CS (A), or an equivalent stimulus that was less trained (B). Following compound training, testing was administered so as to assess the level of conditioning that had accrued to X alone. As can be seen in Fig. 6B, responding to X was less frequent for the group which had had X trained in compound with A than for the group which had received X in compound with B. Comparing Savaadra's results with those of Terry (Figs. 6B and 6A, respectively), it should be noted that the similarity in the decremental effects of training involving either a preceding instance of the same US or of a preceding excitatory CS is again consistent with the assumption that both treatments leave the US representation temporarily in the A2 state, from which it is less accessible for activation to the A1 state.

3. Excitatory versus Inhibitory Learning

If a well-trained excitatory CS is presumed to produce A2 activity in a US node, and not to produce the full sequence of A1 activity followed by A2 activity as would the US itself, pairing a neutral CS with an excitatory CS should have different learning consequences than pairing it directly with the US. The neutral CS should be paired only with that US nodal process that produces *inhibitory* learning, so that the consequence should be an inhibitory linkage, rather than an excitatory or mixed linkage, between the nodes of the neutral CS and the US. Agreeably, the technique that has been known since the reports of Pavlov (1927, p. 76) to be effective in producing an inhibitory CS is the conditioned inhibition paradigm: Some CS, such as A, is reinforced by itself, while the CS of interest, such as X, is presented together with A, and the compound nonreinforced: That is, the contrast A+, AX− is arranged. As a consequence of such training, the X cue can be expected to become effective in reducing the conditioned responding observed to another CS in a summation test and to be retarded in acquiring excitatory, CR-eliciting tendencies itself over a series of reinforced trials. Using such training and testing procedures, conditioned inhibition has been observed with appetitive USs such as salivary conditioning in dogs (Pavlov, 1927) and autoshaping in pigeons (Wessels, 1973) and with aversive USs such as rabbit eyelid and nictitating membrane conditioning (Merchant, Mis, & Moore, 1972; Savaadra, in Wagner, 1971) and conditioned food aversion in rats (Taukulis & Revusky, 1975).

There is a well-known phenomenon wherein an excitatory CS can appear, contrary to the data on conditioned inhibition, to confer excitatory effects on a neutral CS with which it is paired. The phenomenon is, of course, second-order conditioning (Pavlov, 1927). Careful investigation of this phenomenon (e.g., Rashotte, 1981; Rescorla, 1980b), however, suggests that it is accomplished, when it occurs, other than through induction of an excitatory link between the neutral CS and the US with which the excitatory CS has been trained. A principal route, for example, is via an indirect associative link in which the two CSs become associated (as SOP assumes they would), thereby allowing one to access an associate of the other through a mediational bridge. The similarity of the inhibitory learning observed following conditioned inhibition training (e.g., Pavlov, 1927) to that observed by Larew (1986) following backward conditioning, as previously summarized, remains supportive of the assumptions of SOP regarding the nature of the representational activity that may be produced by an excitatory CS versus the US with which it is associated.

III.   Essential Neural Circuit for Eyeblink Conditioning in the Rabbit

Richard Thompson focused the research of his laboratory about 15 years ago (e.g., Thompson *et al.*, 1976) on the neurobiological substrates of Pavlovian eyeblink conditioning in the rabbit. Work with this conditioning preparation was initiated by Kenneth Goodrich, Leonard Ross, and Allan Wagner while collaborating on studies of eyeblink conditioning in the human (Goodrich, Ross, & Wagner, 1957, 1959) at the University of Iowa and was continued by them in conditioning laboratories at Yale (e.g., Thomas & Wagner, 1964) and Wisconsin (e.g., Frey & Ross, 1967). The preparation was further developed and parametrically explored in careful systematic fashion by Isidore Gormezano and his students (see Patterson & Romano, 1987, for a review of this development; see Schneiderman, Fuentes, & Gormezano, 1962, for the first published report of conditioning). It has proved useful in the evaluation of a variety of theoretical issues (e.g., Rescorla & Wagner, 1972; Wagner, 1969a, 1969b, 1971; Wagner, Logan, Haberlandt, & Price, 1968; Wagner & Rescorla, 1972; Wagner, Rudy, & Whitlow, 1973; Wagner & Terry, 1975; Whitlow & Wagner, 1972). The rabbit rarely blinks its eyes, unless directly provoked. However, when a CS, which is typically a brief tone, light, or vibrotactile stimulus, is appropriately paired with a US, which is a puff of air to the cornea or an electric shock to the skin surrounding the eye, the rabbit develops an eyeblink CR (measured as one of a complex of

behaviors, including the bulbar retractor response, the consequent extension of the nictitating membrane over the eye, and the closure of the outer
eyelid) that is similar to the unconditioned reactions to the US.

The essential neural circuit that Thompson (1986) has proposed to be
revealed by the research of his laboratory is shown in Fig. 7. There are,
surely, issues that could be taken with it, given the full range of available
data. There will, even more surely, be modifications required as further
information accumulates in this rapidly advancing research area. Thompson's characterization is, however, a reasonable summary of what we
know at this time about the basic neural circuit involved in eyeblink conditioning in the rabbit. In the following, we describe the brain structures
and anatomical pathways depicted in Fig. 7 and briefly review the find-

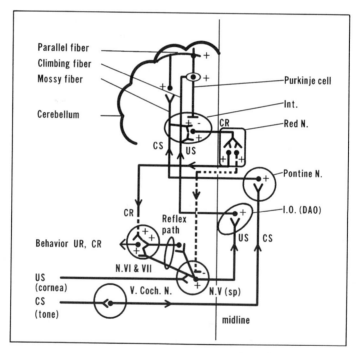

Fig. 7.   Simplified schematic of hypothetical circuit responsible for the conditioned and
unconditioned eyeblink response and other discrete, striated-muscle responses in the rabbit.
The circuit depicts brain structures and pathways making up the CS pathway for auditory
stimuli, the US pathway for corneal air puff, and the pathways for generating the CR and
UR. Abbreviations: I.O. (DAO), inferior olive (dorsal accessory olive); Int., interpositus
nucleus; N.V (sp), spinal fifth (trigeminal) cranial nuclei; N. VI, accessory sixth (abducens)
cranial nucleus; N. VII, seventh (facial) cranial nucleus; V. Coch. N., ventral cochlear
nucleus. From Thompson (1986). Copyright © 1986 by the AAAS. Reprinted with
permission.

ings of neurophysiological experiments that implicate the various components in the Pavlovian conditioning phenomena of interest.

A. THE RESPONSE

The relevant motor nuclei, the accessory sixth and seventh, are shown in the lower left portion of Fig. 7. The eyeblink, nictitating membrane, and/or bulbar retractor responses that are measured are ultimately attributable to activity in these cranial motor nuclei (e.g., Berthier, 1981; Cegavske, Thompson, Patterson, & Gormezano, 1976; Courville, 1966; Evinger, Shaw, Peck, Manning, & Baker, 1984; T. S. Gray, McMaster, Harvey, & Gormezano, 1981; Marek, McMaster, Gormezano, & Harvey, 1984).

B. THE US–UR CIRCUIT

The US, which is assumed here to be a corneal air puff, produces its effects through the spinal nuclei of the trigeminal (fifth) nerve. Results from behavioral, neuroanatomical tracing, stimulation, lesioning, and recording experiments suggest that activation of these structures has consequences for the eyeblink response through two pathways, one relatively direct, the other more circuitous.

1. The Relatively Direct Path

As can be seen in Fig. 7, there are monosynaptic connections between the trigeminal sensory neurons and the motor nuclei of the accessory sixth and the seventh cranial nerves as well as dysynaptic connections between the same nuclei via additional brainstem structures (Harvey et al., 1984; Hiraoka & Shimamura, 1977; Holstege, Tan, Van Ham, & Graveland, 1986; Sanes & Ison, 1979). These routes are what Thompson labels the "reflex path." They provide a relatively direct pathway for elicitation of the eyeblink response by the US.

2. The Relatively Circuitous Path

The relatively circuitous path involves a sequence of brain stem and cerebellar structures. As indicated in Fig. 7, the trigeminal spinal nuclei project to the contralateral inferior olive. Climbing fibers from the inferior olive project back across the midline to the cerebellum, where they contact Purkinje cells in the cerebellar cortex (e.g., to Larsell's HVI) (Yeo, Hardiman, & Glickstein, 1985c) and send collaterals to cell bodies in the interpositus nucleus (e.g., Eccles, Ito, & Szentagothai, 1967; Ikeda & Matsushita, 1974). The output cells of the interpositus nucleus project through the superior cerebellar peduncle to the contralateral red nucleus, which sends projections, via a descending pathway, back across the midline to the motor nuclei (see Houk & Gibson, 1987; Robinson, Houk, & Gibson, 1987; Mauk *et al.,* 1986; McCormick, Steinmetz, & Thompson, 1985). For reasons that will be apparent, Thompson labels the path from the interpositus nucleus to the motor nuclei the "CR" pathway. However, it is important to recognize that this pathway can be regarded as an obligatory branch of the UR pathway. Evidence consistent with this recognition comes from findings that in untrained animals, electrical stimulation in certain regions of the inferior olive (dorsal accessory olive, DAO) produces discrete, striated-muscle responses which are dependent on the integrity of the circuit described, for example, on the integrity of the descending rubral pathway from the red nucleus (Mauk *et al.,* 1986, but see Gibson & Chen, 1988). Somatotopic maps in the DAO have been shown to be preserved in projections to the interpositus nucleus and from the interpositus to the red nucleus (Gellman, Houk, & Gibson, 1983; Gibson, Robinson, Alam, & Houk, 1987). Eyeblink responses can be specifically elicited by stimulation of the rostromedial edge of the DAO (Mauk *et al.,* 1986).

Recent findings by J. Steinmetz (personal communication) lend additional support to the proposal that this pathway contributes a late component to the eyeblink UR. He was able to elicit discrete eyeblink responses reliably by stimulating the DAO using parameters (a single .3-msec, 150-μA pulse) that were more nearly "physiological" than those of Mauk et al. (1986). In this case, the latency of the elicited eyeblink response was on the order of 70 msec, which is a relatively delayed response compared to onset latencies of 20 msec commonly observed for eyeblink responses to an air puff US.

More direct evidence that the circuitous pathway contributes to the eyeblink UR comes from the findings of Welsh and Harvey (1989), who assessed the effects of interpositus lesions on eyeblink CRs and URs. To evaluate the effects of the lesion on the UR, they assessed responding over a wide range of US intensities. In agreement with the observations of McCormick *et al.* (1982), they saw no effects of the lesion on the peak amplitude of the UR to the relatively intense US that was used in the prior conditioning. However, a decremental effect of the lesion could be seen in the peak amplitude URs to weaker-intensity air puff USs.

Given the present characterization of US processing, one might expect to see multiple components of the UR in measures such as eye muscle electromyographic (EMG) activity or motor neuron unit activity and to have the several components differentially decreased via specific lesions. As we previously noted, in a few studies of the human eyeblink response, investigators have identified three components in EMG recordings of eyeblink URs: R_1, which has a latency of approximately 10 msec, R_2, with a latency of 30–40 msec, and R_3, with a latency of approximately 70 msec (Penders & Delwaide, 1973; Sanes & Ison, 1979). It is generally assumed that R_1 and R_2 are generated through what we have designated as the relatively direct pathway, that is, the monosynaptic and dysynaptic projections from the spinal nuclei. The intervening brain structures and pathways responsible for the R_3 component of the UR are unknown, but it is possible that this component originates in the circuitous pathway. Given the larger number of intervening structures in the circuitous pathway in comparison to the relatively direct pathway, we would expect greater variability in the latency and occurrence of the R_3, compared to the R_1 and R_2 components. It remains to be determined whether interpositus lesions that diminish a global UR measure such as peak amplitude (Welsh & Harvey, 1989) have a primary effect through a diminished R_3.

C.   The CS–CR Circuit

The most important thing that we know about the circuitous pathway is that the CR is driven by the cerebellum → red nucleus → motor nucleus portion of the pathway. If an animal is conditioned so that it gives regular eyeblink CRs to, say, a tone CS, lesions to the ipsilateral interpositus nucleus, or the descending rubral pathway (the red nucleus contralateral to the conditioned eye) immediately abolish the CR and make reacquisition impossible (Clark, McCormick, Lavond, & Thompson, 1984; Haley, Lavond, & Thompson, 1983; Lavond, Hembree, & Thompson, 1985; McCormick & Thompson, 1983; McCormick et al., 1981; McCormick, Clark, Lavond, & Thompson, 1982; Madden, Haley, Barchas, & Thompson, 1983; Rosenfield & Moore, 1983; Rosenfield, Devydaitis, & Moore, 1985; Yeo, Hardiman, & Glickstein, 1985a). Figure 8 shows the effects of lesioning the left lateral cerebellum on retention of conditioned eyeblink responses in the rabbit (McCormick, Clark, Lavond, & Thompson, 1982). At the end of the training sequence, in which a tone CS was paired with an air puff US to the left eye, the tone CS elicited large amplitude CRs and the US large URs. After the left interpositus and dentate nuclei and overlying cortex were lesioned, the CR was abolished and did not recover, even with extended training (P1–P4). The UR amplitude remained at near prelesion levels throughout, suggesting that the loss of CRs was not due to general motor impairments. When the airpuff was switched to the right eye (contralateral to the lesioned side), the tone CS quickly developed the ability to elicit a CR at the right eye, indicating that the loss of the CR in sessions P1–P4 was not due to general hearing impair-

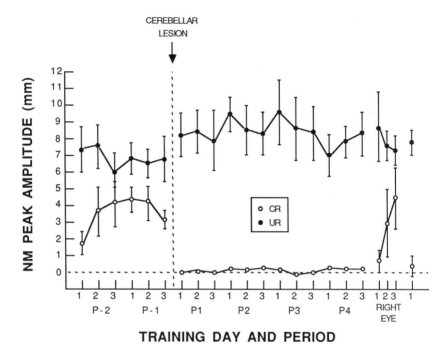

Fig. 8. Effects of lesioning the left lateral cerebellum on the learned NM–eyelid response. Open circles represent the peak amplitude of the conditioned response (CR) and
filled circles the peak amplitude of the unconditioned response (UR). All training was to the
left eye (ipsilateral to lesion) except where labeled ("Right Eye"). Sessions P-2 and P-1
show initial learning on the two days prior to the lesion. Sessions P1–P4 show the results
of 4 days of postoperative training to the left eye. After training on the right eye where
indicated, subjects received an additional day of training to the left eye. Drawn from McCormick, Clark, Lavond, & Thompson (1982); reproduced by permission.

ment. When the US was shifted back to the left eye, the tone CS still
failed to elicit detectable CRs.[1]

Converging evidence that the cerebellum is involved in CR generation
comes from multiple and single unit recordings in the lateral interpositus
nucleus showing increases in neural activity that precede and mirror the

---

[1]The study by Welsh and Harvey (1989) that has otherwise been mentioned raises an
interesting challenge to the picture of cerebellar lesion effects on eyeblink–nictitating membrane conditioned responses shown in Fig. 8. In subjects in which interpositus lesions completely abolished anticipatory CRs, that is, those measured prior to the usual time of delivery of the US as depicted in Fig. 8, Welsh and Harvey observed that the lesions spared
some occasional (14% of the trials) small-amplitude NM responses in the 500-msec poststim-
ulus. This may indicate a CR circuit besides that depicted in Fig. 7, or it may simply reflect
an incomplete lesion. Thompson, Steinmetz, and Chapman (1987) observed no residual CRs
following effective interpositus lesions, even when test trials were extended to 3 sec after
CS onset.

time course and amplitude of the CR (McCormick, Clark, Lavond, & Thompson, 1982; McCormick & Thompson, 1983). Similarly, patterns of neural activity that correlate with the CR can be observed in the cerebellar cortex (Donegan, Foy, & Thompson, 1985; Foy & Thompson, 1986; McCormick & Thompson, 1983). However, there is some question whether lesions in the cerebellar cortex can permanently abolish the CR (see Lavond, McCormick, & Thompson, 1984; Lavond, Steinmetz, Yokaitis, & Thompson, 1987; Yeo, Hardiman, & Glickstein, 1985b). At the present time, the contributions of the cerebellar cortex, relative to the deep nuclei, for CR development and expression are unknown.

In interpreting the results of the lesion experiments, Thompson (1986) emphasized that interpositus lesions abolish the CR without affecting the UR. (As noted above, he proposed that such observations rule out the possibility that CR abolition results from general motor impairments.) Given our above distinction between direct and circuitous UR pathways and the available evidence, we would prefer to say that the designated lesions spare that portion of the UR which is generated through the reflex path and abolish the CR and late component of the UR, both of which are generated through the circuitous pathway.

The tone CS input to the eyeblink CR pathway comes over the route depicted in Fig. 7, that is, from the ventral cochlear nucleus to pontine nuclei (lateral and dorsolateral) that in turn send mossy fibers which terminate in the cerebellum (Steinmetz, Lavond, & Thompson, 1985; Steinmetz et al., 1987). [Mossy fibers project to the cerebellar cortex (synapsing onto granule cells, which contact Purkinje cells through parallel fibers) and appear to send collaterals to the interpositus nucleus (Gerrits & Voogd, 1987; Kitai, McCrea, Preston, & Bishop, 1977; but see P. Brodal, Deitrich, & Walberg, 1986).] Steinmetz, Logan, Rosen, Lavond, and Thompson (1986) have shown that bilateral lesions of the lateral pontine nucleus selectively abolish the CR to a tone CS, while leaving the CR to a light CS unaffected.

D. THE REINFORCEMENT PATHWAY

Neural network models of conditioning typically assume that plasticity responsible for the development of the CR occurs at sites of CS and US convergence (e.g., Donegan, Gluck, & Thompson, this volume; Klopf, 1987; Sutton & Barto, 1981). Work with the rabbit eyeblink preparation from Thompson's laboratory suggests that the information about US occurrence critical for reinforcement converges on the CS–CR pathway through the circuitous circuit: through the trigeminal nuclei → dorsal accessory olive → cerebellum pathway. Conditioning of the eyeblink and other discrete, striated-muscle responses can be obtained using electrical stimulation of the DAO as the US (Mauk *et al.*, 1986, Steinmetz *et al.*, 1985). These authors found that repeated pairings of a tone CS with DAO stimulation resulted in the development of a conditioned response to the tone that was identical to the response elicited by DAO stimulation, while pairings involving stimulation just above or below the DAO that also elicited discrete responses did not support conditioning. Important to an analysis of the eyeblink conditioning circuitry is the observation that stimulation of the interpositus nucleus or the red nucleus, structures further along the circuitous path, does not appear to serve as an adequate US for excitatory conditioning, even though it does produce an eyeblink response (Chapman, Steinmetz, & Thompson, 1988).

There are several experiments that further implicate the DAO as a necessary element in the eyeblink conditioning circuit. Turker and Miles (1986) showed that lesioning the climbing fibers from the DAO disrupted acquisition of the conditioned eyeblink response during reinforced training. Yeo, Hardiman, and Glickstein (1986) found that large lesions in the DAO resulted in an immediate profound decrement in a previously established conditioned response. A most instructive pattern of findings was reported by Mauk, Steinmetz, and Thompson (1986) and by McCormick, Steinmetz, and Thompson (1985). These authors showed that smaller, more focal lesions in the DAO in well-trained animals had little immediate effect on the CR, but that with continued assessment over a series of CS–US pairings following the lesion, the CR gradually disappeared (Mauk, Steinmetz, & Thompson, 1986; McCormick *et al.*, 1985). The findings of McCormick *et al.* (1985) are shown in Fig. 9. Rabbits in two groups initially received three sessions of CS–US pairings. Subjects' performance on the last of these sessions is shown above P3 in Fig. 9. Subjects in the lesion group then received electrolytic lesions of the DAO contralateral to the side of US delivery and were allowed to recover. Subsequently, both groups received several test sessions. Subjects in the control group received extinction training (i.e., CS-alone presentations), while subjects in the lesion group continued to receive CS–US pairings. As expected, CRs from subjects in the control group extinguished. Importantly, the CRs from subjects in the lesion group also declined, even through they continued to receive CS–US pairings. After lesioning the DAO, it appears as though the US is no longer reinforcing, so that a previously acquired CR will extinguish. It is on the basis of such observations that Thompson has referred to the inferior olive → cerebellum pathway as the reinforcement pathway.

E. RECURRENT INHIBITION

Figure 7 shows an inhibitory pathway (dashed line) from the red nucleus to the region of the trigeminal spinal nuclei. Evidence that this path-

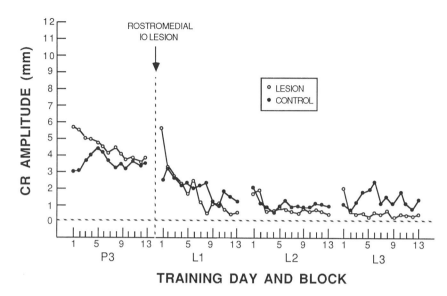

TRAINING DAY AND BLOCK

Fig. 9. Effect of lesioning the rostromedial inferior olive complex on the retention of the classically conditioned nictitating membrane (NM) response. P3 represents the average peak amplitude of the conditioned response (CR) in each of the 13 nine-trial blocks occurring in the training session before the lesion. In postlesion training (L1–L3), subjects in the control group (filled circles) received CS-alone presentations while subjects in the lesion groups (open circles) continued to have the CS paired with the air puff US. Drawn from McCormick, Steinmetz, & Thompson (1985); reproduced by permission.

way is inhibitory comes from findings of Dostrovsky and colleagues that red nucleus stimulation inhibits stimulus-evoked responses in the trigeminal spinal nuclei in cats (K. D. Davis & Dostrovsky, 1986; B. G. Gray & Dostrovsky, 1971); the stimuli included touching and pinching the facial skin and probing of tooth pulp. Similarly, Weiss, McCurdy, Houk, & Gibson (1985) demonstrated that red nucleus stimulation inhibits the response of cells in the DAO to somatosensory input from the limbs and body. They proposed that the red nucleus (magnocellular division) exerts these effects on DAO activity through inhibitory projections to the dorsal column nuclei, the cuneate nucleus in particular. These findings are supportive of the proposal that the red nucleus feedback loop in Fig. 7 is inhibitory, since the trigeminal spinal nuclei are analogous to the dorsal column nuclei for processing somatosensory input from the face and neck.

IV. The Relationship of SOP to the Eyeblink Circuit

As previously noted, an abstract theory such as SOP is not, in principle, partial to any particular neurobiological realization. The A1 and A2 processes could, conceivably, be characteristics of individual neurons, or of unstructured populations of like neurons. However, the relationship between what is known about the essential circuit for eyeblink conditioning in the rabbit, on the one hand, and the major tenets of SOP, on the other hand, might suggest that the fictions of SOP could best be identified with the behavior of complex neuronal circuits made up of specialized interactive components. Figure 10 is intended to indicate a plausible set of correspondences between SOP and the eyeblink conditioning circuit proposed by Thompson and colleagues. The general approach will likely have been anticipated from the preceding outline of the principal features of SOP and the essentials of the eyeblink circuit. The specific relationships can be succinctly summarized as follows.

A. The A1 Process

The A1 process of the US, which corresponds to the initial stages of processing of that stimulus, can be presumed to involve the activity of

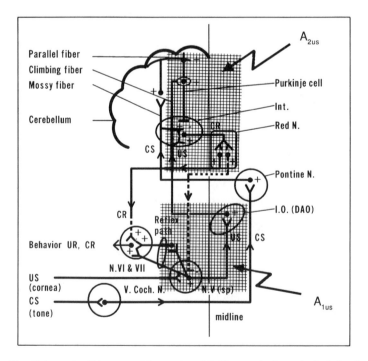

Fig. 10. Schematic of the potential mapping of SOP upon the hypothetical circuit underlying the rabbit conditioned eyeblink response (see Fig. 7). Segments of the US pathway that are taken to correspond to the A1 activation state are shown in the lower shaded area, and the segments of the US pathway that are taken to correspond to the A2 activation state are shown in the upper shaded area.

the trigeminal spinal nuclei, the inferior olive, and climbing fiber input to the cerebellar cortex and deep nuclei. Activity in the sensory components of the trigeminal nerve drives the prominent short-latency UR through the reflex (direct) pathway. Activity in the inferior olive and climbing fiber input to the cerebellar cortex and deep nuclei (the reinforcement pathway), in appropriate pairing with activity in CS pathways, can support excitatory associative learning.

B. THE A2 PROCESS

The A2 process of the US can be assumed to involve the activity of the components of the US–UR circuit in the cerebellum receiving input from the climbing fibers, such as the cells in the interpositus nucleus and the consequent red nucleus. Together, activity in these components of the circuit should drive a longer-latency UR through the more circuitous path and, following conditioning, are responsible for the CR. At present, we cannot be confident where the A1 process stops and the A2 process begins in the cerebellum. This is in part due to our being noncommittal on whether plasticity involved in CR development occurs in the cerebellar cortex, deep nuclei, or both: an issue that has not yet been resolved experimentally.[2]

The A2 process is assumed to have a refractory-like effect on the A1 process, that is, to reduce the ability of the US to generate A1 activity. The inhibitory pathway from the red nucleus to the trigeminal spinal nuclei is an obvious candidate for refractory-like effects on US processing. When an appropriate CS or US activates the red nucleus and generates responding (CR or UR) through the circuitous path, recurrent inhibitory feedback from the red nucleus should act to inhibit subsequent activity in both the reinforcement pathway and the reflex pathway. The circuit is reminiscent of the general manner in which corollary discharges from motor commands feed back to modulate processing of expected stimuli (Bell, Libouban, & Szabo, 1983; Houk & Gibson, 1987).

---

[2]The experimental evidence we have cited points to the cerebellum as a likely structure in which plasticity responsible for the development of conditioned skeletal muscle responses occurs. Although there is no direct evidence that plasticity necessary for the development of the eyeblink CR occurs in the cerebellum, we assume that this is the case for purposes of evaluating the potential capacities of the circuit. We also acknowledge that plasticity contributing to CR development could also occur in structures within the CS–CR pathway afferent to the cerebellum that receive convergent input from the trigeminal nuclei. Although we will not focus on such possibilities, the analysis that we have provided would not change substantially if they also play a role in conditioning.

C. Extrapolations

The preceding, somewhat obvious identifications allow one to give a neurobiological interpretation to a number of the basic conditioning phenomena that are summarized by the abstractions of SOP. What is missing in this picture, thus far, is any direct coverage of the tenets of SOP regarding inhibitory learning. The reason for this is that the possible involvement of the cerebellar–brain stem circuit in inhibitory learning has not been experimentally evaluated. Indeed, there has been little physiological work regarding neural mechanisms of conditioned inhibition (but see Mis, 1977). In this section we nonetheless suggest some extensions of the hypothesized circuit that might allow it, in principle, to generate conditioned inhibition. We can then consider the potential consequences for a variety of Pavlovian phenomena of several physiological manipulations calculated to influence structures associated with the A2 state of US processing. Of particular interest is the way such manipulations might influence both the development of inhibition and the expression of refractory-like effects, as reflected in both conditioning and UR generation.

1. A Possible Locus of Conditioned Inhibition

In spite of the lack of evidence, we can make some educated guesses, guided by SOP, about how an extended version of the circuit in Fig. 7 might be implicated in the phenomena of conditioned inhibition. SOP assumes that inhibitory learning is occasioned by the pairing of a CS with the A2 process of a US, which can be generated by the US itself or by an excitatory CS. Given our identification of the A2 state of US processing with the cerebellum → red nucleus → motor nuclei pathway, one would expect that activity within this branch of the network, occurring in conjunction with activation of CS pathways associated with the A1 state of CS processing, would result in the CS acquiring inhibitory properties. As previously noted, excitatory conditioning is assumed to result from converging activation of CS pathways (here presumably involving mossy fiber input) and US pathways corresponding to the A1 state (here presumably involving climbing fiber input from the inferior olive). It is possible that inhibitory conditioning results from converging activation of the same CS pathways and feedback from structures within the US pathway corresponding to the A2 state (e.g., feedback from the red nucleus to the cerebellum, either directly or via the lateral reticular nucleus) (A. Brodal, 1981). Thus, within the cerebellum, one might find processes underlying both excitatory and inhibitory conditioning. The inhibitory properties of the CS would decrease the ability of it and other concurrent CSs to activate the A2 segments of the US pathway.

2. Experimental Evaluations

The speculations we have allowed ourselves lead to some rather inter- esting experimental possibilities. For example, if the red nucleus has the properties of the A2 segment of the US pathway as described above, then one effect of temporarily inactivating the red nucleus (e.g., pharmacologi- cally or via a cryoblock) should be to prevent activation of the inhibitory feedback loop to the trigeminal nuclei. This should disrupt phenomena that SOP associates with the refractory effects of the A2 state on A1 acti- vation by the US. For example, red nucleus inactivation should interfere with the ability of a US presentation to generate a transient decrement in the amplitude of the eyeblink UR, as observed by Pfautz (1980), as well as interfering with the ability of a pretrained CS to produce a conditioned diminution of the eyeblink UR, as observed by Donegan (1981). Similarly, the decremental effects on conditioning of preceding each CS–US pairing with a presentation of the US, as reported by Terry (1976) should be re- duced by red nucleus inactivation. By the same logic, inactivating the red nucleus during the compound phase of a blocking experiment should interfere with the ability of the pretrained CS to block conditioning to the neutral, target CS with which it appears in compound. Conversely, stimulating the red nucleus prior to a US presentation should decrease the US's ability to generate a UR and diminish its ability to promote con- ditioning to CSs with which it is paired.

Red nucleus inactivation, in addition to disrupting the inhibitory path- way to the trigeminal nuclei, may also disrupt feedback from the red nu- cleus to the cerebellum (which may be direct or via the lateral reticular nucleus). We have previously speculated that a feedback loop to the cere- bellum may be responsible for strengthening inhibitory CS–US associa- tions. If feedback from the red nucleus to the cerebellum does indeed play such a role, then inactivating the red nucleus during extinction train- ing should prevent the CS from activating processes that are necessary to decrease excitatory strength and thus, should protect the CS from ex- tinction. Similarly, inactivation of the red nucleus should prevent a neu- tral CS from becoming a conditioned inhibitor when it is nonreinforced in compound with a previously trained excitatory CS or prevent a neutral CS from becoming an inhibitor when it is paired with a US in an interme- diate backward relationship (Larew, 1986). Conversely, stimulating the red nucleus in an appropriate temporal relationship should facilitate ex- tinction of a previously reinforced CS and cause a neutral CS to acquire conditioned inhibitory properties. We previously noted that stimulation of the red nucleus (or interpositus nucleus), even though it elicits an eye- blink response, is not an effective US for promoting excitatory conditioning of striated muscle responses (Chapman *et al.*, 1985; Chapman & Thompson, 1986). The present view would encourage an evaluation of whether stimulating these structures, taken to correspond to the A2 state of the US pathway, would not, to the contrary, support inhibitory associative learning.

In the preceding examples we have considered how one or the other of the presumed feedback loops from the red nucleus might play a role in Pavlovian conditioning phenomena. It should be clear that in many cases both of these feedback processes may, theoretically, be involved. The most basic instance is the very process of acquisition of Pavlovian conditioned responding, in which one typically observes a negatively accelerating increase in most measures of responding over trials, eventually reaching some asymptote. What produces the slowing of acquisition, that is, the finding that the increments produced by a training trial decrease as the response strength increases? In the rabbit eyeblink preparation we would expect that, over the course of repeated CS–US pairings, the ability of the CS to generate activity in the interpositus → red nucleus → motor nuclei pathway will increase. This should have two consequences in addition to increasing the CR tendency. First, there should be an increased opportunity for inhibition to accrue to the CS. This is assumed to result from the CS's acquired ability to activate the red nucleus → cerebellum feedback loops, as in the preceding analysis of conditioned inhibition. On reinforced trials, these inhibitory effects may be largely masked by the increments in excitatory strength produced by the US but should occur nonetheless. Second, the US should be rendered less effective in promoting increments in the CS's associative strength. This is assumed to result from the CS's acquired ability to activate the red nucleus → trigeminal nuclei feedback loop.

If the circuit indeed behaves in this manner, then inactivation of the red nucleus should allow for more rapid net excitatory conditioning over the course of repeated CS–US pairings. That is, as the CS acquires associative strength, it will not then damp US evoked activity in the spinal nuclei and will not activate feedback loops responsible for decreasing its associative strength. Thus, with the red nucleus inactivated during training, we should see a kind of supranormal conditioning when responding to the CS is subsequently tested with the red nucleus functioning normally. Behavioral experiments have produced such supranormal conditioning by reinforcing a neutral, target CS in compound with a conditioned inhibitor (Rescorla, 1971; Wagner, 1971). Conditioning to the target stimulus (when tested alone) has been observed to be more rapid compared to cases in which the target CS appears in compound with a second, neutral CS (Rescorla, 1971) or compared to cases in which the target CS is trained alone

(Wagner, 1971). According to SOP, the conditioned inhibitor diminishes the ability of the target CS to activate the A2 portion of the US pathway. Inactivation of the red nucleus should have a similar effect. In contrast to supranormal conditioning with red nucleus inactivation, the mapping of SOP outlined above suggests that a retardation of acquisition could be obtained by stimulating the red nucleus shortly before each training trial. The stimulation should be equivalent to presenting a pretrained CS in compound, as in a blocking experiment (Kamin, 1968), or to preceding a training trial by the same US (Terry, 1976), both of which retard conditioning.

In the above examples, we have emphasized, for expository purposes, how activation of red nucleus feedback loops may be responsible for many phenomena of Pavlovian conditioning that SOP ties to activation of the A2 state of the US representation. However, it should be clear that these phenomena could, in principle, be controlled by feedback from structures other than the red nucleus that also correspond to the A2 portion of the US–UR pathway.[3] Our speculations concerning the red nucleus simply illustrate how we may be guided in experiments that can evaluate the roles of this and allied structures in phenomena such as blocking, conditioned inhibition, and supranormal conditioning.

D. THEORETICAL INTEGRATION

The utility of the mapping of SOP onto the neural circuit involved in eyeblink conditioning in the rabbit can be measured, in part, by its ability to suggest extrapolations upon the neural circuit that might allow it to address a broader range of the known Pavlovian conditioning phenomena than have yet been neurophysiologically investigated. Another measure is how it advances the manner of abstract conceptualization of Pavlovian conditioning instantiated by SOP. In this regard, we find that the mapping invites a network expression of the principles of SOP, which may now

[3]For example, the reinforcement effects of a US that may result from activation of the inferior olive might also be diminished by a projection from the interpositus nucleus to the DAO (not shown in Fig. 7) which is thought to be inhibitory (Andersson & Hesslow, 1986; Andersson, Gorwicz, & Hesslow, 1987). This pathway would have the same damping effect as the red nucleus feedback loop on the reinforcement capacities of the US but would not affect the immediate unconditioned response to the US mediated through the direct reflex pathway. If this is the case, then both pathways could contribute to the refractory effects on A1 processing (DAO activation) produced by activation of the cerebellar → red nucleus → motor nuclei pathway prior to US presentation. Consequently, inactivating the red nucleus would presumably attenuate blocking and a conditioned diminution of the UR by preventing the pretrained CS from damping US-evoked activity in the trigeminal spinal nuclei, whereas inactivating the interpositus → DAO pathway would attenuate a blocking effect but not a conditioned diminution of the UR.

seem somewhat more intuitive than their original, stochastic rendering. Figure 11 illustrates one such conceptualization, to which we are guided by the rabbit eyeblink conditioning circuit as well as some theoretical pointings following from cellular investigations of conditioning in *Aplysia* (e.g., Hawkins, Abrams, Carew, & Kandel, 1983).

Figure 11 depicts a CS representation and a US representation, as did Fig. 1. In this case, however, each stimulus is represented by a columnar organization, with a set of initial units, labeled "A1," followed by set of secondary units, labeled "A2." Unconditioned activity dynamics produced by the stimulus that a column represents is taken to involve the activation of some number of A1 units, which in turn activate corresponding A2 units. Active units are presumed to revert to inactivity not only as a result of intrinsic factors but as a result of lateral inhibition by similar-level units in other stimulus columns. This notion of lateral inhibition is consistent both with the original rationalization that the decay parameters p_{d1} and p_{d2} reflect limitations on the number of stimulus representations

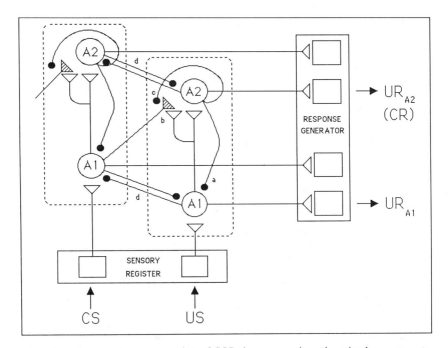

Fig. 11.   A network representation of SOP that summarizes the stimulus representations, associative connections, activation states necessary for excitatory and inhibitory conditioning, and pathways for associative modulation of stimulus processing assumed by the model.

that can be active at any moment (Wagner, 1981) and with the experimental evidence for "distractor effects" on stimulus processing (e.g., Whitlow, 1975). The inhibition is indicated in Fig. 11 by the links labeled "d." It would be assumed that the lateral inhibition is greater between A1 units than between A2 units, giving rise to the specification of SOP that p_{d1} is larger than p_{d2} (Wagner, 1981). Intrinsic to each column are recurrent inhibitory collaterals (labeled "a") from the A2 units to the A1 units. This negative feedback loop is, of course, analogous to the presumed inhibitory loop from the red nucleus to the trigeminal spinal nuclei in the rabbit eyeblink conditioning circuit and is theoretically responsible for the refractory-like characteristics inherent to representational dynamics.

The modifiable connections that are the conventional objects of interest in Pavlovian conditioning experiments are taken to be excitatory and inhibitory links that join the A1 units of CS columns with the A2 units of US columns. They are represented by a single, "mixed" association pathway in Fig. 11. SOP supposes that the CS–US link is made more excitatory as a result of concurrent activation of the A1 process of the CS and the A1 process of the US. The network rendition in Fig. 11 translates this to be the more specific result of the concurrent activation of the modifiable association pathway, driven by the A1 units of the CS, and a "presynaptic" excitatory termination on this link, driven by the A1 units of the US as indicated at the point labeled "b." The abstract relationship that is thus made responsible for excitatory conditioning is patterned after the empirical relationship that Hawkins *et al.* (1983) and Walters and Byrne (1983) have found adequate to produce increments in synaptic efficacy in *Aplysia.* We could as well assume some other mechanism, but we suppose that the "activity dependent synaptic facilitation" (Hawkins *et al.,* 1983) identified in invertebrates is likely to be instantiated in associative learning in vertebrates, and it is a plausible candidate for our purposes.

SOP also supposes that the net excitatory strength of a CS–US link is diminished, and can be made inhibitory, as a result of concurrent activation of the A1 process of the CS and the A2 process of the US. The network rendition in Fig. 11 translates this to be the more specific result of the concurrent activation of the modifiable, "mixed" association pathway, driven by the A1 units of the CS, and a "presynaptic" inhibitory termination on this link from a recurrent collateral driven by the A2 units of the US, as indicated at the point labeled "c." The abstract relationship that is thus made responsible for inhibitory learning is similar, as SOP would suggest it to be, to that presumed responsible for excitatory learning. Mackey *et al.* (1987) and Belardetti, Kandel, and Siegelbaum (1987), in studies with *Aplysia,* have demonstrated that cells in a branch of a US

FRMFamine, which can hyperpolarize the sensory neurons and depress transmitter release. Small, Kandel, and Hawkins (1989) have demonstrated that this inhibitory effect of FRMFamine can be augmented by prior activity in the sensory neuron. It is reasonable to consider that some form of activity-dependent synaptic inhibition may be one candidate mechanism for inhibitory associative learning.

Finally, Fig. 11 makes the general behavior generation rules of SOP explicit by indicating that the A1 and the A2 units of a stimulus representation may each generate responses, with the response to the A2 units being designated as a secondary UR or as a CR, depending on how the A2 units were activated. With the general assumptions of SOP articulated in this manner, we expect that many readers will find it easier to generate some of the behavioral predictions summarized in an earlier section: for example, the pattern of unconditioned and conditioned responding, the refractory-like effects that may be produced by USs and excitatory CSs, and the conditions that produce excitatory versus inhibitory conditioning. Nevertheless, the schematization, without appropriate quantitative specification, would not allow such detailed predictions as those depicted in Fig. 2, which have been important to our conviction concerning the usefulness of SOP (e.g., Donegan & Wagner, 1987; Mazur & Wagner, 1982; Wagner & Larew, 1985). We have begun work on a quantitative, network variation on SOP, patterned after Fig. 11, but cannot yet evaluate the effort. Our colleague, J. W. Whitlow, however, has developed a quantitative, network rendition of SOP (Whitlow, 1986) which has a family relationship to the network in Fig. 11 and which deserves scrutiny.

V. Concluding Comments

There is a satisfying fit between certain of the tenets of SOP and the neuronal circuit, as we know it, for eyeblink conditioning in the rabbit. There must, of course, be a fit at some level. SOP was developed to present an efficient summary of some of the important behavioral regularities in Pavlovian conditioning, and the eyeblink circuit has been elucidated by searching for structures that might be implicated in certain of the basic phenomena of Pavlovian conditioning observed in the particular preparation under consideration. What is satisfying is not only the ease with which the abstract formulation and the neuronal circuit can be related to each other but the conceptual synergy that results.

A model such as SOP is designed to have some generality across different conditioning preparations, with the level of abstraction of the model largely dictated by its scope. The usefulness of the identifications that have been made between the tenets of SOP and the essential neural circuit for eyeblink conditioning should thus extend beyond suggestions for research on the eyeblink circuit, as exemplified in the preceding section. The usefulness should also be apparent in suggestions concerning what aspects of the eyeblink circuit would likely be seen in the circuitry essential to other instances of Pavlovian conditioning. For example, in dealing with a considerable range of conditioning situations, SOP supposes that the A2 process universally acts to reduce the concurrent elicitablity of the A1 process by its adequate US. Refractory-like effects, such as "conditioned diminution of the UR" (Donegan, 1981), "blocking" (Kamin, 1968), "habituation" (Whitlow, 1975), and the like (Terry, 1976; Wagner, 1978) are extremely general. Thus, something like the descending inhibitory pathway from the red nucleus to the trigeminal spinal nuclei ought generally to show up in other Pavlovian circuits, if such pathways generally account for refractory-like effects. In dealing with the same range of conditioning situations, however, SOP implies that the overt behavior generated by A2, and thus appearing as a secondary UR and a CR, will sometimes appear to mimic the behavior generated by A1 and sometimes not. The facts of conditioning suggest that the CR (and secondary UR) is often antagonistic or "compensatory" to the prominent initial UR (Blanchard & Blanchard, 1969; Paletta & Wagner, 1986). Thus, CR circuits involving paths strictly analogous to the excitatory connection from the red nucleus to the motor nucleus that is otherwise more directly driven by the US, as seen in the case of the eyeblink, ought not to be so general. Indeed, in some preparations, one should anticipate a corresponding path that would produce behavior *antagonistic* to that otherwise driven by the US.

A neural circuit, such as that proposed by Thompson and colleagues (see Thompson, 1986) for eyeblink conditioning, is less accountable to the principles of parsimony than to the exigencies of neurophysiology. It is to be expected that some behavioral phenomena that normally covary, and hence are treated as correlaries of a unitary theoretical event, will be dissociable in neurophysiological dissection. For example, SOP assumes that the degree of "reinforcement" for excitatory conditioning occasioned by a US and the vigor of the initial component of the UR produced by the same US will covary, making them common products of the A1 process of the US node. In the eyelid circuit, however, these two effects of a US depend, as previously noted, upon the separable pathways from the trigeminal spinal nuclei to the motor nucleus and to the inferior olive. Variation in the activity of these two pathways may naturally occur together but be experimentally separable, as by lesioning the inferior olive (McCormick *et al.,* 1985). Similarly, SOP assumes that the vigor of the CR and the degree of inhibitory learning occasioned by a CS will covary, making them common products of the A2 activation of the US node. In the eyelid circuit, however, these two effects of a CS undoubtedly depend on partially separable pathways: from the red nucleus to the motor nucleus, in the case of the CR, versus (we have speculated) feedback from the red nucleus of the cerebellum, in the case of inhibitory learning. The network representation of SOP presented in Fig. 11 is the more articulate for expressing these and other distinctions suggested by the eyeblink circuit. It may also be the better prepared, outside of neurophysiological analysis, to deal with the full range of Pavlovian conditioning possibilities in different organisms.

On this note of "scope," we trust it is clear that neither the essential circuit for eyeblink conditioning proposed by Thompson (1986) nor the computational model, SOP (Wagner, 1981), which we have related are assumed to address all learning and performance effects that may be observed in studies of eyeblink conditioning in the rabbit. For example, a major class of phenomena which are not covered are those which involve the modulation of the defensive conditioned and unconditioned eyeblink responses. Brain circuits involving the hippocampus (e.g., Berger, Weikart, Bassett, & Orr, 1986; Moore & Solomon, 1984; Orr & Berger, 1981; Ross, Orr, Holland, & Berger, 1984; Solomon, 1977; Solomon & Moore, 1975), the amygdala (e.g., Davis, Hitchcock, & Rosen, 1988), and numerous other structures (e.g. Bloedel, 1973; Chan-Palay, 1977; Ito, 1984), surely impinge upon and importantly influence the cerebellar and brain stem pathways of Fig. 7. And as surely, our abstract models (e.g., Konorski, 1967) are led by the existing behavioral data (e.g., Brown, Kalish, & Farber, 1951; Davis & Astrachan, 1978; Jenkins, 1985; Rescorla, 1985) to acknowledge the possibility for modulation as well as elicitation. Wagner and Brandon (1989) have offered an extended model, AESOP, that is specifically aimed at accommodating the kind of modulating effect recognized by Thompson, Donegan, Clark, Lavond, Mamounas, Lincoln, Mauk, and McCormick (1987).

ACKNOWLEDGMENT

Preparation of this chapter was supported in part by National Science Foundation Grant BNS-8709680 to Allan R. Wagner.

REFERENCES

Andersson, G., Gorwicz, M., & Hesslow, G. (1987). Effects of bicuculline on cerebellar inhibition of the inferior olive. *Abstract, 2nd World Congress of Neuroscience, Budapest,* 1888P, p. 5631.

Andersson, G., & Hesslow, G. (1986). Evidence for an inhibitory action by cerebellar nuclear cells on the inferior olive. *Neuroscience Letters Supplement,* **26,** S1–S646.

Anisman, H., & Walter, T. G. (1973). Effects of conflicting response requirements and shock-compartment confinement on the Kamin effect in rats. *Journal of Comparative Physiological Psychology,* **77,** 240–244.

Babbini, M., & Davis, W. M. (1972). Time-dose relationships for locomotor activity effects of morphine after acute or repeated treatment. *British Journal of Pharmacology,* **46,** 213–224.

Belardetti, F., Kandel, E. R., & Siegelbaum, S. A. (1987). Neuronal inhibition by the peptide FMRFamide involves opening of S K$^+$ channels. *Nature (London),* **325,** 153–156.

Bell, C. C., Libouban, S., & Szabo, T. (1983). Pathways of the electric organ discharge command and its corollary discharges in mormyrid fish. *Journal of Comparative Neurology,* **216,** 327–338.

Berger, T. W., Weikart, C. L., Bassett, J. L., & Orr, W. B. (1986). Lesions of the retrosplenial cortex produce deficits in reversal learning of the rabbit nictitating membrane response: Implications for potential interactions between hippocampal and cerebellar brain systems. *Behavioral Neuroscience,* **100,** 802–809.

Berthier, N. E. (1981). *The unconditioned nictitating membrane response: The role of the abducens nerve and nucleus and the accessory abducens nucleus in rabbit.* Unpublished doctoral dissertation, University of Massachusetts, Amherst.

Berthier, N. E., & Moore, J. W. (1986). Cerebellar Purkinje cell activity related to the classically conditioned nictitating membrane response. *Experimental Brain Research,* **63,** 341–350.

Blanchard, R. J., & Blanchard, D. C. (1969). Crouching as an index of fear. *Journal of Comparative and Physiological Psychology,* **67,** 370–375.

Blanchard, R. J., Dielman, T. E., & Blanchard, D. C. (1968). Prolonged after effects of a single foot shock. *Psychonomic Science,* **10,** 327–328.

Bolles, R. C., & Collier, A. C. (1976). The effect of predictive cues on freezing in rats. *Animal Learning and Behavior,* **4,** 6–8.

Bolles, R. C., & Riley, A. L. (1973). Freezing as an avoidance response: Another look at the operant-respondent distinction. *Learning and Motivation,* **4,** 268–275.

Bloedel, J. R. (1973). Cerebellar afferent systems: A review. *Progress in Neurobiology,* **2,** 2–68.

Brodal, A. (1981). *Neurological anatomy.* New York: Oxford University Press.

Brodal, P., Deitrich, E., & Walberg, F. (1986). Do pontine-cerebellar mossy fibers give off collaterals to the cerebellar nuclei? An experimental study in the cat with implants of crystalline HRP-WGA. *Neuroscience Research,* **4,** 12–24.

Brown, J. S., Kalish, H. & Farber, I. E. (1951). Conditioned fear as revealed by magnitude of startle response to an auditory stimulus. *Journal of Experimental Psychology,* **41,** 317–328.

Buchanan, S. L., & Powell, D. A. (1982). Cingulate cortex: Its role in Pavlovian conditioning. *Journal of Comparative and Physiological Psychology,* **96,** 755–774.

Castellucci, V., & Kandel, E. R. (1976). An invertebrate system for the cellular study of habituation and sensitization. In T. J. Tighe & R. N. Leaton (Eds.), *Habituation: Perspectives from child development, animal behavior, and neurophysiology.* Hillsdale, NJ: Erlbaum.

Cegavske, C. F., Thompson, R. F., Patterson, M. M., & Gormezano, I. (1976). Mechanisms of efferent neuronal control of the reflex nictitating membrane response in the rabbit (*Oryctolagus cuniculus*). *Journal of Comparative and Physiological Psychology,* **90,** 411–423.

Chan-Palay, V. (1977). *Cerebellar dentate nucleus.* Berlin: Springer-Verlag.

Chapman, P. F., Steinmetz, J. E., & Thompson, R. F. (1988). Classical conditioning does not occur when direct stimulation of the red nucleus or cerebellar nuclei is the unconditioned stimulus. *Brain Research,* **442,** 97–104.

Chesher, G. B., & Chan, B. (1977). Footshock induced analgesia in mice: Its reversal by naloxone and cross tolerance with morphine. *Life Science,* **21,** 1569–1574.

Clark, G. A., McCormick, D. A., Lavond, D. G., & Thompson, R. F. (1984). Effects of lesions of cerebellar nuclei on conditioned behavioral and hippocampal neuronal responses. *Brain Research,* **291,** 125–136.

Courville, J. (1966). The nucleus of the facial nerve; the relation between cellular groups and peripheral branches of the nerve. *Brain Research,* **1,** 338–354.

Davis, K. D., & Dostrovsky, J. O. (1986). Modulatory influences of red nucleus stimulation on the somatosensory responses of cat trigeminal subnucleus oralis neurons. *Experimental Neurology,* **91,** 80–101.

Davis, M. (1970). Effects of interstimulus interval length and variability on startle-response habituation in the rat. *Journal of Comparative and Physiological Psychology,* **72,** 177–192.

Davis, M., & Astrachan, D. I. (1978). Conditioned fear and startle magnitude: Effects of different footshock or backshock intensities used in training. *Journal of Experimental Psychology: Animal Behavior Processes,* **4,** 95–103.

Davis, M., Hitchcock, J. M., & Rosen, J. B. (1988). Anxiety and the amygdala: Pharmacological and anatomical analysis of the fear-potentiated startle paradigm. In G. F. Bower (Ed.), *The psychology of learning and memory* (Vol. 21, pp. 264–306). New York: Academic Press.

Donegan, N. H. (1981). Priming-produced facilitation or diminution of responding to a Pavlovian unconditioned stimulus. *Journal of Experimental Psychology: Animal Behavioral Processes,* **7,** 295–312.

Donegan, N. H., Foy, M. R., & Thompson, R. F. (1985). Neuronal responses of the rabbit cerebellar cortex during performance of the classically conditioned eyelid response. *Society for Neuroscience Abstracts,* **11,** 245.8.

Donegan, N. H., & Wagner, A. R. (1987). Conditioned diminution and facilitation of the UR: A sometimes opponent-process interpretation. In I. Gormezano, W. F. Prokasy, & R. F. Thompson (Eds.), *Classical conditioning* (pp. 339–369). Hillsdale, NJ: Erlbaum.

Drugan, R. C., Moye, T. B., & Maier, S. F. (1982). Opioid and nonopioid forms of stress-induced analgesia: Some environmental determinants and characteristics. *Behavioral and Neural Biology,* **35,** 251–264.

Eccles, J. C., Ito, M., & Szentagothai, J. (1967). *The cerebellum as a neuronal machine.* Berlin: Springer-Verlag.

Estes, W. K., & Skinner, B. F. (1941). Some quantitative properties of anxiety. *Journal of Experimental Psychology,* **29,** 390–400.

Evinger, C., Shaw, M. D., Peck, C. K., Manning, K. A., & Baker, R. (1984). Blinking and associated eye movements in humans, guinea pigs, and rabbits. *Journal of Neurophysiology,* **52,** 323–339.

Fanselow, M. E. (1980). Conditional and unconditional components of post-shock freezing. *Pavlovian Journal of Biological Science,* **15,** 177–182.

Fanselow, M. E., & Baackes, M. P. (1982). Conditioned fear-induced opiate analgesia on the formalin test: Evidence for two aversive motivational systems. *Learning and Motivation,* **13,** 200–221.

Faneselow, M. S., & Bolles, R. C. (1979). Naloxone and shock-elicited freezing in the rat. *Journal of Comparative and Physiological Psychology,* **93,** 736–744.

Feldman, J. A., & Ballard, D. H. (1982). Connectionist models and their properties. *Cognitive Science*, **6**, 205–254.

Fog, R. (1969). Behavioral effects in rats of morphine and amphetamine and of a combination of the two drugs. *Psychopharmacologia*, **16**, 305–312.

Foy, M. R., & Thompson, R. F. (1986). Single unit analysis of Purkinje cell discharge in classically conditioned and untrained rabbits. *Society for Neuroscience Abstracts*, **12**, 518.

Frey, P. W., & Ross, L. E. (1967). Differential conditioning of the rabbit's eyelid response with an examination of Pavlov's induction hypothesis. *Journal of Comparative and Physiological Psychology*, **64**, 277–83.

Gellman, R. S., Gibson A. R., & Houk, J. C. (1985). Inferior olivary neurons in the awake cat: Detection of contact and passive body displacement. *Journal of Neurophysiology*, **54**, 40–60.

Gellman, R. S., Houk, J. C., & Gibson, A. R. (1983). Somatosensory properties of the inferior olive of the cat. *Journal of Comparative Neurology*, **215**, 228–43.

Gerrits, N. M., & Voogd, J. (1987). The projection of the nucleus reticularis tegmenti pontis and adjacent regions of the pontine nuclei to the contralateral cerebellar nuclei in the cat. *Journal of Comparative Neurology*, **258**, 52–69.

Gibson, A. R. & Chen, R. (1988). Does stimulation of the inferior olive produce movement? *Neuroscience Abstracts*, **14**, 757.

Gibson, A. R., Robinson, F. R., Alam, J., & Houk, J. C. (1987). Somato topic alignment between climbing fiber input and nuclear output of cat intermediate cerebellum. *Journal of Comparative Neurology*, **260**, 362–377.

Goodrich, K. P., Ross, L. E., & Wagner, A. R. (1957). Performance in eyelid conditioning following interpolated presentations of the UCS. *Journal of Experimental Psychology*, **53**, 214–217.

Goodrich, K. P., Ross, L. E., & Wagner, A. R. (1959). Supplementary report: Effect of interpolated UCS trials in eyelid conditioning without a ready signal. *Journal of Experimental Psychology*, **58**, 319–320.

Gormezano, I. (1972). Investigations of defense and reward conditioning in the rabbit. In A. H. Black & W. F. Prokasy (Eds.), *Classical conditioning II: Current theory and research* (pp. 151–181). New York: Appleton-Century-Crofts.

Grau, J. W. (1987). The central representation of an aversive event maintains opioid and nonopioid forms of analgesia. *Behavioral Neuroscience*, **101**(2), 272–288.

Grau, J. W., Hyson, R. L., Maier, S. F., Madden, J., & Barchas, J. D. (1981). Long-term stress-induced analgesia and activation of the opiate system. *Science*, **213**, 1409–1411.

Gray, B. G., & Dostrovsky, J. O. (1971). Modulation of the sensory responses of cat trigeminal and cuneate neurons by electrical stimulation of the red nucleus. *Society for Neuroscience Abstracts*, **9**, 247.

Gray, T. S., McMaster, S. E., Harvey, J. A., & Gormezano, I. (1981). Localization of retractor bulbi motoneurons in the rabbit. *Brain Research*, **226**, 93–106.

Haley, D. A., Lavond, D. G., & Thompson, R. F. (1983). Effects of contralateral red nuclear lesions on retention of the classically conditioned nictitating membrane/eyelid response. *Society for Neuroscience Abstracts*, **9**, 643.

Harvey, J. A., Land, T., & McMaster, S. E. (1984). Anatomical study of the rabbit's corneal-VIth nerve reflex: Connections between cornea, trigeminal sensory complex, and the abducens and accessory abducens nuclei. *Brain Research*, **301**, 307–321.

Hawkins, R. D., Abrams, T. W., Carew, T. J., & Kandel, E. R. (1983). A cellular mechanism of classical conditioning in *Aplysia:* Activity-dependent amplification of presynaptic facilitation. *Science*, **219**, 400–405.

Hawkins, R. D., & Kandel, E. R. (1984). Is there a cell-biological alphabet for simple forms of learning? *Psychological Review*, **91**, 375–391.

Heath, C. D. (1976). Simultaneous and backward fear conditioning as a function of number of CS-US pairings. *Journal of Experimental Psychology: Animal Behavior Processes*, **2**, 117–129.

Hiraoka, M., & Shimamura, M. (1977). Neural mechanisms of the corneal blinking reflex in cats. *Brain Research*, **125**, 265–275.

Holstege, G., Tan, J., van Ham, J. J., & Graveland, G. A. (1986). Anatomical observations on the afferent projections to the retractor bulbi motoneuronal cell group and other pathways possibly related to the blink reflex in the cat. *Brain Research*, **374**, 321–334.

Houk, J. C., & Gibson, A. R. (1987). Sensorimotor processing through the cerebellum. In J. S. King (Ed.), *New concepts in cerebellar neurobiology* (pp. 387–416). New York: Alan R. Liss.

Ikeda, M., & Matsushita, M. (1974). Electron microscopic observations on the spinal projections to the cerebellar nuclei in cat and rabbit. *Experientia*, **29**, 1280–1282.

Ito, M. E. (1984). *The cerebellum and neural control*. New York: Raven Press.

Jenkins, H. M. (1985). Conditioned inhibition of key pecking in the pigeon. In R. R. Miller and N. E. Spear (Eds.), *Information processing in animals: Conditioned inhibition*. Hillsdale, NJ: Earlbaum.

Kamin, L. J. (1965). Temporal and intensity characteristics of the conditioned stimulus. In W. F. Prokasy (Ed.), *Classical conditioning*. New York: Appleton-Century-Crofts.

Kamin, L. J. (1968). Attention-like processes in classical conditioning. In M. R. Jones (Ed.), *Miami symposium on the prediction of behavior: Aversive stimulation*. Miami, FL: University of Miami Press.

Kamin, L. J. (1969). Selective association and conditioning. In N. J. Mackintosh & W. K. Honig (Eds.), *Fundamental issues in associative learning*. Halifax, Nova Scotia: Dalhousie University Press.

Kimble, G. A., & Ost, J. W. P. (1961). A conditioned inhibitory process in eyelid conditioning. *Journal of Experimental Psychology*, **61**, 150–156.

Kitai, S. T., McCrea, R. A., Preston, R. J., & Bishop, G. A. (1977). Electrophysiological and horseradish peroxidase studies of precerebellar afferents to the nucleus interpositus anterior. I. Climbing fiber system. *Brain Research*, **122**, 197–214.

Klopf, H. A. (1987). *A neuronal model of classical conditioning* (Tech. Rep. AFWAL-TR-87-1139). Wright-Patterson Air Force Base, Ohio: Air Force Wright Aeronautical Laboratories.

Konorski, J. (1967). *Integrative activity of the brain*. Chicago: University of Chicago Press.

Larew, M. B. (1986). *Inhibitory learning in Pavlovian backward conditioning procedures involving a small number of US–CS trials*. Unpublished doctoral dissertation, Yale University, New Haven, CT.

Lavond, D. G., Hembree, T. L., & Thompson, R. F. (1985). Effect of kainic acid lesions of the cerebellar interpositus nucleus on eyelid conditioning in the rabbit. *Brain Research*, **326**, 179–182.

Lavond, D. G., McCormick, D. A., & Thompson, R. F. (1984). A nonrecoverable learning deficit. *Physiological Psychology*, **12**, 103–110.

Lavond, D. G., Steinmetz, J. E., Yokaitis, M. H., & Thompson, R. F. (1987). Reacquisition of classical conditioning after removal of cerebellar cortex. *Experimental Brain Research*, **67**, 569–593.

Lewis, J. W., Cannon, J. T., & Liebeskind, J. C. (1980). Involvement of central muscarinic cholinergic mechanisms in opioid stress analgesia. *Brain Research*, **270**, 289–293.

Mackey, S. L., Glanzman, D. L, Small, S. A., Dyke, A. M., Kandel, E. R., & Hawkins,

R. D. (1987). Tail shock produces inhibition as well as sensitization of the siphon-with-drawal reflex of *Aplysia:* Possible behavioral role for presynaptic inhibition mediated by the peptide Phe-Met-Arg-Phe-NH₂. *Proceedings of the National Academy of Sciences U.S.A.*, **84**, 8730–8734.

Mackintosh, N. J. (1974). *The psychology of animal learning.* New York: Academic Press.

Madden, J., Haley, D. A., Barchas, J. D., & Thompson, R. F. (1983). Microinfusion of picrotoxin into the caudal red nucleus selectively abolishes the classically conditioned eyelid response in the rabbit. *Society for Neuroscience Abstracts*, **9**, 830.

Mahoney, W. J., & Ayres, J. J. B. (1976). One-trial simultaneous and backward fear conditioning as reflected in conditioned suppression of licking in rats. *Animal Learning and Behavior*, **4**, 357–362.

Maier, S. P., Rapaport, P., & Wheatley, K. L. (1976). Conditioned inhibition and the UCS–CS interval. *Animal Learning and Behavior*, **4**, 217–220.

Marchant, R. G., III, Mis, F. W., & Moore, J. W. (1972). Conditioned inhibition of the rabbit's nictitating membrane response. *Journal of Experimental Psychology*, **95**, 408–411.

Marek, G. J., McMaster, S. E., Gormezano, I., & Harvey, J. A. (1984). The role of the accessory abducens nucleus in the rabbit nictitating membrane response. *Brain Research*, **299**, 215–229.

Mauk, M. D., Steinmetz, J. E., & Thompson, R. F. (1986). Classical conditioning using stimulation of the inferior olive as the unconditioned stimulus. *Proceedings of the National Academy of Sciences U.S.A.*, **83**, 5349–5353.

Mayer, D. J., & Watkins, L. R. (1981). The role of endorphins in endogenous pain control systems. In H. M. Emrich (Ed.), *Modern problems of pharmacopsychiatry: The role of endorphins in neuropsychiatry* (pp. 68–96). Basel: Karger.

Mazur, J. E., & Wagner, A. R. (1982). An episodic model of associative learning. In M. Commons, R. Herrnstein, & A. R. Wagner (Eds.), *Quantitative analyses of behavior: Acquisition* (Vol. 3, pp. 3–39). Cambridge, MA: Ballinger.

McCormick, D. A., Clark, G. A., Lavond, D. G., & Thompson, R. F. (1982). Initial localization of the memory trace for a basic form of learning. *Proceeding of the National Academy of Sciences U.S.A.*, **79**, 2731–2735.

McCormick, D. A., Lavond, D. G., Clark, G. A., Kettner, R. E., Rising, C. E., & Thompson, R. F. (1981). The engram found? Role of the cerebellum in classical conditioning of nictitating membrane and eyelid responses. *Bulletin of the Psychonomic Society*, **18**, 103–105.

McCormick, D. A., Lavond, D. G., Donegan, N. H., & Thompson, R. F. (1982). Neuronal responses of the rabbit brainstem and cerebellum during performance of the classically conditioned nictitating membrane/eyelid response. *Society for Neuroscience Abstracts*, **8**, 315.

McCormick D. A., Steinmetz, J. E., & Thompson, R. F. (1985). Lesions of the olivary complex cause extinction of the classically conditioned eyelid response. *Brain Research*, **359**, 120–130.

McCormick, D. A., & Thompson, R. F. (1983). Cerebellum: Essential involvement in the classically conditioned eyelid response. *Science*, **223**, 296–299.

Mis, F. W. (1977). A midbrain–brainstem circuit for conditioned inhibition of the nictitating membrane response in the rabbit *(Oryctolagus cuniculus).* *Journal of Comparative and Physiological Psychology*, **91**, 975–988.

Moore, J. W. & Solomon, P. R. (1984). Forebrain–brain stem interaction: Conditioning and the hippocampus. In L. R. Squire & N. Butters (Eds.), *Neuropsychology of Memory.* (pp. 462–472). New York: Guilford Press.

Mucha, R. F., Volkovskis, C., & Kalant, H. (1981). Conditioned increases in locomotor activity produced with morphine as an unconditioned stimulus, and the relation of conditioning to acute morphine effect and tolerance. *Journal of Comparative and Physiological Psychology,* **96,** 351–362.

Orr, W. B. & Berger, T. W. (1981). Hippocampal lesions disrupt discrimination reversal learning of the rabbit nictitating membrane response. *Society for Neuroscience Abstracts,* **7,** 648.

Paletta, M. S., & Wagner, A. R. (1986). Development of context-specific tolerance to morphine: Support for a dual-process interpretation. *Behavioral Neuroscience,* **100,** 611–623.

Patterson, M. M., & Romano, A. G., (1987). The rabbit in Pavlovian conditioning. In I. Gormezano, W. F. Prokasy, & R. F. Thompson (Eds.), *Classical conditioning.* Hillsdale, NJ: Erlbaum.

Pavlov, I. P. (1927). *Conditioned reflexes.* Oxford: Oxford University Press.

Penders, C. A., & Delwaide, P. J. (1973). Physiologic approach to the human blink reflex. In J. E. Desmedt (Ed.), *New developments in electromyography and clinical neurophysiology* (Vol. 3, pp. 649–657). Basel: Karger.

Pfautz, P. L. (1980). *Unconditioned facilitation and diminution of the unconditioned response.* Unpublished doctoral dissertation, Yale University, New Haven, CT.

Rashotte, M. E. (1981). Second-order autoshaping: Contributions to the research and theory of Pavlovian reinforcement by conditioned stimuli. In C. M. Locurto, H. S. Terrace, & J. Gibbon (Eds.), *Autoshaping and conditioning theory* (pp. 139–180). New York: Academic Press.

Rescorla, R. A. (1969). Conditioned inhibition of fear. In N. J. Mackintosh & W. K. Honig (Eds.), *Fundamental issues in associative learning.* Halifax, Nova Scotia: Dalhousie University Press.

Rescorla, R. A. (1971). Variations in the effectiveness of reinforcement and nonreinforcement following prior inhibitory conditioning. *Learning and Motivation,* **2,** 113–23.

Rescorla, R. A. (1980a). Simultaneous and successive associations in sensory preconditioning. *Journal of Experimental Psychology: Animal Behavior Processes,* **6,** 207–216.

Rescorla, R. A. (1980b). *Pavlovian second-order conditioning.* Hillsdale, NJ: Erlbaum.

Rescorla, R. A. (1985). Inhibition and facilitation. In R. R. Miller and N. E. Spear (Eds.), *Information processing in animals: Conditioned inhibition* (pp. 299–326). Hillsdale, NJ: Erlbaum.

Rescorla, R. A., & Wagner, A. R. (1972). A theory of Pavlovian conditioning: Variations in the effectiveness of reinforcement and nonreinforcement. In A. H. Black & W. F. Prokasy (Eds.), *Classical conditioning II* (pp. 64–99). New York: Appleton-Century-Crofts.

Robinson, F. R., Houk, J. C., & Gibson, A. R. (1987). Limb specific connections of the cat magnocellular red nucleus. *Journal of Comparative Neurology,* **257,** 553–577.

Rosenfield, M. E., Devydaitis, A., & Moore, J. W. (1985). Brachium conjunctivum and rubrobulbar tract: Brainstem projections of red nucleus essential for the conditioned nictitating membrane response. *Physiology and Behavior,* **34,** 751–759.

Rosenfield, M. E., & Moore, J. W. (1983). Red nucleus lesions disrupt the classically conditioned nictitating membrane response in the rabbit. *Behavioral Brain Research,* **10,** 393–398.

Ross, R. T., Orr, W. B., Holland, P. C., & Berger, T. W. (1984). Hippocampectomy disrupts acquisition and retention of learned conditioned responding. *Behavioral Neuroscience,* **98,** 211–225.

Sanes, J., & Ison, J. R. (1979). Conditioning auditory stimuli and the cutaneous eyeblink reflex in humans: Differential effects according to oligosynaptic or polysynaptic central pathways. *Electroencephalography and Clinical Neurophysiology, 47*, 546–555.

Schneiderman, N., Fuentes, I., & Gormezano, I. (1962). Acquisition and extinction of the classically conditioned eyelid response in the albino rabbit. *Science, 136*, 650–652.

Schneiderman, N., & Gormezano, I. (1964). Conditioning of the nictitating membrane of the rabbit as a function of CS-US interval. *Journal of Comparative and Physiological Psychology, 57*, 188–195.

Schull, J. (1979). A conditioned opponent theory of Pavlovian conditioning and habituation. In G. H. Bower (Ed.), *The psychology of learning and motivation* (Vol. 13, pp. 57–90). New York: Academic Press.

Siegel, S. (1979). The role of conditioning in drug tolerance, In J. D. Keehn (Ed.), *Psychopathology in animals: Research applications* (pp. 143–168). New York: Academic Press.

Siegel, S. (1981). Classical conditioning, drug tolerance, and drug dependence. In Y. Israel, F. B. Sloser, H. Kalant, R. E. Popham, W. Schmidt, & R. G. Smart (Eds.), *Research advances in alcohol and drug abuse* (Vol. 7, pp. 207–246). New York: Plenum.

Small, S. A., Kandel, E. R., & Hawkins, R. A. (1989). Activity-dependent enhancement of presynaptic inhibition in *Aplysia* sensory neurons. *Science, 243*, 1603–1606.

Solomon, P. R. (1977). Role of the hippocampus in blocking and conditioned inhibition of the rabbit's nictitating membrane response. *Journal of Comparative and Physiological Psychology, 91*, 407–417.

Solomon, P. R., & Moore, J. W. (1975). Latent inhibition and stimulus generalization of the classically conditioned nictitating membrane response in rabbits *(Oryctolagus cuniculus)* following dorsal hippocampal ablation. *Journal of Comparative and Physiological Psychology, 89*, 1192–1203.

Solomon, R. L., & Corbit, J. D. (1974). An opponent-process theory of motivation. *Psychological Review, 81*, 119–145.

Steinmetz, J. E., Lavond, D. G., & Thompson, R. F. (1985). Classical conditioning of skeletal muscle responses with mossy fiber stimulation CS and climbing fiber stimulation US. *Society for Neuroscience Abstracts, 11*, 982.

Steinmetz, J. E., Logan, C. G., Rosen, D. J., Lavond, D. G., & Thompson, R. F. (1986). Lesions in the pontine nuclear region selectively abolish classically conditioned eyelid responses in rabbits. *Society for Neuroscience Abstracts, 12*, 753.

Steinmetz, J. E., Logan, C. G., Rosen, D. J., Thompson, J. K., Lavond, D. G., & Thompson, R. F. (1987). Initial localization of the acoustic conditioned stimulus projection system to the cerebellum essential for classical eyelid conditioning. *Proceedings of the National Academy of Sciences U.S.A., 84*, 3531–3535.

Steinmetz, J. E., Logan, C. G., & Thompson, R. F. (in press). Essential involvement of mossy fibers in projecting the CS to the cerebellum during classical conditioning. In C. D. Woody (Ed.), *Cellular mechanisms of conditioning and behavioral plasticity.* New York: Plenum.

Steinmetz, J. E., Rosen, D. J., Chapman, P. F., & Thompson, R. F. (1986). Classical conditioning of the rabbit eyelid response with a mossy fiber stimulation CS. I. Pontine nuclei and middle cerebellar peduncle stimulation. *Behavioral Neuroscience, 100*, 871–880.

Sutton, R. S., & Barto, A. G. (1981). Toward a modern theory of adaptive networks: Expectation and prediction. *Psychological Review, 88*, 135–170.

Taukulis, H. K., & Revusky, S. (1975). Odor as a conditioned inhibitor: Applicability of the Rescorla–Wagner model to feeding behavior. *Learning and Motivation, 6*, 11–27.

Terry, W. S. (1976). The effects of priming US representation in short-term memory on

Pavlovian conditioning. *Journal of Experimental Psychology: Animal Behavior Processes,* **2,** 354–370.

Thomas, E., & Wagner, A. R. (1964). Partial reinforcement of the classically conditioned eyelid response in the rabbit. *Journal of Comparative and Physiological Psychology,* **58,** 157–8.

Thompson, R. F. (1986). The neurobiology of learning and memory. *Science,* **233,** 941–947.

Thompson, R. F., Berger, T. W., Cegavske, C. F., Patterson, M. M., Roemer, R. A., Teyler, T. J., & Young, R. A. (1976). A search for the engram. *American Psychologist,* **31,** 209–227.

Thompson, R. F., Donegan, N. H., Clark, G. A., Lavond, D. G., Lincoln, J. S., Madden, J., Mamounas, L. A., Mauk, M. D., & McCormick, D. A. (1986). Neuronal substrates of discrete, defensive conditioned reflexes, conditioned fear states, and their interactions in the rabbit. In I. Gormezano, W. F. Prokasy, & R. F. Thompson (Eds.), *Classical conditioning III.* Hillsdale, NJ: Erlbaum.

Thompson, R. F., & Spencer, W. A. (1966). Habituation: A model phenomenon for the study of neuronal substrates of behavior. *Psychological Review,* **197,** 16–43.

Thompson, R. F., Steinmetz, J. E., & Chapman, P. F. (1987). Appropriate lesions of the interpositus nucleus completely and permanently abolish the conditioned eyelid/NM response in the rabbit. *Society for Neuroscience Abstracts,* **13,** 802.

Turker, K. S., & Miles, T. S. (1986). Climbing fiber lesions disrupt conditioning of the nictitating membrane response in rabbits. *Brain Research,* **363,** 376–378.

Wagner, A. R. (1969a). Stimulus selection and a "modified continuity theory." In G. H. Bower & J. T. Spence (Eds.), *The psychology of learning and motivation* (Vol. 3, pp. 1–43). New York: Academic Press.

Wagner, A. R. (1969b). Stimulus validity and stimulus selection in associative learning. In N. J. Mackintosh & W. K. Honig (Eds.), *Fundamental issues in associative learning.* Halifax, Nova Scotia: Dalhousie University Press.

Wagner, A. R. (1971). Elementary associations. In H. H. Kendler & J. T. Spence (Eds.), *Essays in neobehaviorism: A memorial volume to Kenneth W. Spence* (pp. 187–213). New York: Appleton-Century-Crofts.

Wagner, A. R. (1976). Priming in STM: An information-processing mechanism for self-generated or retrieval-generated depression in performance. In T. J. Tighe & R. N. Leaton (Eds.), *Habituation: Perspectives from child development, animal behavior, and neurophysiology* (pp. 95–128). Hillsdale, NJ: Erlbaum.

Wagner, A. R. (1978). Expectancies and the priming of STM. In S. H. Hulse, H. Fowler, & W. K. Honig (Eds.), *Cognitive aspects of animal behavior* (pp. 177–209). Hillsdale, NJ: Erlbaum.

Wagner, A. R. (1981). SOP: A model of automatic memory processing in animal behavior. In N. E. Spear & R. R. Miller (Eds.), *Information processing in animals: Memory mechanisms* (pp. 5–47). Hillsdale, NJ: Erlbaum.

Wagner, A. R., & Brandon, S. E. (1989). Evolution of a structured connectionist model of Pavlovian conditioning (AESOP). In S. B. Klein and R. R. Mowrer (Eds.), *Contemporary Learning Theories.* Hillsdale, NJ: Erlbaum.

Wagner, A. R., & Larew, M. B. (1985). Opponent processes and Pavlovian inhibition. In R. R. Miller & N. E. Sperar (Eds.), *Information processing in animals: Conditioned inhibition* (pp. 233–265). Hillsdale, NJ: Erlbaum.

Wagner, A. R., Logan, F. A., Haberlandt, K., & Price, T. (1986). Stimulus selection in animal discrimination learning. *Journal of Experimental Psychology,* **76,** 171–80.

Wagner, A. R., & Rescorla, R. A. (1972). Inhibition in Pavlovian conditioning: Application of theory. In R. A. Boakes & M. S. Halliday (Eds.), *Inhibition and learning* (pp. 301–336). London: Academic Press.

Wagner, A. R., Rudy, J. W., & Whitlow, J. W. (1973). Rehearsal in animal conditioning. *Journal of Experimental Psychology Monograph*, **97**, 407–26.

Wagner, A. R., & Terry, W. S. (1975). Backward conditioning to a CS following an expected vs. a surprising UCS. *Animal Learning and Behavior*, **3**, 370–374.

Walters, E. T., & Byrne, J. H. (1983). Associative conditioning of single sensory neurons suggests a cellular mechanism for learning. *Science*, **219**, 405–408.

Weiss, C. (1986). *The dorsal accessory olive: Inhibitory gating by rubrospinal conditioning stimulation; and physiology of its afferent neurons*. Unpublished doctoral dissertation, Northwestern University, Evanston, IL.

Weiss, C., McCurdy, M. L., Houk, J. C., & Gibson, A. R. (1985). Anatomy and physiology of dorsal column afferents to forelimb dorsal accessory olive. *Society for Neuroscience Abstracts*, **11**, 182.

Welsh, J. P., & Harvey, J. A. (1989). Cerebellar lesions and the nictitating membrane reflex: Performance deficits of the conditioned and unconditioned response. *Neuroscience*, **9**, 299–311.

Wessels, M. G. (1973). Errorless discrimination, autoshaping, and conditioned inhibition. *Science*, **182**, 941–943.

Whitlow, J. W. (1975). Short-term memory in habituation and dishabituation. *Journal of Experimental Psychology: Animal Behavior Processes*, **1**, 189–206.

Whitlow, J. W., Jr. (1986). *Evolution of associative memory*. Paper presented at the meetings of the Society for Mathematical Psychology, Boston.

Whitlow, J. W., & Wagner, A. R. (1972). A negative patterning in classical conditioning: Summation of response tendencies to isolable and configural components. *Psychonomic Science*, **27**, 299–301.

Yeo, C. H., Hardiman, M. J., & Glickstein, M. (1985a). Classical conditioning of the nictitating membrane response of the rabbit. I. Lesions of the cerebellar nuclei. *Experimental Brain Research*, **60**, 87–98.

Yeo, C. H., Hardiman, M. J., & Glickstein, M. (1985b). Classical conditioning of the nictitating membrane response of the rabbit. II. Lesions of the cerebellar cortex. *Experimental Brain Research*, **60**, 99–113.

Yeo, C. H., Hardiman, M. J., & Glickstein, M. (1985c). Classical conditioning of the nictitating membrane response of the rabbit. III. Connections of cerebellar lobule HVI. *Experimental Brain Research*, **60**, 114–126.

Yeo, C. H., Hardiman, M. J., & Glickstein, M. (1986). Classical conditioning of the nictitating membrane response of the rabbit. IV. Lesions of the inferior olive. *Experimental Brain Research*, **63**, 81–92.

SIMULATION AND ANALYSIS OF A SIMPLE CORTICAL NETWORK

Gary Lynch
Richard Granger

I. Introduction

Brain size increased greatly during the course of evolution in two classes of vertebrates, birds and mammals. This occurred independently (i.e., the last common ancestor did not possess a large brain) and resulted in two quite different telencephalic patterns: birds possess an extremely large dorsal ventricular ridge, while mammalian brain is dominated by cortical structures (see Jerison, 1973; Lynch, 1986, for reviews). These observations lead naturally to questions about the advantages and disadvantages of the two organizational designs and what the differences might predict in terms of avian versus mammalian behavior. Surprisingly enough, even preliminary answers to these questions are lacking. This illustrates one of the major problems confronting behavioral neurobiology, namely, the absence of specific and testable ideas regarding the kinds of processing executed by cortical networks. Attempts to account for human behavior in biological terms are particularly affected by this lack of theory, since cortex makes up about 80% of human brain.

Recently, the question of network properties inherent in cortical design has been explored with two types of cortical simulations. The first, which might be termed abstract network modeling, employs theoretical models that use a few assumptions about neurons and their connectivities and then, through computer simulations, seeks to determine if particular, often quite complex, behaviors emerge. The biological postulates are usu-

205

ally simplified so as to allow for mathematical treatment as well as computer modeling. Efforts of this type have produced some impressive results including models that store and associate complex stimuli, reproduce linguistic phenomena, and solve difficult mathematical problems.

The second line of modeling research, biological modeling, seeks to exploit the rapidly growing body of information about the detailed anatomy and physiology of simple cortical networks. With the advent of *in vitro* brain slice techniques it has been possible to describe in great detail the synaptic interactions occurring in hippocampus, including the definition of a form of plasticity that could account for a variety of memorial phenomena. Moreover, neuroanatomical research has served to describe some cortical networks with considerable precision and detail. This information can be incorporated (typically in simplified form) into network models and questions asked about the types of processing that emerge. In biological models, design features are added to simulations for biological reasons only, independent of their potential computational attractiveness or complexity, and the resulting model is not necessarily a tractable subject for mathematical analyses.

The present article is concerned with an attempt to develop a biological simulation of one cell layer in a simple cortical region, that which is concerned with olfaction. Sections II and III describe physiological results that can be used to develop rules by which the network operates and dictates when and where synapses will change during learning, based on the known necessary and sufficient physiological, biophysical, and biochemical conditions for induction of long-lasting synaptic change. As part of the discussion of this material, we will consider the relationship of these rules to those used in more abstract network models. Section IV describes the wealth of known biological parameters of olfactory (piriform) cortex, focusing especially on its anatomical architecture. Having summarized our reasons for selecting olfactory cortex as a model for simulation work, we then review some of the results obtained thus far. Sections V and VI discuss a number of implications of these modeling efforts, including a suggestion that simultaneous categorization and differentiation of inputs resulting from learning is an inherent or local property of simple cortical designs.

II. Operating Rules for Cortical Networks

A. EXCITATORY AND INHIBITORY EVENTS TRIGGERED BY THE ARRIVAL OF INPUT

Figure 1 describes some of the biological circuit operating rules that are involved in dictating the behavior of individual neurons in typical cortical

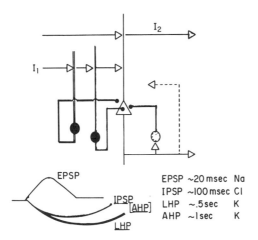

Fig. 1.   Onset and duration of events involved in stimulation of a layer II cell in piriform cortex. Axonal stimulation via the lateral olfactory tract (LOT) activates feedforward EPSPs with rapid onset and short duration (≈20 msec) and two types of feedforward inhibition: short feedforward IPSPs with slower onset and somewhat longer duration (≈100 msec) than the EPSPs, and longer hyperpolarizing potentials (LHP) lasting ≈500 msec. These two types of inhibition are not specific to firing cells; an additional, very long-lasting (≈1 sec), inhibitory after-hyperpolarizing current (AHP) is induced in a cell-specific fashion in those cells with intense firing activity. Finally, feedback EPSPs and IPSPs are induced by activation via recurrent collateral axons from layer II cells.

circuits. These features are undoubtedly found in many brain regions; the points to be discussed have come from anatomical and physiological work carried out in subdivisions of hippocampus and olfactory cortex. The circuit begins with excitatory input from extrinsic sources terminating directly on the principal neurons and interneurons of the target zones (Lorente de No, 1934). These latter inhibitory cells in turn form inhibitory contacts on the principal neurons and thereby generate a feedforward inhibitory circuit (Alger & Nicoll, 1982; Lynch, Jensen, McGaugh, Davila, & Oliver, 1981). They also form a feedback inhibitory circuit, since the feedback axons of the primary cells also contact the inhibitory cell dendrites. The input signal thus generates both excitatory responses (directly) and inhibitory responses (indirectly) in a given target cell.

Abstract network models commonly use positive and negative signals in their inputs to cells, with the response of the target being defined by the sum of the two (i.e., if the positive inputs outweigh the negative inputs then the cell becomes active). Computationally, negative valence input serves two purposes for network modelers: (1) convergence in a cycling system and (2) normalization. Densely interconnected networks with contacts that can range from positive to negative strengths can be shown mathematically and through simulations to cycle in such a manner as to arrive at a condition (convergence) in which a given spatial or temporal pattern of activity is reached and stably sustained until further perturbed by outside inputs (see, e.g., Hopfield, 1982; Shaw, Silverman, & Pearson, 1986). The idea that the value of synapses can go from positive to negative (excitatory to inhibitory) finds no support in neurobiology, but the basic idea could be retained if we assume that activity (e.g., firing frequency) below baseline levels is negative and above baseline is positive (e.g., Kohonen, 1984; Levy & Desmond, 1985). However, this idea encounters a problem in the observation that average firing rates for cells in many areas of telencephalon are quite low (≈ 1–2/sec); accordingly, suppression of activity in one group of afferents would not be likely to balance synchronous excitation in a second, equivalently sized group over the time frame in which neurons sum their inputs. Feedforward inhibitory interneurons of the type occurring in many brain structures (e.g., piriform cortex, CA1 field of hippocampus) certainly provide a means for inserting negative valance input, albeit with a brief delay (about 1 msec) after the arrival of excitation. Whether or not arrangements using direct excitation and indirect inhibition can be used for purposes of convergence remains to be explored.

Normalization refers to the process of constraining the size of the output response (number of active cells) in the face of variable-sized inputs (see, e.g., Grossberg, 1980). The inhibitory postsynaptic potentials (IPSPs) generated in pyramidal cells of hippocampus increase in magnitude as the number of active input axons is increased, presumably because the number of inhibitory cells and/or their response intensity is related to amount of excitatory input. Thus greater input will cause greater excitation in target cells but also greater inhibition, and the amount of excitatory input required to elicit a prolonged response (i.e., a burst of spikes) from a pyramidal neuron will increase with the absolute size of the input vector.

While interneurons may serve to normalize the size of an output, there are several features of inhibition that suggest much more complex and subtle additional functions.

1. IPSP rise time: A short delay will exist between the onset of excitation and inhibition; it also appears that the rise time of excitatory postsynaptic potentials (EPSPs) is more rapid than that for IPSPs. Functionally, this means that later-arriving inputs will be disproportionately reduced.

2. IPSP duration: The time courses for individual excitatory and inhibitory responses are different by about one order of magnitude. EPSPs last ≈ 10 msec while IPSPs are present for 50–200 msec. Thus the symmetry

of positive and negative events used in network models is not found in brain.

3. Three forms of inhibition: At least three known forms of inhibition are set in motion by excitatory inputs.

a. IPSPs: The feedforward IPSP discussed so far is mediated by the well-defined GABA receptor and appears to suppress EPSPs, at least in part, by shunting depolarizing currents (Alger & Nicoll, 1982).

b. LHP: It is now well established that a second inhibitory event mediated by a different receptor is also present in hippocampus and piriform cortex. This event lasts for several hundred milliseconds (the long hyperpolarization, or LHP) and suppresses the effects of the EPSPs by hyperpolarizing the cell rather than through shunting. Thus feedforward inhibition includes a relatively short, extremely effective IPSP and a longer-lasting and less effective LHP, effectively creating a network in which three unequal time steps are set in motion by an input (i.e., the EPSP, the fast IPSP, and the LHP).

c. AHP: Research over the past several years has shown that neurons in various parts of the brain have voltage-sensitive conductances such that when membrane potentials reach certain values powerful ionic conductances are expressed. In the case of hippocampal pyramidal cells, intense depolarization leads to the activation of a calcium current, which in turn triggers a very strong outward potassium current; this results in a profound and long-lasting afterhyperpolarization (AHP) which effectively prevents the cell from firing. The AHP is usually studied by intracellular injections of depolarizing current and there is little work on the patterns of synaptic activation that might elicit it. This is a subject of considerable importance for biological models, since the AHP would functionally eliminate a cell from network operation for hundreds of milliseconds if that cell were to be sufficiently depolarized by its inputs. The utility of this will be discussed in Section V, which deals with our computer simulation work.

From the above it can be seen that excitation is relatively simple but inhibition is complex. In later sections we will develop the idea that inhibitory events, because of their physiological characteristics (longer rise times and greater durations) and multiple nature, will favor certain firing frequencies and patterns of activity, causing networks to act as frequency filters.

B. FEEDBACK

As mentioned above, inhibitory cells respond to activation via collateral axons, as well as responding to their extrinsic inputs. The resulting feedback inhibition could function to normalize the size of the response to different-sized inputs, as mentioned above. That is, the greater the number of cells responding or the greater the intensity of their responses, the greater will be the feedback inhibition they experience. Feedback inhibition might serve to generate a "winner-take-all" cell group of a type commonly used in network models (e.g., Feldman, 1982). That is, if one cell in a small group responds vigorously to an input, it will, through the inhibitory interneurons it contacts, tend to suppress activity in its neighbors.

It seems likely that inhibition in neural networks does tend to isolate active neurons (i.e., winner-take-all in a local group), at least in some brain regions. Pyramidal cells in hippocampal field CA1, for example, are tightly packed, so neighboring cells presumably receive much of the same afferent input. Yet neurons that respond to distinct spatial cues are not surrounded by cells that give similar (or even lesser) responses to the same cues (O'Keefe & Nadel, 1978).

Many regions in cortex and hippocampus contain extensive excitatory feedback networks, and these are, of course, a central feature of many neural network models, both abstract and biological. The version illustrated in Fig. 1, while common, is not universal. For example, the granule cells of dentate gyrus do not project back onto themselves but instead innervate a neighboring group of polymorph cells, which then feed back to the granule cells in an enormously convergent–divergent fashion (i.e., many granule cells project to one polymorph cell, which then distributes its projection to a large number of granule cells). Field CA1 of hippocampus has no excitatory feedback system at all. These variations call attention to the point that functions in brain arise from the interaction of different types of networks and that feedback almost certainly plays different roles in different areas (see Lynch, 1986, for discussion).

Feedback systems inevitably raise the question of timing rules. In the simplest sense, as in Fig. 1, we might assume that the onset of the feedback excitation will occur at a short interval after the beginning of the excitatory input and at about the same time as the two inhibitory inputs. The problem is complicated by the distances over which feedback must travel to reach a particular target neuron. Some well-defined feedback systems (e.g., hippocampus, piriform cortex) are bilaterally symmetrical, in that they are composed of axons from the ipsilateral and contralateral homotopic brain regions. These contralateral fibers are long enough that conduction times are greater than the rise time of the EPSP. Clearly, these effects will mean much more embedded in a highly synchronized system than otherwise. Representing feedback delays and their effects on voltage summation are problems for any biologically constrained network model.

Excitatory feedback systems typically synapse on dendritic trees at different sites than input connections. In piriform cortex, dentate gyrus, and field CA3 of hippocampus, they synapse closer to the cell bodies than do the extrinsic inputs, and this may be a common theme. This raises the point that models need to specify the relative potency (in terms of causing the target cell to spike) of different afferents, that is, the rules by which activity in different inputs will sum in the target cell.

C. ANATOMICAL CONSTRAINTS ON NETWORK OPERATIONS

Here we will mention four anatomical features not illustrated in Fig. 1 that are nonetheless likely to figure prominently in the operations carried out by cortical networks and hence cannot be ignored in models of these networks. First, in most instances, a given axon will form more than one contact with a given target dendrite. This is of interest because of the probabilistic nature of transmitter release at individual synapses. Multiple innervation means that, for a single axon, the probability of quantal release can be multiplied by the number of contacts formed by that axon. In models that incorporate probabilistic synaptic transmission, this will clearly be a point of some significance. It also is a crucial notion in interpreting various forms of synaptic plasticity. Adding synapses will alter the probabilistic character of the response to an individual axon in ways that strengthening existing contacts will not (Lynch, 1986).

A second point of importance for models concerns the distribution of interneuron projections. Excitatory projections in cortical regions extend over considerable distances either as extrinsic afferents or as widely distributed feedback systems. In contrast, inhibitory interneurons have much more limited distributions and connect with perhaps several dozen neighboring cells. In addition, the interneurons are greatly outnumbered by the principal cells and are separated by those cells. These features result in a situation in which a single interneuron may create a local patch of inhibition; doubtless a sizeable degree of overlap exists between patches. Nonetheless, interneurons probably produce a patchwork property in even the most homogeneous of cortical layers.

These anatomical details add to the temporal differences described earlier, emphasizing the asymmetry of inhibition and excitation in cortical networks. Restricted projections are not a necessary feature of interneurons. In dentate gyrus, the polymorph cells, which resemble interneurons in a number of respects, generate an excitatory feedback system that projects over great distances, including the contralateral hemisphere. Conversely, inhibitory connections can project between brain regions; the strio-nigral projections and cerebellar Purkinje cells provide examples.

A third anatomical feature of interest to modelers concerns the density of connections between excitatory connections and their target cells. Network simulations typically use very dense matrices; that is, each input line has a very high probability of contacting each target element. Cortical networks, however, are exceedingly sparse. In piriform cortex and hippocampus, the probability of connections between two cells can be calculated to be something less than 0.10 (Lynch, 1986); neocortex is likely to be at least as sparse. In such a network, any small collection of active inputs will densely innervate only a small subset of target cells; in some senses, sparse networks allow an input to automatically select, or recruit, a set of output elements without using unrealistically high threshold levels (Lynch, Granger, Baudry, & Larson, 1988; Granger, Ambros-Ingerson, Henry, & Lynch, 1989). In any event, sparsity of connections is a necessary feature of a biologically based simulation.

A fourth feature of networks found in brain with strong implications for models is directionality of feedback. In both piriform cortex and hippocampus, feedback connections project much more densely in one direction than the other; for example, in piriform cortex, the axons are directed caudally (Schwob & Price, 1978). In some senses, then, the feedback system is both associative and recurrent in nature (Lynch, 1986; Lynch & Baudry, 1987). The extent to which this is a general feature of feedback connections is unknown but it clearly must be considered in developing biological models. The possible utility of the asymmetry in associative connections will be discussed in Section V.

III. Learning Rules for Networks

A. Hebb Synapses

Network models use learning rules to increase the correlation between activity in an input line and that of a given target element it contacts, thus increasing the likelihood that a previously learned convergent pattern will reappear when the network is excited. The simplest form of a rule to accomplish this is:

$$\Delta T_{ij} = S_i S_j$$

Where S_i is the activity ($+$ or $-$) in the ith input line, S_j ($+$ or $-$) is the activity in the jth target element, and T_{ij} is the strength of the contact between them. S_j is itself determined by multiplying activity of inputs i (S_i) by the strength of their synapses (T_{ij}) with element j, and then summing over all these S_i and T_{ij}. Thus:

$$S_j = \sum_i S_i T_{ij}$$

The synaptic change rule is a conjunctive–disjunctive statement: When input and output are the same, increase synaptic strength; when they are different, decrease synaptic strength. Much has been said recently about the perceived similarity between this rule and one proposed by the psychologist D. O. Hebb and indeed, synapse models that obey the correlational expression are now commonly referred to as *Hebb synapses*. Whether or not Hebb had this in mind, others have gone on to argue that the existence of Hebb synapses in brain is indicated by certain aspects of the hippocampal long-term potentiation (LTP) effect.

When afferents in hippocampus are stimulated at high frequency even for fractions of a second they can increase the strength of their contacts with target dendrites (Bliss & Lømo, 1973). This effect has generated a great deal of interest because the synaptic potentiation persists for extremely long periods (see below) and thus might account for behavioral memory (see Landfield & Deadwyler, 1987, for recent reviews). The idea that an LTP-like process is involved in memory has been supported by recent experiments showing that two quite different pharmacological treatments that block LTP also cause a selective suppression of memory storage (Morris, Anderson, Lynch, & Baudry, 1986; Staubli, Baudry, & Lynch, 1985; Staubli, Fraser, Faraday, & Lynch, 1988).

Intracellular recording studies have shown that the target cell must be intensely depolarized for LTP to develop. Thus, loosely speaking, when the input is very active and the target is very active (depolarized) then synaptic strengthening occurs; if either of these conditions is absent, LTP is not triggered (Wigstrøm & Gustaffson, 1983; Wigstrøm, Gustaffson, Huang, & Abraham, 1986; Malinow & Miller, 1986; Kelso, Ganong, & Brown, 1986).

However, for the notion of Hebb synapses or any other simple correlational rule for synaptic modification to be useful, its predictions must apply across a wide range of physiological situations, and this is clearly not the case. Hebb, for example, addressed himself specifically to the case in which firing of a given input was reliably followed by firing of one of its targets (conjunction); he proposed that with time the synaptic strength between the two would increase. Any number of experiments have shown, however, that single-pulse stimulation of enough afferents to cause a cell to spike does not result in any synaptic change if the pulses are separated by a few seconds. This is true even if the stimulation is carried out for tens of minutes and involves hundreds of pulses and spike responses.

Furthermore, correlational (or "Hebb-like") rules predict that synaptic strength will decrease if S_i is active when S_j is inactive. Clearly, this is not universally the case. For example, a common control procedure in studies of hippocampal slices is to stimulate inputs once every few seconds with a number of afferent fibers too small to cause the target cell ever to spike. Reductions in synaptic strength do not occur under these conditions despite the repeated disjunction in pre- and postsynaptic activity. Even if the inputs are driven at high frequencies and the target cell is maintained in a hyperpolarized state (S_i^+, S_j^-), the maximum possible disjunction, synaptic strength remains constant. Conversely, if the target cell is maximally depolarized and the inputs are kept inactive (S_i^-, S_j^+), S_i does not change its strength.

There is a very substantial body of evidence pointing to the conclusion that disjunctions in pre- and postsynaptic activity do not reduce synaptic strength, at least in the pyramidal cell fields of hippocampus. Moreover, as will be discussed at length below, it is very likely that only very specific patterns of naturally occurring activity produce LTP; saying that this involves a conjunction does not begin to describe the events needed to produce the synaptic change (see Granger, Baudry, & Lynch, 1988, for discussion of these and related points).

While disjunctions per se do not reliably reduce synaptic weights, there is evidence that depression of synaptic strength and reversal of LTP may occur under some circumstances. Early experiments using slices showed that induction of LTP by several seconds of moderate frequency (e.g., 20 Hz) stimulation would often depress other, nonstimulated synapses in the same target region (see Lynch, Gribkoff, & Deadwyler, 1976; Lynch, Dunwiddie, & Gribkoff, 1977). Subsequent work revealed that the optimal stimulation parameters for eliciting LTP had no detectable effect on nonstimulated inputs; moreover, the most reliable and stable depressions were produced by stimulation parameters (e.g., 1–5/sec) that caused little if any LTP (Dunwiddie & Lynch, 1978). The long-lasting heterosynaptic depression is also found in dentate gyrus (Abraham & Goddard, 1983). Desmond and Levy (1983) have described an intriguing variant of depression that in several respects does incorporate the idea of disjunction. Two inputs of very different size to a common cell population were used; LTP was induced in the larger input with high-frequency activity while the small input was stimulated with one of several frequencies. Desmond and

Levy found that lower frequencies weakened synaptic strength in the small input, while high frequencies strengthened it. Finally, it has been reported that long trains of low frequency will reduce potentiated synapses in many cases without affecting "naive" contacts (Barrionuevo, Schottler, & Lynch, 1979). This raises the possibility that specific reversal signals exist.

It must be noted that the above experiments measured depression typically for periods of about 30 min; there are no data indicating that the depressive effects persist for anything like the time periods that characterize LTP. Moreover, the depressive effects that are reported appear not to be as robust or reliable as LTP. Clearly, then, the issue needs to be studied more systematically and with chronic recording.

B. LEARNING RULES DERIVED FROM LTP

Recent studies have gone far towards defining the physiological and chemical processes that produce LTP. This makes it possible to develop learning rules from physiological data in addition to searching LTP for effects that correspond to rules derived from theory.

Neurons in the hippocampus of freely moving animals often fire in short ($\approx$30 msec) bursts of three to five pulses (Fox & Ranck, 1981). Experimental studies have shown that these bursts will induce LTP if they are given repetitively and that the optimal interburst interval is 200 msec: Four-pulse bursts given at higher or lower frequencies were considerably less effective than when applied at five bursts per second (Larson, Wong, & Lynch, 1986). This is an intriguing finding because five per second is the frequency of the theta rhythm, an EEG wave that dominates the hippocampus when animals are moving through or exploring their environments (see, e.g., Landfield, 1976). Further experimentation has provided a likely explanation for the peculiar efficacy of theta bursting in producing LTP. It appears that the short IPSP, once having been triggered, cannot be reintroduced via stimulation for a few hundred milliseconds (Larson & Lynch, 1986; see also McCarren & Alger, 1985). Synaptic activation occuring while the IPSP from that input is still present will be truncated, whereas inputs arriving much later than 200 msec will trigger their own feedforward IPSP, with similar effect. Between these times, a window exists, centered at about 200 msec, during which the feedforward IPSP mechanism is inactive. This absence of the IPSP results in longer lasting EPSPs. For single events this is of no great significance: in fact, the long hyperpolarization (LHP) potential is still very much present at 200 msec and reduces the likelihood that a single response will cause the membrane potential to reach spike threshold. Broadening the EPSP does, however, have substantial effects on the response of the cell to a short burst of synaptic activation because the broader potentials exhibit a far greater degree of temporal summation and thus cause greater net depolarization (Larson & Lynch, 1986, 1988; see also Fig. 2). As noted earlier, intense depolarization greatly facilitates and indeed may be a prerequisite for the induction of LTP; coupling two naturally occurring aspects of hippocampal physiology—short, high frequency bursts and the theta rhythm— provides the conditions needed to produce the depolarization.

The reasons why the enhanced burst response produces LTP are not of essential concern to this discussion and will be only briefly noted. Intense depolarization from theta bursting uncovers NMDA receptors (Larson & Lynch, 1988), allowing calcium to pass into the target dendritic spines (MacDermott, Mayer, Westbrook, Smith, & Barker, 1986); fluctuations in postsynaptic calcium are reasonably well established as an essential step in the triggering sequence for LTP (Dunwiddie & Lynch, 1979; Lynch, Larson, Kelso, Barrionuevo, & Schottler, 1983). Structural changes accompany LTP (Lee, Schottler, Oliver, & Lynch, 1980; Lee, Oliver, Schottler, & Lynch, 1981; Chang & Greenough, 1984; Wenzel & Matthies, 1985; Desmond & Levy, 1983), which is not surprising given the extreme stability of the effect, and these are presumably initiated by chemical processes responsive to elevations in calcium. One candidate for these processes is the partial digestion of membrane cytoskeletal pro-

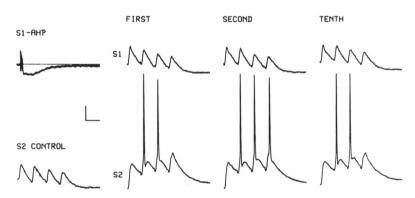

Fig. 2. When short, high-frequency bursts are input to cells 200 msec after an initial priming event, the consequently broadened EPSPs will allow the contributions of the second and subsequent pulses composing the burst to sum with the depolarization of the first pulse, yielding higher postsynaptic depolarization sufficient to cause the cell to spike. From Lynch, Larson, Staubli, & Baudry (1987).

teins by the enzyme calpain (Lynch & Baudry, 1984; Lynch, Larson, Staubli, & Baudry, 1987), a hypothesis that has received recent experimental support (Staubli *et al.*, 1988). In sum, chemical processes have been identified which are fully capable of converting very brief periods of intense depolarization into structural and physiological modifications.

C. ADDITIONAL FEATURES OF LTP-BASED LEARNING RULES

The above discussion led to the conclusion that synaptic strengthening required the occurrence of specific firing patterns (bursting) and a specific rhythm (theta). Several additional features of LTP further constrain its application as a learning rule. These have been discussed elsewhere (Lynch *et al.*, 1987) and will be only summarized here.

First, LTP is accompanied by two types of anatomical changes: modification of existing postsynaptic structures and an increase in the frequency of certain types of synapses. As noted, the second variable affects the statistical properties of communication between a given input fiber and its target dendrite, while the first variable will change the amount of voltage induced by a given amount of input activity at the synapse.

Second, there is evidence that order of arrival of input pulses on a dendrite affects the induction of LTP. That is, when multiple inputs arrive in a given dendritic field in a slightly asynchronous fashion (a situation that is certainly much more realistic than perfect synchrony of arrival), the earliest arrival exhibits the greatest degree of synaptic potentiation (J. Larson *et al.*, unpublished observations), a crucial point for modeling. As noted, in a synchronous system, input synapses will be activated prior to the feedback contacts; the delays could be significant (≈ 10 msec) if the system cycles more than once, especially if contralateral projections are considered. From this perspective, potentiation of input synapses may be aided by later-arriving feedback.

Third, and also crucial for models, the effects of LTP are more pronounced for subsequent single pulses than for bursts of responses. That is, maximum LTP is about a 50% increase in synaptic efficiency as measured by single extracellular responses but is less than half of this when calculated from burst responses (J. Larson *et al.*, unpublished observations). Since bursts are necessary for the induction of LTP, this indicates that previously potentiated contacts do not contribute to the induction of LTP in other synapses to the extent that might be expected. This point emphasizes again the difference in the behavior of the network with regard to single spikes versus bursts and has important implications for the number of synapses modified in response to any single input cue.

IV.   Models of Cortical Networks Based on Olfactory Cortex

A.   DESIGN OF THE OLFACTORY CORTEX

Any brain region that is to be used as a model must necessarily be both simple and well defined. These conditions are difficult to satisfy for neocortex since individual layers of cortex have diverse afferents and a poorly defined feedback system. In essence, the anatomy of cortical layers is neither simple nor well defined. Individual components of hippocampus meet the anatomical and physiological requirements for a model system. However, hippocampus presents a problem that is shared by neocortex: It is (anatomically) distant from the periphery. Because of this, any signals arrive in hippocampus only after considerable preprocessing. This makes it difficult to test satisfactorily, either physiologically or behaviorally, predictions arising from simulations, a second condition for an adequate model system. To elaborate, the response of a brain region to a peripheral stimulus will necessarily reflect its local characteristics as well as the preprocessing of the stimulus by earlier relays. A simulation of the local region thus might produce valid effects that would not be seen in physiological recordings from the selected brain region. The problem is still more acute for behavioral predictions. For example, it is difficult to envision how a simulation of a hippocampal subdivision would reproduce the "spatial" cells found in chronic recording studies without explicit, detailed knowledge of the nature of the inputs to those regions.

These considerations have led us to use the superficial layers (layers I and II) of the olfactory (piriform–entorhinal) cortex as a guide in constructing a simulation of a cortical network. This collection of cells is monosynaptically innervated by the mitral cells of the olfactory bulb (cf. Skeen & Hall, 1977; Schwob & Price, 1978; Haberly & Price, 1977, and references therein), which themselves are the targets of receptor neurons in the nasal epithelium. Thus a layer II cortical cell is disynaptically connected with the cells which detect the physical stimulus for olfaction. Moreover, the anatomy of the system is relatively simple and well defined. Layer II is a collection of densely packed cell bodies, the dendrites of which form layer I. The outer half of layer I is occupied by the terminal field of the mitral cells whereas the inner half is innervated by a feedback-association collateral system (Price, 1973; Luskin & Price, 1983; Krettek & Price, 1977). There are no other major projections (e.g., from other cortical areas) to layers I and II. In a very real sense, layer II cells represent a close approximation to a simple cortical network of the type illustrated earlier in this paper (see Haberly, 1985; Lynch, 1986).

There is reason to suspect that events observed in simulations of the olfactory cortex could be detected in chronic recordings from the cortex or even in behavior. The odor receptors in the nasal mucosa are simply modified dendrites of the neurons situated in that region; processing of the olfactory signals in the periphery must be quite simple, compared at least to the retina, since the receptor cells do not emit extensive collaterals and interneurons appear to be absent (see Shepherd, 1979, for review). The olfactory bulb, which receives the output of the receptor cells, is also a reasonably simple structure. It is composed of mitral cells (which as noted receive the olfactory nerve and project monosynaptically to the cortex), a large subjacent granule cell system that is inhibitory in function, and interneurons (see Shepherd, 1979; Mori, 1987, for reviews). Because of its dense inhibitory granule cell system, the bulb seems well suited to normalize inputs of different magnitude from the receptors (i.e., the greater the signal, the greater the inhibition it elicits). There appears to be a degree of topography in the connections between the receptor sheet and the surface of the olfactory bulb; this suggests that odors are coded spatially on the bulb, a point which is well supported by studies of functional activity (i.e., 2-deoxyglucose uptake) during odor presentation (Lancet, Greer, Kaver, & Shepherd, 1982; Jourdan, 1982). Thus it seems reasonable to assume that the odors stimulate restricted portions of the bulb with the magnitude of the response regulated within reasonably narrow boundaries by a dense inhibitory system. However, this cannot begin to be the whole story since the bulb receives input from many parts of the telencephalon, including those basal forebrain regions that control rhythmic activity in cortex and hippocampus (see Macrides & Davis, 1983; Mori, 1987, for reviews). We assume that these systems change the sensitivity of the bulb and coordinate its activity with the act of sniffing as well as with the physiology of olfactory cortex and hippocampus. This points to an additional advantage of using the olfactory cortex as a model in constructing network simulations: Stimulus sampling by the olfactory system is active, discrete, and occurs within a narrow range of frequencies. Perception of faint odors involves sniffing, a deliberate motor act and one that defines sampling rate. Rats sniff at about 2–6 times/sec, a rate which is quite close to the frequency of the hippocampal theta rhythm (Macrides, Eichenbaum, & Forbes, 1982).

This information leads to the idea that olfactory cortex receives bursts of input from discrete portions of the olfactory cortex activated by specific odors and that these bursts will occur at a frequency near that of theta. Moreover, we can imagine that the number of bulb cells activated by the odor as well as their firing frequency will be normalized across odor intensities to some narrow range of values. These features can easily be reproduced in simulations of the olfactory cortex and indeed were used in the computer modeling work described below. To the extent they are correct, and to the degree that the simulation captures essential features of olfactory cortex, then the simulation should produce outputs (cell firings) that should correspond to those observable in chronic recordings from layer II of piriform–entorhinal cortex. Moreover, since olfactory cortex is the primary recipient of the output of the bulb, it is fair to assume that it plays a central role in all aspects of olfactory perception. It is possible that a correspondence will exist between the events in the cortex and behavior; if so, the computer simulation could also produce interesting predictions about behavior.

It would be difficult to form simplifying assumptions of this type about primary auditory, visual, or somatosensory cortices. The complex nuclei that connect the periphery to these regions carry out important processing steps, and in rats and cats at least, this early processing alone appears to be sufficient for a wide range of behaviors.

B. PATTERNED STIMULATION OF CORTICAL INPUT AS A BEHAVIORAL CUE

The very simple picture of olfactory processing prior to the cortex outlined above may be seriously distorted. It is quite possible that bulbar processing involves mixing of inputs from the brain and the olfactory nerve and that the bulb acts as a unit, rather than as a collection of autonomous patches, in odor perception. Chronic recording studies of the olfactory bulb in freely moving animals engaged in solving familiar olfactory problems are rare. Until extensive work of this type has been conducted, there will be considerable uncertainty regarding appropriate representations and simplifications of the output of the olfactory bulb to piriform cortex. This led us to test the idea that short bursts of activity occurring at the theta frequency in the bulbar–cortical projections (the lateral olfactory tract, or LOT) could be detected as an odor cue by rats.

The likelihood that electrical stimulation of the LOT could be used as an odor cue is increased by the nontopographic nature of the bulbar projections; that is, real odors presumably activate fibers scattered throughout the LOT. Our experiments (Roman, Staubli, & Lynch, 1987) involved training rats on a succession of olfactory discrimination problems until performance had reached asymptote, and then using electrical stimulation as a substitute for one odor in a novel pair; that is, the rat was asked to discriminate between stimulation of the LOT and an odor that had not been previously experienced. The theta bursting cue (the electric odor) was learned quickly and was quickly recognized in recall tests given several days later. This was true whether the electric odor was a positive or negative cue. To test if the electrical stimulation was perceived as more than a vague stimulus, experiments were run in which two electric odors were used, one as a positive cue and the other as a negative cue. The rats were able to form a normal discrimination under these circumstances.

These experiments cannot be taken as strict evidence that the bulbar–cortical system actually uses only theta bursting in normal communications. Additional studies may reveal that a variety of stimulation patterns can be used as substitutes for real odors, and in fact it has been reported that 60-Hz stimulation of the bulb itself is responded to as though an odor were present (Mouly, Vigouroux, & Holley, 1987). Nonetheless, the electric odor experiments do provide a simple input pattern that can be reproduced in simulations and that apparently can be used effectively by the cortex. Note also that coupled with chronic recording from layer II cells, the electric odor paradigm provides a uniquely simple system against which to test predictions arising from simulation work.

A final and intriguing observation made in the behavioral experiments using electrical stimulation was that stimulation produced LTP in the LOT synapses in layer I, but only when it was applied to rats that had experience with natural odors as learning cues. Application of theta bursting to naive rats had no discernable effects on the potency of the LOT synapses.

V.   Simulations

A.   THE SIMPLE MODEL

We have conducted several simulations of olfactory cortex incorporating many of the physiological features discussed earlier. One hundred layer II cells were used with 100 input (LOT) lines and 100 feedback axons. These axons form connections with layer II cell dendrites with a probability of 0.2 and, within certain constraints, at random. The major constraint fixes the number of contacts for axons and dendrites within certain narrow boundaries (in the most severe case, each axon forms 20 synapses and each dendrite receives 20 contacts). The resulting matrix is thus hypergeometric. In our earlier models, inhibition acted globally across the 100 cells (except for the AHP, which is cell-specific). Inhibition rules were approximately as discussed above: The short IPSP was longer than an EPSP but only one-fifth the length of the LHP. Long-term potentiation was represented by a 40% increase in contact strength and was restricted to excitatory connections. LTP occurred when a cell was first primed and then received a burst of pulses sufficiently great to drive it past a threshold value; following from the physiological results, previously potentiated synapses were much less different from naive synapses when driven at high frequency. The simulation used theta burst activation (i.e., bursts of pulses with the bursts occurring at 5 Hz) of inputs during learning and operated according to these fixed time steps rather than continuous time.

The network was trained on sets of "odors," each of which was represented as a group of active LOT lines, as in the electric odor experiments. Usually three or four components were used in an odor, with each component consisting of a group of contiguous LOT lines. We assumed that the bulb normalized the output signal to about 20% of all LOT fibers. In some cases, more specific bulb rules were used; in particular, inhibition was assumed to be greatest in areas surrounding an active bulb "patch."

The network exhibited several interesting behaviors. Learning, as expected, increased the robustness of the response to specific vectors; thus adding or subtracting LOT lines from a previously learned input did not, within limits, greatly change the response. The model, like most network simulations, dealt reasonably well with degraded or noisy known signals. An unexpected result developed after the network had learned a succession of cues. In experiments of this type, the simulation would begin to generate two quite distinct output signals within a given sampling episode; that is, a single previously learned cue would generate two successive responses to successive "sniffs" by an "experienced" network. The first of these response patterns proved to be common to several signals while the second was specific to each learned signal. The common signal was found to occur when the network had learned three to five inputs which had substantial overlap in their components (e.g., four odors that shared ≈70% of their components). It appeared then that the network had begun to produce category, or clustering, responses, and individual, or differentiation, responses. When presented with a novel cue which contained elements shared with other, previously learned signals, the network produced the cluster response but no subsequent individual or specific output signal. Four to five cluster response patterns and 20–25 individual responses were produced in the network without distortion.

In retrospect, it was clear that the model accomplished two necessary and in some senses opposing operations: (1) It detected similarities in the members of a cue category or cluster, and (2) it distinguished between cues that were quite similar. Its first response was to the category and its second to the specific signal. These results reflected the operation of the fast IPSP coupled with the LHP and AHP, as described in some detail below. Together these caused the cells to go through what might be thought of as a series of threshold steps with the earlier steps favoring similarity and the later ones promoting differentiation.

B. ANALYSIS OF CATEGORIZATION CHARACTERISTICS OF THE MODEL

Assume that a set of input cues (or simulated odors) X^α, X^β,...,X^ζ differ from each other in the firing of d_X LOT input lines; similarly, inputs Y^α, Y^β,...,Y^ζ differ in d_Y lines, but inputs from the sets X and Y differ from each other in $D_{X,Y} >> d$ lines, such that the Xs and the Ys form distinct natural categories. Then the performance of the network should give rise to output (layer II cell) firing patterns that are very similar among members of either category, but different for members of different categories. That is, there should be a single spatial pattern of response for members of X, with little variation in response across members, and there should be a distinct spatial pattern of response for members of Y.

Considering a matrix constructed by uniform selection of neurons, each with a hypergeometric distribution for its synapses, as an approximation of the bidimensional hypergeometric matrix described above, the following results can be derived. The expected value of $\hat{d}$, the Hamming distance between responses for two input cues differing by $2d$ axons in the LOT (input Hamming distance of d), is:

$$E(\hat{d}) = \sum_{k=1}^{N_o} \left[\sum_{\substack{i \geq \theta \\ j < \theta}} S_i I(i,j) + \sum_{\substack{i < \theta \\ j \geq \theta}} S_i I(i,j) \right]$$

where N_o is the number of postsynaptic cells, each S_i is the probability that a cell will have precisely i active contacts from one of the two cues, and $I(i,j)$ is the probability that the number of contacts on the cell will increase (or decrease) from i to j with the change in d axons in the LOT; that is changing from the first cue to the second. Hence, the first term denotes the probability of a cell decreasing its number of active contacts from above to below some threshold, θ, such that that cell fired in response to one cue but not the other (and therefore is one of the cells that will contribute to the difference between responses to the two cues). Reciprocally, the second term is the probability that the cell increases its number of active synapses such that it is now over the threshold; this cell also will contribute to the difference in response. We restrict our analysis for now to rostral piriform cortex, in which there are assumed to be few if any collateral axons. We will return to this issue in the next subsection.

The value for each S_a, the probability of a active contacts on a cell, is a hypergeometric function, since there are a fixed number of contacts anatomically between LOT and (rostral) piriform cells:

$$S_a = p(a \ active \ synapses) = \frac{\binom{A}{a}\binom{N - A}{n - a}}{\binom{N}{n}}$$

where N is the number of LOT lines, A is the number of active (firing) LOT lines, n is the number of synapses per dendrite formed by the LOT, and a is the number of active such synapses. The formula can be read by noting that the first binomial indicates the number of ways of choosing a active synapses on the dendrite from the A active incoming LOT lines; for each of these, the next expression calculates the number of ways in which the remaining $n - a$ (inactive) synapses on the dendrite are chosen from the $N - A$ inactive incoming LOT lines; the probability of active synapses on a dendrite depends on the sparseness of the matrix (i.e., the probability of connection between any given LOT line and dendrite); and the solution must be normalized by the number of ways in which n synapses on a dendrite can be chosen from N incoming LOT lines.

The probability of a cell changing its number of contacts from a to $\hat{a}$ is

$$I(a,\hat{a}) = \sum_{\substack{g - l = \\ a - \hat{a}}} \left[\frac{\binom{a}{l}\binom{A - a}{d - l}\binom{n - a}{g}\binom{N - A - (n - a)}{d - g}}{\binom{A}{d} \qquad \binom{N - A}{d}} \right]$$

where N, n, A, and a are as above, l is the loss or reduction in the number of active synapses, and g is the gain or increase. Hence the left expression is the probability of losing l active synapses by changing d LOT lines, and the right-hand expression is the probability of gaining g active synapses. The product of the expressions are summed over all the ways of choosing l and g such that the net change $g - l$ is the desired difference $a - \hat{a}$.

If training on each cue induces only fractional LTP, then over trials, synapses contacted by any overlapping parts of the input cues will become stronger than those contacted only by unique parts of the cue. Comparing two cues from within a category versus two cues from between categories, there may be the same number of active synapses lost across the two cues in either case, but the expected strength of the synapses lost in the former case (within category) is significantly lower than in the latter case (across categories). Hence, for a given threshold, the difference d between output firing patterns will be smaller for two within-category cues than for cues from two different categories.

It is important to note that clustering is an operation that is quite distinct from stimulus generalization. Observing that an object is a car does not occur because of a comparison with a specific, previously learned car. Instead the category "car" emerges from the learning of many different cars and may be based on a prototype that has no necessary correspondence with a specific, real object. The same could be said of the network. It did not produce a categorical response when one cue had been learned and a second similar stimulus was presented. Category or cluster responses, as noted, required the learning of several exemplars of a similarity-based cluster. It is the process of extracting commonalities from the environment that defines clustering, not the simple noting of similarities between two cues.

It is of value to note further distinctions between the clustering that the simulation performs and the "categorization" performed by other network algorithms (e.g., Anderson & Mozer, 1981; Hopfield, 1982). The latter is nonincremental, that is, it requires that the cues to be learned are available to the system in advance of testing. These cues form the categories that will subsequently be used to sort novel input vectors. Any novel vector at testing time will be interpreted as a "degraded" version of one of the learned cues. In essence, then, all of the categories are known to the experimenter and are given to the system initially, by training it only on certain key cues. From that point on, novel cues are interpreted by the system as being in one of the categories defined by the set of learned cues. In contrast, in the task of clustering, it is not known in advance how many categories there are, nor what cues define them. Rather, the system extracts this information as it is learning cues. It is not the case, therefore, that each learned cue defines its own category, as in the other neural network mechanisms described above. Rather, as learning progresses, novel cues are sorted according to their similarities to learned clusters, and learning can proceed incrementally: That is, there is no set learning time versus testing time. The terminology of categorization can therefore misleadingly suggest that the clustering operation and categorization are identical, which is not the case.

An essential question in clustering concerns the location of the boundaries of a given group: What degree of similarity must a set of cues possess to be grouped together? This issue has been discussed from any number of theoretical positions (e.g., information theory); all these analyses incorporate the point that the breadth of a category must reflect the overall homogeneity or heterogeneity of the environment. In a world where things are quite similar, useful categories will necessarily be composed of objects with much in common. The categories formed by the simulation were quite appropriate when judged by an information-theoretic measure, but how well the simulation performs across a wide range of possible worlds has not been addressed.

One area in which the network's behavior seemed less than optimal was in orthogonalizing its inputs. As noted, the first simulation produced both category and individuated responses. Ideally, when confronted with two relatively similar cues, the individuated responses produced by the simulation would have little overlap; with learning, the network should produce very different responses to two very similar cues. The network did differentiate but not to an optimal degree, particularly when processing cues with a 90% overlap. This point was reexamined after constructing different networks that incorporated biological factors ignored in our first simulations.

C. ANALYSIS OF PROBLEMS ARISING FROM THE SIMPLE MODEL

A key problem with the simple model was its lack of adherence to known anatomy of piriform cortex, especially the strong rostral–caudal flow of the collateral axons of layer II cells. Incorporation of this anatomical feature into this model, or any similar model for that matter, gives rise to an immediate problem in principle. In essence, the more rostral cells that fire in response to an input, the more active inputs there are from these cells to the caudal cells, via collateral axons, such that the probability of caudal cell firing increases precipitously with probability of rostral cell firing. Conversely, reducing the number of rostral cells from firing, either by reducing the number of active input LOT axons or by raising the layer II cell firing threshold, prevents sufficient input to the caudal cells to enable their probability of firing to be much above zero.

This problem can be stated formally by making assumptions about the detailed nature of the connectivity of LOT and collateral axons in layer I as these axons proceed from rostral to caudal piriform cortex. The probability of contact between LOT axons and layer II cell dendrites decreases caudally as the number of collateral axons is increasing, given their rostral–caudal flow tendency. This situation is depicted in Fig. 3. Assuming that probability of LOT contact tends to go to zero, we may adopt a labeling scheme for axons and synaptic contacts, as in the diagram, in which some combination of LOT axons (x_k) and collateral axons (h_m) contact any particular layer II cell dendrite (h_n), each of which is itself the source

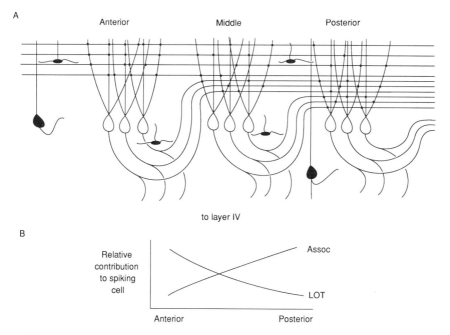

A

Anterior   Middle   Posterior

to layer IV

B

Relative
contribution
to spiking
cell

                                    Assoc

                                    LOT

Anterior   Posterior

Fig. 3. A, Organization of extrinsic and feedback inputs to layer II cells of piriform cortex. The axons composing the lateral olfactory tract (LOT), originating from the bulb, innervate distal dendrites, whereas the feedback collateral or associational fibers contact proximal dendrites. Layer II cells in anterior (rostral) piriform are depicted as being dominated by extrinsic (LOT) input, whereas feedback inputs are more prominent on cells in posterior (caudal) piriform. B, Graphic representation of the relative effect of LOT versus associational input on cell spiking relative to cell location along the rostral–caudal axis.

of an additional collateral axon flowing to cells more caudal than itself. Then the cell firing function for layer II cell h_n is

$$h_n = H \left(\sum_{m<n} h_m w_{nm} + \sum_{k \geqslant n} x_k w_{nk} - \theta_n \right)$$

where x_k denotes LOT axon activity of those axons still with nonzero probability of contact for layer II cell h_n, h_m denotes activity of layer II cells rostral of h_n, θ_n is the firing threshold for h_n, w_{nm} is the synaptic strength between axon m and dendrite n, and H is the Heaviside step function, equal to 1 or 0 according to whether its argument is positive or negative. If we assume instead that probability of cell firing is a graded function rather than a step function, we may eliminate the H step function and calculate the firing of the cell (h_n) from its inputs ($h_{n,net}$) via the logistic:

$$h_{n,net} = \sum_{m<n} h_m w_{nm} + \sum_{k \geq n} x_k w_{nk}$$

$$h_n = \{1 + \exp[-(kh_{n,net} + \theta_n)]\}^{-1}$$

Then we may expand the expression for firing of cell h_n as follows:

$$h_n = \{1 + \exp[-(\sum_{m<n} h_m w_{nm} + \sum_{k \geq n} x_k w_{nk} + \theta_n)]\}^{-1}$$

By assuming a fixed firing threshold, and varying the number of active input LOT lines, the probability of cell firing can be examined. Numerical simulation of the above expressions across a range of LOT spatial activation patterns demonstrates that probability of cell firing remains near zero until a critical number of LOT lines are active, at which point the probability flips to close to 100% (Fig. 4). This means that, for any given firing threshold, given less than a certain amount of LOT input, practically no piriform cells will fire, whereas a slight increase in the number of active LOT lines will mean that practically all piriform cells should fire.

This extreme dependence of cell firing on amount of LOT input indicates that normalization of the size of the LOT input alone will be insufficient to stabilize the size of the layer II response; even slight variation of LOT activity in either direction has extreme consequences. A number of solutions are possible; in particular, the known local anatomy and physiology of layer II inhibitory interneurons provides a mechanism for controlling the amount of layer II response. As discussed, inhibitory interneurons give rise to both feedforward (activated by LOT input) and feedback (activated by collateral axons) activity; the influence of any particular interneuron is limited anatomically to a relatively small radius around itself within layer II, and the influence of multiple interneurons probably overlap to some extent. Nonetheless, the sphere of influence of a particular inhibitory interneuron can be viewed as a local patch in layer II, within which the number of active excitatory cells is in large measure controlled by the activity of the inhibitory cell in that patch. If a number of excitatory cells are firing with varying depolarization levels within a patch in layer II, activation of the inhibitory cells by the excitatory cells will tend to weaken those excitatory cells that are less depolarized than the most strongly firing cell within the patch, leading to a competition in which only those cells firing most strongly within a patch will burst, and these cells will, via the interneuron, suppress multiple firing of other cells within the patch. Thus the patch takes on some of the characteristics of

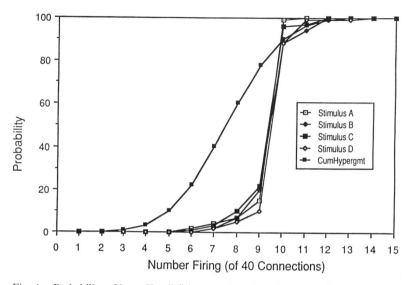

Fig. 4. Probability of layer II cell firing as a function of number of LOT axons active in the absence of local inhibitory patches. The hypergeometric function (CumHypergmt) specifies the probability of layer II cell firing in the absence of caudally directed feedback collaterals, that is, assuming that all collaterals are equally probable to travel either rostrally or caudally. In this case, there is a smooth S-shaped function for probability of cell firing with increasing LOT activity, so that adjustment of global firing threshold (e.g., via nonspecific cholinergic inputs affecting all piriform inhibitory interneurons) can effectively normalize piriform layer II cell firing. However, when feedback axons are caudally directed, then probability steepens markedly, becoming a near step function, in which the probability of cell firing is exquisitely sensitive to the number of active inputs across a range of empirically tested LOT stimulation patterns (A–D in the figure). In this case, global adjustment of inhibition will fail to normalize layer II cell firing adequately: the probability of cell firing will always be either near zero or near 1.0; either nearly all cells will fire or almost none will fire. Local inhibitory control of patches of layer II solves this problem.

a winner-take-all network (Feldman, 1982): Only the most strongly firing cells will be able to overcome inhibition sufficiently to burst, some additional cells will pulse once and then be overwhelmed by inhibition, and the rest of the cells in the patch will be silent, even though that patch may be receiving a large amount of excitatory input via LOT and collateral axon activity in layer I.

D. THE ENHANCED MODEL: TAPERING AND PATCHWORK INHIBITION

The two anatomical features discussed above were built into the second simulation. The lateral olfactory tract "tapers" as it progresses from the rostral to the caudal end of the olfactory cortex: The percentage of the dendritic field of a layer II cell occupied by input grows progressively smaller across the anterior–posterior extent of the cortex; conversely, the associational feedback system grows reciprocally larger (Schwob & Price, 1978). Also mentioned above was the point that the interneurons have quite restricted projection fields. To simulate this, the 100 cells of the network were divided into patches, each of which had its own population of local interneurons.

Two physiological features, probabilistic release and the after-hyperpolarization, were also included in the second model. The first of these requires additional comment. Transmitter is released at the neuromuscular junction in quanta with the number of quanta following Poisson statistics. The appropriate parameters for release are not known in the central nervous system but it has been argued that failures (no release) are common (Redman & Walmsley, 1983a, 1983b). Multiple innervation of a dendrite by a single axon somewhat offsets this; that is, multiple contacts offer several opportunities for a single fiber to depolarize a target cell. Nonetheless, the probabilistic nature of transmission will cause significant variations in the response produced by single inputs. This feature was added to the second simulation.

While work with the new model is still preliminary, it is already apparent that it discriminates (orthogonalizes) inputs much more effectively than did the earlier simulation, without any sacrifice of its clustering ability. Sequential convergence of cluster and individuating responses, so prominent in the first simulation, is also found in the second. However, the more complicated model requires somewhat more stimulus sampling both in learning and performance.

E. EMERGENT CATEGORIZATION BEHAVIOR IN THE ENHANCED MODEL

The probabilistic quantal transmitter-release properties of piriform synapses described above give rise to probabilistic levels of postsynaptic depolarization. This inherent randomness of cell firing, in combination with activity of local inhibitory patches in layer II, selects different sets of bursting and pulsing cells on different trials if no synaptic enhancement has taken place. The time-locked firing to the theta rhythm enables distinct spatial patterns of firing to be read out against a relatively quiescent background firing rate. LTP enhances the conductances and alters the probabilistic nature of communication between a given axon and dendrite (recall that LTP is correlated with added contacts), which tends to overcome the randomness of the cell firing patterns in untrained cells, yielding a stable spatial pattern that will reliably appear in response to the same input in the future and in fact will appear even in response to degraded or noisy versions of the input pattern. Furthermore, subsequent input patterns that differ in only minor respects from a learned LOT input pattern will contact many of the already potentiated synapses from the original pattern, thereby tending to give rise to a very similar (and stable) output firing pattern. Thus as multiple cues sharing many overlapping LOT lines are learned, the layer II cell responses to each of these cues will strongly resemble the responses to the others. Hence, the response(s) behave as though simply labelling a *category* of very similar cues; sufficiently different cues will give rise to quite different category responses.

F.   EMERGENT DIFFERENTIATION BEHAVIOR IN THE ENHANCED MODEL

Potentiated synapses cause stronger depolarization and firing of those cells participating in a category response to a learned cue. This increased depolarization causes strong, cell-specific after-hyperpolarization (AHP), effectively putting those cells into a relatively long-lasting ($\approx$ 1sec) refractory period that prevents them from firing in response to the next few sampling sniffs of the cue. Then the inhibitory winner-take-all behavior within patches effectively selects alternate cells to fire, once these strongly firing (learned) cells have undergone AHP. These alternates will be selected with some randomness, given the probabilistic release characteristics discussed above, since these cells will tend not to have potentiated synapses. These alternate cells then activate their caudally flowing recurrent collaterals, activating distinct populations of synapses in caudal layer Ib. Potentiation of these synapses in combination with those of still-active LOT axons tends to recruit stable subpopulations of caudal cells that are distinct for each simulated odor. They are distinct for each odor because the rostral cells are selected from the population of unpotentiated or weakly potentiated cells (after the strongly potentiated cells have been removed via AHP); hence they will at first tend to be selected randomly. Then, of the caudal cells that receive some activation from the weakening caudal LOT lines, those that also receive collateral innervation from these semirandomly selected rostrals will be those that will tend to fire most strongly and hence to be potentiated.

The probability of a cell participating in the rostral semirandomly selected groups for more than one odor (e.g., for two similar odors) is relatively low. The probability of any caudal cell then being recruited for more than one odor by these rostral cell collaterals in combination with weakening caudal LOT lines is similarly low; the product of these two probabilities is of course lower still. Hence, it is highly unlikely that any particular caudal cell potentiated as part of this process will participate in response to more than one odor.

This means that, when sampling (sniffing), the first pattern of cell firing will indicate similarity among learned odors, causing AHP of those patterns; thus later sniffs will generate patterns of firing that tend to be quite different for different odors, even when those odors are very similar. Empirical tests of the simulation have shown that odors consisting of 90% overlapping LOT firing patterns will give rise to overlaps of between 85 and 95% in their initial layer II spatial firing patterns, whereas these same cues give rise to layer II patterns that overlap by less than 20% on second and third sniffs. The spatio-temporal pattern of layer II firing over multiple samples thus can be taken as a strong differentiating mechanism for even very similar cues, while the initial sniff response for those cues will nonetheless give rise to a spatial firing pattern that indicates the similarity of sets of learned cues, and therefore their category membership in the clustering sense.

VI. Discussion

A. DEVELOPING AND TESTING PREDICTIONS FROM THE MODEL

The simulations so far developed, though quite simple and still impoverished with regard to biological detail, make several psychobiological predictions. Testing these will be greatly facilitated by the development of the electric odor paradigm; the simulation used, as its inputs, a pattern of LOT activation corresponding to that found to be effective when electrical stimulation of the LOT was substituted for real odors in a behavioral experiment (as discussed above; see also Staubli et al., 1988). Experiments are now under way to determine if activity of individual cells in the cortex is synchronized by stimulation to the degree found in the simulation; if intensely firing neurons enter a period of profound suppression (AHP); and if initial responses are more broadly tuned than later ones (i.e., clustering and differentiation). It should also be possible to use extracellular field potentials to determine if several of the fundamental physiological rules identified from experiments on slices and incorporated into the simulations actually hold in the behaving animal or are partially obscured by mechanisms not identified in the in vitro experiments.

Future versions of the model will have to incorporate a more realistic treatment of time and more elaborate input signals, two issues that are interrelated. The electric odor experiments appear to have identified some very minimal conditions needed for the cortex to learn and recognize a cue; the actual messages sent from bulb are certain to be more complex. Some information about "desirable" input signals should emerge from electric odor experiments using a variety of stimulation patterns and multiple stimulating electrodes. Behavioral and physiological results from experiments of this type may point to rules imposed by the cortex concerning what will be processed versus what will be filtered.

Beyond this lies the problem of characterizing the naturally occurring inputs to the cortex. This will require chronic unit recording from identified spatial locations (e.g., sites driven by particular odors) in the bulb of well-trained rats engaged in learning and performing olfactory discriminations. Given the powerful centrifugal influences acting on the bulb, and the active nature of sniffing, it would probably not be appropriate to attempt to use data from acute experiments in a simulation intended to reflect input occurring during behavior. Since the mitral and deep tufted cells (which can be identified by antidromic stimulation of the LOT) project throughout the cortex, while other bulbar cells do not, chronic studies from enough olfactory bulb sites could provide a very direct picture of the type of input sampled by cortical neurons during olfaction.

While detailed predictions about the behavior of piriform units during presentation of natural odors cannot be made in the absence of information about the bulbar output, chronic recording studies are nonetheless being used to test more generalized ideas arising from the simulations. For example, the modeling results indicate that cortex should use sparse coding (i.e., a small percentage of cells should be responsive to any given odor) and that timing rules, presumably locked to sniffing rates, should be in evidence. Early results from chronic recording studies in unrestrained, learning animals have supported these conclusions (J. Larson et al., unpublished observations). The model also predicts that learning will have a stabilizing effect on firing patterns in layer II, and this point is under study in the same chronic recording experiments.

It is appropriate to note here that behavioral studies have identified a number of properties of olfactory learning and performance that constrain ideas about the operation of cortex and that are satisfied by the simulation. For example, detection and recognition of odors by rats is quite fast (<0.015 sec in some studies), which indicates that only a limited number of processing steps in cortex can occur before the response machinery is set into motion. Moreover, olfactory learning can also be extremely rapid in well-trained rats. In studies in which rats are required to learn discriminations between pairs of odors, with a new pair of novel odors being presented each day, it was found that later pairs in a series were acquired in five trials or less (Staubli et al., 1988), indicative of the acquisition of a learning set (Slotnick & Katz, 1974). Only a few training sessions are needed for the network to encode a particular input vector. The olfactory memory system also exhibits great capacity and stability: Rats can learn many odor pairs with no decrease in speed and no increase in interference effects from previous learning (Staubli *et al.,* 1988). Note that rehearsals do not occur in this learning paradigm: The animals appear to encode and maintain memories rapidly without subsequent experience with particular odors, in the face of continuing acquisition of novel odors. These are all properties exhibited by the network simulation. It can also be seen that these are attributes of at least some forms of "everyday memory"; that is, rapid acquisition, reliable encoding without extensive practice, and enormous capacity characterize much of what is commonly thought of as human memory.

B. OTHER OLFACTORY PHENOMENOLOGY

The simulation has thus far been tested using complex odors of constant intensity, using the assumption that the bulb normalizes input signals (odors) of different intensities. It remains an open question as to whether the enormous range of stimulus intensity that is dealt with by the olfactory system can be explained in this way. In any event, it seems unlikely that bulbar operations alone could explain certain other types of olfactory phenomena relating to the detection of observed signals. There is, for example, the problem of identifying a weak odor obscured by a stronger one or identifying the components of a complex odor. That is, the olfactory system seems well suited for synthesizing a unitary perception from a complex of components, but experientially it also appears to have a capacity for analysis or dissection; minimally, it is capable of detecting certain well-known elements even when these constitute a small fraction of the entire stimulus. We have noted that the simulation is able to identify two separate, previously learned odors when these were presented simultaneously by using the assumption that the feedback to the bulb randomly reduced the excitatory center of each odor patch (Lynch *et al.,* 1988). However, this is a specialized case in that the two odor components were of exactly the same strength (i.e., activated the same number of input lines and were members of established categories). Although formal experiments are yet to be conducted, it is doubtful that the network could detect the presence of a weak signal against a strong background. Adaptation at the receptor level might help explain effects of this sort, although it seems questionable whether this would be fast enough. Another possibility is an interaction between cortex and bulb. The anterior olfactory nucleus has topographic connections with the bulb (Schoenfeld & Macrides, 1984) that could be used to suppress the most active patches; coupled with adaptations in the olfactory cortex, a system such as this could exploit the topography of bulb to find weaker signals.

This raises the point that many and perhaps most perceptual and behavioral properties can only be understood by considering interactions between networks of different types. Features will be present in any given cortical network that have little meaning when considered independently of properties in related systems. In the case of the piriform network, it is possible that adjustments of the interneuron system allow the network to sample different frequencies and patterns of activity that are related to different strength signals emerging from bulb during "analysis" of odors.

C. CLUSTERING

In the discussion of physiological rules, the proposal was made that the properties of inhibition were such as to provide cortical networks with multiple thresholds with which to analyze a signal, an amplification device that converts certain patterned inputs into changes in contact strength, and the general property of signal filtering. Simulations indicate that these rules, coupled with certain salient anatomical features of olfactory cortex, result in a network that does a creditable job of clustering and differentiating input cues. A further observation of some potential importance is that behavior of the network improved, at least with regard to differentiation, as more biological detail was added. This is not to say that other models using rules that are only remotely related to neurons could not perform the same operations as the olfactory cortex simulation. We did not, however, design our network with the problems of clustering and differentiating stimuli in mind; quite the contrary, our "bottom-up" simulation work itself suggested these operations as properties inherent in simple cortical networks.

Models of brain networks can use simulations to identify problems that are resolvable by those networks, whereas simulations of more purely theoretical networks typically begin with a problem and then identify parameters needed for a solution. Biological features are incorporated into brain network simulations of the type described here not to add preselected functions but rather to find what properties (or capacities) emerge when these features are added.

Incremental clustering of cues into similarity-based categories is a more subtle process than might be thought, and while it is clear that the networks will execute this function, we do not know how optimal their performance is in an information-theoretic sense relative to some measure of the value or cost of information in the encoding. Building a categorical scheme is a nonmonotonic, combinatorial problem: That is, each new item to be learned can have disproportionate effects on the existing scheme, and the number of potential categories (clusters) climbs factorially with the number of items to be categorized. Algorithmic solutions to problems of this type are computationally very expensive. Calculation of an ideal categorization scheme (with respect to particular cost measures in a performance task), using a measure from game theory termed *category utility* (Gluck & Corter, 1985) and a hill-climbing algorithm using this measure (Fisher, 1987) applied to a problem involving 22 odors, required more than 4 hours on a 68020-based computer. The simulation network reached essentially the same answer as the game-theoretic program but did so in seconds. That is, on this particular set of simulated input data, five trials of training on each of the 22 cues, the network gave rise to first-sniff responses that were nearly indistinguishable (overlapped by more than 90%) for subgroups of cues, effectively partitioning the data into five groups: the same five groups identified as optimal for these cues by the game-theoretic measure mentioned. At the same time, the simulation learned late-sniff response patterns that were unique for each of the 22 cues, none of which overlapped with each other by more than 25%. This task of developing clustering schemes while at the same time retaining differentiated responses to individual cues enables the mechanism to retain hierarchical information about the learned cues. The type of partitioning described occurs in the network whenever a sufficient amount of similarity has been detected. The network may have no group-membership information available, when in fact useful categories are present in the stimulus world. Humans, on at least some tasks, may carry out clustering by building initial clusters and then merging or splitting them as more cues are presented. Thus far, the networks do not pass through successive categorization schemata. However, experiments on human categorization have almost exclusively involved situations in which all cues were presented in rapid succession and category membership is taught explicitly, rather than developed independently by the subject. Hence, it is not clear from the experimental literature whether or not stable clusters develop in this way from stimuli presented at widely spaced intervals with no category membership information given, which is the problem corresponding to that given the network (and that is probably common in nature). It will be of interest to test categorizing skills of rats learning successive olfactory discriminations over several days. Using appropriately selected stimuli, it should be possible to determine if stable clusters are constructed and whether merging and splitting occurs over trials.

Any useful clustering device must utilize information about the heterogeneity of the stimulus world in setting the heterogeneity of individual categories. Heterogeneity of categories refers to the degree of similarity that is used to determine if cues are to be grouped together or not. Several network parameters will influence category size and we are exploring how these influence the individuation function; one particularly interesting possibility involves a shifting threshold function, an idea used with great success by Cooper and co-workers in his work on visual cortex (cf. Cooper, 1984; Bear *et al.*, 1987). The problems presented to the simulation thus far involve a totally naive system, one that has had no developmental history. We are currently exploring a model in which early experiences are not learned by the network but instead set parameters for later ("adult") learning episodes. The idea is that early experience determines the heterogeneity of the stimulus world and imprints this on the network, not by specific changes in synaptic strengths, but in a more general fashion.

ACKNOWLEDGMENTS

This research was supported in part by the Office of Naval Research under grants N00014-84-K-0391 and N00014-87-0838 and by the National Science Foundation under grant IST-85-12419.

REFERENCES

Abraham, W. C., & Goddard, G. V. (1983). Asymmetric relationships between homosynaptic long-term potentiation and heterosynaptic long-term depression. *Nature (London)*, **305**, 717–719.

Alger, B., & Nicoll, R. (1982). Feed-forward dendritic inhibition in rat hippocampal pyramidal neurons studied *in vitro*. *Journal of Physiology (London)*, **328**, 105–123.

Anderson, J. A., & Mozer, M. (1981). Categorization and selective neurons. In G. Hinton & J. A. Anderson (Eds.), *Parallel models of associative memory*. Hillsdale, NJ: Erlbaum.

Barrionuevo, G., Schottler, F., & Lynch, G. (1979). The effects of repetitive low frequency stimulation on control and "potentiated" synaptic responses in the hippocampus. *Life Science*, **27**, 2385–2391.

Bear, M. F., Cooper, L. N., & Ebner, F. F. (1987). The physiological basis of a theory for synapse modification. *Science*, **237**, 42–48.

Bliss, T. V. P., & Lømo, T. (1973). Long-lasting potentiation of synaptic transmission in the dentate area of the anesthetized rabbit following stimulation of the perforant path. *Journal of Physiology (London)*, **232**, 357–374.

Chang, F. L. F., & Greenough, W. T. (1984). Transient and enduring morphological correlates of synaptic activity and efficacy change in the rat hippocampal slice. *Brain Research*, **309**, 35–46.

Cooper, L. N. (1984). Neuron learning to network organization. In *J. C. Maxwell, the sesquicentennial symposium* (pp. 41–90). Amsterdam: Elsevier.

Desmond, N. L., & Levy, W. B. (1983). Synaptic correlates of associative potentiation/depression: An ultrastructural study in the hippocampus. *Brain Research*, **265**, 21–30.

Dunwiddie, T., & Lynch, G. (1978). Long-term potentiation and depression of synaptic responses in the rat hippocampus: Localization and frequency dependency. *Journal of Physiology (London)*, **276**, 353–367.

Dunwiddie, T., & Lynch, G. (1979). The relationship between extracellular calcium concentrations and the induction of hippocampal long-term potentiation. *Brain Research*, **169**, 103–110.

Feldman, J. A. (1982). Dynamic connections in neural networks. *Biological Cybernetics*, **46**, 27–39.

Fisher, D. (1987). Knowledge acquisition via incremental conceptual clustering. *Machine Learning*, **2**, 139–190.

Fox, S. E., & Ranck, J. B., Jr. (1981). Electrophysiological characteristics of hippocampal complex-spike cells and theta cells. *Experimental Brain Research*, **41**, 399–410.

Gluck, M., & Corter, J. (1985). Information, uncertainty and the utility of categories. In *Proceedings of the Seventh Annual Conference of the Cognitive Science Society* (pp. 283–287). Irvine, CA: Erlbaum.

Granger, R., Ambros-Ingerson, J., Henry, H., & Lynch, G. (1989). Partitioning of sensory data by a cortical network. In *Proceedings of the IEEE Conference on Neural Information Processing Systems*. New York: American Institute of Physics.

Granger, R., Baudry, M., & Lynch, G. (1988). Mapping Hebbian psychology onto Hebbian biology. *Trends in Neuroscience*.

Grossberg, S. (1980). How does the brain build a cognitive code? *Psychological Review*, **87**, 1–51.

Haberly, L. B. (1985). Neuronal circuitry in olfactory cortex: Anatomy and functional implications. *Chemical Senses*, **10**, 219–238.

Haberly, L. B., & Price, J. L. (1977). The axonal projection of the mitral and tufted cells of the olfactory bulb in the rat. *Brain Research*, **129**, 152–157.

Harris, E. W., Ganong, A. H., & Cotman, C. W. (1984). Long-term potentiation in the hippocampus involves activation of N-methyl-D-aspartate receptors. *Brain Research*, **323**, 132–137.

Hopfield, J. J. (1982). Neural networks and physical systems wth emergent collective computational abilities. *Proceedings of the National Academy of Sciences U.S.A.*, **79**, 2554–2558.

Jerison, H. J. (1973). *Evolution of the brain and intelligence*. New York: Academic Press.

Jourdan, F. (1982). Spatial dimension of olfactory coding: A representation of ^{14}C-2-deoxyglucose patterns of glomerular labeling in the olfactory bulb. *Brain Research*, **240**, 341–344.

Kelso, S. R., Ganong, A. H., & Brown, T. H. (1986). Hebbian synapses in hippocampus. *Proceedings of the National Academy of Sciences U.S.A.*, **83**, 5326–5330.

Kohonen, T. (1984). *Self-organization and associative memory*. Berlin: Springer-Verlag.

Krettek, J. E., & Price, J. L. (1977). Projections from the amygdaloid complex and adjacent olfactory structures to the entorhinal cortex and the subiculum in the rat and cat. *Journal of Comparative Neurology*, **172**, 723–752.

Lancet, D., Greer, C. A., Kaver, J. S., & Shepherd, G. M. (1982). Mapping of odor-related neuronal activity in the olfactory bulb by high-resolution 2-deoxyglucose autoradiography. *Proceedings of the National Academy of Sciences U.S.A.*, **79**, 670–674.

Landfield, P. W. (1976). Synchronous EEG rhythms: Their nature and their possible function in memory. In W. H. Gispen (Ed.), *Molecular and functional neurobiology* (pp. 389–424). Amsterdam: Elsevier.

Landfield, P., & Deadwyler, S. (1987). *Long-term potentiation: Mechanisms and key issues*. New York: Alan R. Liss.

Larson, J., & Lynch, G. (1986). Synaptic potentiation in hippocampus by patterned stimulation involves two events. *Science*, **232**, 985–988.

Larson, J., & Lynch, G. (1988). Role of *N*-methyl-D-aspartate receptors in the induction of synaptic potentiation by burst stimulation patterned after the hippocampal theta rhythm. *Brain Research*, **441**, 111–118.

Larson, J., Wong, D., & Lynch, G. (1986). Patterned stimulation at the theta frequency is optimal for induction of long-term potentiation. *Brain Research*, **368**, 7–35.

Lee, K., Oliver, M., Schottler, F., & Lynch, G. (1981). Electron microscopic studies of brain slices: The effects of high frequency stimulation on dendritic ultrastructure. In G. Kerkut & H. V. Wheal (Eds.), *Electrical activity in isolated mammalian C. N. S. preparations* (pp. 189–212). New York: Academic Press.

Lee, K., Schottler, F., Oliver, M., & Lynch, G. (1980). Brief bursts of high-frequency stimulation produce two types of structural change in rat hippocampus. *Journal of Neurophysiology*, **44**, 247–258.

Levy, W. B., & Desmond, N. L. (1985). The rules of elemental synaptic plasticity. In W. B. Levy, J. A. Anderson, & S. Lehmkuhle (Eds.), *Synaptic modification, neuron selectivity, and nervous system organization* (pp. 105–126). Hillsdale, NJ: Erlbaum.

Lorente, de No, R. (1934). Studies on the structure of the cerebral cortex. II. Continuation of the study of the amnionic system. *Journal für Psychologie und Neurologie*, **46**, 113–177.

Luskin, M. B., & Price, J. L. (1983). The laminar distribution of intracortical fibers originating in the olfactory cortex of the rat. *Journal of Comparative Neurology*, **216**, 292–302.

Lynch, G. (1986). *Synapses, circuits and the beginnings of memory*. Cambridge, MA: MIT Press.

Lynch, G., & Baudry, M. (1984). The biochemistry of memory: A new and specific hypothesis. *Science*, **224**, 1057–1063.

Lynch, G., and Baudry, M. (1987). *Structure–function relationships in the organization of memory*.

Lynch, G. S., Dunwiddie, T. V., & Gribkoff, V. (1977). Heterosynaptic depression: A postsynaptic correlate of long-term potentiation. *Nature (London)*, **266**, 737–739.

Lynch, G., Granger, R., Baudry, M., & Larson, J. (1988). Cortical encoding of memory: Hypotheses derived from analysis and simulation of physiological learning rules in anatomical structures. In L. Nadel (Ed.), *Neural connections, mental computations*. Boston: Bradford Books.

Lynch, G. S., Gribkoff, V. K., & Deadwyler, S. A. (1976). Long-term potentiation is accompanied by a reduction in dendritic responsiveness to glutamic acid. *Nature (London)*, **263**, 141–153.

Lynch, G., Jensen, R. A., McGaugh, J., Davila, K., and Oliver, M. (1981). Effects of enkephalin, morphine and naloxone on the electrical activity of the hippocampal slice preparation. *Experimental Neurology*, **7**, 527–540.

Lynch, G., Larson, J., Kelso, S., Barrionuevo, S., & Schottler, F. (1983). Intracellular injections of EGTA block the induction of hippocampal long-term potentiation. *Nature (London)*, **305**, 719–721.

Lynch, G., Larson, J., Staubli, U., & Baudry, M. (1987). New perspectives on the physiology, chemistry and pharmacology of memory. *Drug Development and Research*, **10**, 295–315.

MacDermott, A. B., Mayer, M. L., Westbrook, G. L., Smith, S. J., and Barker, J. L. (1986). NMDA-receptor activation increases cytoplasmic calcium concentration in cultured spinal cord neurones. *Nature (London)*, **321**, 519–522.

Macrides, F., & Davis, B. J. (1983). The olfactory bulb. In *Chemical neuroanatomy* (pp. 391–426). New York: Raven Press.

Macrides, F., Eichenbaum, H. B., & Forbes, W. B. (1982). Temporal relationship between sniffing and the limbic (theta) rhythm during odor discrimination reversal learning. *Journal of Neuroscience, 2,* 1705–1717.

Malinow, R., & Miller, J. P. (1986). Postsynaptic hyperpolarization during conditioning reversibly blocks induction of long-term potentiation. *Nature (London), 320,* 529–530.

McCarren, M., & Alger, B. E. (1985). Use-dependent depression of IPSPs in rat hippocampal pyramidal cells *in vitro. Journal of Neurophysiology, 53,* 557–571.

Mori, K. (1987). Membrane and synaptic properties of identified neurons in the olfactory bulb. *Progress in Neurobiology, 29,* 275–320.

Morris, R. G. M., Anderson, E., Lynch, G., & Baudry, M. (1986). Selective impairment of learning and blockade of long-term potentiation by an *N*-methyl-D-aspartate receptor antagonist, AP-5. *Nature (London), 319,* 774–776.

Mouly, A. M., Vigouroux, M., & Holley, A. (1987). On the ability of rats to discriminate between microstimulations of the olfactory bulb in different locations. *Behavioral Brain Research, 17,* 45–58.

O'Keefe, J., & Nadel, L. (1978). *The hippocampus as a cognitive map.* Oxford: Clarendon Press.

Price, J. L. (1973). An autoradiographic study of complementary laminar patterns of termination of afferent fibers to the olfactory cortex. *Journal of Comparative Neurology, 150,* 87–108.

Redman, S. J., & Walmsley, B. (1983a). The time course of synaptic potentials evoked in cat motoneurones at identified group Ia synapses. *Journal of Physiology (London), 343,* 117–133.

Redman, S. J., & Walmsley, B. (1983b). Amplitude fluctuations in synaptic potentials evoked in cat spinal motoneurones at identified group Ia synapses. *Journal of Physiology (London), 343,* 135–145.

Roman, F., Staubli, U., & Lynch, G. (1988). Evidence for synaptic potentiation in a cortical network during learning. *Brain Research, 418,* 221–226.

Schonfeld, T. A., & Macrides, F. (1984). Topographic organization of connections between the main olfactory bulb and pars externa of the anterior olfactory nucleus in the hamster. *Journal of Comparative Neurology, 227,* 121–135.

Schwob, J. E., & Price, J. L. (1978). The cortical projection of the olfactory bulb: Development in fetal and neonatal rats correlated with quantitative variation in adult rats. *Brain Research, 151,* 369–374.

Shaw, G. L., Silverman, D. J., & Pearson, J. C. (1986). Trion model of cortical organization: Toward a theory of information processing and memory. In G. Palm & A. Aertsen (Eds.), *Brain theory* (pp. 177–191). Berlin: Springer-Verlag.

Shepherd, G. M. (1979). *The synaptic organization of the brain* (2nd ed.). New York: Oxford University Press.

Skeen, L. C., & Hall, W. C. (1977). Efferent projections of the main and accessory olfactory bulb in the tree shrew *(Tupaia glis). Journal of Comparative Neurology, 172,* 1–36.

Slotnick, B. M., & Katz, H. M. (1974). Olfactory learning-set formation in rats. *Science, 185,* 796–798.

Staubli, U., Baudry, M., & Lynch, G. (1984). Leupeptin, a thiol-proteinase inhibitor, causes a selective impairment of spatial maze performance in rats. *Behavioral Neural Biology, 40,* 58–69.

Staubli, U., Baudry, M., & Lynch, G. (1985). Olfactory discrimination learning is blocked by leupeptin, a thiol-proteinase inhibitor. *Brain Research, 337,* 333–336.

Staubli, U., Fraser, D., Faraday, R., & Lynch, G. (1987). Olfaction and the "data" memory system in rats. *Behavioral Neuroscience, 101,* 757–765.

Staubli, U., & Lynch, G. (1987). Stable hippocampal long-term potentiation elicited by "theta" pattern stimulation. *Brain Research, 435,* 227–234.

Wenzel, J., & Matthies, H. (1985). Morphological changes in the hippocampal formation accompanying memory formation and long-term potentiation. In N. Weinberger, J. McGaugh, & G. Lynch (Eds.), *Memory systems of the brain* (pp. 150–170). New York: Guilford Press.

Wigstrøm, H., & Gustaffson, B. (1983). Facilitated induction of long-lasting potentiation during blockade of inhibition. *Nature (London), 301,* 603–605.

Wigstrøm, H., Gustaffson, B., Huang, Y. Y., & Abraham, W. C. (1986). Hippocampal long-term potentiation is induced by pairing single afferent volleys with intracellularly injected depolarizing current pulses. *Acta Physiologica Scandinavica, 126,* 317–319.

A COMPUTATIONAL APPROACH TO HIPPOCAMPAL FUNCTION

William B Levy

I. Introduction

This article presents the early, formative stages of a theory of hippocampal function. This theory, while stimulated by the psychological observations indicating a role for the hippocampus in short-term working memory and spatial behavior, develops mainly through consideration of computational issues. These computational issues are related to the psychological viewpoint through physiological and anatomical observations. The critical anatomy which dominates our thinking about the hippocampus is shown in Fig. 1.

In the theory presented here, the hippocampus participates in the prediction of future representations based on past and present representations. All three classes of representations are derived from a multiplicity of sensory modalities, such as auditory, visual, and olfactory signals from neo- and piriform cortices. This fusion of sensory modalities requires recoding because of computational complexity problems.

Figure 2 relates the functional groupings used to explain the theory of hippocampal function to the cells of the hippocampus and entorhinal cortex.

The CA1 region of the hippocampus is postulated to be a prediction-generating layer or tier. This region produces a prediction based on its input from hippocampal region CA3.

The combined hippocampal dentate gyrus/CA3 (DG/CA3) system is

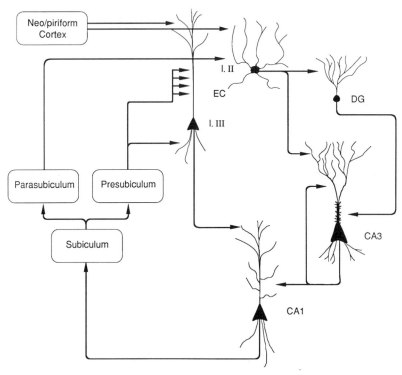

Fig. 1. Limbic system inspiration for the networks: CA1 and CA3 are regions of Ammon's horn (cornu Ammonis) of the hippocampus, DG is the hippocampal dentate gyrus, EC is entorhinal cortex, and l.II and l.III are layers II and III of EC. Copyright © 1989 by William B Levy.

postulated to be a preprocessor serving the CA1 prediction layer. This preprocessor is the focus of the chapter. Computational complexity considerations imply the utility of such recoding as part of signal mixing. That is, from a computational perspective, this preprocessor decreases the statistical dependency of individual representations and increases the similarities between successive representations. These changes al low the CA1 prediction layer to create more accurate predictive repre sentations and predictive representations which predict further into the future.

The computational complexity problems arise from the combinatorial explosion of possible representations resulting when the hippocampus and supporting limbic structures mix representations from multiple sensory modalities. These problems are particularly difficult because both the mixed and unmixed representations occur as sequences which contain information beyond that found within the individual representations.

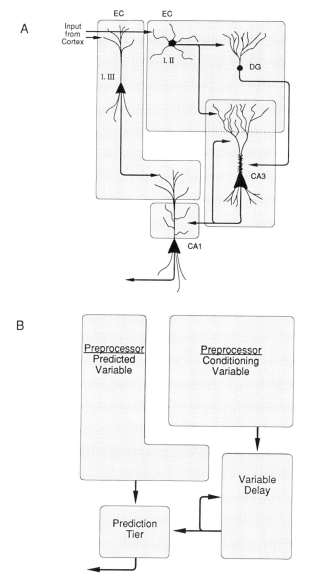

Fig. 2. A juxtaposition of the proposed computational model, B, with its anatomical basis, A. Note that the major subdivisions of the hippocampus and entorhinal cortex depicted in A do not always correspond precisely to the functional units of the model in B. One reason for this imprecise correspondence is that neurons are multicompartmented based on their segregation of afferent termination zones. Layer II of the entorhinal cortex, the dentate gyrus, and the distal CA3 dendritic region correspond to the preprocessor of the conditioning variable. Layer III of the entorhinal cortex and the distal dendritic region of the CA1 pyramids correspond to the preprocessor for the predicted variable. The variable delay resides within the CA3 region. The prediction tier corresponds to the CA1 pyramids. The theory presented here leads up to and discusses preprocessing of the conditioning variable but does not explore preprocessing of the predicted variable. Copyright © 1989 by William B Levy.

A major problem is explaining how the hippocampus computes predictions about these sequences in the face of this combinatorial explosion. The solution advanced here is the generation of an optimal approximate prediction by CA1. The form of this computation is specified by an axiomatic theory of inference called minimum relative entropy (MRE) and by the nature of synaptic modification at the CA3–CA1 synapses. With the specification of a CA1 computation, a desirable preprocessing computation can then be inferred.

The preprocessing computation, a hypothesized function of the DG/CA3 region, produces two results: (1) the reduction of the intrinsic statistical dependency of the CA3 representations, and (2) a variable time shifting of representations which allows predictions to be generated before the event being predicted.

Thus, two problems—time-shifting and complexity—are solved with one preprocessing network. This proposed dual functionality combines with the CA1 prediction function to contribute a theory of hippocampal function in small animals which relates to the theory of hippocampal function in humans. This is true because the network under consideration dynamically represents the present, recent past, and the future. The ability to represent all three time frames seems to be a functional requirement for a working short-term memory. As a result, this computational theory, based on anatomy and physiology, can exist along with psychological theories of hippocampal function for both rats and humans.

The chapter is divided into six sections. Section II provides background for bridging the gap between rat and human hippocampal theories and points out that evolutionary pressure for efficient spatial behavior is also pressure for sensory mixing to form representations and sequences of representations and pressure for accurate prediction of future representations in these sequences as well. Section III sets forth the computational issues in more detail, and Section IV summarizes these issues in the context of Section V. Section V, while giving more details of the model, discusses the anatomical and physiological observations which motivated the specific model. Section VI sketches an algorithm which is the hypothesized computation performed by the DG/CA3 region.

II. Anatomy, Evolution, and Psychology Form a Background to the Computational Theory

At this time there seem to be two, apparently differing, theories of hippocampal function. According to these theories, either the hippocampus provides a distraction-protected, short-term (Squire, 1987) working memory (Goldman-Rakic, 1987; Murray & Mishkin, 1987; Olton, 1978; Raffaele & Olton, 1988), or it is a locus contributing to, and necessary for, competent spatial behavior (O'Keefe & Nadel, 1978). [There are, however, several papers bridging these two ideas (e.g., Breese, Hampson, & Deadwyler, 1989; Eichenbaum & Cohen, 1988; Foster, Christian, Hampson, Campbell, & Deadwyler, 1987; Olton, 1985).] These two formulations are not mutually exclusive and are best related through computational considerations. As a prelude, this section presents a viewpoint which interrelates spatial function and hippocampal anatomy, setting the stage for the computational arguments in the process. Here we advance the idea that efficient signal mixing for sequence prediction, which facilitates efficient spatial behavior, was the original fundamental computation for which the hippocampus evolved.

A. ANATOMY

It is obvious merely from anatomical considerations that the hippocampus and parahippocampal limbic regions bring together, or fuse, diverse sensory signals arising from association areas of neocortex. This sensory signal fusion function is common to all the mammals which have been studied, including primates as well as rodents (Jones & Powell, 1970; Pandya & Kuypers, 1969; see Amaral, 1987; Swanson, Köhler, & Björklund, 1987, for reviews). Therefore, on purely anatomical grounds, it is sensible to infer that one function of the hippocampus and associated parahippocampal cortices is to mix sensory modalities.

With the exception of olfactory inputs, most sensory information entering the hippocampus actually comes from association neocortex via the entorhinal cortex (Insausti, Amaral, & Cowan, 1987; Jones & Powell, 1970; Pandya & Kuypers, 1969; Saper, 1982; Sorensen, 1985; Van Hoesen & Pandya, 1975; Van Hoesen, Pandya, & Butters, 1972, 1975). Most mixing of signals occurs prior to their reaching the hippocampus, within the neocortex and entorhinal cortex (but see Fig. 3). The hippocampus itself receives its multimodal signals from entorhinal cortex, with help from the adjacent subicular cortices, and in turn feeds its signals back to entorhinal cortex (Kosel, Van Hoesen, & Rosene, 1982; Sorensen & Shipley, 1979; Swanson & Cowan, 1977; see Amaral, 1987; Rosene & Van Hoesen, 1987, for reviews). Thus the entorhinal cortex appears to be the ultimate site of fusion of the sensory signals from association cortices while the hippocampus can be seen as a structure supporting the signal mixing performed in the entorhinal cortex. As a support structure, the hippocampus remixes the multimodal signals coming from entorhinal cortex. This remixing, as shown in Fig. 3, occurs primarily through diver-

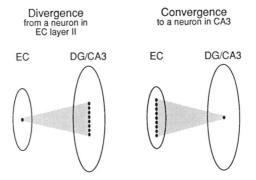

Divergence
from a neuron in
EC layer II

Convergence
to a neuron in CA3

Signal Mixing/Sensory Fusion without CA3–CA3 Feedback

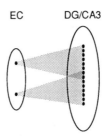

Sensory Signal Fusion of the Two Most Distant Neurons of EC Layer II

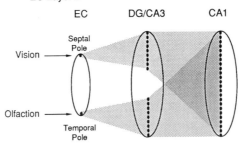

Area of overlapped shadowing indicates region of possible cell to cell convergence in CA1.

Fig. 3.   Schematic illustration of divergence and convergence of signals and their contribution to sensory signal fusion. The entorhinal cortex (EC) may receive signals that are spatially separated across its septo–temporal axis. However, even without CA3–CA3 feedback, it is highly probable that the hippocampal representations of these spatially separated EC inputs will include neurons which are active due to the divergence and convergence of axonal projections. Note, in the bottom panel, the extent of convergence in CA1 even when very spatially separated EC inputs are considered. Such an association of diverse input signals should eventually lead to decreased signal complexity and better prediction. Copyright © 1989 by William B Levy.

gence–convergence of the entorhinal cortical–DG/CA3 projections, the CA3–CA1 projections, and the feedback of region CA3 upon itself (not shown in Fig. 3).

The question to address now is, How are signal mixing and remixing related to efficient spatial behavior?

B. A MATTER OF BACKGROUND: WHOSE HIPPOCAMPUS IS IT, ANYWAY?

Only mammals have a well-defined hippocampus and all mammals have this structure. Thus, it is probable that the stem mammal, a small shrew-like creature, had a hippocampus though its reptilian relatives did not. But why did the hippocampus develop? What purpose did it serve? If we can answer these questions we might be able to imagine how the human and rat hippocampi, although divergent in function, are related.

One outstanding distinction between mammals and reptiles is that mammals exhibit nesting behavior and suckle their young while reptiles do not. Consequently, the mammal with a nest full of young must return home after foraging for food. Thus the prototypical mammal had to find its way upon the earth's surface, constrained by objects which towered over it to form both visual and physical barriers. We should picture this world not from the viewpoint of erect hominids but from the lowly perspective of a small shrewlike animal scurrying through the brush and forests. A small rock or a tuft of grass can tower above a small animal to form wall-like structures. In this case, perception of spatial relations is based not on an all-encompassing, maplike view from above but on sensory sequences involving all senses.

From the above considerations come two main points. The first is that learning-dependent spatial behavior in a maze, as studied in rats and mice today, seems as relevant to the prototypical mammal as to a rat or mouse in the wild. The second point is that studies of spatial behavior essentially require animals to learn and predict sensory sequences.

It was and is a tremendous advantage for a small mammal to get from the nest to a feeding area and back to the nest again as efficiently as possible. This problem of scurrying efficiently to and from the nest is a problem of prediction which requires mixing multimodal sensory signals as these signals arrive sequentially over time. That is, an animal will return home most quickly if it can use sights, smells, sounds and other sensations as they arrive over time in order to predict correctly from moment to moment which way to turn or when to go straight. Note that such prediction is based on sensory input and, in an immediate sense, is just prediction of the set of sensory signals which will follow the set of signals being received at a given time. These sets of signals represent the environmental stimuli bombarding the animal as it makes its way home. To predict the next set of signals in the sequence is effectively to anticipate what is "around the corner."

Maneuvering in a maze or in the wild produces a sequence of sensory inputs involving all sensory modalities: sight, smell, hearing, acceleration, touch, and perhaps even taste. Obviously, the visual input changes as an animal moves about. However, for a small animal with a diminished range of vision, the sense of smell seems at least equally important. Even so, vision and olfaction are not the only senses useful in a maze. Experimenters have found that a rat can use sound cues, such as the sound made by an exhaust fan, to locate itself relative to its surroundings. It is plausible then that our shrewlike animal would be able to use the sound of a babbling brook to orient itself. In regard to touch, we know that we as humans can use the feel of carpet versus linoleum underfoot to locate ourselves. The vestibular sense tells an animal which way it faces as it turns. It is even conceivable that a small animal might lick its surroundings and detect taste differences. Thus we can picture each of the senses solving the same problem: prediction of future multisensory perceptions.

In sum, then, it was the earliest mammal, as distinct from its ancestors, which had the most pressing need to locate itself relative to its present and future surroundings as it moved about. Additionally, in performing this relative localization, all senses are potentially useful.

The evolutionary connection between sensory signal mixing and efficient spatial behavior is further elaborated by using and extending the ideas of Jerison (1973). At the time the first mammals evolved, dinosaurs and other reptiles dominated the land by day, but at night, when it became too cold for these poikilotherms, animals that could regulate their body temperature were free to roam unmenaced by predatory reptiles. In this scenario we picture our prototypical mammal scurrying through a partially darkened maze in which the visual system is much less efficient (though still useful). Thus, the demands of nocturnal life favored the evolutionary development of superior olfactory and sound-localizing abilities to at least match a visual ability already evolved. Development of these other senses and a need to return home after each foray would have fostered the development of a new brain structure that allowed the different modalities to relate to each other.

If we consider the sensory signal fusion problem in more detail, however, our attention is drawn to a very important computational issue. Mere development of multiple, but individual, sensory perceptual abilities is not nearly as useful as an effective combination of these same abilities. It is not efficient to have one sensory system predict that home lies to the left and another sensory system predict that it lies to the right. Efficient functioning requires the combination of multimodal signals to produce a harmonious single prediction pointing the way home. However, this sensory signal mixing is a problem of such computational complexity that it baffles engineers even today.

To illustrate the problem with respect to vision and olfaction, suppose one engineer built the best visual pattern recognition system in the world and another engineer built the best gas chromatograph–mass spectrometer for chemical identification. How should the coded representations of reflected photons and molecules be combined? The answer is far from simple since there is no obvious physical relationship between the physics of light as reflected from macroscopic objects and the reactions or structures of different molecules.

Consistent, predictable relationships between the states of neurons which code sights and the states of neurons which code smells may only exist as higher-order statistics. Such higher-order statistics would be infrequently sampled and quite variable on an evolutionary time scale. This situation contrasts with more peripheral, unimodal coding, which can rely on lower-order statistics that are constant across generations. The higher-order correlations of the multisensory problem are difficult to find because there are so many possible correlations compared with the relatively few important correlations which actually exist. Consequently particular experiences of the protomammal's ancestors would provide little help for constructing a nervous system tied to the specifics of the multisensory relationships they encountered.

Yet even though the problem of multisensory representations is a tremendously difficult one, the hippocampus and associated limbic cortices have managed to meld olfactory and visual signals together into useful multisensory representations. Actually these structures work on an even more difficult problem, that of multisensory sequences.

As mentioned above, the particular sensory signal fusion problem which occurs when traversing a maze is not a static problem involving the "mere" creation of a single multisensory representation which will eventually be recognized or categorized in some other brain region. Rather, the maze problem involves changing multisensory representations which arrive over time as the animal moves both in time and in space. Temporally ordered sets of these changing representations are called sequences. An animal which exhibits efficient spatial behavior by accurately predicting what lies around the corner is just predicting one, or several, successive representations in the current sequence of sensory representations. (E.g., if I turn right at this rock I'll pass by the lilacs and then just down the hill and to the right is the water hole.) From a computational perspective this dynamic problem is even more complex than the already intractable static problem of sensory signal mixing.

Thus we are motivated to study hippocampal function from a dynamic perspective in which this structure predicts computationally complex, multisensory sequences.

In sum, anatomical observations indicate that the hippocampus participates in sensory signal fusion by helping to mix and, in particular, to remix the most highly processed and diverse sensory representations. Evolutionary pressure for new and improved sensory signal fusion capabilities applicable to spatial behavior would have arisen because the protomammal was nocturnal and had a home to which it returned to care for its young. This sensory signal fusion capability facilitates navigation, especially when these fused sensory representations are used for accurate sequence prediction.

The next section gives more precision to the two computational issues introduced here: (1) sensory signal fusion, which lowers signal complexity without losing information and (2) representations of the future, which act as predictions.

III.   Computational Issues

The influence of the computational approach becomes profound when we consider a neural network in terms of two issues: complexity and optimization.

The exponential explosion (complexity) of possible configurations of the environment and, of more relevance, of the activity states of the neurons in the brain implies that exact computations which examine and compare each individual neural representation, one by one or in parallel, are not possible. However, there are methods for maintaining the individuality of representations while simplifying the computations made. Such methods are necessarily approximations. What we have in mind is to describe neurally computable transformations and algorithms which are, in some yet to be defined sense, optimal approximate solutions for the prediction problem.

A.   MOTIVATING THE COMPUTATIONAL APPROACH

There are many reasons for using a computational approach to formulate theories of brain function. To acquaint the reader with the perspectives leading to and inherent in this approach, I will set forth what seem to me to be some of its most important advantages, with the caveat that these thoughts are merely intuitions and lack the support of an airtight logical argument.

1. There have been so many partial models of hippocampal function briefly in vogue over the last 30 years that I have despaired of finding any simple, lasting description of hippocampal function that is specific in its predictions. The computational approach benefits from a precise mathematical language which avoids vague descriptions of how the animal "thinks" by confining itself to questions of signal transformation and statistics. In more than one way, the computational approach advocated here is an extension of the abstract approach advocated by Thompson and Spencer (1966) for the study of psychological processes.

2. Since almost every textbook says that the primary function of the brain is "information processing" an explanation of this phrase would seem to be in order. A computational perspective seems to have a good chance of providing a satisfactory definition of information processing.

3. There should be a way to study only one anatomical region of the brain, such as the basal ganglia, the CA1 region of the hippocampus, or the cerebellum, at a time. If we have to study the totality of all brain areas at once, the job of understanding and explaining the functions of these areas seems hopeless. However, if brain regions can be studied in pieces, and not just from the periphery inwards, then many scientists can work in parallel toward understanding the brain, some concentrating on the piriform cortex, others concentrating on the tectum, and so on.

To carry out such a program successfully we will need a language and a perspective which can encompass all brain regions. An abstract computational approach promises to satisfy these needs.

4. The basic computational issue of prediction is fundamental and easily understood. Rapid, accurate prediction is a continual necessity in our everyday lives. It is the process by which we put past experiences to work in order to anticipate the future and act on our environment. In fact our very survival depends upon it. Inquiry into this realm is aided by the fact that prediction is also a rather well-studied subdiscipline in mathematics and statistical theory.

Good prediction can improve the execution of almost any behavior. It enables the experimental rat to make the correct response and receive its food pellet, the engineer to design a structurally sound bridge (based on the knowledge of stress gained from past bridge building experiences), and the baseball player to accommodate his swing when he recognizes the pitcher's curve ball. [My own thoughts on prediction as a general problem in life were most influenced by the writings of Young (1970) and

Dawkins (1976). In writings on the theory of hippocampal function, prediction is often mentioned by Gray (1982) and Vinogradova (as cited in Gray, 1982).]

When dealing with a complex, multitiered structure such as the brain, we can even consider the issue of good prediction in the context of choosing good transformations, that is, prediction of the utility of a transformation in helping to make a subsequent prediction by the network. In fact this leads to the potentially infinite regress of predicting a good signal transformation in order to help predict a good signal transformation . . . in order to predict about the environment. Happily, such complications are unnecessary because the abstract, computational approach allows us to divide the processing sequence into small pieces. Using such subdivisions we may in effect consider predictions locally, in isolation from subsequent predictions.

At this local or regional level, prediction does not explicitly concern the environment external to the organism, that is, the "real world." Rather, we can and should study prediction in cases in which the environment is the set of neurons afferent to the brain region of interest. When dealing with the hippocampus we consider the environment to be essentially the set of neurons in layers II and III of the entorhinal cortex which are afferent to the hippocampus. Even though the hippocampus receives inputs from many other brain regions, we focus here on the entorhinal cortical afferents because of their high information capacity. We base this interpretation on their numerical dominance and high-frequency firing capabilities relative to other hippocampal inputs.

So we already have a payoff from the abstract, computational approach: Prediction is an important, identifiable issue which we may study in a limited portion of the brain by using an abstract definition of the environment.

B. Computational Questions

Information- and computation-theoretic considerations will allow us to bypass the precise psychological meaning of neuronal signals and still to have viable research questions because these considerations produce their own fundamental and general meaning of neuronal signals. These theoretic considerations provide both research questions and quantitative measures for the study of hippocampal function or, for that matter, the function of any brain region.

One obvious goal of an abstract signal processing approach is to discover the transformation which converts inputs to outputs. For example, suppose the hippocampus performs the general computation f; our goal then is to describe the computation, or transformation, $f: A \to B$.

Here we think of A as a multidimensional input pattern made up of zeros and ones. More technically, $A(t)$ is a sequence of binary vectors over time t where the dimension of these vectors is the number of axons afferent to the hippocampus. Likewise B, with time implicit, is a corresponding sequence of vectors over the efferent axons.

As interesting and challenging as it will be to understand transformation f, this challenge is not enough. We also want to tie this transformation to other questions. On the simplest level, we can ask, Why is it necessary to transform representations such as A into representations such as B?

For the signal mixing and sequence prediction problems, we can outline two general reasons for performing transformations on neuronal signals.

1. The computational problem of prediction of the future based on the past and the present necessitates that representations reflecting the past and present be transformed into representations reflecting the future.

2. The computations which might generate predictions concern problems of large dimension, making them intractable. That is, timely and exact predictions of representations which concern more than 50 neurons are of overwhelming computational complexity. Instead of exact solutions, approximate solutions must be computed. Therefore, signal transformations should be performed to improve these approximations.

Before concluding this introductory material, let us consider two powerful constraints which will influence the evolution and analysis of neural networks.

C. OVERRIDING COMPUTATIONAL CONCERNS: INTRACTABILITY AND OPTIMIZATION

1. Computational Intractability

Computational intractability occurs when the number of possible configurations grows exponentially. Such exponential growth is a very old story (Gamow, 1961). Most of us have heard about the not-so-wise mathematician who asked for payment by having one grain of wheat placed in the first square of a chess board, two grains in the second, four in the third, and so on to end up with 2^{63} grains in the 64th square. As a result of this exponential growth $(2^0, 2^1, 2^2, \ldots, 2^{63})$, the man was owed more wheat than will be produced in 2000 years at current production levels. Not surprisingly, he was put to death by the royal debtor.

When exponential growth characterizes a problem requiring examination of all (or most) possible outcomes, computational intractability results. For example, it is calculated that no computer (Shannon, 1950; Winston, 1977) will ever be able to find the provably unbeatable opening move of a chess game (it is posited that there is such a move, assuming that White, the computer, continues to respond optimally from then on). Finding this move and the subsequent correct responses would require a computer to examine the outcome of every possible chess game, estimated to be more than 2.5×10^{154} games. Thus, even if the computer plays very fast, as fast as one game every femtosecond, it will require 10^{135} years to complete the computation, many times the longevity of the universe.

It is well known that computational constraints, such as the large number of possible decisions, the relatively small number of processors, and a limited memory capacity, are serious concerns in high-dimensional multivariable analysis. (Here we use the term *high-dimension* to mean that the number of variables exceeds 200.) The phrases "curse of dimensionality" (Bellman, 1961) and "combinatorial explosion" (Karp, 1975) are often used to describe the difficulties which arise in high-dimensional problems. A well-known problem which suffers from this explosion is that of minimizing the distance covered by a traveling salesman who must visit a specified set of cities before returning home.

There is an extensive literature on the subject of computational intractability. An early article which emphasizes the intractability of decision-making problems faced by neurallike networks is Ashby (1956). Minsky and Papert (1969) pick up this theme and use it for their own purpose. Barlow (1959 and many other references; see, e.g., 1961a, 1961b), although nontechnical in his discourse, is clearly aware of the importance of this problem and that it must be solved by various brain regions. Recent references to the intractability problem from a computational perspective include Garey and Johnson (1979). Zucker (1981) writes lucidly about how computational constraints limit what can be done in pattern recognition problems. The results of Kirkpatrick, Gelatt, and Vecchi (1983) and Hopfield (1984; Hopfield & Tank, 1985) show that good approximations can be achieved in high dimensions. The 1983 paper by Kirkpatrick and colleagues is particularly influential in advocating the idea that, for a decision-making problem requiring optimization, good approximations in high-dimensional systems are, on average, nearly as good as the set of best possible decisions.

In the case of neural networks, the number of variables present (e.g., processing elements such as neurons) in a simple network can easily number in the thousands. Thus, the sheer number of neurons in the mammalian brain leads to computational intractability there. Figure 4 pictures the exponential growth of the number of possible representations with increasing numbers of neurons. If we consider a neuron as an on–off device, then 1000 neurons can represent 2^{1000} different configurations. For the representations mediated by the approximately 250,000 binary-valued CA1 cells of one rat hippocampus, $2^{250,000}$ different representations could occur. These are unimaginably large numbers (for comparison, consider that there are less than 2^{300} protons and neutrons in the universe). Such a large number of variables and the resulting combinatorial explosion make computations which guarantee exact solutions intractable. Since prediction generation in which a network would have to compare all the alternative possibilities is a computationally intractable problem, a network in the brain will not seek an exact solution to the prediction problem described here. Rather, it is sensible for a network to construct optimal approximations subject to constraints such as available time, number of available computational elements, the computational characteristics of these elements, and the minimally required level of accuracy.

Due to the combinatorial explosion of possible representations, a neural network trying to generate good predictions comes up against at least three insurmountable problems when the perfect, deterministic solution is desired:

1. Time: There is not enough time to compute exact solutions.
2. Processing elements: There are not enough neurons or synapses to store all the statistics needed to describe all possible representations.
3. Samples: There cannot be enough sampling to learn all the probabilities of every representation in such a way that these sample-based estimates, which are just the relative frequency of a representation, converge anywhere near true probabilities.

There are essentially two computational strategies for overcoming intractability. One strategy is to throw out information by decreasing the number of possible configurations which are recognizably different. Pattern recognition, in the sense of categorization and classification, is an example of such a procedure. It is much easier to say ''I see a bird'' than to give a detailed description of the bird you actually see. Discarding information is obviously risky, however, and the efficacy of this method

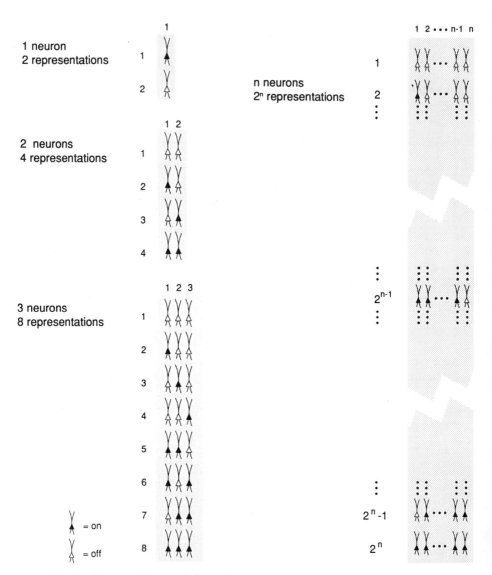

Fig. 4. Exponential growth of possible representations. As the number of neurons increases linearly to n, the number of representations possible increases exponentially as 2^n. The problem of calculating a probability for each of the 2^n representations in a network can, however, best be solved by treating each neuron as if statistically independent and approximating each probability. Copyright © 1989 by William B Levy.

depends on the amount of information lost and its importance. When the importance of any discarded information is unknown and a network or organism is performing poorly, as under mismatch conditions which activate the hippocampus, this strategy seems particularly bad.

The second strategy, which does not throw out information, is to assume statistical independence of converging neuronal activity. If each cell in the network's prediction tier computes a prediction as if statistical independence of its inputs exists, then the computational intractabilities are resolved. However, the usefulness of this approximation is a function of how much statistical dependence exists in the problem under consideration.

If this second strategy is tried and fails to yield acceptable performance, all is not lost as might be if the first strategy is applied. The computation of a prediction can be repeated on a new representation after a suitable transformation. In this case a suitable transformation would be invertible and would yield different statistics than the transformations previously tried. The statistics in question are defined in Section III,C,3, as we discuss a solution to the problem of sparse sampling.

If we are going to argue that a particular approximation is a good procedure, we need some standard for measuring the goodness of an approximation, since there are any number of possible approximation techniques. Thus, at the very least, we need to consider optimal approximations as benchmarks.

2. Optimization and Approximation

In the theory of neural networks, optimization is a pervasive but occasionally misunderstood issue. Engineers working on neurallike networks have an easy problem; they can study optimization from the standpoint of building their own optimal networks. It is more difficult for biologists (see, e.g., Staddon & Hinson, 1983), who must explain the networks found in nature.

We will develop optimization ideas to produce a context for comparing the performance of a particular network in a particular environment to the performance of the best possible network in that same environment. The idea to bear in mind is that a computation which is optimal in one environment may easily fail to be optimal in another environment. Thus, our task as biologists and neuroscientists is to understand when a brain region will produce a good approximation and when it will produce a poor one. To put this perspective to use, recall our local definition of environment for each brain region (i.e., its inputs) and consider the description of an environment as some sequence of states, or even a probability-generating function. Then we can ask, Which probability-generating functions, that is, environments, are expeditiously handled by which particular anatomies and physiologies? If we can answer this question it is natural that we interpret our results under the postulate that the brain is well built. We mean well built in the sense that the appropriate probability-generating functions (environments) are analyzed by those brain regions which do a good job for that class of generators. In other words, we hypothesize not much more than that the visual system of the thalamus and cerebral cortex evolved for analyzing the visual world and that the auditory system of the thalamus and cerebral cortex evolved for analyzing the auditory world. While it is undoubtedly possible for the auditory system to analyze the visual world and vice versa with some good results, it is almost certainly an inferior solution to the computational problems of seeing and hearing. In the present context, then, the argument is *not* that all sequence prediction problems are solved by the hippocampus but that the hippocampus is used when it is better than other brain regions for solving multisensory prediction problems. If the language areas, for example, are better for predicting long linguistic sequences, then the hippocampus will not be used.

The hypothesized statistical environment follows from the problem of sensory signal fusion detailed in Section II. Specifically, the problem is to find information which is in the higher-order relationships, that is, the higher-order statistical moments, or correlations, of the input environment. These information-rich moments are hard to find because they are relatively few in number and are scattered about in an exponentially large space. Furthermore, specific higher-order relationships do not hold constant in the environment from generation to generation, so prewired computational systems cannot evolve to handle them, as they have evolved for the peripheral stages of sensory processing. This hypothesis fits well with the "plain vanilla" morphology of the hippocampus as compared with structures like the retina, the olfactory bulb, and the neocortex which, by virtue of their relative complexity, appear to have inherited more computational biases than the hippocampus.

3. Margination

Because the three resources—time, processors, and samples—are in short supply relative to the pervasive and unavoidable complexity problems and because there is a single approximation technique which solves all three scarcities, we use this approximation technique as a working hypothesis for describing a function which occurs in the hippocampus. The process is called *margination*.

Let us just consider the third difficulty associated with the combinatorial explosion which occurs in multidimensional networks: the problem of sparse sampling. Suppose that $X = (X_1, \ldots, X_n)$ is an n-dimensional random variable, where each component X_i is binary-valued. The values of $X_1, \ldots, X_n$ could represent the zero–one or true–false output of n neurons in a simple network; hence the range space of X consists of 2^n configurations. In the case of small regions of a mammalian brain, n ranges between 1000 and 10,000,000. Even in the case of a moderately large n the presence of noise guarantees that no configuration is sampled, on average, more than once. Furthermore, most configurations will never be sampled because the number of configurations greatly exceeds the number of samples. Thus even in small brain regions there exists a problem of sparse sampling.

A well-known solution to this problem is to reduce the number of components of X by summation so as to obtain meaningful sample sizes. This process is known as margination [see Good (1963) for ideas about generalized margination]. Margination, in contrast to removing configurations from the sample space, is quite conservative since it never allows the network to experience infinite surprise (see below).

Margination can be related to the spatial integration performed by a neuron whose output is either "fire" or "not fire." Consider the set of all subsets of activity patterns which can fire this neuron. This set defines the summation over which margination occurs to create the probability of this neuron's firing.

At this time it is not yet clear which methods are best for selecting the subsets which are the margination process. However, even though mathematicians have not yet offered a tractable, optimal solution to finding these subsets, such methods are a primary concern of the computational approach advocated here.

D. REFINING THE APPROACH: DEFINITIONS AND MEASURES

This section gives some specificity to the theoretical development by defining some terminology and then by introducing some information measures.

1. Current Representations

A neural network can briefly retain information about the current state of the environment (see Fig. 5). This information is represented by the states of the processing elements. If a processing element is a neuron, as opposed to a portion of a neuron, then the state of a neuron means a specific scalar representation, such as (1) the voltage at the axonal initial segment, or (2) whether the neuron fires once within an absolute refrac-

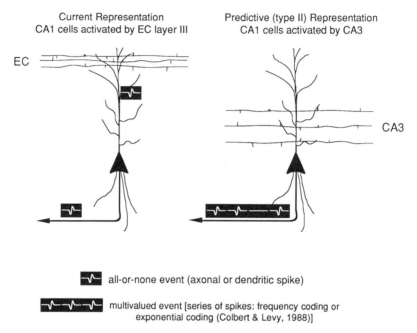

Fig. 5. A single CA1 cell participates in two types of representations: a current representation and a predictive representation. The current representation is monosynaptically activated by the entorhinal cortical (EC) input. The CA1 output of a current representation is pictured as an all-or-none event. In contrast, the predictive representation is monosynaptically activated by the hippocampal CA3 input. A type II predictive representation is illustrated by the multivalued CA1 output; the theory developed in this chapter presumes a type II predictive representation. However, there is no experimental evidence to favor this type of predictive representation over a type I predictive representation (cf. Fig. 6). Copyright © 1989 by William B Levy.

tory period, or (3) the number of firings within some larger, specified interval.

The most general definition of a representation is the state of all neurons in the brain over some very small period of time (e.g., one absolute refractory period). This global representation can be simplified because any subset of a representation is also a representation. For example, the state of all the related neurons of a single structure, such as the state of all CA1 pyramids, is also a representation.

A *current representation* or, more simply, a *representation,* of the environment, means a vector of scalar states of a specified set of processing elements. We will refer to a set of all possible values of such a vector, or the set of neurons which makes this vector, as a *representation space.*

2. Predictive Representations

Since we are interested in networks which generate predictions, or predictive representations (see Figs. 5 and 6), and since communication in these networks is limited by synaptic interactions and the computational

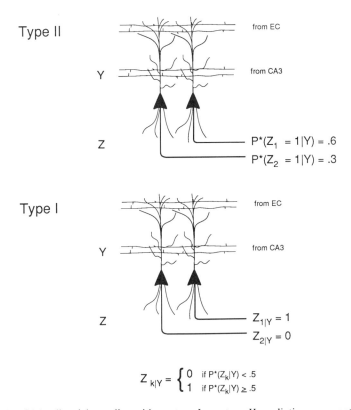

$$Z_{k|Y} = \begin{cases} 0 & \text{if } P^*(Z_k|Y) < .5 \\ 1 & \text{if } P^*(Z_k|Y) \geq .5 \end{cases}$$

Fig. 6. CA1 cells might mediate either a type I or a type II predictive representation as their output. A type I representation (lower panel) is in the form of a binary-state neuronal output (i.e., either fire or not fire). An optimal type I predictive representation would use a CA1 cell's polarization to represent a probability (or a function of this probability). Each cell's output would then be appropriately thresholded to fire or not fire depending on this polarization state. A type II representation (upper panel) requires an output which can be interpreted as a multivalued output by the next set of neurons.

Y is the state of the CA3 input to CA1. Z is the state of the CA1 output. When Y generates the output Z, a type I or II predictive representation results. The type I output is indicated by $Z_{k|Y}$ (the most likely configuration for Z_k given Y) for each CA1 cell k. The type II output is indicated by $P^*(Z_k = 1 \mid Y)$, an inferred probability distribution of Z_k given Y, for each CA1 cell k. Note that the equation at the bottom indicates that the type I predictive representation is generated by thresholding a type II representation. Thus, a type II representation can also be identified with dendritic or somatic depolarization of a cell producing a type I predictive representation. Copyright © 1989 by William B Levy.

constraints inherent in the neurons themselves, we must give serious thought to just what form a prediction can take in a neural network. (However, if we identify a brain region, such as CA1, as producing predictions in conformity with the definition of a predictive representation, these predictions may be quite abstract, with no obvious correspondence between cell firing and an animal's behavior. We would be particularly lucky if, for instance, the abstract predictions coincided with what is identified with a prediction of behavioral relevance such as the head direction-predicting responses identified by Ranck, 1985, in the presubiculum.)

Apparently, only three requirements are needed for a definition of a predictive representation which enables us to identify predictions in isolated brain regions.

1. The prediction occurs before the event being predicted.
2. The prediction is specified such that the network can take advantage of the prediction (i.e., there is a mapping, available to the network, between predictions and later current representations).
3. A predictive representation is not confused with the current representation (i.e., predictive and current representations are distinguishable).

Statements (1) and (2) are natural requirements for a prediction. Note that (1) eliminates retrodictions such as the pattern recognition problem. Requirement (2) ultimately provides for the situation in which a larger network that contains a prediction-generating subnetwork can (a) evaluate the quality of the predictions and (b) use these predictions as a basis for action upon the environment (e.g., to modify the external world to prevent an undesirable event from occurring). Requirement (3) does not seem an obvious necessity, but if the predictive representation space and the current representation space are indistinguishable, then the network cannot evaluate its predictions nor learn from experience, because it cannot separate predictive from current representations. Note, however, that these two spaces must be distinguishable and still satisfy (2). Requirement (2) and the local principle, which prevents memory access by direct addressing, necessitate a mapping between each predictive representation and each current representation by the method of shared representation space. (The neurons which produce the predictive representation must be contained in the set of neurons which produce the current representation: e.g., the CA1 spiny pyramids illustrated in Fig. 5.)

Requirements (1), (2), and (3), taken together, define a predictive representation. Thus, a set of neurons connected within a network in conformity with this definition is a predictive representation space. It is a representation space because of the mapping to a current representation space, and it is predictive because it anticipates a future event.

The definition given above does not attribute accuracy to or require accuracy from a predictive representation, so the quality of the prediction does not affect its identifiability as a predictive representation. Of course, we are really interested in the generation of accurate predictive representations. To assess the quality of the predictions we will need to define some measures. First, however, we will be a little more concrete and describe a subcategory of predictive representations which are of particular interest to us.

There appear to be two types of predictive representations worth distinguishing (see Fig. 6). The most obvious prediction, which we will call type I, is a representation of the one most probable configuration about to occur. Thus, if a current representation can be defined in a multivariate binary space, $\{0,1\}^n$, then a type I prediction occurs in the same multivariate binary space, $\{0,1\}^n$.

While the neurons generating a type I prediction produce a single, multivariate, binary event, the neurons generating a type II prediction produce a probability distribution of all possible such events. Though the type I prediction may seem the most natural form of a predictive representation, it is not the most general form, so it is the type II predictive representation which we emphasize in our theories. The type II prediction is a representation, ideally, on the interval $[0,1]^n$ (although in practice physical realities force the nervous system to make do with a discrete approximation of these n continuous intervals).

This second type of predictive representation attracts our interest for three reasons. First, the type I, most likely configuration, can be directly inferred from the type II prediction, but in general the reverse is not possible. Second, the type II prediction is a necessary intermediate step which the network must derive in order to measure the surprise suffered when an event in the predictive representation space occurs (i.e., the type II prediction is needed to calculate entropies on the relevant space, where a space means a specified set of neurons). Third, although the type I prediction is ultimately necessary for decision making and action on the environment, the type I decision should always be postponed as long as possible in a highly complex multilayered network to avoid the information loss which accompanies such a representation.

The above considerations suggest the following definition: A type II predictive representation is, perhaps implicitly, a vector of conditional probabilities; the conditioned or predicted variable is some future representation, and the probabilities of a type II predictive representation are conditional on the current representation.

3. Information Theory and Prediction

For the discussion which follows we will consider a neuron as a binary device. $P(\ )$ is an unconditioned probability distribution. $P(\ |\ )$ is a conditional probability distribution. $P^*(\ )$ is an inferred probability distribution as opposed to the true distribution. $P^*(A \mid B = b)$ can be read as "the inferred probability of A given B takes on value b," and is the probability distribution over the finite set of events implied by A given that the particular event b in B has occurred. The variable A is the conditioned or predicted variable; B is the conditioning variable.

The choice of probability as the way to quantify predictions is not arbitrary. The set of relationships called probability theory is the only consistent method using a scale from zero to one for quantifying, manipulating, updating, and predicting events (Cox, 1961, 1978; Jaynes, 1978). However, probability is not the only measure we need to consider.

We, and ultimately the network itself, also need a tool for measuring the quality of a network's predictions. This measure turns out to be equivalent to quantifying the information in a prediction. Instead of using the somewhat ambiguous term "information" for this measure, we prefer Hamming's (1980) suggestion of the term "surprise." Surprise, a nonnegative scalar, occurs with each current representation. In the prediction problem, the network is trying to avoid, or minimize, surprise so that surprise is a loss function. The more probable the event which occurs, the less surprise the network suffers. If the network places a probability of one on an event which then occurs, the surprise is zero. If the network places a probability of zero on an event which then occurs, the surprise is infinite. We would like surprise to be monotonic and continuously decreasing in probability, and we would like independent events to have additive surprise. Although a more rigorous justification is possible (see Mathai & Rathie, 1975), in this presentation it is sufficient to define surprise as $-\log P^*(Z = z \mid X = x)$ where P^* is the probability held by the network that representation z in the space of the Z neurons will occur given that representation x in the space of the X neurons has occurred. We identify the Z space with CA1 and the X space with inputs to the preprocessor that is the DG/CA3 region (see Section V).

With the occurrence of each individual sequence pair (Z,X), the information-theoretic loss due to the occurrence of z preceded by x is $-\log P^*(Z = z \mid X = x)$. Over time, then, the performance of the network as a prediction device is the average of this measure:

$$H^*(Z \mid X) = -\sum_{ZX} P(Z,X) \log P^*(Z \mid X). \qquad (1)$$

In an important sense it is the mathematical properties and associated theorems which justify the use of this quantity, average surprise, to characterize the performance of a network. However, we postpone its rigorous mathematical characterization to another time. It is important to note only that we are limiting the theory here to the pure prediction problem, which does not allow a feedback relationship between the network and the environment.

If no prediction is made by the network and we allow a prior unconditioned probability to be built into the network (see, e.g., rule 2 in Levy & Desmond, 1985a), the average surprise of a current representation is Shannon's entropy $H(Z)$ (Shannon & Weaver, 1949).

$$H(Z) = E[-\log P(Z = z)] = -\sum_{z \in Z} P(Z = z) \log P(Z = z), \qquad (2)$$

where $E[\ ]$ denotes expectation. Therefore, $H(Z)$ is the average, naive surprise or, just as well, $H(Z)$ is the average information in a current representation space Z.

Although the network does not need to measure the information loss of preprocessing, the theoretician does. To measure the average information loss of a transformation which takes X into Y, we use Shannon's conditional entropy $H(X \mid Y)$, where X is the set of all possible input signals and Y is the set of all corresponding output signals.

$$H(X \mid Y) = -\sum_{XY} P(X,Y) \log \frac{P(X,Y)}{P(Y)} \qquad (3)$$

$$= H(X,Y) - H(Y). \qquad (4)$$

This conditional entropy has several interesting properties, although for now we note only two. First, when Y is created by an invertible transformation f on X, then $H(X \mid Y) = 0$, the smallest possible value. Invertibly formed representations must have zero information loss, since inverting a transformation, $f^{-1}(f(X))$, to obtain what we started with, X, proves that the transformation f lost no information. Second, when Y is generated without any relationship to X by a uniform random process, then $H(X \mid Y) = H(X)$, the largest possible value. Thus no more information can be lost than was present to begin with.

As an aside, we note that these measures and the associated theorems defining their properties begin to explain what is meant by "information processing." Because of these multiple measures, there is more than one kind of information in a neural network: representation information and predictive information. Thus if someone were to ask how to calculate the information stored at a synapse, we could not answer the question without specifying the kind of information of interest. In either case the calculations show that the information is relative. In the case of a predictive representation, we would produce the difference between $E[-\log P^*(Z \mid X)]$ and $E[-\log P'^*(Z \mid X)]$, where P'^* is calculated with the synapse in question removed. In the case of representation information, we would subtract $H'^*(A \mid B)$ from $H^*(A \mid B)$, where H'^* is calculated for the network with the synapse removed.

Because of the way we hypothesize a network generates type II predictive probabilities, we are interested in the statistical dependence of representation spaces, in particular the representation spaces of CA1 and CA3. The measure of statistical dependence that we use (Watanabe, 1969) quantifies how much all individual neurons Y_j in Y predict about all of Y.

$$\sum_Y P(Y) \log \frac{P(Y)}{\prod_j P(Y_j)} = \sum_j H(Y_j) - H(Y) \tag{5}$$

(This quantity is the obvious extension of Shannon's mutual information, the measure of dependence of a bivariate quantity.) Note that statistical dependence is a nonnegative quantity which is zero when full independence obtains. A deeper appreciation of the properties of this quantity comes from the fact that it is a divergence (Csiszár & Körner, 1981).

Now we put some of these ideas to use.

E.   The Form of Optimal Approximate Inference

1.   Should a Network Preprocess?

Suppose multivariate binary inputs Z and X are given to any neurallike network as a sequence of inputs, first X and then Z. Suppose the network is to predict about Z using X. If we adhere blindly to conventional information theory, we might say the problem is to minimize $H(Z \mid X)$. However $H(Z,X)$ is fixed by some process outside the network and so is $H(X)$, so it seems that there is little the network can do. In fact, anything the network might do—for example, a transformation $f\colon X \to Y$ in order to minimize $H(Z \mid Y)$ instead of the original minimization—risks destroying the predictive information that exists between X and Z, and such a transformation certainly cannot add new information. [In fact, it is relatively easy to produce an analog of information theory's data processing lemma (Csiszár & Körner, 1981) for neurallike networks in this regard.] Yet the brain makes many such transformations. So where has our thinking gone awry?

The problem is that we have forgotten about the combinatorial explosion which forces sparse sampling and approximate computations. As a consequence the network can never know or use the true probabilities required for calculating the entropies of Shannon's information theory. The computational intractability problems discussed previously (see Section III, C) force the network to use an approximation approach. In Section V we hypothesize that this approximation ends up being equivalent to an independence assumption conditioned on each individual neuron whose outputs constitute the predictive representation space.

Since the computation is equivalent to an independence assumption, the closer the statistics of each representation space approach independence, the smaller is the error from the approximation. The trick, then, is to minimize dependence, that is, to approach independence as closely as possible (Levy, 1985). This is done by first preprocessing representations with minimal information loss $H(X \mid Y)$. Then the dimensions (neurons) of these transformed representations are used for prediction in a manner that appears to presume independence.

We now present the final theoretical reason which brings us to accept the computational form which is equivalent to an independence assumption.

2. Optimal Inference of a Probability Distribution from Averages

This section justifies our network's method of forming posterior probability distributions form moment constraints (e.g., adaptively stored means and correlations of the Z and X variables) which are locally available as the synaptic weights (or strengths). In fact, there is essentially only one correct method for generating probability distributions from averages. This method of inference is called minimum relative entropy (MRE) inference (Johnson & Shore, 1983; Shore & Johnson, 1980). [MRE inference is equivalent to maximum entropy inference (Jaynes, 1978) under a uniform prior.] Since we are interested in justifying an optimization procedure, that is, an optimal approximate computation for prediction in the neural network, the results of Shore and Johnson (1980; Johnson & Shore, 1983) are most relevant. They have proven that minimum relative entropy is essentially the only correct optimization criterion to produce a probability distribution when we start with a specified, supporting state space, a prior distribution, and moment constraints. Optimal procedures and results, such as the above claim, depend on the assumptions which are made. We assume that the implied structure and computation of an optimal network is of most interest when it arises from a minimum of assumptions; that is, the optimal results follow from first principles.

For the discrete case, the required axioms are

1. Uniqueness: The optimal inference procedure working from a set of moment constraints (e.g., correlations, variances) must produce a single distribution.
2. Idempotence: Repeated applications of the optimal inference procedure with the same moments do not change the resulting distribution from the first application.
3. System independence: If two sample spaces are disjoint and there are correspondingly disjoint moment constraints, then the optimal inference procedure must produce the same distribution regardless of whether the full joint distribution is formed before or after applying the inference procedure to the moment constraints.
4. Subset independence: If the state space can be decomposed into disjoint marginal subspaces and the constraints can be decomposed similarly, then the probability distribution inferred should be the same regardless of whether the optimization procedure is applied to the full space before or after margination.
5. Invariance: If f is any invertible transformation, and $Y = f(X)$ so that Y is a lossless representation of X, then the optimal inference procedure must produce the same probability distribution whether we work directly with X or work with Y and then apply the inverse transformation $f^{-1}(Y) = X$ to the probability distribution inferred to Y.

These axioms lead to the conclusion that the form of a probability distribution inferred from averages is multiplicative. That is, suppose we have a set of functions, g_i, of the random variable X and their expectations, $\{E[g_i(X)]\}$. MRE then says that the optimal probability distribution is

$$P^*(X = x) = e^{-\lambda_0} \prod_i e^{-\lambda_i \cdot g_i(x)} \qquad (6)$$

where the λ values are parameters which must be determined. Thus, if synaptic modification leads to something that is a good approximation of an average, as we and others posit, the optimal distributional form is of this multiplicative form.

From the computational viewpoint, and particularly for a neurallike network, determination of λ_0 appears to be a computationally intractable problem for arbitrary sets of expectations over a multivariate space because of memory requirements that can grow exponentially with the number of dimensions of the space. However, when the expectations are limited to a particular class of expectations the combinatorial problems disappear. Specifically, the set, or a subset, of the lowest-order marginals leads to a very simple form. For the case of interest to us, in which the expectations are of the form $E[X_i \mid Z_k = 1]$ rather than the unconditioned form of Eq. (6) and the X_i values are binary-valued variables, the probability of the event $X = x$ is

$$P^*(X = x \mid Z_k = 1) = \prod_i E[X_i \mid Z_k = 1]^{x_i} \cdot (1 - E[X_i \mid Z_k = 1])^{1 - x_i}. \quad (7)$$

Here the marginals are summed over half the possible states of the X space. Thus, these are the lowest-order marginals and so avoid the combinatorial explosion. That is, these marginals produce reasonable sample sizes, and they avoid an apparently intractable calculation of λ_0.

It will be obvious to those knowledgeable in statistics that MRE inference applied to such marginals generates a probability distribution which has the independent form. This motivates two comments. First, MRE justifies the independence assumption which is often invoked for computational convenience. Second, it might now appear that we have limited the computational options so severely that a neural network can do nothing to help prediciton. However, this is not the case. MRE gives no prescription that would tell us, or a network, which set of lowest order marginals to use. In fact, when we consider the possibility of permuting the X space, the available choices are on the order of 2^{2^n} different sets of lowest-order marginals. Thus, rather than limiting our options, we may have, at best, an embarrassment of riches or, at worst, another case of computational intractability.

Because our hypothesized computation in CA1 is the MRE-inferred independent form, preprocessing should produce a representation with minimal statistical dependence. In Section VI we outline an algorithm which is hypothesized to be the transformation performed by the DG/CA3 preprocessor. This algorithm minimizes the statistical dependence of the conditioning variable by creating an optimal set of lowest order marginals.

IV. Summary of the Computational Issues Relevant to the Model

We now give a brief summary of the computational theory of the hippocampus in question-and-answer form.

1. *What problem is the hippocampus solving?* The hippocampus solves a prediction problem in which the present environment, here the

signals entering the entorhinal cortex, and the stored statistics of past environments are used to predict a future event. To solve the problem we require the network to generate a predictive representation.

2. *How is the present represented?* The present is represented by the activity state of any subset of neurons, in our case the CA1 spiny pyramids.

3. *How is the past represented?* The past is usually represented in the adaptively modified synaptic weights. In addition, there may be an internal excitability parameter associated with each neuron that is adaptively adjusted by each neuron's activation history.

4. *How is a prediction represented?* A prediction, or predictive representation, precedes a current representation and is the activity vector of a subset of the same neurons that are part of the space used to represent the present (the subset is CA1 itself). However, a predictive representation is directly activated by a different set of inputs, the Schaffer–commissural efferents of CA3, than those inputs which directly activate the representation of the present, the layer III pyramids of the entorhinal cortex. Since the two types of representations share the same neurons, it is possible to map and evaluate the quality of a prediction.

Two types of predictive representations can be envisioned (see Fig. 6). A type I predictive representation is the representation predicted to be the most likely pattern of activity to follow. The type II predictive representation is more sophisticated; it implies a probability distribution over the next set of possible representations. The more sophisticated predictive representation can easily be converted to the maximum likelihood type I representation by a threshold process, $\{0,1\}$, in each neuron. More importantly, a type II predictive representation is converted to a surprise measure when the current representation being predicted finally occurs.

5. *Are there any special physiological characteristics of cells that mediate prediction?* The synapses which evoke the predictive representations should modify as a reinforced system with a special timing requirement for synaptic potentiation: The permissive postsynaptic event can follow but not precede the synaptic activity which it reinforces. If the associative coactivity requirement were not time-ordered, the prediction could get reversed, and the network might end up predicting the past.

6. *How does a neuron calculate a probability?* The physiological input–output function of a neuron produces the multiplications (actually it adds logarithms) required by MRE and by Bayes's equation for inverting (reversing) the conditional probabilities implicitly stored at each synapse. (That is, the synaptic strengths are proportional to the conditional expectations which imply conditional probabilities via MRE.)

7. *What are the characteristics of a predictive representation?* (i) It occurs before the "actual" representation. (ii) It requires circuitry that

performs time-shifting in order to take advantage of associative synaptic modification within a limited time window. (iii) A predictive representation is useful if it is constructed from statistics (i.e., past observations) based on the laws of inference, such as $P(A \mid B) = P(B \mid A)P(A)P(B)^{-1}$. (iv) It can generate outputs almost as if the actual representation has occurred. (v) It can be compared with the actual representation to evaluate the quality of the prediction. Characteristics (iv) and (v) require that there be a one-to-one mapping from the neurons which form the predictive representations to a subset of the neurons which form the actual representations. Furthermore, there is a requirement for a mechanism which keeps the two types of representations distinctive.

8. *What is a preprocessor?* A preprocessor (see Fig. 8) is a system that recodes (transforms) signals in an essentially unsupervised manner. Its synaptic modifications are self-supervised and are not dependent on the specific information content of the next stage in processing.

9. *Why preprocess representations?* There are at least two reasons: to shift a representation in time and to change the form of a representation to make it more compatible with the succeeding computation.

V. The Model

Figure 7 depicts the model we have been developing (Levy, 1988) using abstract blocks which correspond to specific parts of the hippocampus. Except for the prediction evaluation block, the blocks are identified with particular regions of the hippocampus (see Fig. 2A). However, we do not mean to disqualify the possibility that the prediction evaluation generator resides within the limbic system.

The centerpiece of the model is the prediction tier, which consists of the principal neurons of CA1, the spiny pyramids. This group of cells produces two types of representations: a current representation and a predictive representation. When generated as a monosynaptic response to entorhinal layer III pyramidal cell activity, the output of CA1 is a representation of the current environment. When generated as a monosynaptic response to Schaffer–commissural CA3 activity, the output of CA1 is a predictive representation.

Because we are dealing with an abstract idea of prediction, the model works just as well whether we consider the axonal output of CA1 or a dendritic event in the CA1 pyramids as the predicted variable. (In keeping with mathematical usage and the idea that CA1 generates a conditional probability, such as $P(A \mid B)$, the term predicted variable, A in the example, will refer to current representations in CA1; the term conditioning variable, B in the example, will refer to the CA3 Schaffer–commissural

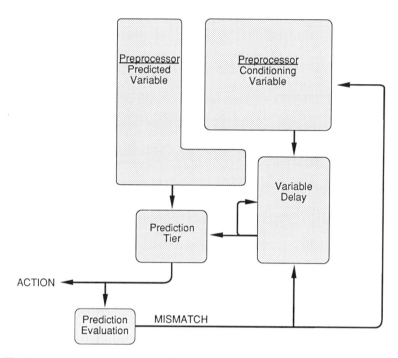

Fig. 7. Here the model network of Fig. 2B is shown with the addition of a prediction evaluation stage, which controls the rate of adaptive modifications Copyright © 1989 by William B Levy.

inputs to CA1; see Fig. 8.) Quite important to the mathematical details of the model here is the postulate that the event being predicted in CA1 is a binary-valued variable for each neuron regardless of which neuronal state is considered to be the predicted variable. Thus, in each CA1 cell, the predicted variable is a threshold-defined event, perhaps the action potential of the soma and initial segment or perhaps a dendritic spike.

There are two preprocessing systems: one for the conditioning variables and one for the predicted variables (see Fig. 8). These preprocessing systems do not correspond neatly to any single tier of principal neurons. For the predicted variable, preprocessing, which includes signal mixing and reducing statistical dependencies, occurs in the layer III cells of the entorhinal cortex, the distal dendrites of the CA1 principal neurons, and within the interneurons of CA1 stratum lacunosum. For the conditioning variable, preprocessing, which involves signal mixing, remixing, reducing statistical dependencies, and time-shifting, occurs in the layer II cells of the entorhinal cortex, the dentate gyrus including its infragranular layer (CA4 of Lorente de Nó), and the CA3 region.

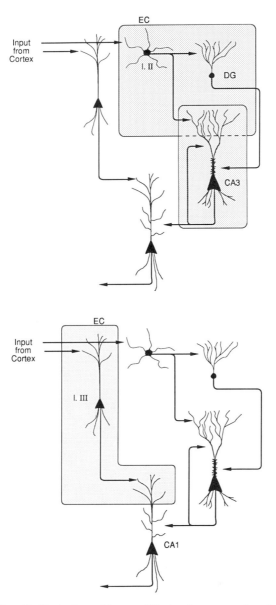

Fig. 8. Schematic illustration of the conditioning (upper panel) and predicted (lower panel) variable preprocessors. In the theory, the CA1 cells generate conditional probabilities and thus constitute the prediction representation space. Such conditional probabilities have two variables, a predicted variable and a conditioning variable, each of which can be preprocessed by the appropriate preprocessor. Copyright © 1989 by William B Levy.

It is also necessary for the conditioning variable preprocessor to perform a type of pattern recognition in order to be robust in its primary preprocessing task. More information about this pattern recognition process is found in Section VI. However, it is worth noting here that the pattern recognition process proposed below is not the information-losing, retrodictive process of categorization or classification that describes the function of many other neurallike networks. Instead it involves shifting the DG/CA3 activity state nearer previously used representations when a mismatch signal exists and when the current environment is similar to a previously experienced environment.

The prediction evaluation generator, as the mismatch-generating subsystem (shown in Fig. 7), keeps a running average of the amount of surprise that results with each successive current representation. When the accumulated, running average surprise exceeds a certain prespecified threshold level, the prediction evaluation generator activates a mismatch signal. To generate the correct amount of surprise, this evaluator needs to receive both current and predictive representations, that is, the outputs from the CA1 prediction tier. A more sophisticated version of the prediction evaluation generator, worthy of both experimental and theoretical investigation, posits a mismatch signal which controls the ease of modifiability and state change along a continuum which varies monotonically with the running average surprise. Because the mismatch detector's output is, in either case, a rather low-dimension signal, it differs from the high-dimension signal used in predictor–corrector systems or back-propagation schemes (Barto, Sutton, & Anderson, 1983; Rumelhart, Hinton, & Williams, 1986). However, the mismatch signal used here is similar to Sutton's adaptive critic (Sutton, 1984) because it quantifies the overall quality of the multidimensional output of the prediction tier. Mismatch generation is central to other theories as well, such as those of Gray (1982), Brooks (1986), and Carpenter and Grossberg (1987).

The mismatch signal is of low information content and should be thought of as a low-dimension output compared to all other signal lines illustrated in Fig. 7. The leading candidate for this signal is the septal input to the hippocampus; other candidates are the various monoaminergic inputs to the hippocampus.

When the statistics of the environment shift, the prediction evaluation generator at the output end of the network signals mismatch (see Fig. 7). If the pattern recognition process triggered in the DG/CA3 region by the mismatch signal fails to find anything recognizable, the CA3 activity state takes a random jump to another state and the mismatch signal allows synaptic modification in the DG/CA3 system.

An ancillary support function is also required of the network by this theory and, like the mismatch signal, may be one of the low-dimension nonspecific neuronal systems mentioned above. Any low-dimension signal, perhaps one mediated through the entorhinal cortex, seems like a reasonable possibility. The required support function, in effect, provides a distinctive label so that the prediction evaluation generator is able to tell the difference between predictive and current representations. This signal's function is to (1) force these two representation types to alternate as they arrive in CA1 and (2) inform the prediction evaluation generator which signal from CA1 is a predictive representation and which is a current representation. Alternation could be at regular or variable intervals without affecting the proposed scheme.

The shared representation space, which has CA1 alternating between predictive and current representations, is the process by which the network satisfies properties (2) and (3) of the definition of a predictive representation (see Section III, D, 3).

With more knowledge, including quantitative anatomy and the appropriate physiological observations, the present hippocampal model could be expanded to incorporate computations performed in the subicular regions (see Fig. 1), entorhinal cortex, and perhaps the modern Papez circuit. Although anatomical and physiological observations may suggest additional computational issues, many of the same types of computational strategies (abstract prediction and preprocessing to mix, time shift, and lower the statistical dependence of signals) would be reapplied. As currently envisioned, the reapplication of these strategies would produce a more interesting theory because of expanded network capabilities. These expanded capabilities extend the range of the predictions so that the predictions being generated concern events further in the future. The added circuitry clearly provides (see Fig. 1) more high-dimension, positive feedback loops which could mediate additional signal remixing and timeshifting.

A.   THE CA1 COMPUTATION

Let the CA3 inputs, j, to CA1 be binary-valued variables, $\{0,1\}$, with the state of the jth input at time t designated as $Y_j(t)$, and suppose that Y is formed from entorhinal or cortical inputs X as $f: X \rightarrow Y$ with an f such that $f^{-1}(f(x)) = X$. Let $Z_k(t+1)$ be a binary-valued variable which denotes the state taken by a CA1 neuron k in response to a layer III input from entorhinal cortex. The strength of the synapse between j and k is denoted as $W_{jk}(t)$. Suppose that synaptic modification of the CA3–CA1 synapses occurs so that each synapse takes on values which are proportional to a conditional correlation. For example suppose, as is detailed below, that this class of synapses modifies according to the equations:

and
$$W_{jk}(t + 1) = W_{jk}(t) + \Delta W_{jk}(t, t + 1) \tag{8}$$

$$\Delta W_{jk}(t, t + 1) = \epsilon \cdot Z_k(t + 1) \cdot [Y_j(t) - c \cdot W_{jk}(t)]. \tag{9}$$

Then synaptic strength will asymptotically converge to $\overline{P}(Y_j = 1 \mid Z_k = 1)$, that is, approximately the value $E[Y_j \mid Z_k = 1]$. Therefore each $P(Y_j \mid Z_k = 1)$ is, at least implicitly, available at each synapse (jk).

At this point Bayes's theorem and MRE inference instruct us to hypothesize one particular computation when we work under the supposition that CA1 generates an optimal type II predictive representation which minimizes average surprise. This computation is defined by Eqs. (10)–(12). For each CA1 neuron k,

$$P^*(Z_k = 1 \mid X) = P^*(Z_k = 1 \mid Y) = \frac{P^*(Z_k = 1, Y)}{P^*(Z_k = 0, Y) + P^*(Z_k = 1, Y)}. \tag{10}$$

The first equality follows from the invertibility of f. The second equality is just Bayes's statement. Equations (11) and (12) follow from MRE inference, from the postulate just above that averages are stored at the jk synapses (see also Section V,B,2), and from the added presumption that the average activity level $E(Z_k = 1)$ is available at each CA1 neuron. (These points and their biological plausibility are discussed in greater detail in Levy et al., in press.)

$$P^*(Z_k = 1, Y) \leq \overline{P}(Z_k = 1) \prod_j \overline{P}(Y_j \mid Z_k = 1)^{y_j}[1 - \overline{P}(Y_j \mid Z_k = 1)^{1-y_j} \tag{11}$$

$$P^*(Z_k = 0, Y) \leq \overline{P}(Z_k = 0) \prod_j \overline{P}(Y_j \mid Z_k = 0)^{y_j}[1 - \overline{P}(Y_j \mid Z_k = 0)^{1-y_j} \tag{12}$$

where $\leq$ indicates the MRE inferred probability which is optimal in the context of Shore and Johnson (1980), and $\overline{P}$ indicates the sample frequency or the Bayesian, sample-based, updated average.

We note that we have a form quite similar to those seen in Hopfield (1987), Hinton and Sejnowski (1983), and Golden (1988) because our assumptions and MRE yield the conditional independence assumed by these other approaches.

The reader has probably noticed that Eqs. (10)–(12) are written in terms of individual cells, k, but that the probability distribution desired, $P^*(Z \mid X)$, is over the aggregate of these individual neurons. If a postprocessing network such as the indicated prediction evaluation generator (see Fig. 7) just adds up surprise across the CA1 neurons, it is essentially making an assumption of independence. We can equivalently think of such an additive function in the prediction evaluation generator as obeying the dictates of MRE when no further information is available. However, a more sophisticated generator might be able to bring further information to bear as it evaluates the output from CA1. If the prediction evaluation generator has stored statistics which indicate some of the dependencies between the CA1 neurons, k, then the outputs of these cells can be appropriately weighted to account for such interactions. Whatever the case, the binary version of the generator generates a relatively low-dimension, mismatch signal when there is too much surprise.

In hypothesizing Eqs. (10)–(12) or their equivalents, as computations performed in CA1, we hypothesize the existence of several neuronal functions which have not been identified nor even looked for by neurobiologists but which seem at least feasible. Equation 11 does not quite look like a computation of a neurallike processing element until we change the multiple products to multiple sums via logarithms and exponentiation. For instance, the multiplicative form is easily accommodated by spatial summation if synapses perform a logarithmic operation. Spatial summation might occur as

$$\log P^*(Y, Z_k = 1) = \sum_j Y_j \log W_{jk}^1 - (1 - Y_j) \log(1 - W_{jk}^1) \tag{13}$$

for Eq. (11), and

$$\log P^*(Y, Z_k = 0) = \sum_j Y_j \log W_{jk}^0 - (1 - Y_j) \log(1 - W_{jk}^0) \tag{14}$$

for Eq. (12) with the appropriate exponentiation following these steps and where

$$W_{jk}^1 = \overline{P}(Y_j \mid Z_k = 1) \text{ and } W_{jk}^0 = \overline{P}(Y_j \mid Z_k = 0). \tag{15}$$

The idea that the synapse performs a logarithm is plausible since the generation of voltage, as described by Nernst and Goldman-type equations, is a logarithmic function of conductance. More unusual is the consideration that an inactive synapse [note the $(1 - Y_j)$ terms] contributes to the computation. To produce this interaction, we hypothesize that the synapses are on dendritic spines and that the nonsynaptic conductance of the spine membrane can act as a current source of some significance.

The denominator in Eq. (10) is notably problematic for the theory since it is not obvious where the terms $\bar{P}(Y_j \mid Z_k = 0)$ are created (however, see Levy *et al.*, in press, for further discussion). We can offer several suggestions including (1) a new modification rule at each synapse *jk;* (2) implicit generation of $P^*(X)$ (see, e.g., Levy & Desmond, 1985a, rule 2) which eliminates the need for $P^*(Y \mid Z_k = 0)$; (3) inhibitory synaptic modification which apparently has the difficult, perhaps impossible, task of sorting and weighting the terms *j* for each *k;* (4) a process which guarantees that the denominator remains constant; or (5) a mathematical short-cut which bypasses the computation in the denominator altogether.

It should be pointed out that if Eqs. (10)–(12) are implemented, each cell *k* can work with any subset $\{Y_j\}$ of the complete set Y and still, via MRE inference, produce a prediction conditioned on the full Y space. Note that the missing Y_j inputs will cancel each other out in Eq. (10) when they assume their MRE value, so full connectivity from CA3 to CA1 is neither postulated nor required.

$\bar{P}(Z_k = 1)$ is postulated to be adaptively encoded at each cell *k*. This is essentially the postulate that a cell knows about its own activity history and modifies its excitability threshold accordingly. In studies of long-term potentiation there is a phenomenon which suggests this postulate. The phenomenon is observed as a shift in the amount of synaptic excitation needed to fire cells and is called an i-o (for input conversion into output) curve shift (see, e.g., Wilson, Levy, & Steward, 1979, 1981). The essential observation of these studies is that, following high-frequency activation of the excitatory inputs to neurons in the dentate gyrus, less synaptic activation is needed to fire the cell than before the induction of long-term potentiation.

B. ASSOCIATIVE SYNAPTIC MODIFICATION

Associative synaptic modification is central to the present theory. Most of our detailed understanding of the characteristics of the rule(s) which govern associative modification comes from electrophysiological research in the dentate gyrus which, by analogy, applies to the CA3 synapses on the CA1 spiny pyramids. To some extent, understanding comes from newer studies in CA1 itself.

1. Self-Supervised Modification

Most of the synapses in the present model are presumed to modify in an essentially unsupervised (perhaps better expressed as a self-supervised) way. The three distinct self-supervised systems in the hippocampus are the entorhinal synapses formed on the cells of the dentate gyrus, on the cells of CA3, and on the cells of CA1. There is abundant evidence for associative modification in the dentate gyrus (see Levy & Desmond, 1985b; Desmond & Levy, 1988, for reviews). Here postsynaptic excitation is permissive for change and presynaptic activity determines the amount and sign of the modification. In CA3 there have been no associative synaptic modification experiments of the entorhinal synapses, but the anatomical similarities between the entorhinal synapses of the dentate gyrus and those of CA3 lead us to hypothesize the identical nature of their associative modifiability. Finally, there are two reports of synaptic potentiation at the entorhinal–CA1 synapses (Doller & Weight, 1985; King & Levy, 1986).

Self-supervised synaptic modification is useful for reducing statistical dependency in representations because such modification tends to combine the effects of converging and correlated inputs on cell firing. This type of modification also assists the pattern recognition aspect of the network.

Even though associative modification in the dentate gyrus appears to be self-supervised, the research in the dentate gyrus can be used as an analog for the reinforced type of modification which is proposed to exist at the CA3–CA1 synapses. This analogy is possible because the experimental paradigms used in the dentate gyrus use a weak and a strong entorhinal input to create many of the characteristics of a reinforced system. Some of these characteristics include (1) the nonlinear, permissive nature of convergent excitation (Burger & Levy, 1987; Levy & Burger, 1987a, 1987b; Levy & Steward, 1979; McNaughton, Douglas, & Goddard, 1978; Wilson *et al.*, 1979, 1981); (2) the existence of a long-term depression which complements long-term potentiation so that an erasure mechanism exists which allows the synapse to function as a running averager (Levy, Brassel, & Moore, 1983; Levy & Steward, 1979, 1983); (3) a specific timing rule which defines the meaning of "associated" in the temporal domain (Levy & Steward, 1983); and (4) a limited amount of interaction along the proximo–distal dendritic axis which defines the meaning of "associated" in the spatial domain (White, Levy, & Steward, 1988).

2. Synaptic Weights as Averages

The experimental observations of Levy and Steward (1979) and Levy *et al.* (1983) using the entorhinal–dentate gyrus synapses directly support a specific class of synaptic modification rules which are related to a variety of earlier proposals (e.g., Amari, 1977; Grossberg, 1976; Kohonen, 1972, 1984). The formulation is best written as Eq. (8) above and as:

$$\Delta W_{jk}(t, t + 1) = \epsilon f(Z_k) [Y_j - cW_{jk}(t)]. \tag{16}$$

Equation (16) is the simplest member of a class of equations which fits the experimental observations and has the properties desired by many theoreticians. The argument t is time in some discrete units and is implicit in terms Z_k and Y_j. The variable W_{jk} is the strength of the synapse formed between afferent j and postsynaptic cell k. The variable $\Delta W_{jk}(t, t + 1)$ is the change in synaptic strength over one unit of time. The variable c is a positive constant of appropriate units so that Y_j and the product $[c W_{jk}(t)]$ have the same units; ϵ is a small positive number; Y_j, the presynaptic input, is nonnegatively valued. If $f(Z_k) > 0$, the difference $(Y_j - c W_{jk})$ determines whether potentiation or depression of synaptic strength W_{jk} occurs. This difference term also keeps the synaptic strength W_{jk} within limits, that is, between 0 and the maximum value of Y/c. The argument Z_k is some postsynaptic event in the kth neuron. The postsynaptic term $f(Z_k)$ is nonnegative and nondecreasing in the argument Z_k so that this term is permissive for change. For an unsupervised system, $f(Z_k)$ is just a function of the inputs and their synapses on k, as $f(Y, W_{.k})$. For a reinforced system, $f(Z_k)$ is a function of a set of inputs and synapses on cell k other than the set described by Y_j. Further details on this distinction between unsupervised and reinforced forms of synaptic modification are found below (Section V,B,3).

If the environment is stationary and strong mixing, it is sensible to average both sides of the equation over time (indicated by expectation operator E[ ] (see Geman, 1981; Levy & Geman, 1982, for examples). Equation (16) then becomes

$$E[\Delta W_{jk}] = E[\epsilon f(Z_k)(Y_j - c W_{jk})] \tag{17}$$

$$= \epsilon E[f(Z_k) Y_j] - \epsilon c E[f(Z_k) W_{jk}]. \tag{18}$$

If ϵ is small enough, W_{jk} changes very slowly. We can then rewrite Eq. (18) as

$$E[\Delta W_{jk}] = \epsilon E[f(Z_k) Y_j] - \epsilon W_{jk} E[f(Z_k)] \tag{19}$$

where c has been given the value of one.

In a stationary, strong mixing environment, $E[\Delta W_{jk}]$ converges to zero so that we have, after rearranging and dividing,

$$W_{jk} = \frac{E[f(Z_k), Y_j]}{E[f(Z_k)]}. \tag{20}$$

Now, if $f(Z_k)$ can only take on the values zero or one, we can write

$$\frac{E[f(Z_k) = 1, Y_j]}{E[f(Z_k) = 1]} = E[Y_j \mid f(Z_k) = 1]. \tag{21}$$

It is notable that, without the term $(-W_{jk})$ corresponding to long-term depression (e.g., Burger & Levy, 1985), this development [Eq. (16)–(20)] would not go through.

The running averager form of synaptic modification just described only coverages to a delta neighborhood determined by the size of ϵ.

A mathematically different class of rules also fits the physiological observations and provides a similar final value of each W_{jk} as does the running averager. This other set of rules is Bayesian in their updating method (Levy & Desmond, 1988). These rules produce changes in synaptic strength which coverage to exact averages. A seeming disadvantage of the Bayesian adaptive form of associative synaptic modification is that, when $f(Z_k) > 0$ after many trials (actually the Bayesian form is most sensible when $f(Z_k)$ can take on values zero or one), new associative events have very little affect on the synaptic weights.

An alternative modification rule, which shares some of the features of the running averager and the Bayesian form, uses Eq. (16) and a dynamically controlled ϵ (t), $0 \leqslant \epsilon$ $(t) \leqslant 1$. The variable ϵ (t) would be controlled by the prediction evaluation generator so as to be identified with a continuous mismatch signal and would be adjusted to larger values in novel environments and to smaller values as more and more time is spent in the same environment. Thus the delta region of approximate convergence which exists in the stochastic averaging method would go to zero. That is, there would be exact convergence when the input environment is stationary in its statistical correlations.

3. Reinforced Modification

A variety of researchers distinguish between unsupervised and reinforced-type supervised modification rules (e.g., Amari, 1977; Kohonen, 1972, 1984). Most important for the development of a network which can perform prediction of future events is an associative synaptic modification rule and appropriate neural circuitry in which the synaptic strength of afferents representing early events is reinforced by converging afferent activity representing later events. The relevant characteristics of a reinforced synaptic modification rule for our model are

1. There should be two distinct classes of excitatory inputs. The two classes are presumably the entorhinal cortical and CA3 inputs to CA1.
2. Sufficient activity of one class of inputs should permit synaptic modification of the other class of inputs. Presumably entorhinal cortical activity is permissive for modification of the CA3–CA1 synapses.
3. The opposite interaction, which reverses the permissive input and the modified input, should not occur. Here the entorhinal–CA1 syn-

apses can remain unmodified even while their activity permits modification of the CA3–CA1 synapses.

An additional characteristic we find useful in our network models is:

4. The permissive class of inputs is capable of self-supervised modification though not necessarily while simultaneously permitting modification in the other class of inputs. (Such unsupervised modifiability of entorhinal–CA1 synapses is suggested by other work from our laboratory.)

The possibility that CA1 is a reinforced type of supervised system follows from the experimental demonstration of these four properties by Moore and Levy (1988; Levy, 1988). These experiments studied associative synaptic modification of CA1 in the hippocampal slice. This study was able to find stimulation parameters such that the CA3 input required an associated distal dendritic excitation for CA3–CA1 potentiation to occur. The reverse interaction, in which potentiation of the distal synapses required CA3 activation, did not obtain, however. These and other observations (King & Levy, 1986) suggest that modification of the CA3–CA1 synapses, as controlled by the entorhinal input to CA1, bears a fundamental resemblance to the reinforced type of supervised synaptic modification.

C. TIME CONSTRAINTS ON ASSOCIATIVE SYNAPTIC INTERACTIONS

The temporal dependencies governing associative synaptic modification are crucial to any theory of the hippocampus as a generator of predictions. Experiments using the bilateral projections from the entorhinal cortex to the dentate gyrus were the first to observe a rather special temporal relationship which defines association at the cellular level (Levy & Steward, 1983; Lopez, Burger, & Levy, 1985; Lopez, Burger, Dickstein, Desmond, & Levy, submitted; see also Levy & Desmond, 1985b, for review). These experiments show that the pre- and postsynaptic activities, Y_j and $f(Z_k)$ of Eq. (16), need not be synchronous so long as their temporal association falls within the constraint of a specific temporal window and has a special temporal ordering. The temporal ordering constraint allows associative potentiation when the presynaptic activity Y_j precedes the postsynaptic excitation $f(Z_k)$. In fact, the two activities need not overlap at all.

Associative long-term potentiation can be induced with as much as 30 msec between the first pulse of a presynaptic train and the beginning of a powerful postsynaptic depolarization. The reverse ordering is not a potentiating condition at all. Rather, long-term depression occurs when the permissive, reinforcing input precedes the associated presynaptic activity. Functionally, then, the rule looks at the preceding $Y_j = 0$ associative with the $f(Z_k) > 0$ rather than the activation of j which follows activation of k.

Similar experiments have now been performed in area CA1. Here the entorhinal input to CA1 is the permissive input for modification of the CA3–CA1 synapses. As in the dentate gyrus, the permissive excitation can follow, but not precede, synaptic activity to produce long-term potentiation at the active CA3–CA1 synapses (Moore & Levy, 1986; Levy, 1988). Figure 9 shows the temporal nature of the pulse trains used in this experiment to induce associative long-term potentiation. The reverse ordering does not produce potentiation.

The ordered timing requirements of an associative synaptic modification rule are useful for constructing a network that learns sequences. For example, if one particular event represented by the CA3 inputs regularly

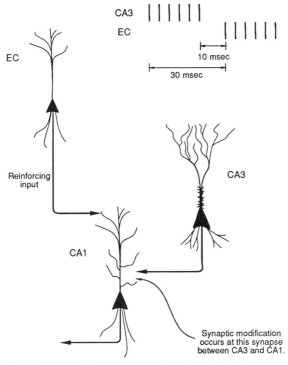

Fig. 9. Associative potentiation can span time. Associative long-term potentiation of CA3–CA1 synapses is induced by the input of entorhinal cortical (EC) neurons. Note the temporal relationship between CA3 and EC activity which induces potentiation; the reverse ordering does not produce potentiation. Copyright © 1989 by William B Levy.

precedes a particular event represented by the entorhinal layer III cells, then the CA3 event can be used to predict in advance, by about 20 msec, the entorhinal event or the CA1 cell firing induced by the entorhinal event. The observed timing requirement thus allows the CA3 input to predict CA1 activity induced monosynaptically by the entorhinal input.

Of course, the rather limited temporal window of 30 msec must be extended to be of behavioral consequence. That is, the temporal window of such associations is too brief to make timely predictions if we consider the whole animal trying to predict its environment in the real world. In this case, a useful predictive representation must be produced many tens, hundreds, or thousands of milliseconds before the event being predicted actually occurs so that the animal can act on its predictions in time. In fact, we interpret the results of these synaptic modification studies as truly limiting, and, therefore, we must consider other mechanisms which might be used to extend the temporal context of the predictions.

D. TIME-SHIFTING FOR ASSOCIATION AND TIMELY PREDICTIONS

1. Delay Lines Shift Representations Later in Time

Although an event which occurs in the real world cannot be shifted in time, it is possible to shift representations of this event in time. The more obvious shift is to move a representation later in time. Shifting a representation later in time is a workable scheme used to produce an association of two events at the cellular level even though these two events are widely separated in time in the real world (e.g., Zipser, 1986). In fact there is a history of research in which sequences longer than two are treated by adding delay lines and feedback (Fukushima, 1973; Grossberg & Kuperstein, 1986; Hopfield, 1987; Kleinfeld, 1986; Kohonen, 1984) to solve pattern recognition problems. However, pattern recognition problems are retrodictions while our interest here is in predictions.

In order to shift representations in time, action potential conduction down an axon could act as a delay line on the scale of 2–4 msec; more important, however, is the capacitance of each neuron. The so-called synaptic delay, usually defined as the time it takes a synaptic event on a dendrite to charge the neuron's cell body, is of the order of 10–12 msec. So, for example, by chaining together a sequence of 10 neurons, a shift in time of 100–120 msec might be achieved. This is still a rather short interval to be of use for many of the sequences encountered in the real environment, such as the sequence of representations generated as a rat moves through a maze.

The top portion of Fig. 10 illustrates a delay line circuit called a tapped delay line because of the multiple delay times available. Such tapped de-

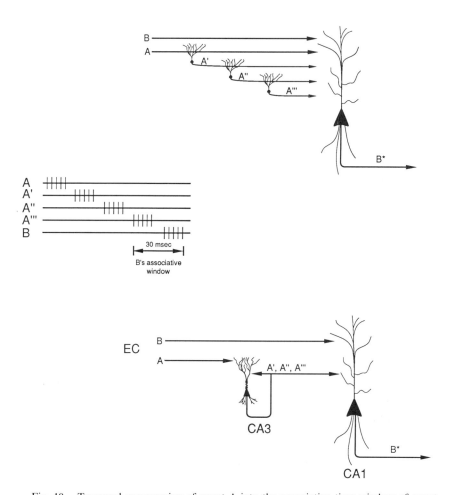

Fig. 10. Temporal compression of event A into the associative time window of event B. Associative synaptic modification spans a short time window. Tapped delay lines (upper panel) allow a multiplicity of delayed representations. In a multidimensional representation, however, such delay lines produce an undesirable delay of predictive representations. In contrast, a positive feedback loop (lower panel) can span longer time windows than the delay lines without delaying prediction generation (see also Fig. 11). Copyright © 1989 by William B Levy.

lay lines are, however, unsuitable for producing a predictive representation in a timely fashion because this same delay circuitry, which brings pre- and postsynaptic events together in time to allow associative synaptic modification, must also delay generation of the predictive representation itself. This undesirable delay is inevitable because the conditioning input *A* which generates the prediction (*B**) is delayed by this same circuitry. As a result, by our definition of prediction (see Section III), an overly delayed prediction is not a prediction at all. Thus, for the prediction problem, as opposed to the retrodiction problem of pattern recognition, this imposed delay must be removed during prediction since the prediction must be delivered in a timely fashion to be a predictive representation.

To be more specific, consider some realistic estimates. A single delay of 10 msec, which just shifts an input into a 20-msec associative window, will create a prediction with 10 msec to spare using the modified synapses. However, if more than 20 msec of delay are interposed to shift a conditioning representation into the associative window, then the prediction later generated by the conditioning representation through this same synapse will not precede the event being predicted (see also Fig. 11 and below).

Thus, to implement the pure delay line strategy not only requires a multiplicity of delays but also requires some way of shifting the delayed response earlier in time or abandoning the originally modified synapse. This problem is solvable for unidimensional signals by using a cascaded sequence of associative modification. For multidimensional signals, however, we have been unable to find an implementation within the spirit of the delay line that does not require too many neurons or too many synapses or that does not violate the local computational principle. The simple picture at the top of Fig. 10 may conjure up the idea that a feedforward input could by-pass the delay circuitry after learning has occurred, but the figure omits the fact that the signals are multidimensional and that successive stages involve thousands of neurons working in parallel while intermixing signals, rather than just the single neurons illustrated.

2. Feedback Networks as Multiple Delay Lines

Networks which can obtain approximately stable states, however, such as the feedback networks of Hopfield (1984), Cohen and Grossberg (1983), and Shaw, Silverman, and Pearson (1985), are suitable for time-shifting delay and for what is effectively reverse time-shifting. That is, if a sequence of representations is highly similar, then associative synaptic modification can occur using the later members of such a sequence, but the modified synapses will be accessed by earlier members of the sequence when the sequence reoccurs as well. Thus feedback networks, including both the short CA3–CA3 loop and the longer limbic loops through subicular cortex (see Fig. 1) (see, e.g., Deadwyler, West, Cotman, & Lynch, 1975), may be able to function as a variable time-shifting device which, in the sense of the similarity approximation achieved, dissolves the arrow of time.

3. Feedback Networks Can Time Shift without the Problems of Delay Lines

The proposed time-shifting mechanism is an approximation scheme which uses preprocessors to make successive signals similar enough that any one signal can substitute for the other to perform prediction but yet different enough that there is no information loss, $H(X \mid Y)$, from this transformation. This idea is illustrated at the bottom of Fig. 10 and in Fig. 11. Figure 10 shows how feedback would shift a representation into the associative window of synaptic modification. Early representations are

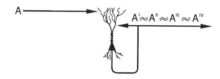

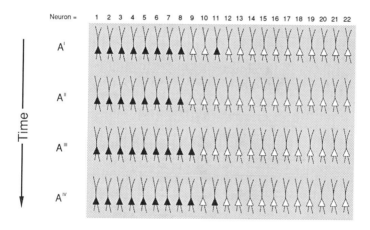

Fig. 11.   Time shifting via approximate sequence stability of CA3 firing patterns. A feedback network such as CA3 can help span longer time windows while still maintaining a sequence of distinct representations. The lower portion of the figure indicates a sequence (A^I-A^{IV}) of output activity patterns of 22 CA3 neurons. Solid neurons are on; open neurons are off. Because the activity patterns A^I and A^{IV} in CA3 are nearly the same, A^I can access almost the same CA1 synapses as A^{IV} including those synapses which have associatively modified. In this way, feedback loops can span longer time windows without delaying the generation of a predictive representation. Copyright © 1989 by William B Levy.

almost identical to late representations (see bottom of Fig. 11), so even
when synaptic modification in CA1 occurs to late (delayed) representations, the early representations will use the same synapses to evoke
timely predictions.

At this point the combinatorial explosion begins to work in the network's favor because, in the high-dimension space (i.e., lots of neurons)
used for neuronal representations, only a very small difference is needed
to distinguish successive signals while the approximately identical nature
of these signals is maintained. That is, perfect signal reproduction is not
needed in a high-dimension space because small differences are a trivial
fraction of the total representation signal. The feedback loop which produces approximately stable representations thus allows the network to
span a variable time range, a long interval for association and little or no
interval for prediction.

Some calculations illustrate how well the feedback network can work.
Suppose we have 10^5 CA3 neurons code a representation with 10% active
and 90% inactive neurons. Of these 10,000 active neurons, let 1% vary
randomly while the network keeps the other 99% at the same high probability of firing. Each successive pattern will be almost like the previous
pattern even though the network has some 2^{100} distinct states available if
the 1% of the neurons undergoing random firing have a 50% chance of
being active. Thus the network can uniquely represent any sequence of
differing patterns, which allows it to avoid information loss [$H(X \mid Y)$],
while the first representation and the last representation remain almost
identical, within 1%. In this way, associative synaptic modification using
the delayed form of the representation is good enough because both the
early, and what we might call the reverse time-shifted, representations
use almost the exact same set of synapses.

Figure 12 depicts a low-dimension example of eight different representations which accomplish temporal compression because they are nearly
identical. Larger groups of neurons will do exponentially better in terms
of the possible number of their distinct representations and their
similarity.

4. Extending the Forecasted Period

In sum, four mechanisms of time shifting have been presented (see Fig.
14): (1) a delay line which uses the RC time constant of neurons to slow
propagation of signals through a network; (2) a high-information content,
positive feedback using a short loop; (3) a high-information content, positive feedback that uses long loops; and (4) the associative synaptic modification rule, which can associate two different inputs across a gap in time.
In the next section we suggest that the feedback circuitry of the hippo-

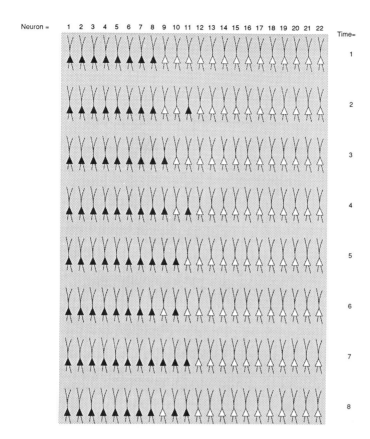

Fig. 12.   One tier of neurons, changing over time, could achieve a highly similar but different series of representations. Solid neurons are on; open neurons are off. Copyright © 1989 by William B Levy.

campus (and associated limbic structures as well) can be used both to create predictions which look farther ahead into the future and to solve the problem of decreasing the statistical dependency of representations.

VI.   An Algorithmic Process as a Hypothesis for the Function of DG/CA3

This section presents the second half of the argument that the function of the DG/CA3 system is to produce a sequence of similar representations. We have just seen that such a sequence is useful for solving the time-shifting problem. Here we sketch an argument which hypothesizes that such a class of sequences can also solve the problem of lowering the intrinsic statistical dependency [Eq. (5)] of the conditioning variable [Y of Eq. (10)].

A. THE TIGHT PACKING ALGORITHM

For the sequence $X(t)$, we are seeking a way to implement a transformation, $f: X(t) \rightarrow Y(t + 1)$, that is provably optimal for reducing statistical dependence. In other words, we want to find an f which creates the smallest $\Sigma \, H(Y_j)$ while preserving information, $H(X \mid Y)$.

Below we outline an algorithm which achieves the desired transformation. Figure 13 illustrates how, after removing enough redundancies by some as yet unspecified process, it is sometimes possible to represent the same information with fewer active neurons. We call this transformation "tight packing" because it allows a reduction in the required size of the representation space.

In fact, there exists a deterministic algorithm which implements tight packing. Just below we prove its optimality in a rather restricted setting. Then we describe a relaxed version of the algorithm which a neural network might be able to implement. We call this approximation method "rough counting." It is easy to imagine that the same DG/CA3 circuitry which performs time-shifting would simultaneously accomplish rough counting. Finally we point out that the algorithm is unsatisfactory in a nonstationary setting and suggest a possible solution to this failing.

The algorithm works for the space, $X \in \{0,1\}^n$, when the space is sparsely sampled, that is, when the sample size $N << 2^n$.

It can be claimed that the mapping which takes an arbitrary sequence $X(t)$ into the sequence $Y(t + 1)$ as illustrated in Table I produces a Y of minimal statistical dependence. It should be clear that the illustrated sequence Y in the third partition of Table I could just be the result of counting a binary starting at zero. This mapping is a tight packing because it minimizes the Hamming distance among the points enumerated. In fact counting up from zero is not the only way to achieve minimal statistical dependence. Any mapping, which may start at any point in Y, minimizes statistical dependence if the mapping minimizes the Hamming distance among the points in Y space.

The proof that statistical dependence is minimized is trivial when the sample size $N = 2^m$, m is an integer, and when probability is taken to be the sampled relative frequency. Suppose $Y = (Y_1, \ldots, Y_j, \ldots, Y_n)$. All those dimensions j which remain unchanged, as in the first and second partitions of Table I, have associated marginal probabilities $\{P(Y_j = 1), P(Y_j = 0)\} = \{0,1\}$. All other dimensions (those in the third partition) have $P(Y_j = 1) = P(Y_j = 0) = .5$. The probability of any sampled Y is 2^{-m}, and this is the same probability as computed from the marginal values as

A Representations in a geometric space

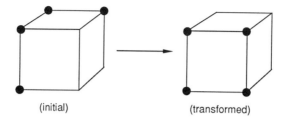

(initial) (transformed)

B The same 4 representations in a neural version of the geometric space

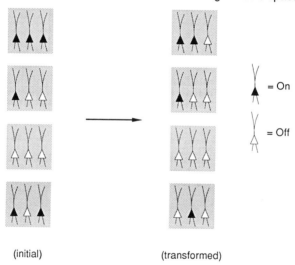

= On

= Off

(initial) (transformed)

Fig. 13. Tight packing can lower the complexity of a representation. A, Four representations (●) in a three-dimensional space (a cube) are transformed into four representations in a two-dimensional space (a face of the cube). B, If a neuron corresponds to a dimension of the cube, three neurons are needed for the four representations scattered around the eight corners of the cube initially. However, only two neurons are needed for the representation after the transformation. Copyright © 1989 by William B Levy.

the product $(1^{n-m})(.5^{-m})$. For the configurations Y of relative frequency zero, the marginal-based calculations give probability zero. Thus we have shown that the mapping produces complete independence under these circumstances because the full distribution $P(Y)$ is reproduced by multiplication of marginal probabilities, $[P(Y_j)]$.

It is too much to expect a neural network to ''count'' in perfect order but this condition can be relaxed.

TABLE I

PARTITIONING OF PROCESSORS AFTER 2^m
SAMPLES

		Partition	
N	First	Second	Third
1	{000...0	111...1	000...00,
2	000...0	111...1	000...01,
3	000...0	111...1	000...10,
4	000...0	111...1	000...11,
•	•	•	•
•	•	•	•
•	•	•	•
2^m	000...0	111...1	111...11}

B. ROUGH COUNTING

1. Sampling in Bunches

Consider the case in which there is a single generating distribution, $P[X(t)]$. Samples are sequences of X drawn in a group, say 2^6 at a time. If a single sampling period covers 2.5 msec, then 2^6 samples represent a sampling period of only 160 msec, so sampling in bunches is quite conceivable for the brain or regions within the brain.

2. The Algorithm Is a Dynamic Partitioning

Suppose there are n processors (about 10^5–10^6 neurons in a subregion of the limbic system that inspires this theory) in the X space, such as layer II cells of the entorhinal cortex, and the same number in the Y space, such as CA3 spiny pyramids. We will now see that there is a dynamic, that is, time-dependent, partitioning of the n processors in the Y space. This dynamic partitioning requires three distinct sets of processors {1,2,3} with $n_1(t)$, $n_2(t)$, and $n_3(t)$ processors in each set in such a way that $2^{n_1} > 2^{n_2} >> 2^{n_3}$ holds. For instance, n_2 might be 1–10% of n_1; n_3 will never be larger than 40 neurons, and 16–20 seems enough for most situations for two reasons. First, the third partition will by itself distinguish the sampled Ys so as to stand in one-to-one correspondence with the X samples. Second, 2^{20} processors allows a unique representation in Y of more than one million samples from X.

The nature of the partitioning of the neurons of CA3 can be described as follows:

1. The n_1 processors in the first partition of Y have never fired.
2. The n_2 processors in the second partition have always been firing.
3. The n_3 processors in the third partition have been on half the time in a very special way.

Specifically then—and here we again assume for simplicity that N is a power of two, say 2^m—$n_3(N) = m$ and no two vectors in Y are the same.

Table I shows such a partitioning of processors after N samples.

When the set of states in Table I is ordered as indicated, the third partition embodies a counting algorithm. As pointed out above, such a countinglike ordering is induced by the way we have ordered the processors Y_j and their partitions for illustrative purposes. Such an ordering does not actually occur in a network so that any numerical label on a processor is just an arbitrary mathematical convenience. [It may also help some readers to note that the transformations under which the measure of statistical dependence is invariant include (1) complementation of any Y_j because $P(Y_j)$ is a binary distribution and complementation does not alter $H(Y_j)$ and (2) permutation of the ordering of the Y_j values because $\Sigma_i H(Y_j)$ is unaffected by permutations of the variable ordering 1, 2, 3, . . ., n.]

Not only is optimization invariant over permutations of neurallike processors Y_j, but it is adequate to count in a rather slipshod manner. Since samples arrive in groups before a prediction is required, the network does not need to do a proper, straight-through job of counting. Any ordering within each group, including a randomly created one, is good enough so long as each group more or less methodically occupies the counting subspace: the third partition.

The dynamic aspect of the partitioning involves shifting a processor from either the first or second partition into the third partition. Tables IIA and IIB show the partitioning after two and four samples respectively. Note that we have suppressed group sampling to make the tables simpler. Tables IIA and IIB precede Table I in that the Table II partitionings later grow into the partitioning shown in Table I. Thus, in this dynamic partitioning, a processor of the first partition has been off (i.e., a zero) for the last N samples and then shifts into partition three by turning on (i.e., a one) for the next N samples. A similar scheme describes the shifting of a processor from partition two to partition three. The size of the third partition thus grows at a logarithmic rate with sample size so that there is more than enough space for any number of samples that may be realistically encountered.

TABLE II

The Growth of the Dynamic Partitioning

	Partition		
N	First	Second	Third
A. After two samples			
1	{000...0	111...1	0,
2	000...0	111...1	1}
B. After four samples			
1	{00...0	111...1	00,
2	00...0	111...1	01,
3	00...0	111...1	10,
4	00...0	111...1	11}

3. Neural Hypotheses

The exact mechanism which would accomplish this algorithm has not been tested. However, the mechanism seems to be compatible with the computations of neurallike processors, particularly feedback networks. The extreme constancy of successive patterns (note that they differ from each other by much less than 1% for the number of processors envisioned) could be produced by a Shaw et al. (1985) network or by a Hopfield (1984) or Cohen-Grossberg (1983) feedback network that has nearly converged. The slight movement away from an absolutely identical sequence of states $Y(t + 1)$ would be guaranteed by the nonconstancy of the input patterns $X(t)$.

C. Nonstationary Environments

A complex environment might contain a sequence of generating functions. In this case even the rough counting algorithm leaves something to be desired. For example, when the environment shifts from one generating process to another and then shifts back again to a previously experienced environment, the preprocessor should be able to shift the dynamic partitioning appropriately. In particular, the network should be able to use the previously acquired conditional expectations in CA1 for predictions in the previously experienced environment. However, it will only be possible to use these acquired expectations and to update them adaptively if the network can return, at least approximately, to the preprocessing state, that is, dynamic partitioning, used for the recurring environment. Unfortunately, naive implementation of the rough counting algorithm can destroy the usefulness of previously acquired conditional expectations because the algorithm can be implemented so as to invalidate the previously acquired expectations.

To put this a little more precisely, we are now considering the problems which result from nonstationary environments. These environments can be thought of as a sequence of generating distributions indexed by r. In such circumstances, rather than seeking overall independence, the network should seek the independence of the representation Y conditional on r. Thus, rather than seek a good transformation f, we are sequentially seeking good transformations f_r.

The added difficulty of prediction in the nonstationary complex environment is how and when to change the transformation $f_r\colon X \to Y$ to another f_r. It is particularly critical to discover a method of changing f_r which allows the network to return to an $f_r = f_s$ when s reoccurs. What is required then is an adaptive version of this dynamic partitioning so as not to destroy previously acquired relationships. The proposed solution to this problem is to interpolate a pattern recognition process between environments r.

One scheme we are considering is described by the following sequence of operations:

tight packing . . . tight packing

$\Downarrow$

mismatch

$\Downarrow$

pattern recognition on the current input r

$\Downarrow$ suppose r is most similar to s, then

choose f_s

$\Downarrow$

begin tight packing algorithm again.

The *tight packing* portion of the algorithm is the rough counting described above. Rough counting continues until a mismatch signal occurs. *Mismatch* means the detection of a series of sufficiently poor predictions such that it is worthwhile to assume r has changed. The prediction evaluation box of Fig. 7 is the mismatch detector. The evaluation process is an adaptive procedure which produces a running average measure of the quality of the predictions relative to the corresponding actual outcomes. Mismatch detection terminates the tight packing mode and switches the network into a pattern recognition mode. The network performs as a *pattern recognition* device on the current environment. This pattern recognition process allows the DG/CA3 system to take advantage of previous adaptive modifications and to shift its preprocessing transformation along with the shifting statistics of the entorhinal cortical inputs. This pattern recognition process also allows the network to return to old transformations when the environment shifts back to previously encountered statistics. If a previously encountered r is sensed, the network configuration moves, that is, shifts its activity state, to a configuration that is similar to the previous representations of r. If a new r is encountered, any configuration that is not associated with any r already observed will do. It is very easy to find a new place to begin tight packing in such a large space ($\sim 2^{100,000}$) because no more than a random selection upon the neuronal activities is necessary to implement the beginning of the three-way partitioning which is, with statistical certainty, a novel configuration. A novel environment would then require synaptic modification to set up relatively stable conditions which are the first and second partitions of the dynamic partitioning.

After the network activity pattern moves to the appropriate configuration of activity, that is, to the first and second partitions appropriate to the environment r, tight packing begins again from about where it left off for this environment, with increases in the number of processors in the third partition as necessary.

In sum, then, we propose that the same mechanisms which are used for time-shifting representations can also be used for solving the sensory fusion problem. The similarities between Fig. 14A and 14B make the same point by juxtaposition. In fact, it is only natural that a system which evolved for helping mammals move to and from the nest as efficiently as possible would have both the capability of sensory signal fusion and of time-shifting representations.

Finally, we can posit a relationship between the psychological theories of hippocampal function and the computational theory presented here. The time-shifting feedback loops which produce sequences of similar representations can be put to other uses. Each of these feedback systems can function as one of the short-term memory systems in the brain. In addition, these short-term memory systems are particularly suited for the signal mixing task of lowering statistical dependence and of connecting the past with the future—functions that could well describe the fundamental computations of a working memory system.

A   **Time Shifting**

B   **Signal Mixing**

1. EC → CA3 → CA1
(a feedforward delay line)

1. EC → CA3 → CA1

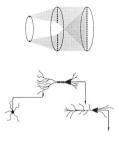

2. CA3 → CA3
(a short feedback loop)

2. CA3 → CA3
(a short feedback loop)

3. EC → EC
(a long feedback loop)

3. EC → EC
(a long feedback loop)

4. Time constraints of synaptic
modification rules.

10 msec

27.5 msec

Fig. 14. Similarities between processes that shift and signal mix. A, Four types of time shifting in the model. Synaptic modification (4) and delay lines (1) can provide a small amount of time shifting and temporal compression of representations. However, feedback networks (2 and 3) can span much longer periods, thereby allowing associative modifications over longer times while still producing a prediction before the event being predicted. B, The same circuitry used for time shifting can also be used for signal mixing. Note that divergence and convergence as in (1) can take place at many successive levels of the system. Copyright © 1989 by William B Levy.

ACKNOWLEDGMENTS

WBL is supported by NIMH RSDA MH00622 and by the Department of Neurological Surgery. John A. Jane, Chairman, provided the environment which allowed me to work on ideas somewhat outside of mainstream approaches to neuroscience. Interactions with F. H. C. Crick stimulated the development of some of the philosophical ideas about prediction. I gratefully acknowledge the suggestions and criticisms supplied by C. M. Colbert, S. Shoemaker, and particularly by N. L Desmond, whose contributions to this paper are pervasive. I am also grateful for help with the more mathematical sections given by my collaborators, D. L. Costa and D. St. P. Richards. J. Sullivan helped develop the figures.

REFERENCES

Amaral, D. G. (1987). Memory: Anatomical organization of candidate brain regions. In F. Plum (Ed.), *Handbook of physiology: Sect. I. The nervous system* (Vol. V, pp. 211–294). New York: Oxford University Press.

Amari, S.-I. (1977). Neural theory of association and concept-formation. *Biological Cybernetics, 26,* 175–185.

Ashby, W. R. (1956). Design for an intelligence-amplifier. In C. E. Shannon & J. McCarthy (Eds.), *Automata studies* (pp. 215–234). Princeton, NJ: Princeton University Press.

Barlow, H. B. (1959). Sensory mechanisms, the reduction of redundancy, and intelligence. In *Mechanisation of thought processes* (Vol. II, pp. 537–559). London: Her Majesty's Stationery Office.

Barlow, H. B. (1961a). Possible principles underlying the transformations of sensory messages. In W. A. Rosenblith (Ed.), *Sensory communication* (pp. 217–235). Cambridge, MA: MIT Press.

Barlow, H. B. (1961b). The coding of sensory messages. In W. H. Thorpe & O. L. Zangwill (Eds.), *Current problems in animal behaviour* (pp. 331–360). London: Cambridge University Press.

Barto, A. G., Sutton, R. S., & Anderson, C. W. (1983). Neuron-like elements that can solve difficult learning control problems. *IEEE Transactions on Systems, Man, Cybernetics, SMC-13,* 835–846.

Bellman, R. (1961). *Adaptive control processes: A guided tour.* Princeton, NJ: Princeton University Press.

Breese, C. R., Hampson, R. E., & Deadwyler, S. A. (1989). Hippocampal place cells: Stereotypy and plasticity. *Journal of Neuroscience, 9,* 1097–1011.

Brooks, V. B. (1986). How does the limbic system assist motor learning? A limbic comparator hypothesis. *Brain Behavior and Evolution, 29,* 29–53.

Burger, B., & Levy, W. B. (1985). Long-term associative potentiation/depression as an analogue of classical conditioning. *Society for Neuroscience Abstracts, 11,* 493.

Burger, B., & Levy, W. B. (1987). An intensity-dependent threshold-like effect controls both LTP and LTD. *Society for Neuroscience Abstracts, 13,* 974.

Carpenter, G. A., & Grossberg, S. (1987). A massively parallel architecture for a self-organizing neural pattern recognition machine. *Computer Vision, Graphics, and Image Processing, 37,* 54–115.

Cohen, M. A., & Grossberg, S. (1983). Absolute stability of global pattern formation and parallel memory storage by competitive neural networks. *IEEE Transactions on Systems, Man, and Cybernetics, SMC-13,* 815–826.

Colbert, C. M., & Levy, W. B. (1988). What is the code? *Proceedings of the International Neural Network Society,* **1,** 246.

Cox, R. T. (1961). *The algebra of probable inference.* Baltimore, MD: Johns Hopkins Press.

Cox, R. T. (1978). Of inference and inquiry, An essay in inductive logic. In R. D. Levine & M. Tribus (Eds.), *The maximum entropy formalism.* (pp. 119–167). Cambridge, MA: MIT Press.

Csiszár, I., & Körner, J. (1981). *Information theory: Coding theorems for discrete memoryless systems.* New York: Academic Press.

Dawkins, R. (1976). *The selfish gene.* New York: Oxford University Press.

Deadwyler, S. A., West, J. A., Cotman, C. W., & Lynch, G. S. (1975). Physiological studies of the reciprocal connections between the hippocampus and the entorhinal cortex. *Experimental Neurology,* **49,** 35–57.

Desmond, N. L., & Levy, W. B. (1988). Anatomy of associative long-term synaptic modification. In P. W. Landfield & S. A. Deadwyler (Eds.), *Long-term potentiation: From biophysics to behavior* (pp. 265–305). New York: Alan R. Liss.

Doller, H. J., & Weight, F. F. (1985). Perforant pathway-evoked long-term potentiation of CA1 neurons in the hippocampal slice preparation. *Brain Research,* **333,** 305–310.

Eichenbaum, H., & Cohen, N. J. (1988). Representation in the hippocampus: What do hippocampal neurons code? *Trends in Neuroscience,* **11,** 244–248.

Foster, T. C., Christian, E. P., Hampson, R. E., Campbell, K. A., & Deadwyler, S. A. (1987). Sequential dependencies regulate sensory evoked responses of single units in the rat hippocampus. *Brain Research,* **408,** 86–96.

Fukushima, K. (1973). A model of associative memory in the brain. *Kybernetic,* **12,** 58–73.

Gamow, G. (1961). *One two three . . . infinity.* New York: Viking Press.

Garey, M. R., & Johnson, D. S. (1979). *Computers and intractability. A guide to the theory of NP-completeness.* New York: Freeman.

Geman, S. (1981). The law of large numbers in neural modelling. *SIAM AMS Proceedings,* **13,** 91–105.

Golden, R. M. (1988). Probabilistic characterization of neural model computations. In D. Z. Anderson (Ed.), *Neural Information Processing Systems* (pp. 310–316). New York: American Institute of Physics.

Goldman-Rakic, P. S. (1987). Circuitry of primate prefrontal cortex and regulation of behavior by representational memory. In F. Plum (Ed.), *Handbook of physiology: Sect. I. The nervous system* (Vol. V, pp. 373–417). New York: Oxford University Press.

Good, I. J. (1963). Maximum entropy for hypotheses formulation especially for multidimensional contingency tables. *Annals of Mathematical Statistics,* **34,** 911–934.

Gray, J. A. (1982). *The neuropsychology of anxiety: An enquiry into the functions of the septo–hippocampal system.* New York: Oxford University Press.

Grossberg, S. (1976). Adaptive pattern classification and universal recoding: I. Parallel development and coding of neural feature detectors. *Biological Cybernetics,* **23,** 121–134.

Grossberg, S., & Kuperstein, M. (1986). *Neural dynamics of adaptive sensory–motor control: Ballistic eye movements.* Amsterdam: Elsevier/North-Holland.

Hamming, R. W. (1980). *Coding and information theory.* New York: Prentice-Hall.

Hinton, G. E., & Sejnowski, T. J. (1983). Optimal perceptual inference. *Proceedings IEEE Conference on Computer Vision and Pattern Recognition,* pp. 448–453.

Hopfield, J. J. (1984). Neurons with graded response have collective computational properties like those of two-state neurons. *Proceedings of the National Academy of Sciences U.S.A.,* **81,** 3088–3092.

Hopfield, J. J. (1987). Learning algorithms and probability distributions in feed-forward and feed-back networks. *Proceedings of the National Academy of Sciences U.S.A.,* **84,** 8429–8433.

302   William B Levy

Hopfield, J. J., & Tank, D. W. (1985). "Neural" computation of decisions in optimization problems. *Biological Cybernetics,* **52,** 141–152.

Insausti, R., Amaral, D. G., & Cowan, W. M. (1987). The monkey entorhinal cortex. II. Cortical afferents. *Journal of Comparative Neurology,* **264,** 356–395.

Jaynes, E. T. (1978). Where do we stand on maximum entropy? In R. D. Levine & M. Tribus (Eds.), *The maximum entropy formalism.* (pp. 15–118). Cambridge, MA: MIT Press.

Jerison, H. J. (1973). *Evolution of the brain and intelligence.* New York: Academic Press.

Johnson, R. W., & Shore, J. E., (1983). Comments on and correction to "Axiomatic derivation of the principle of maximum entropy and the principle of minimum cross-entropy." *IEEE Transactions on Information Theory,* **IT-29,** 942–943.

Jones, E. G., & Powell, T. P. S. (1970). An anatomical study of converging sensory pathways within the cerebral cortex of the monkey. *Brain,* **93,** 793–820.

Karp, R. M. (1975). On the complexity of combinatorial problems. *Networks,* **5,** 45–68.

King, M. A., & Levy, W. B. (1986). Heterosynaptic depression of hippocampal CA3 afferents to CA1 accompanies long-term potentiation of convergent entorhinal afferents. *Society for Neuroscience Abstracts,* **12,** 505.

Kirkpatrick, S., Gelatt, C. D., Jr., & Vecchi, M. P. (1983). Optimization by simulated annealing. *Science,* **220,** 671–680.

Kleinfeld, D. (1986). Sequential state generation by model neural networks. *Proceedings of the National Academy of Sciences U.S.A.,* **83,** 9469–9473.

Kohonen, T. (1972). Correlation matrix memories. *IEEE Transactions on Computers,* **C-21,** 353–359.

Kohonen, T. (1984). *Self-organization and associative memory.* Berlin: Springer-Verlag.

Kosel, K. C., Van Hoesen, G. W., & Rosene, D. L. (1982). Non-hippocampal cortical projections from the entorhinal cortex in the rat and rhesus monkey. *Brain Research,* **244,** 201–213.

Levy, W. B. (1985). An information/computation theory of hippocampal function. *Society for Neuroscience Abstracts,* **11,** 493.

Levy, W. B. (1988). A theory of the hippocampus based on reinforced synaptic modification in CA1. *Society for Neuroscience Abstracts,* **14,** 168.

Levy, W. B, Brassel, S. E., & Moore, S. D. (1983). Partial quantification of the associative synaptic learning rule of the dentate gyrus. *Neuroscience,* **8,** 799–808.

Levy, W. B, & Burger, B. (1987a). An intensity-dependent threshold-like effect controls both LTP and LTD. *Society for Neuroscience Abstracts,* **13,** 974.

Levy, W. B, & Burger, B. (1987b). Electrophysiological observations which help describe an associative synaptic modification rule. *Proceedings IEEE First Annual International Conference on Neural Networks,* IV, 11–15.

Levy W. B, Colbert, C. M., & Desmond, N. L. (in press). Elemental adaptive processes of neurons and synapses: A statistical/computational perspective. In M. A. Gluck & D. E. Rumelhart (Eds.), *Neuroscience and connectionist models.* Hillsdale, NJ: Erlbaum.

Levy, W. B., & Desmond, N. L. (1985a). The rules of elemental synaptic plasticity. In W. B Levy, J. Anderson, & S. Lehmkuhle (Eds.), *Synaptic modification, neuron selectivity and nervous system organization* (pp. 105–121). Hillsdale, NJ: Erlbaum.

Levy, W. B., & Desmond, N. L. (1985b). Associative potentiation/depression in the hippocampal dentate gyrus. In G. Buzsaki & C. H. Vanderwolf (Eds.), *Electrical activity of the archicortex* (pp. 359–373). Budapest: Akadémiai Kiadó.

Levy, W. B, & Desmond, N. L. (1988). Characteristics of associative potentiation/depression. In H. L. Haas & G. Buzsaki (Eds.), *Synaptic plasticity in the hippocampus* (pp. 93–95). Berlin: Springer-Verlag.

Levy, W. B, & Geman, S. (1982). *Limit behavior of experimentally derived synaptic modification rules* (Reports in Pattern Analysis No. 121). Providence, RI: Brown University, Division of Applied Mathematics.

Levy, W. B, & Steward, O. (1979). Synapses as associative memory elements in the hippocampal formation. *Brain Research, 175,* 65–78.

Levy, W. B, & Steward, O. (1983). Temporal contiguity requirements for long-term associative potentiation/depression in the hippocampus. *Neuroscience, 8,* 791–797.

Lopez, H., Burger, B., Dickstein, R., Desmond, N. L., & Levy, W. B. (1989). *Long-term potentiation and long-term depression in the hippocampal dentate gyrus: quantification of dissociable modifications.* Manuscript submitted for publication.

Lopez, H., Burger, B., & Levy, W. B. (1985). The asymptotic limits of long-term potentiation/depression are independently controlled. *Society for Neuroscience Abstracts, 11,* 930.

Mathai, A. M., & Rathie, P. N. (Eds.). (1975). *Basic concepts in information theory and statistics.* New York: Wiley.

McNaughton, B. L., Douglas, R. M., & Goddard, G. V. (1978). Synaptic enhancement in fascia dentata: Cooperativity among coactive afferents. *Brain Research, 157,* 277–293.

Minsky, M. L., & Papert, S. A. (Eds.). (1969). *Perceptrons.* Cambridge, MA: MIT Press.

Moore, S. D., & Levy, W. B. (1986). Association of heterogeneous afferents produces long-term potentiation. *Society for Neuroscience Abstracts, 12,* 504.

Moore, S. D., & Levy, W. B. (1989). *Heterogeneous synaptic activation can permit long-term potentiation in the hippocampus.* Manuscript submitted for publication.

Murray, E. A., & Mishkin, M. (1987). Experimental studies of memory in monkeys. Implications for understanding human memory disorders. *National Forum, 67,* 33–37.

O'Keefe, J., & Nadel, L. (1978). *The hippocampus as a cognitive map.* London: Oxford University Press.

Olton, D. S. (1978). Characteristics of spatial memory. In S. H. Hulse, H. Fowler, & W. K. Honig (Eds.), *Cognitive processes in animal behavior* (pp. 341–373). Hillsdale, NJ: Erlbaum.

Olton, D. S. (1985). The temporal context of spatial memory. *Philosophical Transactions of the Royal Society of London, Series B, 308,* 79–86.

Pandya, D. N., & Kuypers, H. G. J. M. (1969). Cortico–cortical connections in the rhesus monkey. *Brain Research, 13,* 13–36.

Raffaele, K. C., & Olton, D. S. (1988). Hippocampal and amygdaloid involvement in working memory for nonspatial stimuli. *Behavioral Neuroscience, 102,* 349–355.

Ranck, J. B., Jr. (1985). Head direction cells in the deep cell layer of dorsal presubiculum in freely moving rats. In G. Buzsaki & C. H. Vanderwolf (Eds.), *Electrical activity of the archicortex* (pp. 217–220). Budapest: Akadémiai Kiadó.

Rosene, D. L., & Van Hoesen, G. W. (1987). The hippocampal formation of the primate brain. A review of some comparative aspects of cytoarchitecture and connections. In E. G. Jones & A. Peters (Eds.), *Cerebral cortex* (Vol. 6, pp. 345–456). New York: Plenum.

Rumelhart, D. E., Hinton, G. E., & Williams, R. W. (1986). Learning internal representations by error propagation. In D. E. Rumelhart, J. L. McClelland, & the PDP Research Group (Eds.), *Parallel distributed processing, explorations in the microstructure of cognition* (Vol. 1, pp. 318–362). Cambridge, MA: MIT Press.

Saper, C. B. (1982). Convergence of autonomic and limbic connections in the insular cortex of the rat. *Journal of Comparative Neurology, 210,* 163–173.

Shannon, C. E. (1950). A chess-playing machine. *Scientific American, 182,* 48–51.

Shannon, C. E., & Weaver, W. (1949). *The mathematical theory of communication.* Urbana: University of Illinois Press.

Shaw, G. L., Silverman, D. J., & Pearson, J. C. (1985). Model of cortical organization embodying a basis for a theory of information processing and memory recall. *Proceedings of the National Academy of Sciences U.S.A.* **82,** 2364–2368.

Shore, J. E., & Johnson, R. W. (1980). Axiomatic derivation of the principle of maximum entropy and the principle of minimum cross-entropy. *IEEE Transactions on Information Theory,* **IT-26,** 26–37.

Sorensen, K. E. (1985). Projections of the entorhinal area to the striatum, nucleus accumbens, and cerebral cortex in the guinea pig. *Journal of Comparative Neurology,* **238,** 308–322.

Sorensen, K. E., & Shipley, M. T. (1979). Projections from the subiculum to the deep layers of the ipsilateral presubicular and entorhinal cortices in the guinea pig. *Journal of Comparative Neurology,* **188,** 313–334.

Squire, L. R. (1987). *Memory and brain.* New York: Oxford University Press.

Staddon, J. E. R., & Hinson, J. M. (1983). Optimization: A result or a mechanism? *Science,* **221,** 976–977.

Sutton, R. S. (1984). *Temporal credit assignment in reinforcement learning.* Unpublished doctoral dissertation, Amherst, MA: University of Massachusetts, Department of Computer and Information Science.

Swanson, L. W., & Cowan, W. M. (1977). An autoradiographic study of the organization of the efferent connections of the hippocampal formation in the rat. *Journal of Comparative Neurology,* **172,** 49–84.

Swanson, L. W., Köhler, C., Björklund, A. (1987). The limbic region. I: The septohippocampal system. In A. Björklund, T. Hökfelt, & L. W. Swanson (Eds.), *Handbook of chemical neuroanatomy* (Vol. 5, pp. 125–277). Amsterdam: Elsevier.

Thompson, R. F., & Spencer, W. A. (1966). Habituation: A model phenomenon for the study of neuronal substrates of behavior. *Psychological Review,* **73,** 16–43.

Van Hoesen, G. W., & Pandya, D. N. (1975). Some connections of the entorhinal (area 28) and perirhinal (area 35) cortices of the rhesus monkey. III. Efferent connections. *Brain Research,* **95,** 39–59.

Van Hoesen, G. W., Pandya, D. N., & Butters, N. (1972). Cortical afferents to the entorhinal cortex of the rhesus monkey. *Science,* **175,** 1471–1473.

Van Hoesen, G. W., Pandya, D. N., & Butters, N. (1975). Some connections of the entorhinal (area 28) and perirhinal (area 35) cortices of the rhesus monkey. II. Frontal lobe afferents. *Brain Research,* **95,** 25–38.

Watanabe, S. (1969). *Knowing and guessing. A quantitative study of inference and information.* New York: Wiley.

White, G., Levy, W. B., & Steward, O. (1988). Evidence that associative interactions between afferents during the induction of long-term potentiation occur within local dendritic domains. *Proceedings of the National Academy of Sciences U.S.A.,* **85,** 2368–2372.

Wilson, R. C., Levy, W. B., & Steward, O. (1979). Functional effects of lesion-induced plasticity: Long term potentiation in normal and lesion-induced temporodentate connections. *Brain Research,* **176,** 65–78.

Wilson, R. C., Levy, W. B., & Steward, O. (1981). Changes in the translation of synaptic excitation to dentate granule cell discharge accompanying long term potentiation. II. An evaluation of mechanisms utilizing the dentate gyrus dually innervated by surviving ipsilateral and sprouted crossed temporodentate inputs. *Journal of Neurophysiology,* **46,** 339–355.

Winston, P. H. (1977). *Artificial intelligence*. Reading, MA: Addison-Wesley.

Young, J. Z. (Ed.). (1970). *The life of mammals*. Oxford: Clarendon Press.

Zipser, D. (1986). A model of hippocampal learning during classical conditioning. *Behavioral Neuroscience,* **100,** 764–776.

Zucker, S. W. (1981). *Computer vision and human perception*. Paper presented at the Seventh Joint International Conference on Artificial Intelligence, Vancouver.

INDEX

CONTENTS OF RECENT VOLUMES